W9-DFB-790

CHICAGO AND NATIONAL HISTORIC LANDMARK DISTRICT

Wicker Park

FROM 1673 THRU 1929

AND
WALKING TOUR GUIDE

Elaine A. Coorens

Assisted by
Mary Ann Johnson

Edited by
Larry E. Clary

Published by

Old Wicker Park Committee

P.O. Box 477580, Chicago, Il 60647-7580

F 548.68 .W52 C66 2003
Coorens, Elaine A.
Wicker Park

MCKINLEY PARK BRANCH
1915 WEST 35TH STREET
CHICAGO, ILLINOIS 60609

Copyright @ 2003 Elaine A. Coorens

All rights reserved. No part of this publication may be reproduced, stored in a retrieval system or transmitted in any form or by any means, electronic, mechanical, photocopying, recording, scanning or otherwise, except by permission under sections 107 or 108 of the 1976 United Sates Copyright Act, without prior written permission from the copyright holder.

Library of Congress Card Catalog Number 2002096948

Library of Congress Cataloging-in-Publication Data:
Coorens, Elaine A.

Wicker Park, Chicago: Chicago Historic District
Wicker Park, Chicago: Walking Tour Guide
Chicago: Wicker Park Historic District
Chicago: Walking Tour Guide, Wicker Park
National Historic Landmark District: Wicker Park, Chicago

        p. cm
        Includes index
        ISBN 0-9726811-0-8

Cover Design and Illustration by ANNE FARLEY GAINES
Book Design by DAN PATERNO
House Tour Sketches by CHAR SANDSTROM
Historic Wicker Park District and Landmarks Maps by JOHN JOYCE

R07127 28718

Dedicated to
**Those who enjoy knowing the past for knowledge, fun, and/or as a foundation
for actions today and tomorrow...**

and

In honor of
Neighborhood pioneers from the past, present and future.

REMEMBER TWO LESSONS OF HISTORY:

Through decades and centuries, immigrant issues remain the same
AND
We own nothing...we are but caretakers

E. A. COORENS

Table of Contents

Foreword

Throughout its long existence, the Wicker Park community has managed to do something that is remarkable for an urban neighborhood. It has changed with the times, but still remains the same.

Saying that Wicker Park has remained the *same* certainly doesn't mean that it has stood *still*. Its entire existence could be described as a great urban square dance, with ever-changing partners of ethnic identity and economic circumstance.

Pride is one of the principal factors in Wicker Park's long-term endurance. Whether it was a modest worker's cottage or a thundering brick mansion, the distinctive older buildings of the community were always given something extra by the people who built them. Whether it was an ornamental turret, a profusion of wood scrollwork, or ornamental iron railings on an otherwise modest front porch, the things built by the residents of the community represented pride in themselves and their community.

Another factor is respect. The Wicker Park community has shown amazing restraint in resisting the temptations to change its unique identity to accommodate fleeting fads and changing tastes. In part, this phenomenon can be attributed to common-sense practicality, and adherence to the time honored saying, *"If it ain't broke, don't fix it."* The neighborhood's vitality, however, derives from much more than just frugality and stoicism. It takes a special kind of mindset to appreciate and respect what most people take for granted.

Anybody visiting Wicker Park cannot help but be impressed by its tree-lined streets and picturesque buildings. But to people in the know, the essence of the Wicker Park community is in the people who have called it — and continue to call it — HOME.

Timothy J. Samuelson, Cultural Historian
City of Chicago Cultural Historian

JUNE, 2003

i

Preface

When referring to an historic landmark district such as Wicker Park, people always focus first on buildings. Therefore, it seemed natural that the Old Wicker Park Committee's Historic Book Committee started this publication's plan with a walking tour and other brick and mortar information.

Discussions moved to city infrastructure questions such as, "How did people get to the center of the city?" and "What was the story of the 'L' that ran parallel with North Ave.?" Then an explosion of questions began. A question like "Where did people go for grocery shopping?" led to "How did the Park fit into people's lives?" then "What institutions were available to residents?" and on to "What were the people like?"

Suddenly we were faced with an even bigger dilemma. How do we tell the **complete** Wicker Park Neighborhood story from the beginning to the 21st century and include a walking tour? The answer, **"WE DON'T!"** We are limited by budget and time.

Following is a series of stories that will give you an opportunity to meet some people from the past, see where they lived and worked, get a feel for life and the environment in Wicker Park. The stories begin the year Marquette and Jolliet stepped foot on land by Lake Michigan and the Chicago River and end in the midst of prohibition when the country was poised on the brink of a financial disaster. The time span is 1673 through 1929.

As you journey back in time through these pages, we hope that:

- you totally enjoy your visit
- you share the wonderment and emotions these stories have raised
- you do additional studying about your home community or ours
- you contact me at book@cci.biz about any information you have or know about that can add to our knowledge about people and places in the Wicker Park District.

EAC
JUNE, 2003

Acknowledgements

PRODUCTION:

Praise to the Old Wicker Park Committee's History Book Committee which included, in addition to myself, the following people: Alice Prus, Char Sandstrom, John and Carol Scheidelman, and the late Marion Smith. It was their passions, visions, and insights that started this publication on the road to reality.

To those who did the research and writing, BLESS YOU! They include: Joe DuciBella, Susan Keyser, Neil Levendusky, Arlene Murphy, Diedre Papp, Joe Ricchio, Wanda Rohm, Harriet Sadauskas, Char Sandstrom, Carol Scheidelman, John Scheidelman, Cheryl Smalling, Nick Sommers, Mary and Ed Tamminga, and Rev. Ruth VanDemark.

Mary Ann Johnson, friend, former neighbor and Executive Director of Jane Addams Hull House Museum at the University of Illinois, helped give a perspective to data and the process of producing this body of work that was priceless. The Institutions' section and the Milwaukee Ave. story have the depth they do because of her extensive knowledge and willingness to share.

Very special thanks and appreciation goes to Larry Clary who served not only as editor extraordinaire, but gave me encouragement when needed and tolerated the endless hours devoted to this project instead of my business and personal life!

Thanks to Richard Tilley for proof reading and to three final readers. They are all detail oriented women who are long time friends: Pat Lloyd, architect and former Wicker Park resident; Donna Langlois in Santa Fe, NM; and Pat Knoop in Rockbridge, OH.

Architect George Sorich was my building hero. He literally walked the streets verifying copy on various buildings in the House Tour section. In addition, Sheldon and Sally Kahn were kind enough to spot the buildings for the walking tour guide.

To former resident and longtime supporter, Pablo DeLeon, thank you for giving of your artistic talent, your community knowledge, and on-going encouragement. Without Dan Paterno, this publication would never have been "put to bed." Anne Gaines has put the "frosting on the cake" with her cover design and other drawings, capturing the essence of the book.

Without these marvelously giving people, I could not have brought this project to the level of professionalism that it deserved. Thank you one and all!

RESOURCES:

To the countless number of people who have assisted us in researching our material, thank you so very much. They include but are not limited to the staff in the Municipal Reference Collection, particularly Ellen O'Brien and Shah Tiwana, Social Sciences Division, and Special Collections and Preservation Division at the Chicago Public Library-Harold Washington Library Center; staff at the Newberry Library; and Natalia U. Wilson at the NAES College and Chicago Academy of Sciences, Chicago Botanic Gardens, Morton Arboretum, Field Museum, Illinois Geological Survey, and Illinois Natural History Survey and City of Chicago Dept. of Sewers staffs also aided us in our quest for accurate data.

Chicago Historical Society's three key contacts that made much data and graphics available were Russell Lewis, Paula Murphy, and Rob Medina. Russell's support and encouragement were very helpful. Without Paula, many a fact would have gone undiscovered. Rob and Aimee Marshall.were most helpful with images.

Neighborhood Contributors

There are three men who were instrumental in helping Wicker Park get the historic district statuses and preserve the look of the original community from the mid 1970s. Their efforts and those of so many others, too numerous to list, are what gives everyone living in or visiting this area the opportunity to enjoy the ambiance of days gone by while experiencing a vibrant revitalized urban community. To them we say "GOOD JOB! THANK YOU!"

Julia Bachrach, Chicago Park District, introduced me to the wonderful world of Park District history which intertwines with so many Chicago neighborhoods and people.

Historian John Swenson went way beyond being courteous about verifying facts and sharing information. The depth of his knowledge about early Chicago is awesome.

John Notz was most generous with his time, information, and photos concerning the Uihlein family. Jim Schulz, great grandson of Mathias Schulz, participated in our quest for historical information and oral history. Mitzi Isador's help went beyond assistance with Sarah and Jacob Isador because she introduced me to Joy Sigal Frank. Mitzi, who grew up in Logan Square, and Joy are truly Chicago treasures.

Diane Miskiewicz of Palatine, IL and Lynn Horn of Huntington Beach, CA were great sources of information about Wicker Park places and families from decades ago that is not recorded or readily available.

Our long time police officer and friend William (Bill) Jaconetti and fire department guru, Ken Little, were both most helpful.

Richard Kujawa of the Polish Museum gave freely of his extensive knowledge of the Polish community, John Smulski, and Ignance Paderewski. Norwegian Archivist, Jennifer Johnston at Vesterheim Norwegian-American Museum in Decorah, IA. was very helpful relative to the Norwegian community.

Blessings to the very smart people of the forerunner of Chicago Title and Trust Company, who, when the 1871 fire was shooting its destructive tongues of doom about the city, had the sense to move their land tract deed books out of harm's way. Thanks also to CTT's present staff for making them accessible.

Special thanks to Mary Jo Doyle at the Roger's Park/West Ridge Historical Society, for sharing her knowledge about producing and marketing a neighborhood publication.

Joe DuciBella spearheaded hours of work by a legion of the "pioneers" of the 1970s as the historic recognition battles spread throughout the neighborhood, first to Washington, D.C. and then to Chicago's City Hall.

Lonn Frye gave of his professional design expertise, working with People's Gas and Light Company and the Park District to construct buildings in the 1990s that keep the feel of the Victorian architecture while providing for the physical demands of the current times.

Marion Smith fought for the rights of the community, whether for beautification of the neighborhood, proper fencing around the park, restoration of the original park fountain, community signage, or a myriad of other issues. Marion lost a long fought battle with cancer during the creation of this book, though he was contributing ideas to the very end. He was always generous with his energy, knowledge and support for honoring our heritage and making the "hood" a great place in which to live. For this we honor him. We will miss him, and his legacy will continue, thankfully, to impact our community.

Patrons

Seed money for this publication was vital to its creation. We give loud applause to the State of Illinois' Illinois First Program. Thanks to Brian Pendrak and his committee of fundraisers for bringing in additionally needed funds. The Patrons are, of course, our angels that made sure the thousands of hours of research and writing were published.

Platinum ($500 and up)

Alice Prus

Gold ($250 to $499)

BigFin Properties
Butler Development
Cloister of Wicker Park
Nick's Beer Garden
The Note
Nancy Wicker
Leland Wilkinson

Silver ($100 to $249)

Betancourt Realty
Thomas Black & Ann Lanphear
Michelle Booz
Rafer Caudill
Conrad Cwiertnia
James Ferguson
Holiday Club
Alvin Joyner

Matthew Kudrna
Michael Lorimer
Claudia Mastro
North Clybourn Group
Northside Café
Brian & Bridget Pendrak
Peterson & Assocates
St. Mary Hospital

John Scheidelman
Silver Cloud
Nancy Stark
Cheryl Smalling
Subterranean
Ed & Mary Tamminga
Jane Wenger

Bronze ($50 to $99)

William & Fay Corbett
Jody & Steven LaVoie
Club Lucky
J.K. Expert Developers
Amy Lehman
Sheri Katz

Thomas Kmiecik
Manik Motor Sales
Don & Patricia McNichols
Alfred Mojica
Arlene Murphy

The Beginning

Plate 1.1
DEER AMID BIG AND LITTLE BLUE STEM, ASTERS,
GOLDENROD, SWITCH GRASS, COMPASS PLANT, AND CATTAILS.

Travel Through Time...
Chicagou* Struggles for Life Then Grows Explosively

Plate 1.2

THIS IS A SAVANNAH THAT WAS PROBABLY TYPICAL OF WOODED AREAS SUCH AS AROUND ELK GROVE AVE.

To understand Wicker Park's history, imagine yourself standing at the intersection of Milwaukee, North, and Damen, the heart of Chicago's Wicker Park neighborhood. Take a journey back in time.

Close your eyes and watch the calendar move backward in time...2000, 1950, 1900, 1850, 1800, 1750, 1700, stopping at 1673.

Open your eyes and view the vast panorama. Gaze in all directions. You are surrounded by prairie with sparse woods to the southeast. This landscape is already ancient. To get a better view, take flight.

Soar to the east and look south. In about a mile, a ribbon of water meanders from north to south. Follow the river (Chicago) south, then east. A huge body of water (Lake Michigan) is straight ahead. Though

*There are at least 39 different spellings and 11 different etymologies relative to the origin of the word Chicago. Names include: "Chicagoux", "Checagou", "Chicougou", and "Chicaou". Meanings include: "something great", pole cat, skunk, leek, wild onion, and wild garlic. Based on research from original documents, John Swenson stated in 1999 that "Chicago" was derived from the Indian word, chicagoua. Chicagoua was the native garlic plant (Allium tricoccum) that abundantly grew along the wooded banks of this area's waterways.

there is no visible indication, this vast area will be known as downtown Chicago. Look back to the northwest at the area from which you just came.

All of this area is part of the Chicago Lake Plain. This was the bottom of what was the Glacial Lake Chicago, formed when water from the melting glacier pooled between upland ridges (moraines) on the west and the glacial ice to the east. One of the moraines that formed the lake is named Valparaiso. It starts its reverse "j" shape at the south end of Lake Michigan, swings west of what will become Wicker Park, and heads north further than you can see to an area that will be known as Wisconsin.

From your current location, look to the south and to the west. In the wet seasons you'll see the water encroaching well inland in the area that will become the heart of the city.

Remember the layout of the modern streets as you wing your way south to what will become 47th St. and head west to Harlem Ave. Look north and east. See the shallow depression about five miles in length and of irregular width (Harlem and West 47th to the area of Kedzie Ave. and West 31st St.). It is filled with grasses in dank and sticky muck.

Head north to 45th. This is the beginning of what is known as the Chicago Portage. The Illinois Indians discovered this shortcut many moons ago. During the dry season it is a land link between the DesPlaines River (which further south flows into the Illinois) and the south branch of the Chicago River. During the wet seasons, the spillage from the DesPlaines generally floods over the land, creating a water passage.

As you head north, the flat, drier prairie now appears to the north and east. Tilt your wings and head northeast toward Howard and Damen. Observe that the prairie expanse is broken by a trail. One of the earliest paths that brought man down from the north is the Green Bay Trail. Follow this trail (southeast) to what is now Foster and Clark, then south to Michigan Ave. and the River. Follow the river west and note that there are no bridges, but there is another trail breaking the prairie landscape at the river's edge. In about 150 years that trail will be known as the Milwaukee Plank Road. Follow it to the northwest

until you arrive at your starting spot.

At ground level, you would have recognized various types of forestation, wild life, and social organization.

During the period of the 1600s, trees tended to populate the side of water opposite the fire source. Prairie fires were the trees' major enemy (while being the prairie's friend), thus forests on the plains were fairly rare. Instead, you see clusters of trees occur along lakes, rivers and creeks. Hazelnut and oak predominate in these areas. Open savannas (prairies with occurrences of trees) are more prevalent. Groves, another type of tree cluster, vary in size with undergrowth that is woodland-like. You flew over more savannahs and groves than forests.

In prairie areas, tall grasses, typically big and little blue stem as well as Indian and switch, flourish in the rich soil. Nature adds texture with the broad leaf plants such as compass plant and prairie dock. Brown-eyed Susans, goldenrod, and asters provided the color for the broad expanses, throughout three of the four seasons.

Low swampy areas are populated with such plants as cattails, bulrush and other water-loving species. In between the high and low areas, there are saw or cord grasses.

The abundant variety of birds and fowl living in this area provide food for human inhabitants. These feathered creatures include: passenger pigeons, prairie chickens, swans, geese, grouse, eagles, hawks, wild turkey, and several types of ducks including tiny water-witch, blue winged teal, mallard, and canvasback.

Many fowl dine on wild rice and insects while the birds forage among the grasses and trees for seeds, berries, insects, and small animals.

Though mastodon bones will be found on the south side of Wicker Park in 1885*, the animals in residence here in 1673 are much different. Drinking from rivers and streams, bear, wolf, fox, beaver, and herds of deer move across these prairies, providing food, skins, and pelts to residents and fur traders. It is possible that there were stray bison (also known at the time as buffalo, oxen, and Illinois cattle) from south of Chicago roaming close by.

*Found under 13 to 15 feet of silt, part of a jaw, teeth, and fragments of a few other bones were given to the Chicago Academy of Sciences.

Among the humans, there is struggle for survival and dispute over territorial "ownership." Stream after stream of Native American nations have made their homes in this area: Illinois, Sioux, Sauk, Mesquakie (Fox), Miami (a branch of the Illinois tribe), Ojibwa (or Chippewa), and Ottawa. One group, often in fear of another, moves on to another territory. Villages are often a mix of tribes and occasionally non-Indian people live in these Chicago district communities.

Plate 1.3
LOUIS JOLLIET

The causes of these mixed communities vary: captives brought back from warfare; inter-tribal marriage; migration of whole tribes; and epidemic diseases. Non-Indians are from European and African origins. Some are "business partners" in trading, others are captives, and some inter-married. As long as they live in the ways of the community they are accepted as relatives and kinfolk. Children are raised like the tribal children.

Plate 1.4
FATHER JACQUES
MARQUETTE

In this year of 1673, the area's civil jurisdiction is under France's Province of Nouvelle France headquartered in Quebec.

Louis Jolliet and his fellow explorers, including Father Jacques Marquette, are returning to Canada after their exploration of the Mississippi. According to many accounts, they are the first white men to set foot on the land next to the joining of the River (Chicago) and the Lac des Illinois (Lake Michigan).

Jolliet, an organist, is a college-educated man whose plans to enter the priesthood were changed by his intense interest in mathematics and geography. That interest resulted in his heading west, where his brother Adrian, a fur trader, was living. Marquette, a linguist, is known to be a learned, talented man who is a devoted priest interested in missionary work.

Seeing the Chicago, Jolliet sees the great commercial potential for joining Lake Michigan and thus the other inland waterways with the Gulf of Mexico via the Mississippi. He makes this recommendation to French authorities in Montreal.

Move slowly forward. It's now 1675 and Marquette dies at age 38. Father Jean Claude Allouez picks up his missionary efforts. Not until 1696 will another, bigger wave of French missionary efforts occur in this area.

La Mission de L'Ange Gardien (the Guardian Angel Mission) is founded by Father Pierre Francois Pinet. (The mission was probably located where the present-day Merchandise Mart stands.) Father Julian Bineteaut came with Pinet; they are joined by Father Jean Mermet. In a few years, a Miami Indian village with 150 cabins will surround the mission. A trading post will be built nearby. All will flourish.

By 1712, the Fox, who have been friendly with the French (their power being centralized in Detroit under Antoine Laumet), join the efforts of the Iroquois against the French, disrupting community development from Chicago, through the Illinois River valley, and down to the Mississippi. In fear of repeated Indian raids, people flee the mission, village, and trading post.

As you move forward through time, seasons, people and area "ownership" come and go. Weather continues to alternate between extremes of hot and cold temperatures; from no air movement to gale-like conditions; and from ground parched of all moisture to wallowing in mud from snow or rain.

In February of 1763, the French and Indian war ends and England takes over the Province of Quebec with the provisional government in Quebec. Slow down at 1769. Note that the Potawatomies conquer the Illinois at Starved Rock and become the dominant tribe of upper Illinois.

In 1773, William Murray and a group of fellow English subjects purchase Indian land that extends up the Illinois River to "Chicagou or Garlick Creek." It includes most of what is now Chicago. This purchase will be determined to be null and void by the U.S. Supreme Court. It will be determined that Indian-owned frontier land could only be sold to a government. Murray forms the Illinois Land

Company. He continues his efforts to regain rights to this land. Ultimately these efforts will fail.

Plate 1.5

JEAN BAPTISTE POINT DE SABLE'S CABIN IS DEPICTED ON THE RIGHT BANK OF THE RIVER IN THIS PENCIL DRAWING BY KATE BACON BOND, DURING 1933 TO 1934.

On June 22, 1774, the English Parliament passes an act formalizing British rule over France's former territories. Notice that the Revolutionary War begins in 1776. By December 9, 1778 Virginia, with its seat of government in Williamsburg, claims all of Illinois to the 41st degree (just south of Chicago). Chicago remains as the western edge of Connecticut. Jurisdiction changes again. It goes to the United States on Sept. 23, 1783, with a provisional government in Philadelphia.

Continue to move forward in time. Jean Baptiste Point de Sable, a free born black man, becomes the first non-Indian resident of modern-day Chicago, sometime around the mid 1780s. His residence is a prosperous house and farm at the mouth of the Chicago River (close to where the current Chicago Tribune Tower stands), probably owned by licensed British trader, William Burnett of Detroit. Being a time of barter for goods and services, it is easy to understand why Point de Sable is called a "trader," when in reality he is a farmer. Though many later writings will credit Point de Sable with having a trading post in Chicago approximately 10 years earlier, it was located in what is now Michigan City, IN.

Many of the "facts" of Point de Sable's life are uncertain or disputed, including the date and location of his birth, the identity of his parents, the spelling of his name, and his successes and failures. By all accounts, he is well known and sociable.

As we come to 1795, the U.S. government recognizes Chicago as a significant factor in the security of the western frontier. Battles in the East against the British and the Indians that started several years ago culminate in a resounding victory by General Anthony Wayne (a.k.a. "Mad Anthony" and "The Tempest"). On June 16, a council of American officials and many Indian nations' representatives begin a fifty-six day meeting. It concludes with the Treaty of Greenville (Ohio).

Among many other points, the treaty states that there will be free use of the Chicago and Illinois rivers and portage, and that the Indian nations will vacate reservations at Chicago, Peoria, and the mouth of the Illinois. The Indians cede to the United States "one piece of land six miles square, at the mouth of

Plate 1.6

FIRST FORT DEARBORN, BUILT IN 1803, IS BURNED IN 1812 AND REBUILT IN 1816.

Chicago River, emptying in to the southwest end of Lake Michigan, where a fort formerly stood." (Though not surveyed, this will become Fullerton on the north to 31st street on the south, the lake on the east and Cicero Ave. (48th Ave.) on the west.)

From this moment, the stage is set. The country will expand. Chicago will become a transportation hub for distribution of goods.

Let's move forward to 1803. Construction of Fort Dearborn at the mouth of the Lake and the River begins under the control of Captain John Whistler who commanded a company of infantry from Detroit, MI. The Louisiana Territory is purchased from France. Many can now see the possibility of connecting the Hudson with Lake Erie, Lake Michigan, the Illinois, and the Mississippi down to the Gulf of Mexico. Jolliet's vision of more then 125 years earlier is being put into action.

It takes another nine years, but John C. Calhoun, Secretary of War, submits a report to the Congress urging the construction of a canal across the Chicago Portage. This year of 1812 also brings many peace treaties with the northwestern tribes as well as tragedy to Fort Dearborn.

It is a sunny warm morning on August 15, 1812. A "militia" of twelve, plus fifty-five regular soldiers, nine women, and eighteen children in two oxen drawn wagons file out of the fort. Heading to the lake shore on the way to the Fort Wayne road, they are escorted by thirty Miami, brought from Fort Wayne by Captain William Wells to assist in the retreat. Suddenly, from behind sand hills there is a band of warriors heading toward the column of travelers. The Miami desert the column almost immediately. Captain Heald leads his men in a bold return attack but most are massacred in the battle. The remaining twenty nine soldiers, two men and six children will be tortured and killed before the warriors leave for their homes after burning the Fort.

Four years later, in 1816, the Fort is rebuilt. A non-military settlement is also built. Life in these communities is hard. There are few resources. The few women who live in the community try to bring some social life to it. Cabins are sparsely filled. Homespun cloth from homespun wool is used for clothing while home-grown food is supplemented with pork, beef and occasional wild game. Fruit occasionally comes in from Indiana travelers and traders. Schooling is irregularly available as is religious counsel.

As we move to 1818, we can celebrate statehood for Illinois. Though the northern boundary was to have been the bottom point of the lake, it is moved north allowing for commercial access to Lake Michigan. This is the final step that insures Chicago of being a major player in the growth of the country.

Move forward to 1827. Congress grants Illinois a section of land in a five-mile wide strip along either side of the canal for the purpose of aiding its construction. In 1829, the State Legislature makes provision for a three-person canal commission with powers appropriate for the perceived work. Their first action is to lay out the towns of Chicago and Ottawa, at either end of the proposed route.

Archibald Clybourne builds the first meatpacking plant up the River's

Plate 1.7

LAST COUNCIL OF THE POTTAWATOMIES, 1833, ORIGINALLY PAINTED BY LAWERENCE EARLE, DEPICTS THE SEPTEMBER MEETING AT WHICH THE POTTAWATOMIES AND REPRESENTATIVES OF OTHER NATIONS CEDE THEIR LAND AND AGREE TO BE OUT OF THE TERRITORY IN TWO YEARS.

North Branch between North and Armitage, around 1829*.

You will count the population of Fort Dearborn as being between thirty and forty in 1830. It covers an area that will later be known by streets named State west to Halsted and Madison Ave. north to Chicago Ave. Since more than half of the area is north of the river, surveyor James Thompson proceeds to lay out the town plat for the area northward from Madison to Kinzie and westward from State to Des Plaines. The area east of State to the lake and south of the River is where Fort Dearborn is located. The plat is filed on August 4, 1830. Public auction of lots brings a modest income the next month. Two 80-acre parcels sell for $1.25 per acre while 126 lots average $35 per lot.

The Illinois General Assembly creates Cook County, with Chicago as the permanent county seat, in 1831. All troops leave Fort Dearborn.

As we move to spring, 1832, Du Page, Des Plaines, and Chicago area residents, faces stricken with fear, rush into the protection of the Fort Dearborn. News of Black Hawk warriors coming into Illinois spreads through the area like wild fire.

The population increases five fold. Confusion is increased by the arrival of Michigan militia and regular soldiers. Food supplies become inadequate during the Indian war. July brings General Scott, on the first steamships into Chicago, with several hundred East Coast soldiers, along with Asiatic cholera. The Fort becomes a hospital. Chicago empties overnight, the fear of cholera being greater than of Indians.

We see people returning in fall as a result of the victory over Black Hawk, reducing fear of Indian attacks; the beginning of real estate interests along the canal; and reports of fertile land.

Better times unfold for Chicago as it incorporates as a town in August 1833. The community is one of a frontier settlement. Animals roam about unrestrained. The first public building is a pen to keep livestock until their owners claim them. Then a building is constructed for the sick, both residents and non-residents. Next there

Plate 1.8

It is 1833, Chicago is about to have buildings added to its sparse existence.

is a non-military jail. A lumber mill goes into operations near Clybourne's meatpacking facilities. The mill's finished products begin to replace logs as Chicago's main building material.

Early fall brings the treaty signing with the Potawatomies and other Indian nations. They agree to leave the state in two years.

The Erie Canal opening in 1825 is now beginning to impact Chicago. Ambitious eastern residents learn about Chicago's commercial potential. Returning soldiers tell of the entrancing wilderness of northern Illinois and southern Wisconsin as well as the beauty and wealth of natural resources. They believe that Chicago will be a key for world-wide trade.

The "school section" (between State and Halsted from Madison south to Roosevelt Road) is sold at auction. At an average price of $6.72 per acre, the 144 blocks are each approximately four acres.

While Chicago began the year with log huts and one frame building, it will end with dozens of frame buildings. Congress, in March, votes to expend $25,000 for a Chicago harbor, and Chicago, as a viable shipping capital, begins. The force of the water rushing to the Lake, after the sandbar at the mouth of the river is cut open next year, will dredge the channel deep enough to allow the passage of the heaviest ships.

The town of Chicago is formed in 1833, though the Illinois legislature will not recognize that

*Danckers, in Early Chicago, gives land tract information that puts into question the exact year and location of this plant.

status until 1835.

As you pass through 1834, note the extreme real estate frenzy that occurs, not just in Chicago but all around the Lake Michigan shores. Watch the bubble burst in 1837. This is a small step backwards as Chicago's growth begins to explode. The population of 1833 of 150 is now up to 4170. The 100-ton schooner *Illinois* glides into the river, greeted by cheers of residents lining the banks. Chicago incorporates as a city on March 4, 1837, the same day Martin Van Buren takes the oath of office as President of the United States.

Plate 1.9

BY 1869, WATER TRAFFIC IN AND OUT OF THE RIVER AT LAKE MICHIGAN IS BUSY, AS SEEN FROM THE RUSH STREET BRIDGE VANTAGE POINT.

Not much happens until 1843 when the population takes another leap forward to a population of 7,580. It doubles again over the next three years. Notice that the first permanent school building is erected in 1845.

Slow down as you pass through 1847. Robert McCormick moves the McCormick Reaper Factory from Cincinnati, Ohio to Chicago, locating it just east of what will later be Michigan Ave., between North Water St. and the Chicago River.

In 1848, Jolliet's vision of opening the inland waterways to world traffic is realized when the canal is completed. Telegraph services begin by linking Milwaukee and Chicago. In addition, the old wood burning steam engine, *Pioneer*, chugged its way from Oak Park to Galena and back on October 25, 1848. On November 20, it brought wheat from the DesPlaines River into Chicago on Chicago's first railroad, the Galena and Chicago Union.

By 1850 the population is up to 28,260. Gas lamps are erected on Lake St. and several adjacent blocks. Chicago area's first university,

Northwestern, is founded in 1851. The police department is expanded in 1855 and Fort Dearborn is demolished the next year. Livestock, lumber, and grain are major factors in the economy. Manufacturing operations such as meatpacking, tanning, soap-making, lumber milling, and flour milling expand the need for factory workers. Chicago has become the hub of major transportation routes and the gateway to the West.

The population grows to 93,000, by the end of 1857. The city boundaries continue to expand.

People with emerging industrial and handicraft skills as well as those with all types of abilities and talents are drawn to the city that is becoming a center for almost every major industry. Agricultural products and major industry distribution develops outside the city while industry and commerce grow within.

With the context of Chicago and the world behind us, it is time to end this journey and move to the creation and growth of the Wicker Park neighborhood.

— *Elaine A. Coorens*

Neighborhood Ownership and Boundaries Change

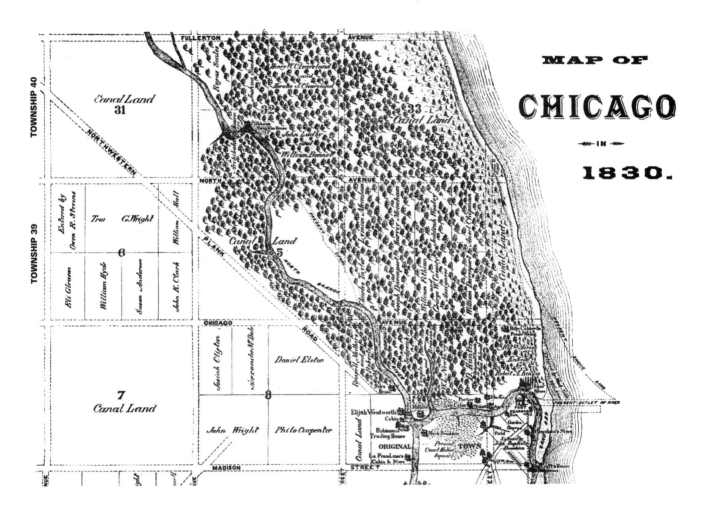

Plate 1.10

MAP OF CHICAGO IN 1830 SHOWS THE SECTIONS IN TOWNSHIP 39 AND 40 THAT MAKE UP THE WICKER PARK DISTRICT WITH THE NAMES OF THE SUPPOSED PROPERTY OWNERS IN THAT YEAR.

Though the original "ownership" of the Wicker Park District and the rest of Chicago goes back to at least the Archaic people (in the area until about 1000 B.C.), the Native Americans inhabited the area for many centuries while many foreign countries claimed ownership. France took possession in 1671 with the seat of government being Quebec. England claimed sovereignty in 1763. In December 1778, Virginia claimed Illinois south of Chicago. But Chicago remained the western edge of Connecticut. The United States claimed ownership on September 23, 1783.

From 1787 to 1818, territorial boundaries (Northwest, Indiana, and Illinois) shifted around

Chicago. When Illinois declared statehood in 1818, it included Chicago. County boundaries continually changed around Chicago until 1831, when it was declared part of Cook County.

Organization of Chicago began in 1833 when five trustees were elected from a population of approximately 350 to serve on a village board. They met and drew up the town's boundaries for incorporation on August 10. Nineteen blocks within the village and 80 adjoining acres were sold to visiting New Yorkers, Arthur Bronson and Charles Butler.

It was two years later, on February 11, 1835, that Chicago's 1833 incorporation as a town was endorsed by the Illinois General Assembly. Population had grown to approximately 3,265 people. Individuals bought 370,000 acres of public land in 1835 and another 202,364 in 1836. Land set aside for schools was sold, by demand of 95% of voters. It sold for less than $39,000.

Incorporated as a city in March 1837, the city's original western boundary was Wood St. and its northern boundary, west of Ashland Ave., was North Ave. Ten years later (First Extension by Act of Feb. 16, 1847) Western Ave. became the city's western boundary* while North remained the northern boundary. The Third Extension by Act of Feb. 13, 1863 extended the city's northern boundary from North to Fullerton Ave., between Western and Ashland. The western boundary, south of North, was moved to Kedzie in 1869, as determined by the Fourth Extension (Act of Feb. 27, 1869). It was another twenty years before the western boundary, north and south of North, moved further west.

Structure for the city was set up to be Wards. Initially there were six wards, which increased to fifty by 1921. Cook County in 1850 established twenty-seven townships and divided Chicago into three sections, North, South, and West.

Though it is not known when Wicker Park neighborhood boundaries were established or by whom, the *Greater Chicago Magazine* February, 1929 issue states, "The section of Chicago bound by Western (2400 W.) Avenue on the west, Ashland (1600 W.) Avenue on the east, and Augusta (1000 N.) Street to Armitage (2000 N.) Avenue on the south and north, respectively, is known as the Wicker Park District..."**

As per the Survey Plat maps of 1821, the Wicker Park District is part of two townships.

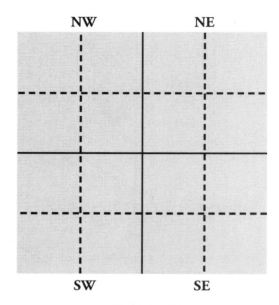

Illustration 1

EACH TOWNSHIP SECTION IS ONE-MILE BY ONE-MILE SQUARE. THAT SQUARE IS THEN DIVIDED INTO FOUR QUADRANTS: NORTHEAST (NE), NORTHWEST (NW), SOUTHEAST (SE), AND SOUTHWEST (SW). EACH OF THOSE SQUARES IS DIVIDED INTO FOUR SQUARES. THIS PRODUCES A GRID OF SIXTEEN 40-ACRE PARCELS.

Each township is bounded by Western on the west and Ashland on the east with a dividing line between them at North Ave. Township 40 is north of North Ave., and Township 39 is south of North Ave. In Township 40, the Wicker Park District occupies the Southwest and Southeast quadrants of Section 31 and the Northwest and Northeast quadrants of Township 39 Section 6. The land in Township 40 was Canal Land and was the last District land to be developed. Township 39 land was Federal land.

---

*Some records show this date to be 1851, we are using the original designation as per the Act of Feb. 16, 1847.

**In this book, based on historical facts, the Wicker Park District boundaries are Armitage on the north and Division on the south, with Ashland and Western being the eastern and western boundaries, respectively.

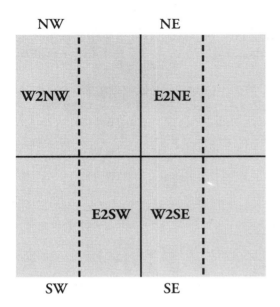

Illustration 2
WHEN REFERRING TO SECTION QUADRANTS,
"2" INDICATES "HALF."

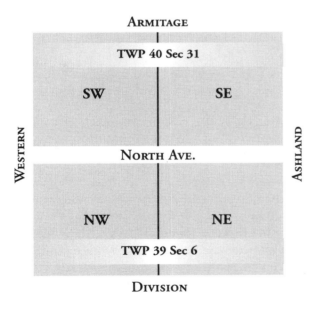

Illustration 3
WICKER PARK CONSISTS OF THE SOUTHERN HALF OF
TOWNSHIP 40, SECTION 31 AND THE NORTHERN HALF
OF TOWNSHIP 39 SECTION 6.

The earliest map of land ownership is the Chicago 1830 Map. (See *Plate 1.10.*) The information on that map, in the Illinois Public Land Tract Sales database, and in the original Tract Books do not totally agree.

As seen on the 1830 Chicago map, all of the land in this area was undeveloped, though it is possible that people had settled on or used some of this property prior to the land sales that began on June 15, 1835. Those people were called "pre-emptioners." Notice to Pre-emption Claimants published in the *Chicago Democrat* on March 25, 1835 read:, "Persons claiming the right of pre-emption to any of the aforesaid land, are required to prove the same to the satisfaction of the Register and Receiver prior to the date of sale." The "aforesaid land" included the Wicker Park District.

The charts below list the original "purchasers" of the land that make up the Wicker Park District. The information was brought together from the original land Tract Books and the Illinois Domain Tract database. Notice that all purchase dates in Township 39 are prior to 1835. They were pre-emptioners. Only the Wicker Park quadrants are shown.

*N = NORTH; S = SOUTH; E = EAST; W = WEST;
2 = HALF (EXAMPLE: W2SW (BELOW) INDICATES WEST
HALF OF THE SOUTHWEST QUARTER OF TOWNSHIP 39,
RANGE 14, AND SECTION 6)

TOWNSHIP 39, RANGE 14E, AND SECTION 6
(FEDERAL LAND)
(North, Chicago, Western, and Ashland)

PURCHASER	LOCATION DESCRIPTION	ACRES	PRICE PER ACRE	TOTAL PRICE	DATE
Hall, William	E2NE	80.00	1.25	100.00	11/22/1832
McNeely, James	W2NE	80.00	1.25	100.00	11/15/1834
McNeely, Isaac	W2NW	80.00	1.25	100.00	11/15/1834
Stevens, Orrin R	W2NW	79.95	1.25	99.94	06/13/1835

TOWNSHIP 40, RANGE 14E, SECTION 31
(CANAL LAND)
(Fullerton, North, Western and Ashland)

PURCHASER	LOCATION DESCRIPTION	ACRES	PRICE PER ACRE	TOTAL PRICE	DATE
Pierce, Asahel	N2SW	80.00	35.00	2800.00	09/09/1848
Lytle, William	S2SW	80.00	1.25	2800.00	09/09/1848
+Bronson, Arthur	SWSE	40.00	10.00	400.00	11/18/1841
+Bronson, Arthur	SESE	79.95	1.25	99.94	06/13/1835

+It is not clear on the Public Domain database whether Bronson purchased 80 or 160 acres.

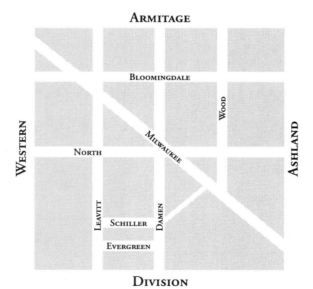

ARMITAGE

BLOOMINGDALE

WOOD

WESTERN

NORTH

MILWAUKEE

ASHLAND

LEAVITT

SCHILLER

DAMEN

EVERGREEN

DIVISION

Illustration 4
**SHOWS BOUNDARY OF WICKER PARK DISTRICT
AND SOME MAIN STREETS.**

Take note of the increase in price per acre from the $1.25 in the 1830s to $35.00 more than a decade later.

By 1867, streets had been laid out in the original incorporated area bounded by North, Ashland, Division, and Wood as well as the area bounded by North, Leavitt, Division, and Western. Street development had occurred in the area bounded by Armitage, Ashland, Bloomingdale, and Western as well as the Bloomingdale, Ashland, North, and Milwaukee area. The two areas most referred to as "Wicker Park", Bloomingdale, Milwaukee, North, and Western, and North, Wood, Division, and Leavitt had no laid out or developed streets.

In 1868 the area bounded by North, Milwaukee, the alley south of Evergreen, and Leavitt was laid out as the D. S. Lee Addition. The streets were not laid out in the area bounded by Bloomingdale, Milwaukee, North, and Western until 1892.

As streets were developed, other services were also delivered, including sewers, gas and water.

Researched by Elaine A. Coorens and Mary Ann Johnson
— Elaine A. Coorens

WICKER PARK BOUNDARIES UPDATE

Although the Neighborhood Map of the City of Chicago shows the southern boundary of the Wicker Park District to be Augusta Blvd., Wicker Park residents, by the mid 1970s, considered the neighborhood's southern boundary to be Division St. (1200 N.). The area south of Division was considered part of Ukranian Village.

Realtors started promoting the area between Damen and Ashland, from Armitage to North, in the late 1980s as part of the Bucktown neighborhood. The Wicker Park and Bucktown community organizations and the Chamber of Commerce agreed to drop Wicker Park's northern boundary from Armitage to the railroad tracks at Bloomingdale Ave. at the time the new millennium arrived.

When historical district designations (National Register for Historic Places as of June 20, 1979 and Chicago Landmarks as of 1991) were given, neither included the entire community nor were their boundaries identical. See the map at the back of this book.

The University of Chicago sociologist, Louis Wirth, set about grouping wards together for purposes of statistical comparisons in 1938. At that time, he and his students defined seventy-five communities within the city of Chicago. The groupings were based on: settlement growth; local identity; local trade districts; membership in local institutions; and natural and artificially created barriers. This project resulted in the Local Community Fact Book, which is republished approximately every ten years. Wicker Park was included in his West Town community.

For purposes of this book, the Wicker Park neighborhood boundaries are Armitage on the north and Division on the south, with Ashland and Western being the eastern and western boundaries, respectively.

— *Elaine Coorens*

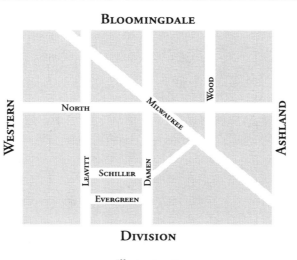

Illustration 5
DISTRICT BOUNDARIES AS PER 2000

Piecing Together Wicker Park Land Development

To get a bird's eye view of the Wicker Park District's land sales and development, one needs to think of layers of maps.

Creating these layers required piecing together information from various sources such as the 1830 Chicago Map, Illinois Domain Tract database, Tract Books, and post-fire Fire Insurance Maps. The Great Chicago Fire (1871) wiped out all real estate records including tract books, and related documents such as deeds, mortgages, etc. Fortunately, employees of Chicago Title and Trust's predecessor had the good sense to move their set of Tract Books outside the reach of the fire.

The pre-fire Tract Books and the Insurance Maps are the most valuable sources. Hundreds of real estate transactions listed between 1830 and 1860 pro-vide clues about the land as well as the early developers that began shaping the neighborhood. From time to time these information resources raise questions as well as provide answers.

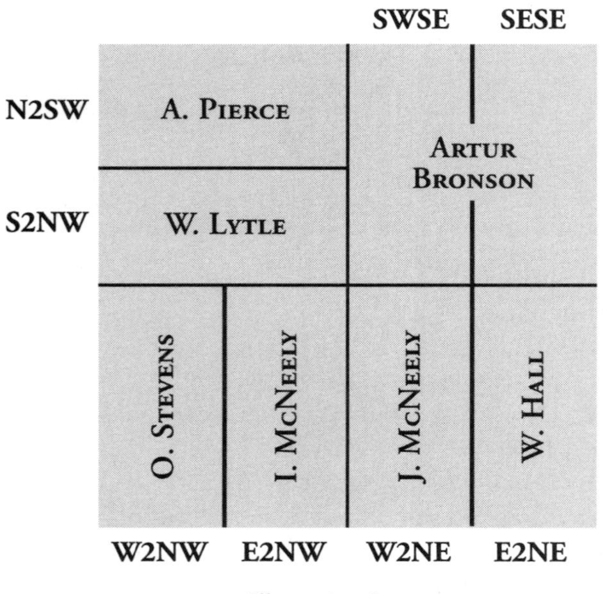

The 1830 Chicago Map, for example, shows Truman G. Wright as the owner of a large parcel of land south of North Ave. In fact the Tract Book shows that. Wright acquired two previously owned parcels that made up that area seven years after the map's date. Within seven months of his purchase, T. G. gave a mortgage to Charles S. Wright, followed by a quit claim in 1857. There is some lack of clarity about ownership of this property because there are many other transactions, over a period of several years, showing parts of those parcels deeded by and to other owners, including D. S. Lee.

The basic survey of 1821 (for the southeast and southwest quadrants of Township 40 Section 31 in Range 14E and the northeast and northwest quadrants of Township 39 Section 6 in Range 14E) is what will be considered to be layer one. (See *illustration 3*.)

Layer two consists of the original purchasers of that land. South of North they were William Hall, James McNeely, Isaac McNeely, and Orrin Stevens. North of North, they were Asahel Pierce, Wm. Lytle, and Arthur Bronson.

South of North, prior to breaking up the original purchases into subdivisions, many new names were involved in transactions for Hall's parcel (Ashland to Wood) as well as J. McNeely's and I. McNeely's (Wood to Leavitt). They are: Cyrenius Beers; Henry Carrington & wife; George T. Cline; Norman Clark; John E. Cone; Robert Gracie; Edward H. Haddock & wife; Elijah K. Hubbard and wife; J. W. Jewett & Azel Dorathy; David S. Lee; Charles G. Meletta; Adamson B. Newkirk; Hiram Pearsons; Solomon L. Sharp; Martin O. Walker; Charles S. Wright; and Truman G. Wright.

Illustration 6

SHOWS ORIGINAL PURHASERS OF LAND IN THE WICKER PARK DISTRICT. TOWNSHIP 40 SECTION 31 IN RANGE 14E IS SHOWN IN TOP HALF AND TOWNSHIP 39 SECTION 6 IS SHOWN IN THE LOWER HALF.

In the two quadrants of land north of North (Township 40 Section 31 in range 14E), Asahel Pierce purchased the north half of the southwest quadrant (N2SW) in 1848. William Lytle bought the second half of that quadrant (S2NW). It appears that Arthur Bronson bought the entire southeast quadrant in 1841.

Layer three, beginning in 1850, shows the early subdividing into "Additions" or "Subdivisions." Layer four takes layer three and divides those parcels into smaller Subdivisions.

In June of 1856, pre-emptioner Orrin Stevens' holding from Leavitt to Western (W2NW in Township 39) was made into the George Watson, William A. Tower & John W. Davis Subdivision. By 1886 the Robinson Insurance Map shows four smaller Subdivisions, within the large Subdivision, for Ham B. Bogue, and one each for C. M. Smith and John W. Davis.

James McNeely's parcel (W2NE) became part of Picket's Addition, Picket's Second Addition, Adam Och's Addition, part of D.S. Lee's Addition, part of Baird & Bradley's Subdivision, Joseph Peacock Subdivision, Beygeh's Subdivision, J. W. Cochran's Subdivision, R. P. Hamilton Subdivision,

J. P. Clarkson's Subdivision, Clarke and Blake's Subdivision, and O. N. Allen's Subdivision as well as George Raithel's small Subdivision within D. S. Lee's Addition.

Isaac McNeely's section (E2NW), in 1886, was broken into part of D. S. Lee's Addition, Waterman's Subdivision, and part of Baird & Bradley's Subdivision. In addition, a small portion of D. S. Lee's portion is shown as John Buehler's Subdivision, while William D. Kerfoot has two Subdivisions in Baird & Bradley's section.

William Hall's former quadrant (E2NE), by 1886, consisted of: McReynold's Subdivision, created in 1853; part of Picket's Second Addition; Bauwan's & Hoffman's Subdivision; Fish's Subdivision; Thompson's Addition; Moorman's Addition; and Spear's Addition. William Herman's Subdivision is shown as part of Spear's Addition and F. A. Hoffman's Subdivision is shown as part of Bauwan and Hoffman's Subdivision.

In Township 40, Pierce's property was changed to be Pierce's addition to Holstein in 1854. By 1886, Robinson's map shows that Pierce's Addition has two subs: Mary Parrot's and Marshall Field's second sub. Only three areas of Lytle's section, which was sold to Eliz. H. R. Allen the same year it was purchased, are shown as laid out. One is bounded by Wabansia, Leavitt, North and Claremont and is divided into Subdivisions for Monroe; J. N. Mason; W. T. Johnson, and Morley and Allen. The second area is Bradwell's Addition, which is bounded by Bloomingdale, Damen, Wabansia, and Milwaukee. The third area is Mather and Taft's Addition, which is bounded by Wabansia, Damen and Milwaukee.

Bronson's southeast quadrant is considered to be Part of Sheffield's Addition. Its Subdivisions are: Chicago Land Co, created in 1868; Matthew Marx, established in October 1859; William Wernecke; Charles Quentin, setup in July of 1855; Joseph F. Lawrence, created in July 1855; E. Randolph Smith, as of October, 1853; Orrin J. Rose, created in November 1853; J. G. Keenon; and John Fitch, established in October 1867.

In reviewing these many transactions in the Tract Books, one notices that some developers

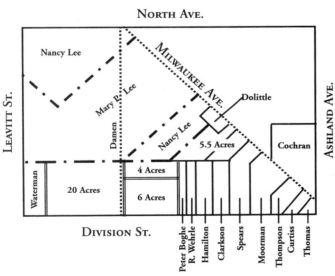

Illustration 7

THIS REPLICATES AN INSERT IN THE TRACT BOOK FOR NE1/4 AND E2NW OF SECTION 6, TOWNSHIP 39, RANGE 14E. CIRCA 1861, IT SHOWS LAND OWNERSHIP.

focused on certain areas and that others had patterns of working with others. Transactions of the Wicker brothers are examples of both. Charles focused on property west of Leavitt and Joel on property in the D. S. Lee Addition.

Joel agreed to purchase specific lots in the D.S. Lee Addition, totaling eighty-four acres, from Simon Reinemann in June of 1868. He received the deeds to that property two years later and sold them two years after that in 1872. Other people who purchased multiple lots in the D. S. Lee Addition were William L. Ewing, Edwin Fowler and J. E. Tyler.

Between June 1868 and March 1869 Charles Wicker appeared to have worked with William Kerfoot, and Adolph Loeb in buying and selling property in Orrin Stevens' parcel (West from Leavitt and south of North). Wicker purchased specific lots and Kerfoot purchased tax deeds on the same properties. They would subsequently both sell their interests to Adolph Loeb.

Having looked at the land transactions, one wonders who these early purchasers and developers

Plate 1.11
WILLIAM D. KERFOOT

were. Five names have been mentioned many times over the years when community history has been discussed: T. G. Wright, David S. Lee, Mary L. Stewart, Charles Gusavus Wicker, and Joel H. Wicker.

According to *Fergus Directory of the City 1839*, Truman G. Wright boarded at the Tremont Hotel and was classified as a speculator. Subsequent directories did not list him, though Wright sold property in 1856.

Plate 1.12
CHARLES G. WICKER

It is possible that he was one of the earliest examples of people gobbling up land, selling it, and moving on in search of other opportunities.

Listed in the 1850 Census, New Jersey born David S. Lee was shown as being thirty-five years of age and his Pennsylvania born wife Mary at twenty-nine. Lee began purchasing land in the area in 1847. Within ten to twelve years he owned a great deal land in the E2NW and W2NE quadrants of Section 6 Township 39. Several city directories listed his law office on Lake St. and his home at 59-60 Randolph.

After D. S. Lee's death in 1860 in Northampton, MD, his wife Mary P. Lee and mother Nancy Lee held ownership of the property. Upon the death of Nancy in 1868, her interests went to Mary, who at an unknown date married R. Stewart and became known as Mary L. Stewart. *Bailey's City Directory of 1864-65* and *1865-66* list her as a widow living as a boarder at 287-89 Illinois. The D. S. Lee property was recorded as an Addition in 1868 and was divided into sixteen blocks of lots. She deeded D. S. Lee's Addition, Block 7, Wicker Park, to the city in September of 1870. Mary L. Stewart's name appears as the seller of many parcels of land in this neighborhood through the 1880s. Yet, little is known about her.

Like so many of Chicago's first business and real estate developers, the Wickers came from New England. Vermonters, they came from humble beginnings. Joel's and Charles' father, a minister, died in 1822. Joel moved from New York to Ohio and opened a general store. Charles, in 1836 at the age of 16, worked as a mule boy on the construction of the Erie Canal before joining Joel as a store clerk. Coming to Chicago in 1839, Charles

Illustration 8
ADDITIONS AND SUBDIVISIONS OF THE WICKER PARK DISTRICT AS SHOWN
ON THE 1886 ROBINSON INSURANCE MAP.

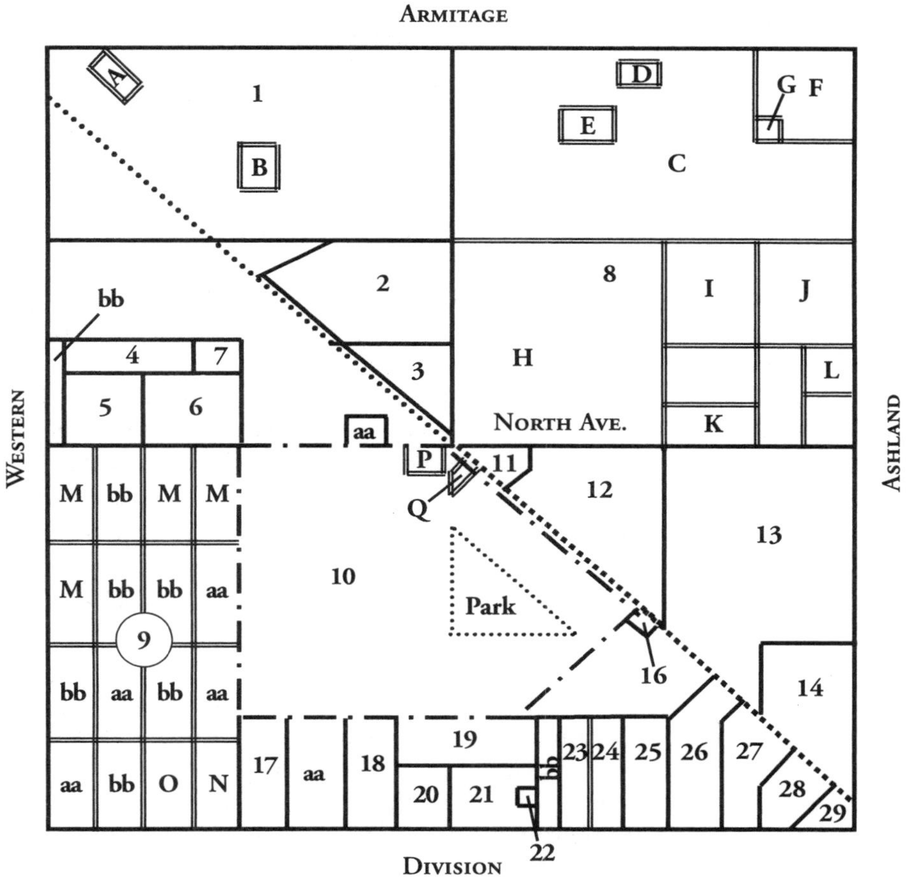

1. Pierce's Addition to Holstein
A. Mary Parrots Sub
B. Marshall Field's Second Add
2. Bradwell's Addition
3. Mather and Taft's Addition
4. Monroe's Subdivision
5. J.N. Mason's Subdivision
6. W. T. Johnson's Subdivision
7. Morley and Allen's Subdivision
8. Part of Sheffield's Addition
C. Chicago Land Co's Sub
D. Wm. Wernecke's Sub
E. M. Marx Sub
F. Quentin's Sub
G. Lawrence's Sub
H. E. R. Smith Sub
I. Rose's Sub
J. J. G. Kennon's Sub
K. John Fitch's Sub
L. Burr Public School
9. Watson, Tower & Davis Subdivision
M. H. B. Bogue
N. C. M. Smith
O. J. W. Davis
10. D. S. Lee Addition
P. John Buehler Sub
Q. John Raithel's Sub
11. O. N. Allen's Subdivision
12. H. E. Picket's Second Addition
13. McReynold's Subdivision
14. Bauwan & Hoffman's Subdivision
15. H. E. Picket's Addition
16. Clarke and Blake's Subdivision
17. Waterman's Subdivision
18. Adam Och's Addition
19. Baird & Bradley's Subdivision
20. Wm. D. Kerfoot Subdivision
21. Joseph Peacock's Subdivision
22. Beygeh's Subdivision
23. J. W. Cochran's Subdivision
24. R. P. Hamilton's Subdivision
25. J. P. Clarkson's Subdivision
26. Spear's Addition
27. Moorman's Addition
28. Thompson's Addition
29. J. P. Fish's Subdivision
aa. Lots laid out but no sub name
bb No lots laid out

NUMBERS = INITIAL ADDITIONS AND SUBDIVISIONS
LETTERS = SUBDIVISIONS OF ADDS AND SUBS
DOUBLE LETTERS = DEVELOPMENT
NO LETTER OR NUMBER = NO LOTS OR STREETS LAID OUT

MILWAUKEE AVE.
D.S. LEE ADDITION

once again worked for Joel. The *Fergus Directory* lists them as grocers at 87 Lake.

The 1844 directory lists their residence as the Tremont. An advertisement for the business in the same year reads: "Cheap Cash Store, No. 94 Lake St., C.G. Wicker & Co., Wholesale & Retail

Dealers in Dry good, groceries, leather, glass, nails, produces, etc." At this point Charles pursued his own interests. He moved into the political arena in 1861 and became well known for championing the unpopular cause of saving the downtown lakefront property for public use. He served as Third Ward Alderman for two terms in the late 1860s. Nothing else is known about Joel.

An 1890 biographical sketch, written by an employee of Charles, states, "In 1867 he bought, in connection with others, what was known as the 'Lee tract' on Milwaukee avenue, subdivided it, fenced it, laid out streets, made ditches, etc., and improved and set apart as a gift to the city the beautiful tract now known as Wicker Park." There is no transaction in the tract books to support this statement.

Though the Wicker brothers had interest in the community, there was no evidence found that either brother ever lived in the district that bears their name.

The backgrounds of other early developers point out that diversity of people involved with the neighborhood started from its inception. Pre-emptioner William Hall is listed as a lumber merchant, in 1842. He was a border at the City Hotel. At the time of his death in 1894 he was 83 years of age.

Research produced no information about Orrin Stevens, Isaac McNeely, and James McNeely except their land transactions. Appearing in the 1843 directory, William Lytle is listed as a clerk at Hamilton and White.

A listing in the *Fergus Directory for 1855-56,* shows Nathan Allen as an attorney at 32 Randolph with his home at Milwaukee "near city limit." *D. B. Cooke & Company's Directory for 1858* lists Nathan Allen as a lawyer at Milwaukee Ave. near Wood. Other directory listings have Allen's office consistently on Randolph and his residence around Milwaukee and North. In the *Lakeside Directory of 1874-75* Allen's office is not listed, but his residence address is 931 Milwaukee (old numbering system).

Arthur Bronson was a New Yorker who began purchasing Chicago land in 1835.

In 1839, Asahel Pierce was listed as a plow and wagon maker at 18 Market. In 1844, Pierce's trade is listed as blacksmith on South Water by Lake and Randolph. His home was on Lake St. Involved in politics, he was one of the first aldermen (4th ward) elected in the city.

With the exception of Allen, it appears most early purchasers and developers did not live in the community. That changed, however, starting in the 1880s, when residents purchased and sold single and multiple lots. An example of this is Edward Uihlein who lived in the 2000 block of Pierce (then Ewing Place). He had a subdivision in the D. S. Lee Addition that included 2119 to 2129 W. Pierce, which he purchased in 1887. From Sept. 1887 to March 1888, he sold them to Charles Frees, Frederick Mueller and Julius Schuldt. Other property records show purchases and sales among neighbors. In addition there was lending of money, neighbor to neighbor.

In the Recorder of Deeds office, the Chicago Tract Books show transactions beginning with 1871. The pre-fire tract books reveal the names and transactions that occurred, property by-property from, in some cases, before the government started selling the land in 1835. Since track books only record land transactions, it is not possible to learn about any buildings on the land or any agreements that were not recorded with the property.

— *Elaine A. Coorens*

Development

Plate 2.1
THE ELECTRIC STREETCAR MARKED "NORTH AVE LINCOLN PARK & HUMBOLDT PARK" IS HEADING EAST ON NORTH,
ABOUT TO CROSS THE INTERSECTION WITH MILWAUKEE AND DAMEN.
VIEW IS FROM THE SOUTH SIDE OF NORTH, WEST OF MILWAUKEE PRE 1906.

Gentry and Working Class Immigants —Why Did They Come?

Overview

Since development of a city and neighborhood occurs at many levels at the same time, reconstructing information about Wicker Park's development is like putting a multi-level jigsaw puzzle together. The clearest way to deliver this information seems to be by covering the elements that went into neighborhood creation and growth. Those elements are: ethnic groups, businesses, the Great Fire of 1871, transportation, Prohibition, and the advent of city services. Then show how the neighborhood's main artery, Milwaukee Avenue, mirrored that development.

The following stories provide information about these elements and lay the backdrop for this book's next section about life in the Wicker Park District.

Plate 2.2

ETHNIC GROUPS OFTEN MAINTAINED THEIR OLD WORLD TRADITIONS AFTER SETTLING IN CHICAGO. HERE NORWEGIAN CHILDREN CELEBRATE SYTTENDE MAI (MAY 17) IN WICKER PARK.

Regardless of where they came from, immigrants in Chicago during the 1800s were generally fleeing from something. And, they were seeking something in their new country: greater economic opportunity, freedom of religion and politics, the chance to live and work where they wished, and/or social equality. Immigrants were from all social and economic backgrounds and they came with an array of values, beliefs, abilities and resources.

Geographically and geologically Chicago was ideally positioned during this period for development. Natural resources for commerce and industry were at her door. Building materials, food, energy sources, and other raw materials could be accessed by foot, water, horse, or train. Chicago's growing commercial, manufacturing and industrial concerns attracted human resources with a wealth of knowledge, skill, talent, ingenuity and ambition. During the 1800s Chicago was a magnet for development, attracting new residents from parts of America and countries throughout Europe.

After the Chicago Fire of 1871, the Wicker Park District became home to a series of European immigrant groups. Although many people settled in the community during the 19th century, the largest groups were the Germans and Norwegians first, and later, the Poles and Eastern European Jews. Other groups that settled in the district at that time were the Irish, Danes, Swedes, and Serbians. Newly arriving groups faced many of the same issues: economic survival, discrimination, assimilation, preservation of ethnic identity and patriotism among them.

The newest arrivals were generally employed in the lowest paying jobs. Many were unskilled laborers who worked in sub-standard conditions for long hours at low pay. Often nationality groups would cling together, claiming a part of the city as their own, creating institutions, organizations and societies based on their traditional cultures.

Some members of the various ethnic groups were eager to assimilate into American society as quickly as possible, while others sought to maintain native languages, values and traditions. Within each community there were many opinions about where to stand and what course to take on issues of bilingual education of children, the maintenance of cultural customs, and the observance of religious and ethnic traditions.

Germans

Although Germans began immigrating to the United States in the 17th century, it wasn't until the 1850s and 60s that masses of people from Germany began settling in Chicago. By 1860, Chicago's German-born residents represented more than twenty percent of the population and were more than forty-one percent of the foreign born. Their numbers continued to swell during the 1870s. The 1884 Chicago School Census reported that one-third of the city's population was first or second-generation German.

Initially, German immigrants came mainly from the southern part of Germany. Social and economic changes induced by the Industrial Revolution, agricultural reform, and overpopulation in rural areas

Plate 2.3
GERMAN WORKERS AT THE HORN BROS. FURNITURE COMPANY PREPARE FOR A STRIKE JUST BEFORE THE HAYMARKET LABOR INCIDENTS IN 1886, ILLUSTRATING HOW LABOR CONFLICTS SOMETIMES PITTED MEMBERS OF THE SAME ETHNIC GROUPS AGAINST EACH OTHER.

made it hard to maintain traditional ways of life and in response, many Germans began emigrating to other countries. Most of these emigrants were craftsmen, farmers and small shopkeepers. Once in Chicago they often entered into the trades as shoemakers, coopers, bakers, butchers, cigar makers, cabinet makers, upholsterers or wagon makers. Other Germans during this period were professionals or intellectuals who emigrated for political reasons after the failed 1848 revolution in Germany. By the 1880s Germans were coming primarily from the northern part of the country and were generally less skilled workers, often day laborers and servants.

The Germans who came to Wicker Park in the 1870s and 80s were both first-generation and second-generation immigrants. Some families had previously lived in other neighborhoods in Chicago and, having been burned out by the Fire, were relocating to Wicker Park for a fresh start or as a move up, socially and economically. Others were new arrivals from Europe, and Wicker Park was their first area of settlement.

The variety of occupational, regional and reli-gious backgrounds of the Germans made a very heterogeneous group. Despite a common language and national heritage the Germans in Wicker Park represented a great variety of attitudes, life styles and beliefs. Some were Catholic, Protestant or Jewish, while others were considered "club Germans," those whose main allegiance was to secular organizations rather than religious ones. Some in the neighborhood were elite business owners, while others were skilled workers or common laborers. Some aspired to assimilate into elite American society while others sought to change the system through participation in trade unions or socialist, communist or anarchist movements.

As will be seen, the Germans in Wicker Park were great institution builders. In addition, they influenced mainstream organizations. By the 1860s they were able to institute the teaching of the German language in the public schools. The Germans left their mark in the neighborhood through their hospitals, schools, businesses, organizations and distinctive architecture.

NORWEGIANS

The Norwegians came to Wicker Park at about the same time as the Germans. Because of their country's extensive coastline that faces to the west, Norwegians have long been seafarers, explorers, and colonizers. They claim to have settled in North America as early as the 13th century, although this has been disputed by some scholars. An early group of fifty-two Norwegian immigrants voyaged from Stavanger, Norway to New York in 1825. Mainly Quakers and religious dissenters from nearby rural districts, they sailed on a small sloop named "Restauration" (the Restoration) and were called "sloopers." The trip took a little more than three months. On the way over captain Lars Larson's wife gave birth to a daughter, two months after leaving Norway.

During the 19th century Norwegians, about eighty percent of who were peasants, had strong beliefs about liberty, human rights, national identity, and self-determination that conformed to old Nordic ideals. By the mid-1800s many began to seek social equality as well. America, with its prospects of free or cheap land, comparatively high wages and promise of social equality regardless of occupation or background, became an attractive destination. As with all immi-grant groups, economic and demographic pressures also played a major role in their decision to emigrate. During the 19th century, no other country except Ireland contributed so large a proportion of its population to settling the United States. Most of the emigrants left Norway between 1840 and 1915, with the 1880s being a peak decade.

Once in Chicago, Norwegians initially settled along Milwaukee Ave. near Chicago Ave., building their first church at Superior and Wells. In the 1870s members of this group moved up Milwaukee Ave. and into the Wicker Park District. The Chicago School Census of 1884 reveals that 80 percent of first- and second-generation Norwegian immigrants lived in three wards on the city's Northwest Side, while a canvassing of the district in the immediate area of Wicker Park indicates that about half were German and a quarter Norwegian.

Wicker Park Norwegians were upper-middle class, middle-class professionals, and working-class people. The upwardly mobile Norwegian elite built mansions and elegant homes in the area and called the community "Homansbyene" after an exclusive section

Plate 2.4
**NORWEGIANS OF ALL AGES HEAD WEST ON NORTH AVE. PAST ST. PAUL'S CHURCH (UPPER RIGHT)
ON THEIR WAY TO HUMBOLDT PARK TO CELEBRATE SYTTENDE MAI (MAY 17TH).
THE VACANT LAND IS THE SOUTHEAST CORNER OF NORTH AND LEAVITT.**

of Oslo. Middle-class residents were often business owners, shop keepers or professionals. Working class Norwegians lived in more modest housing in the neighborhood and worked as carpenters, joiners, cabinet makers and painters, trades that were in great demand as the city rebuilt itself after the Great Chicago Fire. Unlike nearly all other ethnic groups, the Scandinavians did not advocate the teaching of their native languages in the schools. According to the editor of their major newspaper, *Skandinaven,* they wanted their children to learn English - not foreign languages. Expressing values of frugality and stability, most had a desire to own their own homes rather than rent, and it was said that

their places of businesses were among the most neatly kept in the city.

The Norwegians maintained a strong ethnic identity through the proliferation of numerous societies based on regional loyalties and identities, and through the celebration of national holidays such as Syttende Mai on May 17th. This holiday celebration was originally held in Wicker Park, but as it grew it was moved to Humboldt Park where eventually "ten thousand spirited Norwegian Americans" were in attendance on a single occasion. By the turn-of-the century Norwegians were moving west along North Ave. into new areas of settlement in Chicago.

POLES

Although the Poles were less than one percent of the population of Chicago from 1850 to 1870, their numbers grew dramatically during the late 19th century. By the mid-1880s Chicago had a population of 40,000 Polish people and was known as the American Warsaw. By 1900 the Chicago Polish community was the largest one in the United States.

During the 19th century, as the capitalist system spread across Europe, profound changes in the economic and social conditions of Polish territories caused large numbers of people to emigrate. In the period after 1865 most Polish immigrants were peasants who left their home country for economic and religious reasons. In Poland these people were called *za chlebem* (for-bread) emigrants. They attached particular importance to the possession of land, which to

them meant security. During this period, many Poles came to Chicago hoping to make money and then return to Europe better equipped to purchase property in their homeland. In the 1870s and 80s the *Kulturkampf,* or "struggle for culture" was instituted by the government to weaken the hold of the Roman Catholic Church in the German-dominated territories of Poland. As a result, many Polish Catholics, especially the clergy, emigrated to America to establish new institutions.

Chicago became a major destination for Poles in the late 1800s because of the great employment opportunities for unskilled workers that were developing in industries here, but also because of the freedom the city offered to establish national Catholic parishes. Unlike eastern American cities, whose Catholic hierarchy was dominated and controlled by the Irish,

Plate 2.5

THE POLISH ARMY WAR VETERANS AND THEIR FAMILIES GATHER IN FRONT OF THEIR HEADQUARTERS ON WOOD ST. IN THE 1920S. THIS BUILDING WAS CONSTRUCTED FOR THE MARKS NATHAN ORPHANAGE IN 1906.

Chicago's Catholic Church struggled to accommodate a plethora of ethnic groups by the late 1800s and permitted the establishment of parishes based on nationality and native language.

Although Polish immigrants in Chicago came from a variety of independent areas in Europe, most of them had certain basic things in common: they spoke Polish, they were primarily Catholic, and they came from a communal society. The last characteristic, which meant that individual's personal goals were subordinated in order to achieve the common good, was carried over and maintained in Polish settlements in Chicago, becoming a fundamental principal of this group's institutions, organizations and cooperative self-help societies.

Polish immigrants first began moving into the Wicker Park District in the 1880s. Their initial settlement around St. Stanislaus Church at Noble and Potomac (Bradley) had expanded dramatically in the 1870s, spawning several new churches, a Polish high school, an orphanage and other institutions. As a result, Poles began moving up Milwaukee Avenue, replacing the earlier German and Scandinavians settlers in the community. Eventually Division Street was so dominated by this group's businesses, organizations and entertainment spots that it was called the "Polish Broadway."

JEWS

Jewish people came to Wicker Park after the-turn-of the century. By 1915 they were one of the major groups in the community and the largest ethnic group served by the social services of Association House of Chicago. The Jews who moved to the Wicker Park District around 1900 century were pri-

Plate 2.6
THESE JEWISH MEN, LARGELY FROM THE WICKER PARK DISTRICT, WERE FOUNDERS OF THE MARKS NATHAN ORPHANAGE ON WOOD ST. SECOND FROM THE RIGHT IN THE THIRD ROW IS NICHOLAS J. PRITZKER.

marily Eastern European immigrants from Russia, Poland, Lithuania and other countries. They were distinguished from Chicago's German Jews, who had come to the city in the 1850s and 60s. The German Jews had been merchants and civil servants in small towns and cities in Germany. Once in America they became engaged in various businesses and commercial operations and by the 1880s they were quite well assimilated and established in Chicago society. A handful of German Jews lived in the Wicker Park neighborhood in the early days as a part of the general German community. In the 1870s and 80s they moved further west to the newly established community of Humboldt Park.

The immigration of Eastern European Jews (generally referred to as "Russian Jews") began in the 1870s and increased tremendously between 1880 and 1925. In the 1880s anti-Semitism, the horrors of the Russian draft (that often tied up young Jewish men for many years) and the institution of murderous pogroms against Jewish people in Eastern Europe, led to a mass emigration to America and other countries. Eastern European Jews were generally people whose life in the shtetl, a small Jewish town or Jewish part of a larger town, was bound by strict Orthodox law that governed all aspects of life including religious practices,

social behavior and dietary customs. Once in America, many tended to identify themselves as Jews and cling to their traditional ways, although there was still a great deal of variety in this group's approach to American society.

The first Eastern European Jewish settlement in Chicago was on the west side in the "Maxwell Street" area. This was a neighborhood characterized by overcrowding, poverty, disease and deteriorated housing. As immigrants in this area began moving out into other parts of the city in search of better living conditions, Wicker Park became a destination for many.

The Jews who moved to the Wicker Park District during this period were a diverse group. A significant number were involved in progressive social movements, identifying themselves as members of the labor movement or as socialists or communists. Others became successful business people, establishing large stores and manufacturing concerns along Milwaukee Ave. The Jews in Wicker Park established many retail establishments, institutions and organizations during their brief period of residence in the community. By the 1930s Jews were moving out of the neighborhood and into other areas of Chicago.

— *Mary Ann Johnson*

Industries Are Born and Opportunities Abound

Lumber District, Chicago, Ill.

Plate 2.7

LUMBER WAS A MAJOR CHICAGO INDUSTRY, FIRST TRANSPORTED BY WATER THEN BY RAIL. WICKER PARK FURNITURE AND CONSTRUCTION COMPANIES AS WELL AS LUMBERYARDS USED THIS RESOURCE.

Moving to the Chicago area in the 1800s was like putting the first footsteps on new fallen snow. Chicago's first entrepreneurs had the opportunity to imprint their ideas and ways on a brand new community at the edge of civilization. Natural resources were bountiful and location was ideal. Human resources not only became plentiful, but were eager to succeed. In addition, many were skilled craftsmen. With each ethnic wave came more resources with which a powerful city was built and the Wicker Park District was created.

Chicago's industries grew out of fur trading, shipping, grain, lumber, livestock, stones and minerals, and railroads. Many tended to locate along the waterways for transportation and the use of water. Each industry created other businesses. Byproducts from livestock alone included: meatpacking, glue, gelatin, fertilizer, soap, buttons, tanning, and many more. Grain accounted for the grain elevator and mill businesses as well as flour and other food-product companies. Lumber's contribution included lumberyards, furniture, prefabricated buildings, and along with limestone, the construction industry. Manufacturing brought major contributions to this area and the world, including everything from farm implements to building products, as well as food and clothing.

The service needs of these various businesses and residents opened more avenues for ways to earn a living. Service businesses included: legal, financial, commercial trading, medicine, education, communication, distribution, retailing, lodging, and entertainment, to name but a few.

Early city directories listed people with many different occupations. Following is a partial list: blacksmith, boot and shoemaker, capitalist, clerk, canal contractor, carpenter, compositor, cooper, dentist, drayman, gardener, grocer, gunsmith, hairdresser, hostler, lighthouse keeper, house mover, laborer, pawn broker, portrait painter, phrenologist, pressman, publisher/editor, real estate dealer, tailor, school teacher, stage coach ticket agent, and teamster.

INDUSTRIAL BEGINNINGS

Fur traders and innkeepers were among the first to establish businesses in Chicago. An invoice dated April 13, 1833, for products shipped from Chicago to eastern markets, according to Chicago historian A.T. Andreas, was considered to be the beginning of Chicago's major involvement in trade and commerce.

Manufacturing plants started opening their doors in 1833. Tyler K. Blodgett built a kiln and opened a brickyard on the river's north bank between Clark and Dearborn. Though sawmills opened along Hickory Creek in 1832, it appears that a full-range mill was not available until a steam-powered sawmill, located on the Chicago River near Clybourn Ave., opened in 1834.

Establishment of one type of business often resulted in another. Asahel Pierce, newly arrived from Vermont in early October 1833, when he started to build a small blacksmith shop at Lake and Canal. Unable to obtain the lumber he needed in Chicago, he hauled it from Plainfield, IL, forty miles away. His capital nearly depleted, he bought an old set of blacksmithing tools from Rev. Mr. See. In January of the next year he obtained an order from John T. Temple & Co. for doing the ironwork on the first stage line from Chicago to St. Louis. By spring he was manufacturing "Bull" plows, which became the first farm implement made north of Springfield, IL. Pierce went on to make improvements on his products and produced the first steel and self-scouring plow in the West. And, in 1848 he became a Wicker Park District land owner.

Briggs & Humphrey, early in 1834, began manufacturing vehicles for the horsepower available on

North Branch of Chicago River, looking North from Division Street Bridge, Chicago, Ill.

Plate 2.8
LOOKING NORTH UP THE RIVER FROM THE DIVISION ST. BRIDGE, MANY COMMERCIAL FACILITIES MAY BE SEEN, 1909-12.

Plate 2.9
ROLLING MILL STEEL WORKS PROVIDED THE FIRST INDUSTRIAL IMPACT ON WICKER PARK. THIS PAINTING DEPICTS THE ROLLING OF STEEL RAILS.

the farm and then the highway. In the same year on the West Side, William H. Stow and David Bradley built the first foundry. Lyman and Gage Flour Mill opened in 1836 on the west bank of the Chicago River at about VanBuren. A year later, Ira Miltimore established a sash, door, and blind factory and retail store along the South Branch. In 1837, Charles

Morgan started making furniture on Lake St. Many other businesses such as candle and oil manufacturers, tanneries, and brewers and distillers were also opened.

Companies made it through the financial panic of 1837 and continued to grow in numbers and size. Cyrus McCormick, who built his first reaping machine in Virginia in 1831, moved his plant to Chicago in 1847.

Plate 2.10
ROLLING MILL STEEL WORKS BECAME ILLINOIS STEEL COMPANY IN 1889. THIS VIEW WAS PROBABLY TAKEN IN THE EARLY 1900S AFTER THE PLANT HAD ESTABLISHED A BRANCH ON THE SOUTH SIDE.

HOME OF THE **BEN BEY**
GROOMES & ELSON CIGAR FACTORY
CHICAGO

Plate 2.11
GROOMES AND ELSON CIGAR
FACTORY STATES ON THE BACK
OF THIS CARD, 1909-12: "MOST
SANITARY AND MODERN CIGAR
FACTORY KNOWN, CAPACITY
80,000 CIGARS DAILY, LOGAN
SQUARE AND HUMBOLDT PARK
'L' ROADS; MILWAUKEE AVE.,
ARMITAGE AVE., NORTH AVE,
AND ROBEY ST. LINES
CONVENIENT MEANS OF
TRANSPORTATION, SITUATED
AT CORNER OF ROBEY
AND WILMOT STREETS"

The advent of the railroad turned Chicago into a transportation hub with ten trunk lines, by 1856. Rail transportation provided faster distribution of products and materials that were delivered more reliably and predictably than by water or horse-drawn vehicle.

It was not until 1857, however, that industry impacted the Wicker Park District. Located north of North and east of Ashland, Rolling Mill steel works was the impetus for development of the northeast corner of the Wicker Park District. This factory re-rolled iron railroad tracks and is said to have made the first Bessemer steel rail in the country in 1865. It became part of a larger organization, the North Chicago Rolling Mill Company, in 1869, and consolidated with two other steel factories to form the Illinois Steel Company in 1889. Like other industries that sprang up along the north branch of the river, it attracted new immigrants to the area, originally Irish and German, and later Polish.

Chicago business development flourished in the 1860s, in great part due to the Civil War. Three facilities— Camp Douglas, a prisoner of war camp, and the induction and training center for Camp Fry Troop— were major purchasers of food and military supplies.

The Great Fire of 1871 caused near complete destruction of Chicago. Rebuilding, however, brought a boon to the construction industry and pushed commercial and residential development further out from the city's center.

Old industries rebuilt and new ones sprang up. Activity in Chicago's manufacturing and commerce sectors was so intense that the Panic of 1873 did not have the same effect in Chicago as elsewhere in the country. The pre-fire product value of 1870 nearly doubled to $176,000,000 in 1873.

Tobacco manufacturing was one of the industries badly hurt by the disaster, as most were located in the downtown area. Prior to the fire all varieties of tobacco products were made here, including cigars, snuff, and cigar boxes. Wicker Park became home to several of those cigar factories by the 1890s. One was on Division east of Ashland, another was on Milwaukee between Division and North. Grommes and Elson Cigar Factory, home of the Ben Bey, came after the turn of the century to Damen and Concord (Robey and Wilmot).

Two Chicago companies were soon engaged in a new approach to sales, which became known as direct catalog marketing. Aaron Montgomery Ward started this type of merchandising in 1872, followed by Sears, Roebuck & Company. These companies became the retailers for many companies, including the Schulz Piano Company. Mathias Schulz, who became a Wicker Park post-fire resident, founded the M. Schulz Company in 1869. It made sewing machine cabinets, pianos and other contract cabinetry, adding organ cabinets when the reed organ gained popularity.

While making sales calls one day, Schulz was shocked and horrified to learn that one of his best customers, for whom he had hundreds of organ cabinets completed or in progress, was declaring bankruptcy. He hired the organ company's superintendent and arranged to complete the organs. He then had the dilemma of how to sell them. Mathias's grandson Otto, Jr. tells the rest of this story in his memoirs:

"Someone told him there were two men on Jackson Boulevard who sold watches and furniture by mail... so... he went to the partner in charge of sales, Mr. Sears. His partner was in the rear of their space in a loft building, fixing watches. He was Mr. Roebuck. Mr. Sears said an organ was a pretty big item for them to sell but he admired the pictures my grandfather brought and said he would give it a try. Needless to say, they offered them at a low price as my grandfather was anxious to realize what he could from his inventory. At any rate, they sold, and that started a relationship that lasted for 10 or 15 years."

Many well-known companies outside the Wicker Park District were owned and operated by Wicker Park residents.

In 1868, A. P. Johnson pooled resources with F. Herhold and A. Borgmeier, to purchase a cane seat factory, changing it to a wood seat chair manufacturing company called Herhold, Johnson & Borgmeier. In 1877 Johnson bought out Herhold and asked his brother Nels to join the firm, changing its name to A. P. Johnson & Co. Incorporating in 1883, it became the Johnson Chair Company. Their business continued to boom, causing them to add to their building continually. Then they built new buildings. By 1905 they had in excess of 180,200 square feet for the com-

pany, plus lumber sheds, stables, etc. It was located at Green and Ancona (Phillips), and they expanded to Halsted (south of Chicago Ave.). Both Johnson and Borgmeier also became Wicker Park residents.

During the infancy of brewing in Chicago, Edward Uihlein accepted a position as Agent with brewer Joseph Schlitz to open up the Chicago market in 1872, two years before the Joseph Schlitz Brewing Co. was incorporated. Edward's brothers were already working with Schlitz in Milwaukee. Edward was very successful by the time Mr. Schlitz was killed in a ship disaster in England three years later. Related to Schlitz through marriage, the Uihlein brothers were put in charge of the company. In his memoirs, Edward reports on the business's progress:

"In the brewery, everything progressed well; all debts were paid, all necessary equipment was present, and the machinery was in the best condition. There was a continually growing supply of malt, hops and beer. We could, now, turn to investing funds in the improvement of other facilities and opening in new cities. I was instructed to inspect likely sites in Chicago, for the purpose of large new outlets. In the beginning, I often consulted my brother August about these possibilities, but with experience, my judgment became dependable. For our own purposes, we often invested funds by financing our customers. In this manner, we not only reached higher sales figures, but we also insured our customers against competition. We could set our own prices, but, of course, we never took unfair advantage of this situation. When we rented to a merchant who handled our products, exclusively, we were very sure of his reputation and his compliance

Plate 2.12

HORN BROS. FURNITURE COMPANY OPENED THEIR DOORS IN 1875 UNDER THE NAME OF HORN BROS. MANUFACTURING CO. AS SHOWN ON THIS PIECE OF STATIONERY.

Plate 2.13
**RONNE'S WHOLESALE DISTRIBUTION BUSINESS WAS HOUSED
IN THIS BUILDING ON ONTARIO.**

problem renting all available space. The final result was the respect of all Chicago's business sector. Eventually, all original land purchases proved to be most prudent, and great profits were made when they were sold. Now that my 'plan' was crowned with success, my brothers August, Henry, and Alfred decided to invest their private funds with me, and I was told to buy more lots in Chicago, which, eventually, attained a worth of several million dollars."

J. C. Horn and his brothers entered the furniture manufacturing business in 1875 on Superior under the name Horn Bros. Manufacturing Company. They later changed it to Horn Furniture Company.

In the wholesale sector, Wicker Park's Christian H. Ronne, a sugar broker, was known as the Sugar King. His wholesale business was located on Ontario.

In the Wicker Park District, William Thoresen, at the age of 25, opened his first building cornice factory on Western Ave. and secured a contract with the Board of Education with the assistance of his Wicker Park neighbor on Caton St., Ole Thorp. Thorp was on the Board of Education. Over the next five years, Thoresen developed an interest in metal ornamentation. He started studying, then designing and making ornaments. By 1897 he abandoned the cornice business, devoting their manufacturing to architectural sheet-metal ornaments. His increasing business relocated to a multi-building complex on Wabansia between Damen and Western. However, the demand for product was so great that he built his own building on 1914-1916 W. North (formerly 419-421), near the intersection of Milwaukee and Damen.

According to the 1892 Rascher Insurance

with all laws and ordinances. A respectable merchant need not have feared an increase in his rent, unless an increase in taxes or the costs of maintenance made it necessary. Needless to say, our policies were not highly regarded by the competition. However, after some time, when we had achieved a reputation for keeping to our contracts and the most inconsequential of promises, we had no

Plate 2.14
**LUDWIG DRUM
COMPANY FIRST
OPENED FOR BUSI-
NESS ON DAMEN
AVE. IN 1910,
ADDING BUILD-
INGS TO ITS COM-
PLEX AS NEEDED.**

Map, the Busch & Epps Malting Company was located south of Bloomingdale and west of the railroad
tracks near Ashland. One of the brewers with facilities
in the district in 1910 was Stenson Brewing Company
at Winchester and Bloomingdale.

William F. Ludwig, Sr, played his first Chicago drumming date in 1893 and opened his manu-

facturing plant, Ludwig Drum Co., in 1910. Over the
years their building complex would grow to cover over
two-thirds of a block with the address of 1728 N.
Damen. Their original inventions were said to include:
separate tension rods, portable pedal-tuned tympani,
floor-model drum pedal, throw-off snare release, chromat-
ic bell lyra, plywood shells, and triple flanged hoops.

OTHER BUSINESSES

Farmers and realtors were probably the first
businesses in what would become the Wicker Park
District; and unfortunately, not much is known about
those who farmed in this area. People involved with
real estate during the 1860s and 1870s appear not, for
the most part, to have lived in this area. (See Page 14.)
They ran the gamut, from people interested in development to those merely interested in "flipping" property ownership, for short-term profit.

Initial commercial establishments serving the
residents were probably merchants in small shops,
taverns, and small manufacturers whose work occurred
on the premises where they lived, or behind or above
other business establishments. The intersection of
Milwaukee, Ashland, and Division is probably where

the first businesses opened. Though, because of the
Rolling Mill plant east of Ashland near Cortland,
there were, no doubt, businesses in that area beginning
in the late 1850s. Initially, buildings were sparse in
number throughout the area. The lots filled in as the
years rolled forward toward 1900.

Businesses included: tailor shops, sausage-
makers, coal and wood yards, stone yards, coal and
lumber yards, livery stables, blacksmiths, photogra-
phers, laundries, greenhouses, milk depots, grocers
(general stores), furniture upholstery shops, bakeries,
drug stores, dye works, and eventually large department stores.

Types of businesses such as groceries are, of
course, familiar to us. Services and items offered have

changed rather dramatically. For example, an 1875 advertisement for Marbach's Grocery shows they offered feed, pressed hay and weighing services.

Some businesses were actually multiple businesses. Jensen Bros. at 1574 Milwaukee was an optician and jeweler. One of their advertisements offered a free eye exam using the "latest appliances for scientific examination of eyes." They sold diamonds, watches and jewelry as well as "spectacles or eye glasses correctly fitted." Albrecht Bros were printers and publishers at 1632 N. Winchester. They offered "Club, society, job and commercial printing" services. They began publishing the monthly newspaper, *Wicker*

Park Eagle, in 1900. Their masthead stated: "Published in the interest of Wicker Park and North-West Side" and "The North-West Sides Most Exquisite Newspaper. Spicy and Clean."

Mademoiselle M. Samuel at 1311 N. Western placed an ad in the *Wicker Park Eagle* in 1910 that reminds many women of how grateful they are that some products are no longer used very often. The ad read: "Notice to Ladies… Corsets made to order at reasonable prices. Perfect fit guaranteed. People with deformities also fit. All corsets made by me kept in repair free of charge for one year. Repairing also done."

In another 1910 ad, Panter Bros. at 1368 Milwaukee was appealing to "Fashionable and Dressy Ladies" with the news "We have established the most reliable and up-to-date Cloak Store… Consisting of high class Cloaks, Suits, Skirts, Dresses, Waists, Furs, etc."

Many business owners lived and worked in the same building or very close to it. The H. N. Lund Coal Company was a good example. Located at the southeast corner of Wabansia and Leavitt, its southern wall became a privacy wall for several homes facing Caton. In fact, one of those homes, 2152 W. Caton, belonged to the Lunds. To get to work, Mr. Lund merely crossed his backyard and entered a door in the south wall of his business. Schroeder's Piano Manufactory on Ashland seems to have been an example of having a business beneath one's living space.

By 1927 Chicago was said to be the "Great Central Market" when, according to the Association of Commerce and the U.S. Census Bureau, Chicago's dollar value of manufactured products rose ten percent and the number of industrial establishments increased by eight percent in two years. The increase of Chicago's 9,112 manufacturing plants to 9,886, in that time frame, was considered to be remarkable as there were many mergers and expected loss in number of plants nationally. Retailing and service businesses were also flourishing and growing in number.

— *Elaine A. Coorens*

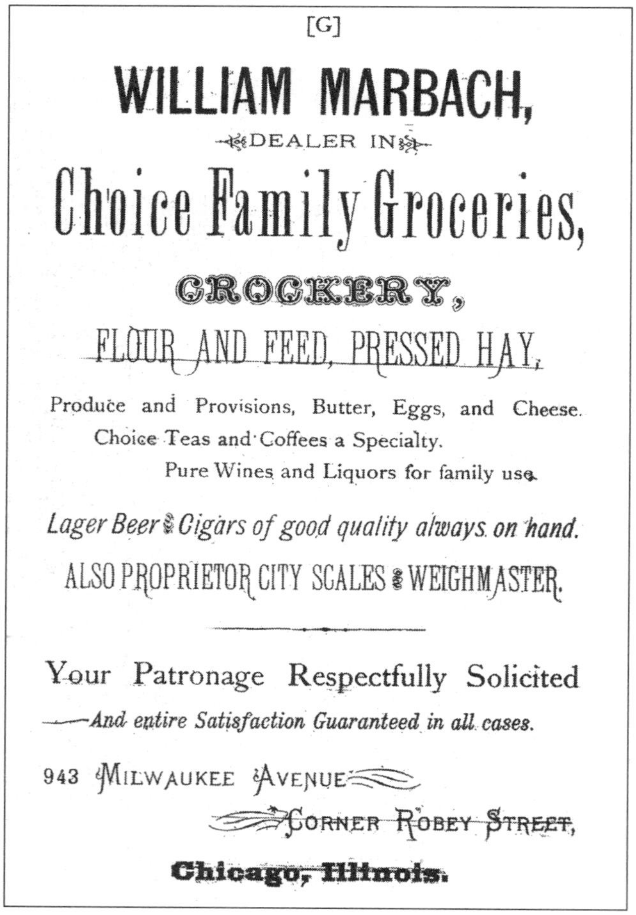

[G]

WILLIAM MARBACH,
⸙DEALER IN⸙
Choice Family Groceries,
CROCKERY,
FLOUR AND FEED, PRESSED HAY,

Produce and Provisions, Butter, Eggs, and Cheese.
Choice Teas and Coffees a Specialty.
Pure Wines and Liquors for family use.

Lager Beer & Cigars of good quality always on hand.

ALSO PROPRIETOR CITY SCALES & WEIGHMASTER.

Your Patronage Respectfully Solicited
——*And entire Satisfaction Guaranteed in all cases.*

943 Milwaukee Avenue
Corner Robey Street,
Chicago, Illinois.

Plate 2.15
THIS WAS AN 1875 ADVERTISEMENT FOR A MILWAUKEE AVE.
GROCER, WILLIAM MARBACH.

Plate 2.16
THE WICKER PARK EAGLE
WAS PUBLISHED AND PRINTED ON
WINCHESTER. THE RAILROAD
CROSSING AT BLOOMINGDALE AND
WINCHESTER IS ONE AND A HALF
TO TWO BLOCKS NORTH OF THE
ALBRECT BROS. BUSINESS,
BUT THIS SHOWS THAT THE STREET
WAS A MIX OF BUSINESS
AND RESIDENTIAL BUILDINGS.

Plate 2.17
IT APPEARS THAT SCHROEDER'S "PIANO-MANUFACTORY" WAS AN EXAMPLE OF BUSINESSES BEING LOCATED
BENEATH RESIDENCES, LOCATED AT 1800 N. ASHLAND IN 1895. NOTICE THE WOODEN SIDEWALK.

FINANCIAL INSTITUTIONS WERE A BIG PART OF GROWTH

Several Wicker Park residents such as John Buehler, Paul Stensland, Joseph R. Noel, and John Smulski were involved, over the years, with financial institutions in and out of the District.

Ethnic financial institutions were an important part of the various ethnic communities. These banks often started as small enterprises that also provided other services or products such as real estate sales, rail and steamship ticket sales, and insurance agencies. Unlike the bigger banks, the small banks solicited people's business for such services as transmitting money overseas and small loans. Often these small banks would loan money to business, churches, and benevolent institutions at lower rates. They, too, were always contacted for charitable fund raising purposes. Unfortunately, this "fellow countrymen" loyalty caused many to loose their money because of the dishonesty of bankers.

Norwegian Paul Stensland and Milwaukee Avenue State Bank are examples of this misplaced trust. Starting as a private bank, Stensland's bank grew and became a state bank. A successful banker for many years, Stensland's personal wants and desires caused his bank to fail. Many people lost their hard earned money. Worst yet, one of Stenland's popular tellers, Frank J. Kowalski, a Pole, was so disgraced that he committed suicide. Another ripple effect was that it was impossible for Joseph Noel to get enough investors to permit him to open his business as a state bank instead of a private bank.

Plate 2.18
NOEL STATE BANK BUILDING IS LOCATED ON THE NORTHWEST CORNER OF NORTH AND DAMEN. ITS IMPACT ON THE COMMUNITY WAS AS IMPRESSIVE AS ITS PHYSICAL STRUCTURE.

The history of the Noel State Bank in *Greater Chicago Magazine* gives a bit of Chicago's banking history as well as what this institution's influence was on the growth of the district:

"North West Savings Bank, (as the Noel state Bank was originally called), began business October 28, 1905, with a capital of $25,000,000, which was increased in May 1907, to $50,000,000.

February 1906, the bank moved into its own building at the intersection of Milwaukee and North avenues, the present site of the North West Tower. The neighborhood was cosmopolitan, and became more so as numerous industries and manufacturing plants established themselves in the vicinity.

Officials of the bank in 1906 were Joseph R. Noel, proprietor; H. B. Berentson, cashier and Frank W. Hausmann, assistant cashier. Under the wise direction for these officers the bank was able to weather the panic of 1907.

Public announcement was made in October 1908, by these officers, of the intention to organize a state bank, and a charter was issued to the North West State Bank January 26, 1909. The state bank began business February 1, 1909 with deposits of $285,000. The first officers were: Joseph R. Noel, president; H. B. Berentson, vice-president; A. S. Boos, cashier and Frank W. Hausmann, assistant cashier.

Wm. B. Conklin was elected vice-president in 1912, and Mr. Hausmann was appointed cashier following the resignation of Mr. Boos in 1915.

...The bank's position had become so definitely secure in 1914, that it was elected to affiliated membership in the Chicago Clearing House Association. In 1923 it was elected to direct membership in the Association. Only 30 banks of the 233 in Chicago hold direct membership in this Association, and the advantages of the connection are many. The Federal Reserve Bank was started in 1914, and the North West State Bank joined it in 1917, as the thirteenth member in Chicago.

The name of the North West State Bank was changed to the Noel State Bank, February 1917, and public announcement was made that a new building would be erected for its use. A site was chosen on an adjoining corner to the old bank and the new and present building was opened with a public reception July 30, 1921.

It is interesting to contrast the fortunes of the great institution today with its modest beginnings. Deposits on the first day, October 28, 1905, amounted to $252,000, today it has a paid in capital of $1,000,000.00 and a surplus of $400,000.00. This surplus has all been taken out of profits.

There are many highlights in its history.

One year from the opening day its deposits reached the gratifying total of $1,000,000. The first million in deposits was reached in the spring of 1911.

Mr. Noel became chairman of the board of directors, January 1928. Frank W. Hausmann, succeeding Mr. Noel as president, has had twenty-three years of service with the bank. He was elected vice-president in 1917, and at that time was the youngest bank vice-president in Chicago.

Mr. Hausmann is respected by all who know him for his judgment and knowledge of securities and credit. He is a member of the Bankers' Club, the American Institute of Banking, a director of the Chicago Association of Credit Men, a member of the Chicago Association of Commerce, the Wicker Park Chamber of Commerce and the Ridgemoor Country Club.

Otto J. Hartwig, vice-chairman of the present board of directors, has been associated with the bank twenty-one years. He was the first chairman of the board of directors in 1909 and held this position for nineteen years. Mr. Hartwig is in the drug business at 1570 Milwaukee avenue*, and has been in the same location forty years.

James Davis has been a vice-president and a director of the bank since it was organized as a state bank in 1909. Mr. Davis is the president and founder of James Davis, Inc., wallpaper and painters supplies—an old, established neighborhood firm— 1400 Milwaukee avenue."

Then, like now, financial institutions worked together in efforts to market their services. A committee of bankers in 1913, according to a June *Wicker Park Eagle* article, was undoubtedly interested in getting children properly educated in saving money. Led by chairman J. R. Noel, they went before the School Management Committee of the Board of Education urging them to adopt Chicago School Savings Banks. This activity apparently was the result of the American Bankers' Association's adoption of a miniature banks program in schools aimed at children saving their pennies and nickels.

The Father Gordon Building and Loan Association at 1734 W. Cortland was one of the largest Polish building and loan associations in Chicago according to the *Greater Chicago Magazine* No. 2 1929.

Organized in 1910, its assets were $944,384.83, with a membership of 2,100 shareholders on October 1, 1928. The 1928 report also showed there was an increase of shares to 22,304 that were divided into three classes.

In 1926, Mr. Joseph P. Malick, secretary of the

*Believed to have been old numbering system. (See Page 41)

association and former president of the Building Association League of Illinois, constructed the Cortland building to meet the increased needs of the association.

The officers and directors were: August Marlowski, President; Thomas Malinger, Vice-President;

Philip Sadowski, Treasurer; Joseph P. Mallek, Secretary; and directors Joseph F. Greby, Thomas S. Gordon, Frank Witkowski, Frank Urbanski, and Walter Modjeski.

— *Elaine A. Coorens*

TAILORING COMPANY DRESSES FOR SUCCESS

A novel sales plan aimed at encouraging people to "dress for success" was the 1929 Fall focus of wholesale tailors, G.W. Holmes Tailoring Company at 2302 W. Wabansia Ave.

In an interview with Holmes' Charles Moderow, responsible for the new approach, the *Greater Chicago Magazine* reported:

"This firm of wholesale tailors has been supplying the demand for superior custom-tailored men's clothing for the past thirty-five years. Fulfilling this need to the satisfaction of customers all over the United States meant the opening of a clean, clear road to permanent success for this company.

The unique sort of service recently made available consists in offering two suits or a suit and an overcoat or topcoat for the price of one garment. A saving of about forty per cent is thus effected for the purchaser. The directors of the Holmes Tailoring Company had their 'ear to the ground' and took account of the trend toward a wide range in style, color and pattern which men's clothing is enjoying this fall. The two-for-one plan makes it possible for any man to double the size of his wardrobe at a nominal cost, as the prices fit any purse.

The considerable saving is possible due

to the direct selling methods used. The company contracts with big woolen mills to take their entire output. The clothes are tailored in a great modern factory to the exact measure of the customer. Efficient methods are employed and there are not middleman's profits to add to the cost. Garments of individuality are produced and no customer need finally accept them unless they satisfy in every particular. Men of judgment know that a good custom-made suit will win hands down any time as against the ready-made article....Representatives call on customers, displaying samples, taking measurements and attending to all details."

Promotion for this plan was based on the concept that "modern Americans" attach a great deal of importance on being well dressed and that "good clothes" and "good Americans" are terms that go together.

The *Greater Chicago Magazine* article ended with "Grit your teeth, Mr. Man, throw back your head and say: 'Happen what will, I am going to be prosperous.' And you will be, provided you 'dress' and 'look' the part. It's up to you."

— *Elaine A. Coorens*

Plate 2.19
G. W. HOLMES TAILORING PLANT, 2302 WABANSIA AVE., WAS SAID TO BE HEADQUARTERS FOR ONE OF CHICAGO'S LARGEST CLOTHING ENTERPRISES.

LIFE- AND DEATH- RELATED BUSINESSES POPULATED THE AREA

In addition to the hospitals and physicians who provided health care services in the Wicker Park District, there were also commercial businesses that dealt with health and death. Notable among them were proprietary medicine producers, druggists, ambulance services, and undertakers.

Milwaukee, WI, native Charles F. Elsner came to Chicago to attend the Chicago College of Pharmacy and then opened his pharmacy at 1401 N. Milwaukee. At the time of his death in 1913, it was stated that he had served the community for over thirty years.

Though Theophilus Noel learned of a curative natural product mined in the southwest before the Civil War in 1860, it was not until 1883 that he introduced it as "Damonia." At first the Theo Noel Company marketed it as a dry powder, then as a liquid. In about 1885 he changed the name to "Elixir Vitae." Unfortunately the product froze when shipped in cold weather and bottling was expensive. So, he changed the product back to a dry powder about two years later, giving it the name "Vitae Ore."

Uniformity was a problem with the natural product and customers complained. It took until 1896, however, before Noel could, by working with a chemical company, produce a manufactured formula. Called "Concentrated Compound Extract of Vitae Ore Elixir," the consistent product pleased customers and sales began to exceed those of the original "oxidized" Vitae Ore. Packaged in envelopes, the product was more easily distributed via direct mail rather than through drug stores. In addition, distribution was accomplished

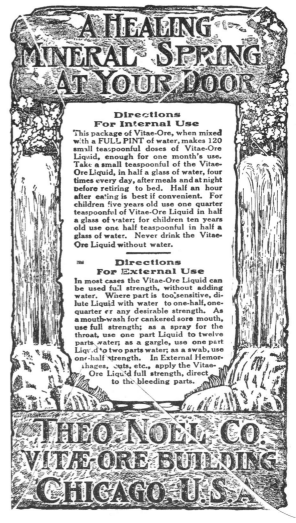

Plate 2.20
THEO NOEL COMPANY'S DETAILED INSTRUCTIONS FOR INTERNAL AND EXTERNAL USE OF VITAE ORE WERE SURROUNDED WITH GRAPHICS.

Plate 2.21
THE VITAE ORE PACKAGE CONSISTED OF AN OUTER ENVELOPE, A GUMMED LABEL, AN INNER ENVELOPE, A WAXED PAPER ENCLOSURE, AND ABOUT ONE-HALF OUNCE OF THE OF THE DRY POWDERED OF VITAE ORE.

through selected drug stores and "local canvassing agents."

Success began to occur in the late eighties and early nineties mainly because of Theo's acquaintance with Joseph Medill of the *Chicago Tribune*. Medill gave him a great deal of publicity, stating that Vitae Ore was "specific for diphtheria." As Joseph Noel, Theo's son who began working in the company in 1897, later stated:

"Although he (Medill) did not fully understand the technical meaning of the word 'specific', nor that of 'antiseptic', he made bold claims for Vitae Ore being both, asserting that there had never been a case of diphtheria in which Vitae Ore had been tried, which it did not cure. This was just prior to the introduction of diphtheria antitoxin."

Sales soared, reaching a peak of $438,000 for Vitae Ore and other V. O. products by 1904, when the office was located in the 2100 block of W. North. Then, popular publications of the time, *Colliers Weekly* and *Ladies Home Journal* began campaigns against proprietary medicines; and the Food and Drug Act became law. Soon publications that Noel used for advertising would not accept proprietary medicine

Plate 2.22 And Plate 2.23

OTHER PRODUCTS IN THE LINE INCLUDED OINTMENT, PILLS AND, BY 1915, A EUCALYPTUS OIL.

advertisements. Though Vitae Ore products continued to be sold, Noel set up another company in 1909 and produced a new product called "Bodi-Tone." Never as successful as Vitae Ore, Bodi-Tone, "…especially because in 1921, 'Bodi-Tone' advertising matter was emasculated as a result of an agreement reached with the authorities in Washington, D.C," according to Joseph Noel.

Otto Hartwig opened a drug store in 1889 in an unfinished building at Milwaukee and Western, four years after his graduation from the University of Illinois College of Pharmacy and following an apprenticeship in a drug store at Chicago and Milwaukee. The land was previously owned by C. Herman Plautz, former city treasurer, founder of Chicago Drug and Chemical Co., and Wicker Park resident.

Surrounded by barren fields, the location was initially outside the city (just west of Western Ave.). Utility service charges were therefore more expensive.

Hartwig's telephone bill, alone, was two hundred dollars higher than that of the business across the street. There was no mail delivery, forcing Hartwig to go to Bandow grocery store, which also served as a post office, opposite the Armitage Ave. car barns.

The Wicker Park Livery Stable, at the corner of Hoyne and Concord (Alice Place) also offered hearses in addition to other carriages.

In 1897 Hochspeier Funeral Home opened its doors in a two-story frame building just west of the North and Western intersection at 2408 W. North. Though probably the first such establishment in the district, it was not the first in the city. However it was the first to have all the components that became the norm for such businesses including: chapels, embalming rooms, hearses, limousines, and more.

With an eye to the future, Mr. Hochspeier built a completely modern business that attracted

Plate 2.24
CARRIAGES AND HEARSES WERE PART OF THE EARLY 1900S OFFERINGS FROM THE WICKER PARK LIVERY STABLE AT SOUTHEAST CORNER OF CONCORD AND HOYNE

the attention of undertakers as far away as Milwaukee, WI. The business grew so much by 1913 that the original building was jacked up and moved to a vacant lot in the rear, and a new modern building was built.

Expansion was in part due to Hochspeier meeting the need for speedy medical service on the northwest side. He established the first ambulance service in Chicago in 1902, taking it from horse-drawn to motorized vehicles in 1912.

A progressive businessman, Hochspeier noticed that advertising on a large scale was the coming trend and began placing ads in church bulletins. He also led the way for advertising in the streetcars and other forms of Chicago's surface transportation. Though Mr. Hochspeier died in 1918, the business continued to serve the city.

— *Elaine A. Coorens*

Plate 2.25
AMBULANCE SERVICES WITH HORSE-DRAWN VEHICLES BEGAN IN 1902. HOCHSPEIER SWITCHED TO MOTORIZED VEHICLES IN 1912.

Plate 2.26
HOCHSPEIER FUNERAL HOME BEGAN WITH HORSE-DRAWN HEARSES BUT MOVED INTO THE MODERN MOTORIZED VEHICLES.

Wicker Park Is Neighborhood's Namesake

Wicker Pk

Plate 2.27
COMMUNITY CHILDREN AND ADULTS GATHER AROUND THE 1895 FOUNTAIN.

Originally established in 1868, Wicker Park had entrances topped with arched wooden gateways, carved with "Wicker Park," by 1870. Beyond the entrances was an idyllic setting of a 4.3-acre triangle of land bordered by Damen, Schiller, and Wicker Park Ave. The area was protected by a wooden fence, boardwalk and entrance posts, from cattle going to and from pastures. Winding paths, landscaped shrubbery, and a large oblong pond, spanned by a rustic bridge, presented a tranquil scene inside the enclosure. This serene location was home to swimming swans and chirping birds perched in a quaint wooden structure on an island located at one end of the pond. Named Wicker Park, it became the namesake of an entire community.

On September 19, 1870, Alderman McGrath presented and moved for approval of a resolution for Wicker Park improvement. It stated:

"Resolved. That the Board of Public Works be and they are hereby requested to extend the water pipe to Wicker Park, erect a fountain, lay out walks and otherwise improve said park, during the present season, to the extent of its share of the appropriation made for park purposes for the East Division, provided a good and sufficient deed of the same be given to the city for that purpose."

According to the Land Tract Book, this condition was met one week later. D. S. Lee Addition's Block 7, Wicker Park*, was deeded to the City of Chicago by Mary L. Stewart (D. S. Lee's widow) on September 26, 1870.

Chicago parks were intended to be places for people of all economic levels to relax and enjoy fresh air. In February of 1869 three acts had created three Park Commissions: Lincoln Park, South, and West Side. The Governor was given the duty to appoint seven members per commission for seven years. The West Side Commission was empowered and given the duties to open the contemplated parks and the boulevards leading to them. Wicker Park was put under the West Side Board's auspices in 1885. John Buehler, Wicker Park resident, served as treasurer from 1879-1884. Over the years, other community residents served on the West Park Commission Board, including Edward Uihlein (1894-1899), George Rahlf (1879-1887), John F. Smulski, (1908-12, 1917-20), and Herman Weinhardt (1891-1898).

The park, like the community, began experiencing change early in its existence. In 1885, park control was passed from the City of Chicago to the West Park Commission. Sidewalk areas were filled to grade, a few trees were planted and some landscaping was done. In 1886, a police shelter building, removed from Washington Boulevard, was repaired and placed near the center of the park. A small number of seats were added for visitor use.

That same year the police dug much of the park up in a futile attempt to find bombs they thought anarchists had planted. The park bore silent witness to the unrest of the times, and to the funeral procession for the five convicted labor leaders that

Plate 2.28
Pergolas were added to the parkscape in 1908, encircling the fountain area.

*When talking of the history of the Park over the years, it has been stated repeatedly that the Wickers donated the land to the city for park purposes. According to the Land Tract Books, it is unclear whether the Wickers ever owned that block of land. Based on writings in 1890 and the fact that the park bears their name, it seems likely that Charles G. and Joel H. Wicker were involved with the park's planning and creation.

Plate 2.29
CHILDREN SPLASH IN THE WADING POND THAT JENS JENSEN INTRODUCED TO THE PARK IN 1908.

died as a result of the Haymarket Riot on Black Friday, November 13, 1887.

The whole image of the park began to change again in 1889. Recreational areas became more of a priority for the park as the land around it filled up with homes and became more citified. That part of the mini-lake that was north of the bridge was filled in and the bridge was removed. The rest of the pond was partially filled in to give it a symmetrical look. Two years later, another plan was executed to reconstruct the park completely. The pond was filled, turning that area into an open lawn. Walks were paved and electrically lighted. A pavilion was built in 1893, in time for the Columbian Exposition of 1893.

"Gurgoyle" (Spanish form of gargoyle), a cast iron fountain as illustrated in the 1883 J. L. Mott Iron Works Catalog, was installed in the Park in 1895.* Then in 1898 the electric light system was renovated and put into working order. An 1898 park plan also shows a comfort station on the Schiller side of the park. According to the "Historical Register of the Twenty-two Superseded Park Districts," published by the Works Progress Administration and Chicago Park District in 1941: "At the turn of the century it was in a very presentable appearance and in fact, it was beau-

tifully kept for the remainder of the West Chicago Park District regime."

A flagpole was added in 1906 at the same time that walks were resurfaced, the pavilion painted and the landscaping improved. In 1905 Olmstead and Burnham started a movement in south-side parks to open the parks' usability by turning fountains into wading ponds. That influence spread to the north side in 1908 when Jens Jensen, as the West Park System Superintendent, removed the 1895 fountain. A new water system was installed and the space was changed to a children's wading pool. In the same project, Jensen built trellis-like structures (pergolas) and planted additional trees and shrubs. His tree requests were for catalpa, elm and gleditschia. His shrub plans included twelve selections: "hawthorns, Russian mulberry, philadelphus, viburnum opulus and letago, cornus Siberica, syringa persica, forsythia, ligustrum ibota, berbieris thunbergi, delavilla rosea, and showberries."

A year later the walks were entirely reconstructed. Evening band concerts were illuminated when an expanded electrical system was installed in 1918.

Researched by Elaine A. Coorens and Char Sandstrom
— Elaine A. Coorens

*Though the original "Gurgoyle" was removed in 1908, another was made from the original J.L Mott molds, and was dedicated on May 11, 2002.

Fire of 1871…Imprints Horror on Residents but Brings Growth

Plate 2.30
THE GREAT CONFLAGRATION OF 1871 IS SHOWN IN THIS DRAWING.

By 1871, Chicago had seen tremendous growth in population and industry. Structures were everywhere. Growing numbers of homes and commercial establishments had not only expanded the boundaries of the city but also increased the density of people and buildings in the downtown area. More substantial buildings had replaced small shacks and modest homes and business establishments. Banks and other entities, in an attempt to show their strength, stability, and security, built solid stone and brick structures. Many of those pre-fire structures were considered to be fireproof.

The Wicker Park District had pockets of development that included: the area around the intersection of Ashland, Milwaukee, and Division; along Ashland toward Armitage (close to the Rolling Mill steel works on the River east of Ashland); along North, Milwaukee, Division, and Damen; plus a few areas off the main streets and avenues. Primarily, Wicker Park was still considered to be "country" property, to some degree.

On Sunday, October 8, 1871, at approximately 8:30 p.m., the Great Conflagration began. Safe in his little factory on West Chicago Ave. on October 9, Edward Uihlein, who would the next year join Joseph Schlitz's Brewing Company and later in the decade be a Wicker Park resident, and his friend

Gundlach were so fascinated by the news of the fire that they rushed downtown to see the event firsthand.

Thinking the fire line was at Madison and Clinton, they were surprised to find it at Canal and Polk Streets. In his memoirs, Edward relates:

"We had crossed the bridge, when the Fire, in less than ten minutes, spread across the River, taking its course in a Northeasterly direction. We hurried along Wabash Avenue, only to find that Monroe, Adams, and Washington were reached by the Fire, and if we undertook to proceed further North, we would absolutely, be cut off and would perish...So, we turned south, again, and found our way, via the 12th Street bridge, and reached home at 436 Milwaukee Avenue at about 2:00 a.m.

Reports came that the Courthouse was gone and the Waterworks on Chicago Avenue was on fire. Hundreds perished in the LaSalle Street

Plate 2.31

SOME OF THE HUMAN PANIC CAN BE SEEN IN THIS DRAWING OF PEOPLE FLEEING FROM THE TONGUES OF THE RAGING FIRE OF 1871.

Tunnel, so that there was no question that all that part of the South Side and the whole North Side, to Lincoln Park, was doomed.

Although the neighboring towns and cities including Milwaukee, Joliet, Peoria, Galesburg, etc., sent fire apparatus of all kinds, nothing could check the elements in their fury. All that they could do

was defend the West Side, where the River gave a good opportunity to help. On the South Side, south of Harrison, whole blocks were blown up with dynamite, to check the Fire from going further south, with fairly good success."

According to Cassius Milton Wicker (not believed to be related to C. G. and J. H. Wicker) who was working as a guard, possibly military, after the fire:

"All day long, part of the night before and in many cases, Monday night, hundreds and thousands of people lay out on the sand in the wind strong enough to blow a chair, left alone, clear across the park. The air was so full of dust and sand that it was impossible to see the fire, and there, utterly exhausted, lay the lowly and the proud."

Others crammed into remaining structures beyond the ring of fire, and dispersed out into the country.

Wicker related part of his Sunday night activity:

"The Post Office, Tribune, Chamber of Commerce, Safety Deposits, Union Depot and many other buildings, just as fireproof as they could be made, all crumbled to the ground. Even buildings that were lathed with fire doors and sash of same were driven to the ground with the intense heat. The old part of the Court House, being built of sand stone, stood long and well against the flames, but the wooden cupola was too much for it. As I passed it on the north last Sunday night about 2 o'clock, the flames were leaping the street from the Chamber of Commerce, and in a moment had gone from it over my head, to the Sherman House. It was frightful.

Roughs and thieves from all parts of the country flocked here for plunder. Many fires have been started, but in most cases the party caught in the act has been shot on the spot. Their hopes were to burst open the safes, of which there are thousands through the burned district, but Gen. Sheridan promulgated a Death Proclamation to everybody found on the burnt district after dark.

Thinking (people in) Milwaukee would be off their guard, many started for that city and we put them off the train when, for the sake of plunder, they attempted to throw a train off the track, but so far without success. Every block in the city is guarded strongly by the citizens. As an instance of our quiet time, Wednesday night while on watch between 8 & 2, I heard but 19 shots fired. Many, I hope, were false alarms, but it shows what little mercy is shown.

Evidently roughs do not like their treatment. The largest slaughter was by Catholic priests guarding a church, when seven men went under the wing and attempted to start a fire and were all shot.

Plate 2.32 & 2.33
The Chamber of Commerce Building is depicted before and after the Great Fire.

They had just failed in their attempt to set the front steps of a row of dwellings on fire.

Friday night while I was on watch between 12 & 2, the long-looked-for rain commenced – fine at first, but at last pouring right down as I thought it never could again, all day yesterday and during the night until a fearful wind came up and drove the clouds away and dried up much good effects of the rain, but now that the long span of drought is ended I hope we may not suffer more. Yet our city is far from being out of danger for we have but little water on the West Side….no gas on the South Side and there is no North Side – beautiful North Side all destroyed in a night."

Though the ruins smoldered for some time, the massive burning ended on October 10th. The fiery, wickedly ferocious, uncontrollable flames of

destruction had turned the city into a smoking pile of twisted rubble. Structurally Chicago's main population areas were destroyed.

The people of Chicago, with their internal fires for survival and success, began almost immediately to create the city again. With the exception of the loss of life, the City might be said to have gained from being leveled. Its original rapid growth allowed for no development plan. The re-builders, on the other hand, had forty years of knowledge and experience to guide them in laying out a new city and then erecting buildings that met certain guidelines. Among the evolutionary steps that were initiated at this time, frame buildings were banned within a perimeter of the central part of the city. (Wicker Park was not in the area.)

Immediate need for housing, a desire for less density of surroundings, and shortage of money for all-masonry construction, were influential factors in driving people to build residences and establish commercial enterprises further out from the central business district. Wicker Park, with sparsely developed areas, soon grew in the numbers of its buildings, residents, and businesses.

— *Elaine A. Coorens*

Transportation Is Big Growth Factor

Plate 2.34
**LOOKING NORTH AT THE CHICAGO AND NORTH WESTERN RAILWAY CLYBOURN STATION, THE TRACKS SPLIT,
GOING NORTH AND NORTHWEST NEAR CORTLAND AND ASHLAND AT ABOUT 1900.**

By 1830, land trails and waterways started Chicago on its journey toward beoming the transportation hub that it would become with the passing of time.

Roads began to connect Chicago to other cities. A long-used Indian trail from Detroit, the Great Sauk Trail, was just a horse path in 1820, but was adopted by the government as a postroad in 1825. Coming up from the south was the Vincennes Trace (Vincennes, IN) on the Wabash River up through Danville and Iroquois to Chicago. It became a state road by act of the General Assembly. The Trace was surveyed and marked with milestones in 1832 and 1833.

Originally water traffic flowed primarily from the east to the west for both passengers and freight. In

1839 a regularly scheduled steamboat line ran round-trip, Buffalo to Chicago; and by 1841 there were seventy-five arrivals annually from Buffalo alone.

When the first passengers from Chicago to New York completed their trip in only six days, many considered this a miraculous accomplishment. The trip required steamboat travel from Chicago to Buffalo, then railroad and steamboat to Lewiston and Syracuse, then rail to Albany, and on to New York via another train. (An Act of Congress later declared Chicago a port of entry, on July 16, 1846.)

Dominance of roads and waterways for transportation in the Chicago area was about to end as the 1850s began. Though the first railroad left Chicago in 1848, it was not until 1852 that direct rail communication was opened between Chicago and New York. It reduced the time required for the trip from six days to thirty-six hours. By 1856 Chicago was at the hub of ten trunk lines and nearly three thousand miles of track, a giant spider-web of rails that connected Chicago to points east and west, north and south. Irish and German immigrants, fleeing conditions in their homeland, began bypassing New York, the main port of entry, and heading straight for Chicago.

The development of two railroad lines in particular affected the Wicker Park neighborhood. The Chicago and North Western Railway, the first railroad westward from Chicago, established its Wisconsin branch through the northwest side in 1854. The Chicago, Milwaukee and St. Paul Railway, established in 1864, originated in Union depot at Canal and Adams streets and provided a direct line between Chicago and St. Paul/Minneapolis. This line cut through the neighborhood, east to west at Bloomingdale, and became a popular mode of transit that helped increase development here and in the suburban areas further west.

Within the city, transportation modes ranged from foot to horse, wagon, buggy, omnibus, horse-car, streetcar, "L," and then automobile by 1920. Each new transportation advancement moved the perimeter of developed neighborhoods further from the downtown center. Streets like Milwaukee, Ogden, Grand, and North became immigrant corridors reflecting greater prosperity.

— *Elaine A. Coorens*

Street Railways Open Roads for City Expansion

Mass transportation began its slow growth shortly after the establishment of four different railroad lines and their stations in Chicago during 1852.

Coaches began transporting people from one train station to another. When they had space, they picked up other people who needed to get to other destinations along the route. The profitability of these trips was sufficient that regular routes were established.

Privately owned and operated, the omnibus businesses were unregulated, and their numbers began to increase. The vehicles were unheated coaches, some of which were open to the weather. Seats were generally benches and the suspension systems were quite primitive. People were willing to experience the discomfort for short rides because it was easier, cleaner and safer to ride than walk. Middle-class people who were willing to pay a nickel per ride were the primary passengers. Wealthier people had their own buggies, and poor people walked because they could not afford the fare.

Though this transportation mode solved problems for some, it was not without problems. Aside from being uncomfortable, omnibuses were often unreliable. Driver reliability, fierce competition and terrible street conditions were major problems. Streets and roads were often in terrible condition, and it was not uncommon for omnibuses to slip off the planked streets. Sometimes this was caused by competition for fares. Omnibuses could be seen careening down streets determined to get the next rider before the plodding horses for the street railways arrived. Schedules were then severely hampered, as it took a team of horses and several men to get a coach back on the road.

Horse-drawn vehicles on rails, sometimes also called horse-cars, came onto the scene in New York in 1832 and started to be discussed in Chicago in 1854. It was not until St. Valentine's Day in 1859 that the State legislature gave Chicago City Railway Co. (created by a group of investors headed by Franklin Parmalee) their charter. Shortly thereafter another

Plate 2.35

THIS IS ONE OF FRANKLIN PARMELEE'S FIRST OMNIBUSES. IT CARRIED FEW PASSENGERS AND LACKED COMFORT, BUT WAS FASTER AND SAFER THEN WALKING. PARMELEE BEGAN SERVICES BETWEEN RAILROAD STATIONS IN MAY 1853 WITH THIRTY HORSES, TWELVE EMPLOYEES, AND SIX WAGONS ADAPTED FOR CHICAGO'S MUDDY CONDITIONS.

group headed by railroad executives Ogden and Turner received a street railway charter under the name North Chicago City Railway. In 1861 a third charter was given to the Chicago West Division Street Railway, which began operations in July, 1863 when City Railway sold their west side operations.

Though they were a lightweight version of the omnibus, horse-cars required that rails be laid to prevent the vehicles from sliding off the streets. As larger coaches were built, they could carry up to thirty people. Still unheated with no internal illumination, the ride was made somewhat more comfortable when straw was strewn on the floors for warmth and oil lamps were hung in the early and late hours of the day and night. Despite the fact that the speed was roughly three miles per hour, riders preferred that pace over drudging on foot through the mud and filth.

Service by horse-car entered the Wicker Park district in 1873 when the Milwaukee Ave. car (inaugu-

rated in 1863 from State St. to Augusta Blvd.) was extended to Division St. In the next two years it was extended twice more to North and then to Wabansia. They located the West Chicago Noble Street Barn and the Center Headquarters on Division Street Railroad at Western. Citizen's Line, owned by A. Steinhouse, provided omnibus service in Wicker Park starting about 1874. According to *Holland's 1875-76 Directory of Milwaukee Avenue*, Citizen's enhanced the popularity of the business district along Milwaukee Ave. and was far better than the horse-drawn street railway.

North, on the other hand, had a horse-car line that began in 1875, running between Damen and California. Twelve years later it was extended east to Clark St., and another five years brought it west to Kedzie. In 1885, Noble had horse-car service from Milwaukee via Noble, Blackhawk, Greenview, North, Ashland, and Cortland to Wood. In 1896 it was changed from horse-cars to streetcars, and the service was cut to run from Milwaukee and Noble to North and Ashland. Service along Ashland ran from Roosevelt to Paulina then Lake back to Ashland and up to Cortland.

By 1880, four-legged horsepower was in need of replacement technology. Not only had the population soared from 109,000 to 503,000 in 1880, but the square mileage of the city had grown from 17.5 to 180. Horses as a traction engine had two major problems: they were not cost efficient, and they posed health concerns. Cable cars overcame the problems associated with horse-drawn vehicles. They were more efficient, and did not have the sanitation issues associated with horse-drawn vehicles. However, they were too expensive to operate on anything but major routes, and they posed interesting problems of their own.

The cable car moved on a track, like the horse-drawn streetcar. However, instead of horses pulling the car, a cable located underground pulled the cab. In the middle of each set of tracks was a slot about three-fourths of an inch wide, under which a heavy steel cable ran, constantly in motion. Cable cars were put in service on Milwaukee in the late 1880s.

And, a powerhouse (used to keep the cables in motion) was built at Milwaukee and Cleaver St.

The cable car operator, called a gripman, had an attachment that extended down through the slot and hitched onto the moving cable when he wanted the car to start. When he wanted to stop, the gripman released the cable and applied his brakes. In an effort to increase speed on the line, the starting and stopping of the cars was often very abrupt.

The cable car initially created quite a sensation since it appeared to run by itself without visible means of locomotion. It proved to be hazardous and unreliable however. The cables, which were only about one and five-sixth inch in diameter, broke frequently causing long delays. In addition, mischievous young boys learned to hook wires to the cable and attach blocks of wood, tin cans, or bunches of rags, for the amusement of watching them go speeding along the middle of the tracks, scaring horses and people alike. People were often maimed. Henry L. Hertz, a well-known Wicker Park politician for whom the district was called "Hertzville," lost a foot in a cable car incident on Milwaukee Ave. on April 4, 1893.

It took until 1890 for electrification to come to street railways in the city. The first electric elevated

Plate 2.36
THIS PHOTO WAS TAKEN SHOWING THE FIRST HORSE-CAR ON THE WEST DIVISION STREET LINE.

Plate 2.37
A BENSON AND RIXON CLOTHING ADVERTISEMENT APPEARS ABOVE THIS ELECTRIC CAR.

railway was built above the street in 1892 in Chicago. It was a freight line that served the Armour Meat Packing Plant.

Each of these transportation advancements meant that workers could spend the same amount of time commuting greater distances to their jobs. People often did not want to live next to industrial plants because of dirt, grime, and sometimes air quality. As workers' incomes increased, so did their distance from home to work. Managers and clerical workers were the first who were willing to pay to ride. It was faster and less perilous than walking along streets and sometimes sidewalks that could be grossly filthy, to say nothing of dangerous.

— *Elaine A. Coorens*

"L" MOVES MASSES HIGHER AND FASTER

Chicago's public transportation in 1890 could be described as redundant. Multiple transportation options were available on popular streets. Congestion on downtown streets was a problem. Solutions were sought to "rise above" the crowded streets.

In 1883, State Senator George E. Adams sponsored legislation that required elevated rail companies to receive permission of two-thirds of the property owners along each mile of the line in order to build. Consent was negotiated through bribes with the local property owners.

This prohibitively expensive practice was bypassed to some extent by building the "L" in the alley. It required the rail companies to pay more initially to buy their own alley. But this was substantially less expensive than bribing the property owners to build it on the street. This encouraged overextending lines into sparsely populated areas where property owners were eager for development. Corrupt politicians and land speculators influenced where a line might run, oftentimes placing it in an area that would not be profitable. The initial expense and lack of profit associated with running an elevated was a reason for the resistance to public ownership of the lines.

In 1892, steam-powered elevated lines were introduced on the South Side. As was the case with most mass transportation systems in Chicago, this was a privately-owned and operated line. The Metropolitan West Side Elevated Railroad, the city's third elevated line, was incorporated on March 9,

Plate 2.38

THE HUMBOLDT PARK ELEVATED TRAIN RUNNING BEHIND THE "OLD GRAY HOUSE" ON THE NORTH SIDE OF NORTH AVE. BETWEEN HOYNE AND LEAVITT PRIOR TO 1902.

1892. Known as the Polly "L" or more commonly the Met, its route contributed to development in the Wicker Park area. The City of Chicago granted the company a fifty-year franchise license. The line lived up to its financiers' credo of "Nothing but the best" with several of their innovations.

The Met line started at Wells and ran west over the South Branch of the Chicago River to Marshfield between Ashland and Wood. In order to cross the South Branch of the Chicago River, the Met created a special drawbridge that was built exclusively for the "L". It was the only "L" company to own and operate a drawbridge.

The Met branched out into four lines. The Douglas Park branch ran south to 21st St. and then west. This allowed access to the Cubs games on the West Side Grounds. The Garfield Park (Forest Park) branch ran west to Cicero Ave. The northwest branch ran north to Milwaukee, and then northwest to Austin Blvd. The fourth line, called the Humboldt Park Branch, was to branch out of the Northwest line just north of North at Damen and ran west to Harlem Ave.

The first section of the Metropolitan West Side Elevated Railway opened on May 6, 1895. It went to Damen (formerly Robey). By the end of 1895, the line was extended to Logan Square. The Humboldt Park Branch extension starting at Damen stopped at Humboldt Park. The Humboldt extension was substantially shorter than planned, stopping far short of Harlem Ave. The only addition to the line was on November 11, 1902, when a station at the Humboldt Blvd. stop was created, in response to residents' complaints that the other stops, two blocks away, were too far away. Nevertheless, realtors and land speculators continued to advertise that the line would soon extend past the current terminal. In fact, elevated operators cooperated with real estate companies in order to create and increase the customer base of the elevated.

The Metropolitan West Side Elevated Railway was planned as a steam line, but the design was converted to an electric traction line just prior to construction, adopting the design of the electric lines that were used at the 1893 Columbian Exposition World's Fair. At the time, most lines that were electric drew their current from overhead cables. This line used the "third rail," as it was found in the World's Fair design. It became the nation's first permanent third-rail line. The third-rail design was put to the test in a heavy snowstorm during the first winter after it was built. While most of the surface and overhead electrical lines were shut down, the Met continued to run. Though rider-ship dropped during the warmer summer days. Operating expenses were favorable. It cost twenty-two and one-half cents to operate per mile compared with forty-six cents per mile for a steam-operated alley elevated. All "Ls" built after this line in Chicago followed the example of an electric traction line; the third-rail design is in use throughout the elevated system to this day.

Some other firsts for the Met included streamlined fare collections. Instead of buying a ticket and giving it to a conductor, a nickel was given directly to the conductor who recorded the transaction with a streetcar-type fare register. Bicycle storage racks were installed at the station, and space was available on the trains for mothers to park their baby carriages. Employees announced incoming trains in the station waiting rooms.

Metropolitan signed an agreement to discontinue its own efforts and work with the United Elevated Railroad Company to build downtown terminal facilities. Local traction magnate Charles Tyson Yerkes, who controlled United Elevated, got other elevated lines with access to downtown to sign the deal, too. The "loop" was completed in October, 1897.

Unfortunately, the Met quickly fell into financial difficulties. Debt associated with initial cost of construction, completion of Yerkes' Lake Street Elevated and other trolley lines, and low population densities in outlying areas caused financial strain on the organization. In 1898 this line went into bankruptcy. Up to that point it had 23.9 million riders and $1,179,363 in revenue. The cost of building the sixteen and one-half mile long line was nearly $16 million. Right-of-way acquisitions alone cost more than $5 million. It went into receivership and was reorganized as the Metropolitan West Side Elevated Company.

— *John Scheidelman*

TUNNELS BECAME SOLUTIONS FOR SURFACE AND SHIP TRAFFIC

Development of Chicago's North and West Sides, including Wicker Park, occurred later than "downtown" and the South Side because it was difficult to cross the river. At first there were no bridges, then there were rickety bridges with tenders who were often unreliable. After the issues of bridge stability and tender unreliability were resolved, traffic on the river became so great that bridges were opened at a frequency that made it almost impossible to get across. Tunnels were first considered as the solution in 1837. The city's first mayor, William B. Ogden, obtained an estimate of

$130,000 in 1844, and all discussions ceased.

River and surface traffic continued to increase. In the 1850s more plans and proposals came and went. Finally in July 1866, the Common Council passed an ordinance that there was to be a tunnel under the River at Washington St, between Clinton and Franklin. It was to be financed by a new tax. A contract was let for $271,646 and ground was broken in October 1866. By May 1867 construction halted for lack of an extra $1,500 that the contractor needed and the new Board of Public Works was unwilling to pay.

Plate 2.39

A SHIP STEAMS AWAY FROM THE RANDOLPH BRIDGE IN THE TOP PART OF THIS LITHOGRAPH AS THE WASHINGTON ST. TUNNEL IS DEPICTED IN THE LOWER TWO FRAMES. THE PEDESTRIAN PASSAGE IS NOT SHOWN.

Plate 2.40
LOOKING EAST, THIS WAS THE WASHINGTON ST. TUNNEL NORTH SIDE ENTRY POINT IN ABOUT 1878, PRIOR TO ITS USE BY STREETCARS. WICKER PARK RESIDENTS USED THIS TO GET TO DOWNTOWN CHICAGO.

Despite damage to the structure already underway and financial issues, new financing was put in place to cover a new contract of $328,000. Struggling through floods and bad weather, the Washington Tunnel was opened on January 1, 1869 with a final accounting of expenditures at $517,000.

It was the world's first underwater highway tunnel for pedestrians and vehicles. This engineering marvel was constructed of brick masonry with two wagon roads and an 810-foot pine-planked pedestrian passage. The overhead river depth was fourteen feet, which was considered to be adequate for the vessels of the time.

When the city tested the grades with loaded wagons, they found that the horses had to work harder to get the loads up the incline. The added burden on the horses was considered preferable to waiting for bridges to open. There was one flaw, however, that caused varying amounts of distress and expense; the tunnel leaked. Though not unpleasant in the summer, the dripping water produced icicles and patches of ice on the roadways during colder seasons. Accidents occurred, causing property and bodily damage. The tunnel, however, was deemed a success in alleviating many of the traffic problems. It was, in fact, so well received that a second tunnel was planned for LaSalle St.

The LaSalle St. Tunnel, from Randolph to Hubbard, differed from the first tunnel in that the steepness of the grade was to be reduced by extending its length; and the depth was three feet greater, with an added two feet in height. It opened in June 1871 at a cost of $566,276. Virtues of this tunnel were recorded as "well-lighted with gas, well-ventilated, and as neat, clean and free from dampness as could be desired." Surface traffic congestion was lessened and all went well until the night of October 8, 1871, when both tunnels provided an escape route for thousands from the devastating flames. The LaSalle St. Tunnel was the site of hundreds being consumed by fire.

During the rebuilding of the city, the tunnels helped to absorb traffic that resulted from the loss of seven bridges. Post-reconstruction traffic declined, and the tunnels went into disrepair. In 1884, the city engineers declared the Washington Tunnel unsatisfactory.

An ordinance was passed in 1886 that granted Chicago Passenger Railway Company the right to build a cable-car on the West Side and to bring it through the tunnel to downtown. Various political maneuvers occurred involving the city and Charles T. Yerkes, but Wicker Park residents were able to use the Milwaukee Ave. cable car through the Washington St. Tunnel beginning in August 1890.

Plate 2.41
MILWAUKEE AVE. STREETCARS ARE SEEN COMING AND GOING ON THE DOWNTOWN SIDE OF THE WASHINGTON ST. TUNNEL.

As 1900 approached, the seventeen-foot channel depth was no longer adequate, and twenty-two feet were required for the new bigger ships. After six years of court cases, the tunnels were taken out of service in 1906; and with it there was an end to cable cars, as they were replaced by electric cars. The tunnels were lowered and the Washington St. Tunnel reopened for electric railcars in 1911.

Vivid memories of the ride through the tunnel were probably shared by generations of passengers that had the experience. In the Chicago Historical Society's publication "Chicago History" Vol. 4 No. 3, Frank J. Piehl shares his memories of a ride on a hot summer day:

"You boarded the red Milwaukee Avenue car and paid your 7 cent fare to the conductor on the back platform. You scrambed past the wicker seats, followed the conductor's rope to the front platform, and maneuvered yourself alongside the open window next to the motorman. As the car angled toward the Loop, you began to smell the lake air rushing through the open window. The car turned south on Des Plaines street and then east on Washington street. At Clinton Street, the gaping black hole of the tunnel loomed beneath the Chicago and Northwestern Railroad tracks. The car tipped down into the dingy tunnel. The walls were damp and the lighting came from ancient incandescent lamps, but the air was cool and refreshing. The car plummeted down the steep track, the motorman applied the brakes by turning his black-handled lever, you hear the hiss of the compressed air, and you worried about whether the brakes would hold. As the car neared the bottom, the brakes were released—they did hold, after all—and the car picked up speed. You were at the bottom of the tunnel, under the river, shivering at the idea that the inky black water might pour in on you. Then the car headed up the other side, the electric motor straining and whining to pull the huge load up the steep incline. The motorman pressed a little lever. The air hissed again, this time releasing a stream of sand to the tracks below to provide more traction for the climb. You glanced with admiration at the brave motorman in his navy-blue uniform with the metal buttons, staring straight ahead, intent on his dangerous task. The tiny patch of sky ahead grew larger as you neared the top of the long climb. And the motorman stomped on his bell with his left heel with a clang of authority, for he had the right-of-way on the street above. At last you burst into the bright sunlight and smiled sheepishly at the motorman. Brave as you were, you had been frightened—just a little bit."

— *Elaine A. Coorens*

City and Private Services Vital to Growth...
Streets Provide Highway for Other Services

Plate 2.42

THIS RESIDENTIAL STREET PHOTO IS TYPICAL OF HOW MUCH THE STREETS WERE RAISED AND HOW SOME HOMEOWNERS DEALT WITH THE NEW CHALLENGES. IF THERE WAS ENOUGH SPACE FROM THE STREET TO THE BUILDING, OTHERS BUILT STEPS DOWN TO THE PREVIOUS LOT LEVEL. (SEE *Plate 4.22*)

Wicker Park, like most of Chicago, lies on marshy soil barely above the level of Lake Michigan. As for all early Chicago settlers, this caused constant problems for the Wicker Park residents for both street construction and public sanitation. The land was frequently flooded. Drainage was unmanageable.

The original city streets were dirt tracks, prone to becoming mud pits in wet times, and rutted tracks in dry times. Several, including Milwaukee, Ogden, Elston, and Grand Avenues, were originally Indian trails. In 1847, at the time when the Chicago city limit had just been expanded west to Western Ave. along North Ave., John Lewis Peyton, a visitor to Chicago, wrote, "On the outskirts of the town...the highways were impassible, except in the winter when frozen, or in the summer when dry and pulverized into the finest and most penetrating of dust. At all other seasons they were little less than quagmires."

Another visitor, the famous essayist Ralph Waldo Emerson, wrote in 1853, "If we step off the short street, we go up to the shoulders, perhaps, in mud… " This reputation for muddy roads gave rise to an often-told anecdote. A pedestrian, who noticed the head and hat of a well-known person showing above the mud, yelled, "You're in pretty deep, do you want some help?" The reply was, "It's my horse, who's under me, that I'm concerned about!"

The first attempts to make better roads and sidewalks involved planking. Several planked toll roads, developed by private companies, helped bring farm produce into the city. One of these, the Northwest Plank Road, which was planked in 1849, extended along what is now Milwaukee Ave. from the Chicago River out to Wheeling.

Although these had the advantage of presenting a drier surface, water would collect under the planks. It putrefied, and became a breeding ground for mold and vermin. As Peyton describes:

"under these planks the water was standing on the surface over three-fourths of the city, and as the sewers from the houses were emptied under them, a frightful odour was emitted in summer, causing fevers and other diseases… "

As the planks became warped and loosened, they became unstable. The pressure of wagons passing over the uneven surface would sometimes result in filthy water squirting out at those standing next to the road.

In an attempt to keep streets passable and to drain away waste, neighborhoods, including Wicker Park, dug ditches sloping towards the Chicago River. Since Wicker Park is some distance from the river, the minimal slope meant stagnant and standing water. The ditches and the River both became chronically polluted.

Since it proved impossible to drain sewerage through the network of drainage ditches, the City in the 1850's decided to solve the problem by building a system of sewer pipes which would gradually allow the sewage to flow to the Chicago River. In 1852 a Drainage Commission was incorporated. The 1854 cholera epidemic and the constant outbreaks of typhoid fever from 1860 to 1900 were the obvious results of the drainage problem.

In 1855 William B. Ogden, a land developer and former Mayor of Chicago, was appointed to head the commission. Ogden brought Boston engineer Ellis S. Chesbrough to Chicago to design a system of underground sewers. For the next 30 years, Chesbrough, as the Chief Engineer of the Chicago Board of Sewerage Commissioners, was involved in designing and building the first comprehensive system of underground sewers in the United States.

By the spring of 1856 the Chicago Board of Sewerage Commissioners had decided that the only effective way to drain the City sewers would be to lay them on top of the current streets, and raise the street level to cover them. The increases in street level height ranged from four to fourteen feet, depending on how much height was needed to maintain a slope that would cause the sludge to flow into the Chicago River.

The installation of sewer lines in Wicker Park occurred from 1872 to the 1890s. In 1872 sewer lines, pavement, and curbs were in place on Milwaukee. The section between North and Division had sidewalks and lampposts. Ashland had sewers near Division in 1872, and by 1874 the line extended past North. Many of the streets between Ashland and Milwaukee — such as Pierce (formerly Ewing), LeMoyne, Honore (formerly Girard) and Elk Grove — had sewers installed in 1879 and 1880. Damen (formerly Robey) had sewers in 1883 and 1886. Schiller (formerly Fowler), Evergreen, Potomac, and Crystal were installed in 1886 just west of Damen. The sewer installations traveled west block by block during the 1880s with Hoyne in 1886, Bell in 1887, Oakley in 1888 and finally Western in 1889. The first water distribution system and the first sewerage drains were constructed of oak. Later sewers were made of brick or vitreous tile.

The City laid gas and water mains at the same time, covering all three systems with soil dredged from the Chicago River. The Chicago Hydraulic Company began water distribution in 1836. By 1858 the company was delivering 3,000,000 gallons of water daily, and by 1863 the company was delivering 6,400,000 gallons daily. To respond to increased demand for water, and to attempt to avoid the polluted water near to shore, a two-mile underwater intake tunnel was completed in 1867. Construction on the Chicago Ave. pumping station, now recognized as the landmark "water tower" at Michigan Ave. and Chicago, began in 1867 and was completed in 1869.

The Chicago Gas Light and Coke Company was legislated in 1849. By 1855, there were seventy-eight miles of pipe supplying 2,000 customers with natural gas. Both water and gas distributions were greatly enhanced by the ability to lay "above ground" pipes and bury the pipes by raising the streets.

Landowners were caught in a new kind of quagmire because of higher streets. The disruption was incredible. For most buildings, what had been the second floor was now at street level, and the first floor became the level of a basement.

There were three ways to deal with the problem. The first option was to do nothing. As the surrounding streets filled in, one could fill in the lot area around the building and treat the first floor as a basement, or leave the lot at its original level and build

stairs to climb up to the new street height. Examples of this can be seen at 1410 Elk Grove, 1540 Honore, and 1440 Wood. Since the Great Fire did not come this far west, these buildings are still standing, whereas locations destroyed by the fire were rebuilt at the new grade level.

The second option was to raise the building. One of the most famous of the Chicago building raisers was George M. Pullman, a house mover from Albion, New York, who made his name and early fortune by raising buildings in Chicago. One of his most famous jobs was raising the six-story Tremont Hotel while all the guests continued to occupy the building. Pullman used the money earned from raising buildings to invest in the enterprise that equipped railway cars with sleeping facilities, and later to develop the planned community of Pullman. Many Wicker Park streets have buildings that were raised. They are identifiable by simple first floor facades and ornate second stories.

The third option for dealing with the street ele-

Plate 2.43
THIS VIEW SHOWS HOW, IN SOME CASES, A BUILDING WAS RAISED TO THE NEW STREET LEVEL (TALL CENTER BUILDING) WHILE OTHERS PROVIDED RAMPS OR STAIRS TO ORIGINAL ENTRANCES AND CREATED NEW ENTRANCES ON A HIGHER LEVEL OF THE BUILDING.

vation was to move the building to another location, on a new foundation. A visitor to Chicago at that time wrote, "Never a day passed that I did not meet one or more houses shifting their quarters. One day I met nine. Going out Great Madison Street in the house-cars, we had to stop twice to let houses get across."

The elevation of streets took two decades to complete throughout the City. It was a significant improvement in transportation for the area. This incredible engineering effort also had significant benefits for the delivery of major City services, and waste disposal. The other significant contribution for improved waste disposal was, of course, reversing the flow of the

Chicago River, which was completed in 1900. By 1908 the typhoid death rate had dropped 91%.

Although many of the streets in Wicker Park are still sized for horse-drawn carriages rather than automobiles, the materials that make up the streets have progressed from the parallel wooden timbers of the planked roads to cedar blocks, cobblestone, and macadam. In 1892, North, Ashland, and Milwaukee were paved with cedar block, Leavitt was still not paved, and Caton was paved with macadam. By 1929, most Wicker Park streets and alleys were paved.

— *Mary and Ed Tamminga*

FIRE AND ANGRY MOB DESTROY A SNELL TOLLGATE

Fire and mob demolition of one of ten Snell tollgates in 1881 began the decline of Amos Snell's tollgate business, according to an article in *The Chicago Daily News* in 1906. In protest of pricing, an unknown source set fire to the *Chicago Gate,* at Fullerton and Milwaukee. When the fire did not totally destroy the gate, hundreds of men completed its

demise and then hauled off the remains. Response to the fire alarm was slowed by firemen's sympathy for the anti-toll people.

William Landshaft, a businessman who relied on customers getting to his establishment over Snell's road, rallied fellow business owners, friends, residents and farmers in the surrounding county to a meeting to

Plate 2.44
SNELL'S TOLLGATE AS IT APPEARED IN THE CHICAGO DAILY NEWS ARTICLE IN 1906.

address problems with Snell's tollgate, at Turner Hall on Milwaukee Ave. Snell owned considerable land along the city's western edge. He had a government charter that allowed him to take tolls on all roads through his farms, provided he kept the roads in good condition.

When asked about the issues, Landshaft was reported to have said: "Snell charged for every person and animal that passed through his gates. However, roads were so bad it was almost impossible to get around. Mud, often a foot deep, prevented traffic from moving. Scores of teams were delayed daily. Horses died after vainly attempting to drag their wagon over the sticky roads.

Even funeral trains were frequently stopped. Hearses had to be unloaded so the horses could pull the wagons out of the muck. Then, mourners had to gather around their dead at the side of the road."

Travelers not only had to endure terrible conditions, but they had to pay for the privilege. Rates were: two cents per mile for one horse; three cents for two; and fifty cents per round trip for funeral carriages to the Bohemian cemetery.

According to the keeper of Milwaukee and Elston's *Main Gate*, William Ringlier, who manned his post for fourteen years, his biggest revenue day was $790.00. "It was a Sunday and the Polish/Bohemian picnic was being held at Niles and Des Plaines. Several new cemeteries opened near Dunning that day too. An average day brought in about $400.00."

Snell later tried to construct another tollgate at Milwaukee and California but Landshaft and his anti-toll people tore down the posts and removed the lumber before it could be completed. Landshaft explained, "People would have had to pay a toll to go to their grocer and butcher."

Wicker Park business people, residents, and visitors were affected by the *Chicago and Main* gates. Made of stout hickory poles, the gates were swung open and shut by gatekeepers who kept a vigilant eye for teams of horses, cattle, sheep, and other travelers approaching the crossing. Snell provided a cabin for four gatekeepers and their families at an annual cost of little more than $1,000 per family.

— *Elaine A. Coorens*

WATER AND ICE PROVIDED BY SERVICES

Water was initially provided by wells or service businesses. Like dairy products, water and ice were mainly delivered items from service businesses. Though there were several such companies, the Chicago Artesian Well Company occupied forty acres at Chicago and Western and no doubt serviced many in the Wicker Park District.

The water and ice business began in 1863, through the efforts of four people: Thomas J. Whitehead and A.E. Swift, two spiritualists from the state of Maine; Abraham James, clairvoyant; and Caroline Jordon, a medium who wrote instead of spoke the messages from "those on the other side." They met at the Chicago and Western site to try to locate petroleum.

The spirits told them that there were both petroleum and water resources in this area. Though they never located petroleum, they did locate water.

Even at one hundred feet above Lake Michigan, there was a substantial water force (head) and 600,000 gallons per twenty-four hours flowed from their wells. Their goal was to sell water at half the city's price for

Plate 2.45
ICEMAN DELIVERS LARGE BLOCKS OF ICE IN 1908.

water. Claiming curative possibilities from the water's pureness, they also opened a sanatorium and fountain house along with a large horse shed. Their first well was four feet wide. Later they drilled a second well five feet wide; and later still they increased one of the wells to between fifteen and twenty feet in width.

Twenty-five acres of their forty-acre site were devoted to providing ice to the public throughout the year, which could be delivered to or picked up by the customer. Ponds, flooded in the winter, provided enough ice to fill a 210 by 232 foot ice house which held up to 40,000 tons of ice.

At an original storage cost of ten to fifteen cents per ton, the following price schedule would indicate a tremendous profit, but expenses increased and other competition forced them to the decision for demolition. (See *Illustration 9*.)

Their ice house was doomed for demolition, according to *The Morning News* on June 2, 1891. An almost thirty-year tradition was being brought to an end for residents of Wicker Park and surrounding areas.

Four artesian wells were sunk during 1871 by Chicago in areas where Chicago water pipes were not laid: Central Park at 1220 ft.; Douglas Park at 1165 ft.; Humboldt Park at 1155 ft.; and the last was Humboldt Blvd.

— *Elaine A. Coorens*

W. T. B. READ'S & SONS DELIVERED ICE RATES

Illustration 9

POUNDS	CONTAINER	COST
15	Pail	.50 per week
20	Pail	.60
30	Pail	.80
50	At one time	.40 per 100 lbs.
100	At one time	.30
200	At one time	.25
Groceries, Saloons, & Sm. Customers		.20
Markets, restuarants, & Lrg. Customers		.15
On Platform and Ice House		.00

GARBAGE DISPOSAL CHALLENGED MANY SENSES

Initially, disposal of garbage in Chicago was totally unregulated, thereby having to pass the carcass of a cow or horse on the street was not unusual. Between 1837 and 1881 the Chicago Municipal Code charged the Commissioner of Health with the responsibility of employing "…from time to time as many persons and companies as he may deem necessary for removal of garbage, offal, swill and ashes." Dumps were the main choice for the ever-increasing problem.

From the Commissioner's Office of the Department of Public Works in 1905, a report on Garbage Disposition revealed much about the problem —garbage disposal.

"Those who have interested themselves in the problem of garbage disposal in Chicago are agreed on this proposition: The dumps must go.

Dumps poison the air for miles around, and if ground made by dumping is dug up years afterwards it is found still putrid. Dumping is a barbarous anachronism for a twentieth century city.

There is also agreement that garbage must be collected daily from all homes in the city. For while fresh swill, under twenty-fours old, is comparatively inoffensive and harmless, stale swill which has been left to decay for two or more days quickly becomes unpleasant and dangerous to health. Especially is this true in hot weather."

The report goes on to discuss the many ways available to handle disposal and what entity should handle that disposal, looking at the costs and possible income from the processes. It ends with the following:

"Again, if the city lets out garbage collection by contract, there will remain for disposition

Plate 2.46
**SERVICING THE WICKER PARK DISTRICT, THIS OPEN GARBAGE DUMP, LOCATED AT WEBSTER AND ELSTON,
WAS STILL IN USE IN 1908.**

ashes, rubbish and street dirt. Should the city abdicate these municipal functions also? If not it must go into the teaming business for itself, buy land where necessary, build stables in various parts of the city, buy horses, and hire drivers.

The past system of hiring leaky wagons and worn-out, half-dead horses from political favorites at the rate of $4.50 per day has been a joke—and an expensive one to the city. It must be said in fairness, however, that no team owner would send a good horse into the dump where a cut from a piece of old glass or can will allow the poison from the decayed swill to enter the blood of the horse and kill him.

I, therefore, respectfully suggest that the city go into the teaming business and append estimates of cost from Assistant Superintendent of Streets Fox and William Hard."

In 1928 the cost of 1905 garbage disposal doubled and the quest for less costly solutions continued. Whether in Wicker Park or elsewhere in the city, the issues were the same though technology was changing—keeping the city clean and safe for the least amount of money.

— *Elaine A. Coorens*

THEY SERVE AND PROTECT — POLICEMEN AND FIREMEN

Neither police nor fire protection was part of the first Chicago town charter in 1833, though the town government was given general jurisdiction over disorderly conduct. Chicago Trustees, in 1835, were empowered to appoint constables and instructed to "regulate the police of the town" as well as to establish night watches.

Authorization for a constable per ward was given in 1837 and two years later a night patrol was created. By 1847 one police constable was to be elected in each ward at the annual election, and in 1848, nine constables were chosen in the annual election.

A volunteer Fire Department was established in 1835. Volunteers were part of this "city service" until 1867.

POLICE DEPARTMENT

During the mid-1800s the police stations served mainly as neighborhood complaint and welfare centers. As there were no telephones, people brought complaints about family quarrels, unruly adolescents, noisy neighbors, and crimes (often petty) to the police station.

In 1855, the Chicago Police Department began to focus on providing service continuously, not just in the evening. Badges changed over the years from stars to shields. Leather badges, though short

Plate 2.48

HOUSED IN A CALLBOX (*see below*), THE CLOCK-LIKE ALARM FACE ALLOWED POLICEMEN A WAY TO SEND IN DIFFERENT CALLS. THE CLOSE UP (*above*) ILLUSTRATION SHOWS THE DETAIL OF ONE OF THE EARLY ALARM DEVICES.

Plate 2.47

POLICE PATROL WAGON RESPONDS TO AN OFFICER'S ASSISTANCE CALL FROM A CALLBOX WITHIN THIS CALLBOX STATION.

lived, were the idea of Mayor John Wentworth who served as Mayor in 1857-58 and 1860-61. Though probably designed earlier, most officers did not adopt uniforms until 1858. They carried heavy canes as batons and some carried firearms, though guns were not officially issued during the early years. Prior to whistles, officers carried a "creaker" to call for assistance

Officers walked their beats, cut off from their

stations. If you wanted a policeman in the 1860s, "…you would have to go to a lamp post and knock on it till a policeman came. If you did it for fun, you would be arrested and fined $5.00 and costs next day," according to an article written by a retired Wicker Park mail carrier, Rudolph R. Albrecht, in the February 1929 *Greater Chicago Magazine*.

In 1861 the state legislature passed a law setting up a Chicago police board. Three new police commissioners were given sole authority over the department, giving the mayor no opportunity to control the police force. The law was revised in 1875 as a result of police corruptions charges in the 1860s and 1870s. The police commissioners were abolished and a single police commissioner was to be appointed by the mayor with approval of the city council.

In the beginning of the 1880s call boxes and horse-drawn patrol wagons were introduced. Telegraph and then telephone technology made it possible for an assistance call to go into the police station from call boxes placed around the city. In the Wicker Park District, they were located on the: northwest corner of Damen and Armitage; Damen and Schiller; southwest corner of Division and Ashland (Rawson); southwest corner of Division and Wood; northwest corner of Milwaukee and Nobel (Rawson); northeast corner of Milwaukee and Oakley; southwest corner of Milwaukee and Paulina; Milwaukee and Western; southeast corner of North and Ashland (Rawson) northeast corner of North and Leavitt; southwest corner of North and Noble (Rawson); northeast corner of North and Western; southwest corner of North and Wood; Hoyne and Evergreen; and southwest corner of Wabansia and Paulina.

It was hoped that this connection to the sta-

tion would also provide a way to monitor patrolmen's performance. John Flinn in *History of the Chicago Police* implies that the strong resistance of the patrolmen (regarding reporting their activity) was because many spent time on duty socializing in saloons or sleeping in favorite hiding places. As it turned out, this new requirement did not change the behavior of

Plate 2.49

BUILT IN 1895, THIS POLICE STATION WAS LOCATED ON THE NORTHEAST CORNER OF OAKLEY AND NORTH.

the patrolman, since the men at the station house soon learned to cover for the failed hourly reports from the field.

Over the years, the Wicker Park District fell under different police districts and precincts. The neighborhood was covered by the 4th Precinct, located at 1123 W. Chicago (formerly 233 W.) in 1868. In 1875 that station became known as the 3rd Precinct. In August 1883 the West North Ave. District was established and a patrol wagon put into service. Patrol wagons did not patrol but served as transports for taking prisoners to jail and taking sick people to hospitals.

It covered the area from Armitage on the north to Augusta on the south, Ashland on the east to the western city limits.

Five of the men assigned to the North Ave. station patrol wagons in the earlier period reflected the composition of Chicago's Finest. They were: George W. H. Roycraft, Elef Danielson, Michael Burns, John Hanrahan, and John R. Looby. Born in Cork, Ireland, in 1847, Roycraft became a tanner in Chicago in 1866. Appointed to the police force in 1873, his wagon took the body of the first Haymarket victim, Officer Mathias Degan, from the scene of the riot. Danielson was born August 22, 1894, in Norway. A patrolman, he joined the force in 1873. Born in Wisconsin in July 1842, Looby was assigned to the West North station in 1883. Driver of the wagon, Burns had a reputation as a "skillful handler of the ribbon in fast driving." Born in Ireland, the twenty-three year old transferred to the Wicker Park location in June 1883. Hanrahan, another Irishman came to Chicago at the age of twenty-seven, joining the force in1870. He participated in the suppression of 1877 labor riots and the anarchist troubles of 1886. In 1881, a thief shot him in the wrist.

Prior to the patrol wagons it was often difficult for policemen to get prisoners to walk to a station; thus occasionally prisoners were put in wheelbarrows for transportation.

According to the Police Department Report of December 31.1886, the cost of the 2021 W. North (formerly 480 W.) station was $11,522.40. It included: $2,000.00 for the land (31 feet of lots 47 and 48 of Block 1, D.S. Lee Addition –31' x 162'); $6,000 for a two-story brick building with a brick barn; and $3,522.40 for furniture, fixtures, stationary, stock, and apparatus.

Construction of the Metro elevated line, which opened in 1895, caused that Station to be moved from 2021 W. North to 2300 W. North. At that point, it was the 4th Division 24th Precinct and the cost was $20,963.45. It included: $6,500.00 for the land (Lots 20 & 21 of Block 1, Johnson Sub –49' x 130'); $11,730.35 for a two-story brick and stone basement station house and patrol house; and $2,733.10 for furniture, fixtures, stationary, stock, and apparatus.

The 35th Precinct was housed in a new facility at 2174 N. Milwaukee (formerly 1780 N.) at the cost of $10,308.65. It included: $4,000.00 for the land (So. 3 SubBlock 2 Attrills Sub of lots 4 to 9); $4,500 for a two-story frame station house and one-story patrol house; and $1,808.65 for furniture, fixtures, stationary, stock, and apparatus.

The following story appeared in a 1910 issue of the Wicker Park Eagle:

BURGLARIES VERY NUMEROUS
Police kept busy rounding in suspects

Chief Stewarts blue coats are kept busy these days gathering in suspicious looking characters accused of numerous hold-ups and robberies. The North West side seems to be getting more than its share, for never before have there been so many cases reported to the police.

On Feb. 7th burglars gained entrance to Harry Levy's saloon, 1467 Milwaukee Ave. by forcing open a rear door and stole numerous cigars and liquors. The following night they crawled through the coal-hole in front of the saloon and again gained entrance.

When Fred Siemers awoke in this home, 1905 W. North Ave. on Thursday afternoon, Feb. 17th, he found a man of very large proportion standing near the foot of his bed. He was so frightened that he could not speak, but finally when he regained his power of speech the man had jumped through a side window and disappeared. He did not get away with anything.

For a time it seemed as if the man might have been an agent from some secret organization, for rumor had it that Fred was in love with a young lady in California, and this may have been his rival.

Burglars tried to gain entrance to the saloon of Henry Schoknecht, 1700 N. Robey St. (Damen Ave.), but were frightened away by bakers employed across the street."

In 1916, the District was covered by 16th Ward 33rd precinct and 28 and 15 Ward 34th precinct. By 1921 coverage was from Division 23 and Division 22.

FIRE DEPARTMENT

Plate 2.50

MEMBERS OF THE FIRST COMPANY OF ENGINE #35 SIT IN FRONT OF THEIR FIRST HOUSE AT 2019 W. NORTH. AUGUST SCHUBERT, THEIR CAPTAIN, IS SECOND FROM LEFT IN THE FIRST ROW IN 1885 OR 1886.

An act passed by the Illinois Legislature in January 1831 authorized the trustees of any incorporated town or village in the State to organize fire companies, not exceeding thirty members, and exempting them from jury service, or military service except in time of war. Even so, Chicago did not have a Fire Warden until an ordinance was passed on Nov. 6, 1833. In 1835 legislation was passed to allow for people, not more than forty, to form fire companies, and still no fire department was created. In October of that year, however, a major step was taken toward creating a working fire force. An order was placed for the purchase of two fire-hooks with chains and ropes, two ladders sixteen feet long, four axes and four handsaws, for a total cost of $29.63. An ordinance creating the first regular fire department passed on Nov. 4, 1835.

Run primarily by volunteers, it would not be until 1867 that volunteers were phased out of service in the Chicago Fire Department. But even with professionals, nothing would stave off the destruction from the Great Conflagration of 1871. Afterward a fire district was set up in which there were to be no frame buildings. However, the City had to build shelter for more than 100,000 homeless people, violating their own rules. They called the frame structures "relief shelters."

Located at 1318 W. Concord Place, the first fire station in the Wicker Park District was created in 1872. Engine 20 was situated near the Rolling Mill steel works area. Two years later on July 14, 1874, another major event occurred in Chicago. This event consumed the south end and west of the loop. Some 812 buildings were destroyed, and frame construction was again the target of further restrictions. The following year, hook and ladder #7 organized at 455-57 Grand (Grand and Wolcott), and Engine #26 formed in 1875. Haddon and Ashland was home for Engine #30's organization in 1880.

The heart of Wicker Park got its first fire station when Engine #35 organized Dec. 31, 1885 at 2019 W. North. Though some insurance maps showed this building to be made of wood, it was built of brick. Because of the construction of the Metro Elevated Railway for the L, the North Ave. property was sold nine years later.

On July 1894, Engine #35 and company moved to its second home, 1627 N. Damen, and an addition was built in 1903. Organized Oct. 31, 1904, Truck #28 (hook and ladder) called the Damen building home, too.

Plate 2.51

THE ENGINE #35 HOUSE AT 2019 W. NORTH PROBABLY LOOKED LIKE THIS ENGINE #36 HOUSE BUILT IN 1886.

Plate 2.52
ENGINE #35's SECOND HOME AT 1625-27 N. DAMEN. IT WAS ONE OF TWO FIRE STATIONS IN THE CITY WITH THE SEAL.
NOTE THAT THE SEAL IS SLIGHTLY DIFFERENT THAN THE CITY SEAL NOW USED.

Plate 2.53
THE WICKER PARK DISTRICT WAS PART OF THE FIRE
DEPARTMENT'S FOURTH BATTALION'S AREA.
FOURTH BATTALION CHIEF CHARLES HEANEY IS
PICTURED HERE IN HIS BUGGY WITH DRIVER.
CHIEF'S CARS, TO THIS DAY, ARE CALLED "BUGGIES."

Plate 2.54
ENGINE #35 IN 1920
(1917 AHRENS FOX)
PARKED AT CONCORD
AND DAMEN.

Plate 2.55
IN FRONT OF 1625 N.
DAMEN, ONE OF THE FIRE-
MEN HOLDS THE REINS OF A
HORSE HITCHED TO A
BUGGY..

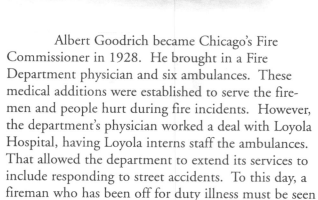

Plate 2.56
TRUCK #28 IN 1920 (1918 WHITE
TRUCK CO.) WITH A FIRE DEPT.
FRAME, MODIFIED FROM HORSE-
DRAWN TO HORSE POWER DRAWN.
PICTURE TAKEN AT DAMEN AND
CONCORD.

Albert Goodrich became Chicago's Fire Commissioner in 1928. He brought in a Fire Department physician and six ambulances. These medical additions were established to serve the firemen and people hurt during fire incidents. However, the department's physician worked a deal with Loyola Hospital, having Loyola interns staff the ambulances. That allowed the department to extend its services to include responding to street accidents. To this day, a fireman who has been off for duty illness must be seen and given a certificate to return to work.

— *Elaine A. Coorens*

Temperance Led to Prohibition and Economic Changes

Plate 2.57

Bolit's Tavern *(See Page 162)* **on Hoyne Ave. had no liquor visible on the bar in the early 1920s.**

Alcohol consumption had been an issue in many countries before Wicker Park was a community. In the United States the average annual per-person consumption of pure alcohol was seven gallons in 1870. As the decades rolled forward, many people believed that increases in poverty, violence and crime were directly related to liquor consumption. Political and religious leaders received increasing pressure to address these problems, as citizens were banding together in movements aimed at temperance and then prohibition.

In 1873 a "Women's War" broke out, and women marched from churches and other meeting places to saloons where they prayed, sang, and demanded saloonkeepers to give up their business. Many Wicker Park organizations aimed their efforts at temperance.

Amid the frustration and behavioral problems, accusatory fingers were pointed at many who were seen as the sources of the problem. The meat packing businesses were among the accused. In 1918, one of the three volumes of *Manufacturing and Wholesale Industries of Chicago* states:

"…it has been pointed out that these districts are usually hemmed in almost solidly by rows of saloons which subsist by the patronage of the workers themselves who support them of their own free will and accord. This is a matter coming under the control of the municipal authorities and cannot be blamed on any of the great employers of labor. It is a field, indeed, wherein the reformers may well expend their efforts and work for a citywide prohibition of the saloon evil to the benefit of all the inhabitants. Perhaps to many a "dry Chicago" is an unthinkable state of affairs, but by degrees it is becoming more and more apparent to every thinking man or woman that this is 'manifest destiny,' and we may live in hopes of seeing the time when the saloon evil will join the limb of many other 'old, unhappy, far-off things,' that have afflicted our welfare in the past.

Compare the situation in this respect with that of another large and populous city on the Pacific coast… (It) has taken this particular 'bull by the horns,' and cast the beast out of its municipal limits. In an article recently published in McClure's Magazine, descriptive of conditions in Seattle, it is said: 'Here is one of the best demonstrations of what prohibition can do for a city. I doubt if there is one man in Seattle who would want the town to go back to liquor. Up to the time when the present war law went into effect, individuals could, ship in specified quantities; but today Seattle is bone dry, and saves a million dollars a month that was formerly spent for alcoholic drinks."

From the viewpoint of the temperance proponents, saloonkeepers took money from the workmen, causing wives and children to starve and sometimes suffer beatings. Many also believed that crime, civil unrest, and other corruption such as prostitution were all tied to alcohol. The opposing view was that a bar was an escape from the pressures of daily life, a place for camaraderie of fellow travelers of life's highway where friendly bartenders would listen and give advice on almost any subject. In fact many establishments were places where families gathered for food, drink, and family entertainment.

To address increasing demands for making the sale of liquor illegal, Congress passed the 18th amendment aimed at prohibiting the sale and transportation of intoxicating liquors which was ratified on Jan. 16, 1919 and would take effect at midnight one year later, Jan. 16, 1920.

The Volstead Act, on October 10th, 1919, further enforced the amendment.

In preparation for the prohibition effective date of midnight on January 16, 1920, people were using everything from chauffeur-driven cars to baby buggies to aid in stocking their cupboards with as much liquor as possible. Subsequently, the results of the Amendment and Act appeared to some to be worse then the original problems. A new type of lawlessness came on the scene with the help of gangsters—boot-legging and speakeasies.

The impact of this legislation on Wicker Park was significant. Many of the beer barons that lived and owned property in the district saw their fortunes melt away. They chose to give up large homes, making large parcels of land available. Land purchasers were intent on constructing multi-unit buildings that insured greater neighborhood density and included little or no landscaping, changing the cityscape. Saloonkeepers, in order to maintain their businesses, had to change their businesses to ice cream parlors, restaurants, or illegal speakeasies, or to close their establishments. Loss of fees and taxes from the sale of liquor reduced public spending and required charging for such things as soap at the free bathhouses.

Though there appears to be no written documentation about the illegal activities of this era in Wicker Park, there is physical evidence and oral history. For example, there are at least two tunnels under the intersection of North, Milwaukee, and Damen. One crosses from the North West Tower building to the south side of North. The other goes from the southwest corner of North and Milwaukee to the northeast corner of North and Damen. Those tunnels apparently were used as entrances and exits for people to go from one hidden establishment to another, whether illegal or legal. Another speakeasy was apparently located on the west side of Damen just south of Division, while a brothel and possibly a speakeasy was located on the south side of Division in the 1700 block.

Remnants of what was probably an illegal still are in a five-car brick garage in the 2100 block of Pierce. The death of the homeowner was purported to have resulted from a house fire caused by lightning. Local lore and weather records show the day to have been clear and sunny, suggesting that the fatal fire might have had a human cause rather than an act of nature.

— *Elaine A. Coorens*

Milwaukee Avenue Mirrors Development

Plate 2.58

VIEW LOOKING NORTHWEST ON MILWAUKEE AVE. AT EVERGREEN, AROUND 1900, REVEALS IMPOSING BUILDINGS FROM THE 1880S AND 90S AND THE DENSITY OF THE COMMERCIAL DISTRICT.

For nearly two hundred years the path of Milwaukee Ave. has been a corridor of migration and trade, linking up what is now downtown Chicago with the city's outlying northwest territory. The presence of Milwaukee Avenue, a great, diagonal thoroughfare that traverses the community from southeast to northwest, has been an important catalyst for development of the Wicker Park District. As the boundaries of Chicago expanded through the years, an increasing number of small communities along the avenue were brought within the city limits and the street developed into a major urban transportation artery.

Long before Chicago's incorporation in 1835, a narrow crooked trail served Native Americans as a route for their journey from the current Milwaukee (Wisconsin) area to what is now Chicago. The northern part of their trail followed along a low sandy ridge, roughly thirty-to-forty feet above the lake level, and only ten-to-twenty feet above a surrounding area that was largely swampland, to the north and west of today's Jefferson Park in Chicago. Although Milwaukee Ave. eventually became a busy corridor, transporting waves of immigrant groups outward from the city's center, the history of the street actually begins at its other end. It originated when outlying settlers struggle to connect with the emerging Chicago community by transporting farm produce and other wares into its growing markets.

1830s and 40s
Footpath Becomes Road

In the early 1800s John Kinzie Clark, one of the first Caucasian settlers in the area, built a log cabin on the old Milwaukee trail. The Native Americans called him "Nonimoa" or Prairie Wolf. Soon other simple dwellings dotted the frontier, and the old Milwaukee trail was widened to permit the passage of oxcarts and horse-drawn vehicles.

In 1832 George M. Powell entered claim for one hundred and sixty acres, a quarter-section of land, under patent from the United States Government, for property that is now just west of Western Ave. at Armitage Ave. He soon built a large inn on the property to accommodate travelers headed from the north to the newly incorporated village of Chicago to the southeast. The old Powell inn became a landmark in the area and a popular stopping place for farmers driving their wagons along the muddy Milwaukee trail.

Another early settler named Kimbell established a homestead about a mile and a quarter northwest of the Powell house. By 1837 the Kimbells and the Powells were running a market-gardening business together; they transported their produce along the Milwaukee trail to the burgeoning little town of Chicago some five miles away. Eventually they supplied fresh vegetables to a large proportion of homes in the city.

In time a wagon track was established, connect-

Plate 2.59

The Powell Hotel at the corner of Milwaukee Ave. and Armitage Ave. in the 1870s. This building was constructed on the site of the original Powell Inn, established in the 1830s by George M. Powell. The idealized illustration reveals transportation modes of the 1870s including the horse-drawn omnibus that ran along Milwaukee Ave. and terminated at this location.

ing downtown Chicago, at Kinzie St., out through Jefferson Township, to parts northwest. Because each settler coming across the prairie set his/her own course — trying to avoid holes, wagon ruts, sloughs and other obstacles — a series of tracks running parallel to each other developed. When roads were good it was a four-day trip to get from Chicago to Northfield, but when the weather was wet and the roads were muddy, it could require eight days or more for the same trip. In the springtime the Milwaukee trail became totally impassable, and often remained that way for several months.

In an effort to improve travel on the Milwaukee thoroughfare, Silas W. Sherman, a prominent resident of Northfield, petitioned the State Legislature in 1848 to have the road surveyed and designated as a permanent highway. His request was approved.

George Powell, whose country inn was a thriving business by this time, was eager to insure that the newly surveyed road went directly past his establishment. In anticipation of the surveying party, Powell raised a flag above his property and announced that if the new road hit this spot he would open his hotel to the workers, offering them the very best he had in food, wine and whiskey, with enough, in addition, to carry them on to the next tavern further north. Needless to say, the road hit the mark; and according to Chicago historian A. T. Andreas "the boys had a good repast."

Also in 1848, nearby landowners initiated and organized the Northwestern Plank Road Association. The charge of this organization was to grade and plank the Milwaukee road from Wolf Point in Chicago all the way to Wheeling, and to assume responsibility for its upkeep and maintenance. In return the association was given legal control of the highway, along with the right to establish toll gates at numerous points along its course. In 1849 construction of the Northwestern Plank Road began. During this period chartered companies planked nearly all the main roads entering Chicago. By June 13, 1851 the Northwestern Plank Road was completed from Kinzie in Chicago to two and one-half miles beyond Dutchman's Point (in Niles). Construction cost for the first twenty-three miles of the road, together with all toll houses, gates and one bridge, eventually totaled $51,000.

1850s
TRANSPORTATION ALONG THE ROAD

During the 1850s a number of early speculators in the Jefferson Township section promoted improvement of transportation to their area. This resulted in the establishment and intersection of two major rail lines in the community: the Chicago and North Western Railway, and the Chicago, Milwaukee and St. Paul Railway. As hoped, this development stimulated land speculation in the area. Investors, realizing the possibility of commuting from Chicago, began to subdivide their property, taking land out of farming and dividing it into small lots for residential use.

Amos J. Snell settled in Jefferson in 1852 and established a general store. In addition, he had a contract with the Chicago and North Western Railway to furnish wood for both railroad ties and fuel. In 1854 Snell purchased the system of toll roads and the franchise in the area near Wicker Park. One gate was located where Milwaukee crossed Fullerton, and the other at Milwaukee and Elston. A government charter permitted him to exact a toll on all roads through his property, as long as he kept the roads in good condition.

Establishment of the Chicago and North Western Railway lines in the 1850s also led to development at the southeast end of Milwaukee Avenue, near the river at Grand and Kinzie. Here railcar repair shops were built which in turn led to the construction of workingmen's homes and boarding houses in the area. Many of these buildings were of frame construction, and some were mere shacks.

During the 1850s Polish immigrants began moving into Chicago's northwest side to work in the railroad yards and factories that sprang up along the west bank of the Chicago River and on Goose Island. This community would eventually grow to become the largest Polish settlement in the world outside of Europe. In later years Poles migrated up Milwaukee Ave., as did many other groups, to become a major ethnic population in the Wicker Park neighborhood. During the 1850s, however, there were only patches of settlement along the southern end of the avenue.

1860s
DEVELOPMENT BEGINS

During the 1860s, the decade of the Civil War, the banks of the North Branch of the Chicago River and Goose Island were inundated with manufacturing plants, tanneries and other industries. These new businesses attracted and employed thousands of immigrants who were pouring into Chicago from countries throughout Europe. At the other end of the city, farms in Jefferson Township continued to be divided into smaller and smaller parcels, while side streets north and south of Milwaukee Ave. were being laid out and developed. As a consequence of both *pressure outward* from the city's center and *movement inward* from the outlying areas, Chicago developed in a direction along Milwaukee Ave. during this decade. Reflecting this growth, the northern boundary of the city was extended to Bloomingdale as far west as Western Ave., through action of the state legislature in 1863.

In 1869 the newly established West Park Commission created the fabulous 207-acre Humboldt Park at California, North Ave., Kedzie and Division St. At the same time it laid down an extensive boulevard system that connected this park to other major parks on the west side and throughout the city. After 1869, it is said, the Milwaukee Ave. corridor began to develop rapidly. Intentionally or not, Humboldt Park and the boulevard system lent a tremendous impetus to development of the city's northwest side, and strengthened the role of Milwaukee Ave. as the area's major thoroughfare.

Plate 2.60

PHOTO OF THE MILWAUKEE AVE. HORSE-DRAWN STREETCAR OR "HORSE-CAR ON RAILS" TAKEN IN THE 1870S. THE "NORTH AVE." SIGN ON TOP OF THE CAR PRESUMABLY INDICATES THAT THE LINE RAN TO NORTH AVE. AT THIS TIME.

1870s
POST-FIRE GROWTH

The Great Chicago Fire of 1871 and the decade of the 70s brought many significant changes to the city and specifically to the northwest side. Milwaukee Ave. became a major urban thoroughfare exploding with new businesses and carrying waves of ethnic groups out from the city's center.

In the early 1870s the Avenue was paved with Nicholson blocks, from its beginning at Kinzie St. to its intersection with Damen (Robey) and North in the

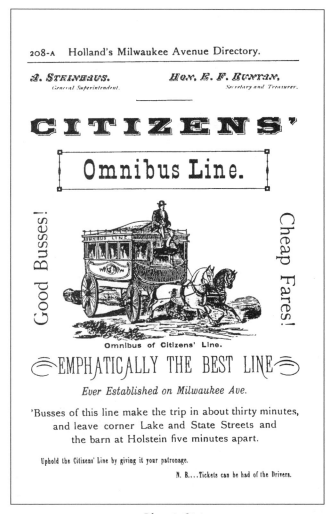

Plate 2.61
ADVERTISEMENT FOR THE CITIZEN'S OMNIBUS LINE ESTABLISHED BY A. STEINHAUS ON MILWAUKEE AVE. SHORTLY AFTER THE CHICAGO FIRE.

Plate 2.62
ADVERTISEMENT FROM THE *Holland's Directory of Milwaukee Ave.* PUBLISHED IN 1875 TO PROMOTE BUSINESS ACTIVITY ALONG THE STREET.

heart of Wicker Park. This improvement ushered in a "new era" for businessmen and residents. Real estate values soared, with lots selling at double their value before the paving was completed.

In 1873 the Chicago West Division Railway Co., a horse-drawn streetcar, installed tracks and began service on Milwaukee to Division St. By 1874 the streetcar system was extended to North Ave. Although this system was a great improvement, it still had its drawbacks. A Chicago newspaper article offers a neighborhood resident's recollection of some of the difficulties:

"All cars in those days were drawn by horses or mules. Some were drawn by one horse and some were drawn by two. The trips were infrequent and the service slow. In winter, with the thermometer down to twenty below zero, traveling up Milwaukee avenue in an unheated car was no joy ride. The cars creaked and lunged, and the horses pulled and tugged through the snow. The driver and conductor had to get off frequently to shovel snow off the tracks. The end of the run was a barren and wind-swept prairie with scarcely a house in sight, and it was here that the crew was allowed to stop twenty minutes for lunch."

An alternative omnibus service, called the "Citizen's Line," was established by a Mr. A. Steinhouse on Milwaukee Ave. according to *Holland's Directory of Milwaukee Avenue for 1875-76*:

"Although a few years ago the avenue was almost destitute of street traveling accommodations, we are now able to boast of having one of the best omnibus lines in the city. They have an immense barn and buildings contiguous, which are used as harness shop, blacksmith shop, coach factory etc. They make all their own busses, do all repairing, horse shoeing on the premises; have 26 busses and over 200 head of good horses.... Barn and factories at Nos. 1058

to 1059 Milwaukee Ave.... This line is in competition with the street car company which uses old worn out cars, worse than useless horses... and consumes the whole day in getting to and from town."

The *Holland's Directory* gives a remarkably detailed picture of the street in 1870s:

"A large number of stores and buildings of a superior order have been erected, till now the avenue presents an almost unbroken front from Kinzie St. to North Ave. Many of the stores are really elegant buildings, in which are kept immense stocks of everything used by families or individuals in almost any station in life."

After the Fire of 1871, many well-to-do business families, whose homes had been destroyed by the great conflagration, rebuilt their residences in the Wicker Park district. Wealthy Germans and Scandinavians, who had made fortunes in breweries, lumber yards, tanneries, furniture factories and other industries located along the river, began moving into previously undeveloped lots surrounding the park.

Holland's Directory indicates that a large proportion of businesses on Milwaukee Ave. were

Plate 2.63
VIEW NORTHWEST ALONG MILWAUKEE AVE. FROM THE ASHLAND AVE. INTERSECTION ABOUT 1900, CAPTURES THE BUSTLING, MULTI-ETHNIC CHARACTER OF THE AREA, SHOWING WOODEN SIDEWALKS, MUD STREWN STREETS AND STREETCARS VISIBLE IN THE DISTANCE.

Plate 2.64

THIS POST CARD SHOWS A MORE SANITIZED VIEW OF MILWAUKEE AVE. LOOKING NORTHWEST FROM DIVISION STREET AROUND 1910. ON THE RIGHT IS A STRIKING, WHITE TERRA COTTA BUILDING THAT EVENTUALLY HOUSED THE ALLIANCE PRINTERS AND PUBLISHERS (AN OFF-SHOOT OF THE POLISH NATIONAL ALLIANCE) THAT PUBLISHED TWO POLISH NEWSPAPERS THE WEEKLY ZAGODA (HARMONY) AND THE DAILY DZIENNIK LUDOWY (ALLIANCE DAILY NEWS.)

owned by Germans in 1876, along with a mixture of Scandinavians and other groups. William Marbach, a Chicago resident since 1851 established himself in the neighborhood in 1872. He was listed as city weigher and dealer in flour and feed, pressed hay, canned goods, vegetables, poultry, pure wines, liquors, and beer at the corner of Milwaukee and Damen with his residence at the same address. His listing promised "good goods and entire satisfaction guaranteed." John A. Mayer was "proprietor Wicker Park drug store, and Deutsch apotheke (German apothecary), pure drugs and medicines, perfumery, brushes, sponges, toilet articles, pure wines and liquors, physicians prescriptions carefully compounded, corner Milwaukee and North Aves." Miss Hoffmann was "dressmaker, 923 Milwaukee." Paul Hermann's listing stated: "butcher, all kinds of fresh and cut meats of best quality kept, and none other, also hams, pork,

bacon, dried beef, sausages, lard, 959 Milwaukee near Robey."

A Norwegian business, Helmke and Petersen, established in 1872, was listed at two locations on Milwaukee: "dealers in choice family groceries, flour, provisions, canned goods, crockery, glass, wood and willow ware, fine teas and coffees a speciality."

In a class by himself was John Beuhler, the German banker, former Chicago Alderman and State Senator of Illinois. According to the Directory:

"Mr. Buehler has been for many years a well known and respected resident of Chicago and has spent 19 to 20 years of his life on Milwaukee Ave. At No. 316 the bank of Mr. Buehler is located, in which he does a general banking business, buys and sells exchange, and issues drafts on the principal cities of Europe... He is also of the firm of Buehler and Schack, whose office is in the bank building, where they jointly deal in real estate very extensively.... He owns the building in which he conducts his business... Mr.

Buehler proposes to erect other buildings in the coming season... He owns about 150,000 dollars worth of real estate on this street amounting to a total frontage of some 400 feet, added to which may be mentioned a splendid lot on Robey Street cornering on Milwaukee avenue, of about 350 feet frontage, upon which his residence is situated."

At the same time that well-to-do Germans and Scandinavians were moving into Wicker Park, building elegant homes to demonstrate their status and privilege, Chicago was undergoing another dramatic transformation in its population. After the Great Fire, masses of European immigrants poured into the city to work at

rebuilding Chicago and to take jobs in its exploding and expanding industries. As the major Norwegian newspaper, the *Skandinaven*, described it, there was, "an enormous influx of people from all four corners of the world... mostly working people with blue overalls and a dinner pail... and there was no lack of work at good pay." During this period newly arrived workers from Germany, Scandinavia and later Poland, began making their way up Milwaukee into the Wicker Park neighborhood.

The devastation of the Chicago Fire resulted in an ordinance that prohibited construction of

Plate 2.65

A SCENE ON MILWAUKEE AVE. NEAR ASHLAND AVE. AROUND 1915, REVEALS A MIXTURE OF BUILDING STYLES SPANNING SEVERAL DECADES. THE CONTINENTAL CLOTHING COMPANY ON THE CORNER SIGNALS THE DOMINANCE OF THE RETAIL CLOTHING BUSINESS, WHILE THE PRESENCE OF AN AUTOMOBILE AMID HORSE DRAWN VEHICLES FORECASTS A NEW ERA OF TRANSPORTATION ON THE STREET.

cheap, frame dwellings within a prescribed limit in the central city. The Wicker Park neighborhood, which lay outside these fire limits, escaped restriction. The fire ordinance caused poorer residents to seek homes away from the center of the city and to begin relocating on the outer fringes. This phenomenon gave impetus to the movement of immigrants up Milwaukee into the Wicker Park neighborhood and led to development of the community as home to both well-to-do business families and the working class.

By 1878 the Milwaukee Ave. streetcar line was extended to Western Ave. with the terminal barns built on Armitage. This final extension resulted in further development of the surrounding area by working-class people, mostly Germans, who settled in close proximity to the end of this transportation line.

JAMES DAVIS.
1400-1406 Milwaukee Avenue, Chicago.
Artistic Wall Paper and Painters Supplies.
This entire Building, containing 45,000 feet of floor space, dedicated to the art and beauty of Home Decoration.

Plate 2.66
ADVERTISEMENT POSTCARD FROM THE DAVIS WALL PAPER AND PAINTERS SUPPLY BUSINESS ON MILWAUKEE AVE AND WOLCOTT (LINCOLN). ON THE BACK, APRIL 1, 1914, DAVIS WROTE TO A CUSTOMER: "OUR LINE IS PROVING THE GREATEST SUCCESS ALL OVER THE COUNTRY. HAVEN'T HAD ANY ORDERS FROM YOU YET. WHAT IS THE MATTER?"

1880S AND 90S
IMMIGRATION AND EXPANSION

An 1881 Chicago newspaper article, titled "The Story of Milwaukee Avenue," reveals the progression of ethnic groups along the street at the time:

"As we proceed northwest we notice that the buildings are mostly one and two stories in height.... The names on the signs change. Most of them are German now and saloons with family entrances are numerous. Groceries, tailor shops, and drug stores, fortune-tellers, with an occasional dry good or hardware store or carpenter shop make up the business activities.... As we go on slowly we find the buildings are farther apart, the vacant lots more numerous, fewer stores, more residences. Looking west we catch glimpses of the prairie extending westward, which affords pasturage for the cows that many families still keep.... Nearing North Avenue we find the buildings grouped more thickly about the street intersections, more stores, fewer German and more Scandinavian names. Passing North Avenue we pass few buildings until we reach Western Avenue, where there is quite a settlement. At our right on Armitage Avenue is the old Powell House, now used as a residence.... At this time there are not many people living west of Milwaukee Avenue north of North Avenue."

In addition, a vivid description of Milwaukee Ave. in the 1880s is given by an individual named Salmonsen as quoted in *A Century of Urban Life, the Norwegians in Chicago Before 1930*:

"The Avenue was most characteristic during the early morning hours between six and seven, when the rush of workers to shops or other places of employment began. They came by the thousands, young and old of both sexes... Their occupations could usually be determined by how they were dressed. There was the bricklayer in his coarse overalls... The carpenter in similar attire, but of finer, blue material, the ditch digger carrying a shovel over one shoulder, the tailor dressed in clothes of good quality and cut, the shoemaker with polished shoes, barber apprentices with pomaded hair and clean fingernails, waiters in clean linen, coach men with gloves to protect their hands... Most of the women were young girls on the way to a tailor's workshop... hatmaker... or cigar factory. But in the crowd one also saw elderly women who carried their work clothes on their way to a large establishment where they worked as cleaning women or to the large laundries where the strong heat long ago had given the women their pallid yellow skin color."

Another description from the time, quoted in *Haymarket Revisited,* confirms this general impression:

"The workday began in the dark hours of the early morning, as early as 4 a.m. for those with over two or three miles to walk (since they could not afford Yerkes' streetcars that cost 10c, which was two hours wages for the women and children). By six o'clock thousands of men, women, and children were trudging down streets like Milwaukee Avenue... Dinner buckets in hand, not to return until early evening. In 1882 bakers were found working 15 to 17 hours a day around hot ovens, with little time for food or rest. Brewery employees labored from 3 a.m. to 6 p.m. in the busy season."

The cable car was introduced to Chicago in the 1880s and put in service on Milwaukee Ave. in the late 1880s. A powerhouse, that kept the cables in constant motion, was built at Milwaukee and Cleaver Street.

In 1889 Chicago's boundaries were expanded dramatically when several outlying towns were annexed to the city, even beyond the reach of Milwaukee Ave. These included Cicero, City of Lake View, Town of Lake, Village of Hyde Park and the Town of Jefferson. By this act, approximately 126 square miles were added to Chicago, resulting in the area of the city being enlarged to 169.8 square miles. As a result, the northwest boundaries of the city were extended to Harlem and Howard, bringing well within the city limits the town of Jefferson that lay just beyond the neighborhood of Wicker Park. Many new subdivisions opened in this area and old ones became revitalized, while the population here increased rapidly. From this point on, the Wicker Park community was no longer located at the northwest edge of Chicago. Instead it became more of a central city neighborhood; and Milwaukee Avenue continued, all the more, to be a corridor for ethnic groups moving northwest out from the center of the city.

In 1892 the Milwaukee Ave. car line was extended to Logan Square, and to Lawrence Ave. in 1895. Shortly thereafter an extension of a few blocks connected it to the Chicago and North Western Railway, while a temporary line was laid to the city limits giving people a means of reaching St. Adalbert's cemetery at Niles. St. Adalbert's, a huge Polish and Bohemian cemetery, had been organized along Milwaukee Ave. in Niles in 1872.

1900 — 1920S
THE BOOM BEFORE THE CRASH

By 1900 Milwaukee Ave. and its side streets from Division to North, were being inundated by Poles and other Eastern European immigrants. Scandinavians and Germans, who had dominated the area in earlier times, were moving further northwest, while the Poles, Ukranians, Slovaks, and finally Jews were slowly replacing the earlier businesspeople in the area. In 1905-06 the Milwaukee Ave. cable car line was electrified, and a safer more reliable means of transportation took people all the way to Lawrence Ave.

The Goldblatt Brothers opened their first store on Chicago Ave. at Ashland in 1914, and soon Jewish merchants replaced German and Scandinavian businesspeople along Milwaukee. In an interview con-

ducted in the 1970s, long-time neighborhood resident, Mrs. Bohnsak, recalls the early stores:

"Wieboldt's had one of their first stores there. The store used to be called the Lion's Store - and Mr. Wieboldt himself would frequently be there. Then there was Koop Store, the Molar Store (for dry goods,) Spangler's Dry Good on Robey and Milwaukee, Mansels Hardware and many hat shops. By 1917 or so, Jews began moving into the neighborhood, although for several years, they had already been in business on Milwaukee Ave."

By the 1920s Milwaukee Avenue was a well-established commercial center, but it was becoming a light manufacturing area as well. Above shops and along the side streets, various small industries were gaining a foothold. A

Plate 2.67

LOOKING NORTHWEST ON MILWAUKEE AVE. IN THE 1920S. THE WIEBOLDT STORE, ALONG WITH OTHER NEIGHBORHOOD BUSINESSES, MADE THIS A LIVELY RETAIL DISTRICT ACCESSED BY AUTOMOBILE AND THE ELECTRIC STREETCAR.

Chicago newspaper in 1922 reported:

"One of the greatest clothing manufacturing districts in the world has Milwaukee Avenue for its axis. Here, also, is one of the largest glove manufacturing districts in America and one of Chicago's busiest shopping centers and a growing manufacturing district... The stretch between Division St. and North Ave. is Milwaukee Avenue's busiest shopping center. The street is lined with modern department stores, big furniture stores, numerous millinery shops, shoe stores, clothing stores and speciality shops of every nature. Saturday nights in this section produce as dense shopping crowds as the loop at its busiest, for the foreign born residents cling to the tradition of 'market day' and do most of their shopping on Saturday."

Plate 2.68
1228 N. MILWAUKEE AVE., CORNER OF MILWAUKEE AND ASHLAND, IN 1919.

CONCLUSION

The 1920s continued to be a boom time for Milwaukee Ave. In 1921 the new Noel State Bank Building was built at the corner of Milwaukee, North and Damen while a ten-story, $800,000, Medical Arts Building (later called the Tower Building) was planned for the corner of Milwaukee and North, increasing the importance of this intersection. In 1927 the avenue was widened and paved for two and one half miles. A detailed map of the businesses along Milwaukee Avenue in 1929 reveals a mixed ethnic character with Polish and Jewish names predominating: Lenard Restaurant, Zwiefka Brothers Haberdashery, W. Wieczoreks Drugs, Kaufman Clothes, Rusnak Brothers Furniture, George Horwitz Frocks and Lingerie, and Kaplan Department Store are examples.

By 1930 a Chicago newspaper article emphasized both the commercial and industrial nature of Milwaukee Avenue. "At Division Street we find a busy retail business district... Passing North Ave. we find a manufacturing district, along the Milwaukee and St. Paul Railroad."

Through the years Milwaukee Avenue had a profound effect on the history of the Wicker Park District. It provided an axis of transportation, served as a backbone for development of its residential communities, supported the development of a vital business community, created jobs through small industry and manufacturing, and served as a corridor for the movement of a succession of ethnic groups through the city.

— *Mary Ann Johnson*

Life in Wicker Park

Plate 3.1

THIS PORTRAIT OF THE NOEL FAMILY WAS PROBABLY TAKEN IN ABOUT 1907. JOSEPH R. NOEL IS ON THE LEFT, NEXT TO DAUGHTER, HARRIET, WITH THEOPHILUS, THE PATRIARCH, IN THE MIDDLE. JOSEPH'S YOUNGEST DAUGHTER VIRGINIA IS NEXT TO THEOPHILUS WITH JOSEPH'S WIFE ALICE ON THE RIGHT.

Wicker Park Institutions and Cultures

Overview

WHAT WAS IT LIKE TO LIVE IN WICKER PARK DURING THE LATE 1800'S AND EARLY 1900'S ?

Unlike other Chicago neighborhoods at this time, the Wicker Park District was a model for blending ethnic groups residentially, commercially and institutionally. That blending of immigrant groups was visible in the community's schools, and in many institutions and organizations. Whether these groups came with the intention of returning someday to their previous homelands, or they knew they were here to stay, it's evident that they stayed and left their mark.

Many of the institutions created during this time still survive and thrive. The schools, hospitals and churches demonstrate clearly that the community's residents felt the bonds of religion and national ancestry. Other organizations in the District stand as proof that social activism had arrived in Chicago by the 1890s, during the earliest days of the settlement house movement in this country, for the general purpose of assisting all of the ethnic groups as they arrived.

The public theaters, taverns, bathhouses and even social organizations that the neighborhood's residents enjoyed together demonstrate that they were willing to mix to some degree. Most visible in the District today is the housing supply they created, which still reflects the presence of entrepreneurs and workers, often as next-door neighbors. They also appear to have chosen not to live in isolation, according to their ethnic identification.

Fortunately, residents took pictures, sent postcards, and created other written records of who they were and how they lived. Perhaps they understood that they were leaving behind reminders of family bonds and the existence of "community." Lucky for us.

We hope you enjoy meeting some of the early residents of the neighborhood, and the community they helped create.

— Larry E. Clary

Institutional development in the Wicker Park District followed the settlement of ethnic and cultural groups in the neighborhood. As a result, the area's institutional history is as rich and varied, as colorful and dramatic, as multi-layered and diverse, as the people who populated this remarkable urban community.

Although an early map of Chicago indicates that streets were laid out in parts of the Wicker Park neighborhood by 1867, there is evidence of only one institution. According to Chicago Board of Education records, the Rolling Mill Primary School was established on Ashland Ave. (Reuben St.) near Wabansia Ave. in 1866. The school was named after the Chicago Rolling Mill, a plant that rolled railroad tracks. Located along the North Branch of the Chicago River north of North Ave., it was established in 1857, attracting Irish immigrant workers to the area and triggering institutional development.

1871 — ANNUNCIATION SCHOOL AND CHURCH BEGIN

On October 2, 1871, just six days before the Great Chicago Fire destroyed vast areas of the city, Rev. T. J. Edwards and the Sisters of Charity of the Blessed Virgin Mary opened Annunciation Parochial School on Marshfield Ave. (formerly 42 Commercial Ave.) near Wabansia in the Rolling Mill area. Rev. Edwards, who apparently was associated with the Jesuit parish of Holy Family located on Chicago's Near West Side, had been ministering to Irish immigrants from County Clare in this area for several years. An 1876 *Chicago Times* article, quoted in *Catholicism Chicago Style (1993)*, emphasized attempts by the church to influence the lifestyles of the area's working-class immigrants in 1866:

> "The people were largely Catholic in name, but in name only. They paid little or no regard to the outward ordinances of religion, and cared less for its principles. To a great extent they were quarrelsome and dissolute....Father Edwards saw that the people in this part of the city needed the restraining and the purifying influences of the church, and he resolved to supply this need. There was no place of worship, and there were practically no worshipers. He undertook to build the one and supply the other. In both of these attempts he has been remarkably successful."

The Annunciation Parochial School was a three-story frame building containing thirteen schoolrooms and an assembly hall. Run by the disciplined and exacting Sisters of Charity of the B. V. M., the school set a standard for excellence in the neighborhood, offering instruction in basic Catholic doctrine as well as an elementary curriculum. By 1876 the school enrolled 500 students. While plans were being made for a new church building, church services for the community were held in the basement of the school, a common practice in this early period of Catholic institution building.

The cornerstone for the Church of the Annunciation was laid at the corner of Paulina St. and Wabansia on August 16, 1874, "with all the pomp and ceremony which is usually brought to bear on such occasions in the Catholic Church," according to a *Daily Inter Ocean* newspaper report. Like most of the newly built Catholic churches after the Great Fire of 1871, it was constructed of brick or stone rather than wood. A grand procession, an assembling of all the prominent Catholic societies, and a long march in the heat of the day, with over 1,000 people participating, is described. The societies that participated were: Married Men's Sodality of the Holy Family, 300 men; Father Mathew's Total Abstinence and Benevolent Society, 100 men; Holy Family Cadets and band, 50 young men; Holy Family Temperance Society with band, 100 men; St. Boniface Society with band, 100 men; St. Stanislaus Kostka with band, 300 men; St. Joseph (Polish) Society and band, 150 men; The Emeralds No. 1, 150 men; The Emeralds No. 4 with band, 125 men; Emeralds No. 7, 60 men, and Emeralds No. 8 with band, 150 men.

Beginning at the corner of Milwaukee and Union at three o'clock, the procession made its way northwest and arrived at the church at five o'clock. There, on a temporary platform created for the occasion, prominent Chicago Catholic priests (including Bishop Foley and Father Edwards) performed an elaborate exercise and ritual. "The altar was blessed, and the foundation sprinkled with holy water, after which the Bishop recited the forms of the church preparatory to laying the stone. The Bishop took the trowel and went through the appropriate form, when the stone was lowered to its place," stated the *Daily Inter Ocean*.

The Church of the Annunciation was built in a classic gothic style at a cost of $75,000. The parish soon numbered 800 and supported many organizations such as the St. Vincent de Paul Society, the Hibernians, the Foresters and the Total Abstinence Society. The new church (also known as the Rolling Mill Church) was an Irish Catholic church established under the authority of the Chicago Archdiocese that had been established in 1844. As such it was a territorial church, that is, its parish was defined as a specific geographical territory of the city. Although most of its parishioners were originally Irish, eventually some German and Polish Catholics attended Annunciation. The Church of Annunciation was the dominant Catholic institution in this part of the neighborhood until St. Mary of the Angel's Church, a Polish national parish, was established in 1899. A calendar, published by Annunciation in 1912, indicates that even at this late date, there were still many Irish church members located in the Wicker Park neighborhood, particularly on Wabansia, Paulina, North, and Damen (Robey).

1873 — St. Paul's Church Established

Norwegians and other Scandinavians began to come into the Wicker Park District about the same time as the Germans, and originally many of them also settled in the area around the park. Recognizing a need to address the increasing numbers of Norwegians moving from downtown to new developing areas, such as Wicker Park and Humboldt Park, the Lutheran Norwegian Synod created a home mission venture.

In 1873, Rev. J. L. Krohn of Our Savior Lutheran Church at Erie and May gave assistance in forming a new congregation to some of his members, who had moved to Wicker Park. St. Paul's Church was established during a two-day meeting on May 11-12, 1873

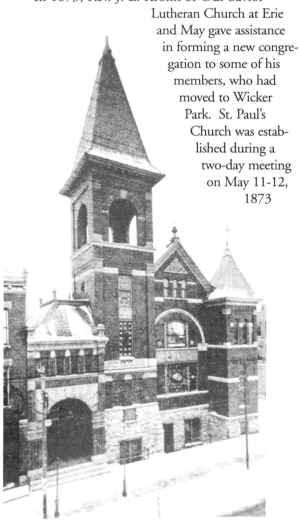

Plate 3.2

St. Paul's Evangelical Norwegian Lutheran Church was built on North Ave. near Leavitt and dedicated in 1892. This early view shows the church before North Ave. was widened.

when a constitution was adopted and officers elected. It was also decided to petition the Norwegian Lutheran Synod for finding and supporting a permanent pastor.

The Synod agreed, and newly ordained pastor, Rev. I. L. P. Dietrichsen, became St. Paul's first pastor. Among his first year's regular pastoral duties, Dietrichsen oversaw the construction of a church on Wicker Park Ave. (Park St.).

In March 1874, the Synod's missionary efforts resulted in the founding of St. Peter's Church. Dietrichsen guided the establishment of their Sunday school in a chapel on the corner of Campbell Ave. and Hirsch St. (just west of Western). Dietrichsen left both churches in 1876, followed by a series of pastors who came and went.

Although St. Paul's had originally been formed as a Norwegian-language parish, by 1886 it offered two English-language and four Norwegian-language services a month. Eventually the Sunday school and most of the church services were conducted in English, although the formal Norwegian church language continued to be heard for another generation.

Becoming pastor to both churches in 1887, Rev. O. O. C. Hjorth set about merging St. Paul's and St. Peter's. The congregations agreed. By July 1, 1889, a revised constitution had been approved and the two congregations incorporated as St. Paul's Evangelical Norwegian Lutheran Church, and land was purchased on North near Leavitt St. for the church and parsonage. The cornerstone for the sanctuary was laid August 24, 1890 and the congregation moved into the church's completed basement later that year.

Work continued and the building was finished and dedicated on November 13, 1892. The new St. Paul's Church was designed by architect G. Isaacson and built at a cost of $12,000, twice the estimated cost and a serious blow to the young church's finances. It is said that its interior was meant to replicate an inverted ark. The church's sturdy pews and beautifully carved wooden altar came from the First Norwegian Lutheran Church of Chicago, which was located at one time on Franklin. In 1906 a pipe organ was installed by the prestigious Austin Organ Company of Hartford, CT, and a parsonage was built on the west side of the church.

1874 — Wicker Park School Constructed

By 1874 the Rolling Mill School consisted of two two-story frame buildings with one classroom on each floor. A new brick school was built at 1621 Wabansia and named Jonathan Burr, after an early Chicago real estate investor, banker and financial speculator. On January 13, 1874, the Board of Education approved the relocation of two frame buildings and out houses to the 2000 W. Evergreen block. Mr. Jacob Becker received the contract for $425.00. In February of that year, the old Rolling Mill School buildings at Ashland and Wabansia were picked up and moved. Residents of this part of the neighborhood had urged the Board of Education to relocate the school to the Evergreen site and were thus supporters from the beginning.

On February 24, Miss Eliza Lundegreen, the principal of the Holstein School, was placed in charge of the new school with a salary of $1,200 annually. Later that year, it was officially named the Wicker Park Primary School, with the Holstein School a branch of Wicker Park. The school was soon overcrowded, however, and the Board of Education was forced to rent space in a nearby church for $22.00 a month. In June 1877, the first group of students graduated, some of them with grades high enough to be admitted to high school. Since there was only one public high school in Chicago at the time, this was an accomplishment. In 1879 the Board leased a two-story brick building at 2020 W. Evergreen (formerly 141 W.), east of and adjoining the school, to accommodate new classes. At this point, the study of German was typically offered in the Chicago public schools. In 1879 enough students wanted to study German at Wicker Park School that a teacher was requested for this purpose.

As the population of the Wicker Park District continued to increase after the Fire, education of children became a growing problem. The Wicker Park School on Evergreen Ave. was seriously overcrowded by 1880 and a

CHICAGO PUBLIC SCHOOLS.

IN REMEMBRANCE OF THE SCHOOL YEAR 1883. *Wicker Park School.*

Plate 3.3
This was probably the Wicker Park School building that was erected in 1882 and pictured in 1883.

new fifteen-room school was planned. In June two additional lots to the west were purchased, and the new building was ready for occupancy in1882. Overcrowding continued to be a problem, however, and it was therefore necessary to renew the lease on the church at Hirsch and Seymour for another year. In 1885 Von Humboldt Grammar School (grades four through eight) was opened at Hirsch and Rockwell, and the Andersen Grammar School at Division and Honore was opened in 1886. The Wicker Park School was changed to a "Primary" school (grades one through three) as the student population and faculty continued to increase. In 1896 a nine-room addition was completed, and Wicker Park became a grammar school again.

Principals for the school were: 1874-85, Eliza Lundegreen; 1885-86, William C. Dodge; 1886-87, Henry D. Hatch; 1887-90, Helen Blanchard; 1890-1904, Agnes M. Brown; 1904-06, Elizabeth T. H. Spieker; 1906-07, Charles D. Lowry; 1907-08, Kate S. Kellogg; 1908-15, Fred E. Smith; 1915-21, Frank H. Chase; 1921-26, Roland O. Witcraft; 1926-28, William R. Hornbaker; and 1928-32, Dora W. Zollman.

1879 — WICKER PARK LUTHERAN CHURCH ORGANIZED

In the late 1870s Edmund Belfour, the founder and pastor of Holy Trinity Church at Dearborn and Erie Streets, advanced the idea of organizing another English-speaking Lutheran congregation in the Wicker Park District. In 1879 he called a meeting of neighborhood Lutherans, including John Buehler and A. C. Lausten, at the home of Dr. Niles Quales. As a result of this meeting the Wicker Park Lutheran Church was organized as a congregation within the Pittsburgh Synod.

The church was incorporated, and a constitution was signed on August 24, 1879, at Dr. Quales' home. Representing a mixture of nationalities, the signatories of the constitution were: Rev. Belfour; John Buehler, banker and politician; Niles Quales, physician and civic leader; J. A. Greiner, manufacturer; George Murbach, flour and feed; Franz Schack, real estate and alderman; Bryngal Olson, contractor; Lewis Iverson; W. J. Hamilton, salesman; A.C. Lausten, manufacturer; Nels Nelson, dentist; Fred Belz, freight superintendent; P. W. Gilbertson, railroad; Ed Warnecke, sewing machine manufacturer; Peter W. Bandow, grocer; and Louis Martin, lumberman. The group acquired title to an unfinished frame structure at the corner of Hoyne and LeMoyne by paying off a $3,000 mortgage.

The congregation grew rapidly during the first weeks, as illustrated by its rising Sunday school attendance: 80 boys and girls the first Sunday, 148 the second, and 225 the third. In the meantime $4,000 was raised to complete the building that was dedicated on January 18, 1880. This frame structure (See *Plate 4.13*), reportedly one of the largest on the northwest side, served the congregation until it was razed to build a new stone building in 1906.

Wicker Park Lutheran Church's new structure was built in the Romanesque style, modeled after the twelfth century Holy Trinity Church in Caen, France. The large, grey mica-flecked stones used in constructing the new church came from a house of "ill repute" on Michigan Ave. When questioned about the appropriateness of using this stone, the pastor replied: "It has served the devil long enough, now let it serve the Lord."

This church was, for many years, a social and spiritual center for the neighborhood's immigrant elite, mostly Scandinavian and German families.

Plate 3.4

THE SECOND WICKER PARK LUTHERAN CHURCH BUILDING WAS BUILT ON THE NORTHWEST CORNER OF HOYNE AND LEMOYNE IN 1906. IT WAS CONSTRUCTED IN A ROMANESQUE STYLE AND MODELED AFTER THE TWELFTH CENTURY HOLY TRINITY CHURCH IN CAEN, FRANCE. SUNDAY SCHOOL ATTENDEES WERE TRANSPORTED TO CHURCH IN THIS STYLISH HORSE-DRAWN CARRIAGE.

1884 — ST. ALOYSIUS PARISH ORGANIZED

Many people living in the Wicker Park District in the 1870s identified themselves as Germans. In spite of a common language and national heritage, these people represented a great diversity of backgrounds, attitudes, life styles and beliefs. The German Catholics became conspicuous in the Wicker Park District during the late 1800s because they were great institution builders. A tradition of German Social Catholicism that was developed in Europe in the nineteenth century prompted them to social action and charitable work in the United States.

In 1884 Chicago's Archbishop Patrick A. Feehan appointed Rev. Aloysius J. Thiele to organize a parish for German Catholics settling near the intersection of North, Damen and Milwaukee. Rev. Thiele called a meeting of neighborhood German Catholics at the home of Adolph Borgmeier, who lived at 2132 W. LeMoyne (then 99 Thompson) to discuss plans for the new church. John

Brausch, Albert Vogler, Joseph Resch, Nicholas Ireman, Borgmeier and Rev. Theile attended this meeting, and determined that the intersection of North and Western would be the central point of the new parish. Peter Lagoni, a tavern owner at this site, loaned a piece of property and within days the group had acquired the necessary lumber and constructed a one-story frame building with a cross on the top. The little frame building (See *Plate 4.10*.) was located on the northwest corner of the intersection and was built at a cost of $450.

On June 20th, Rev. Thiele established St. Aloysius Church here, naming it after his patron, St. Aloysius. The dedication ceremony included a gospel in which Rev. Thiele pointed out that "lack of religious guidance makes life barren as the desert" and vowed to serve as a good shepherd, leading this almost forgotten flock back to the fold. Officially, the boundaries of the new parish were:

Plate 3.5

ST. ALOYISIUS' FIRST PERMANENT CHURCH (SECOND BUILDING FROM THE LEFT), SCHOOL AND RECTORY BUILT IN 1884 ON THE WEST SIDE OF CLAREMONT (DAVIS) JUST NORTH OF LEMOYNE.(THOMPSON). THE BUILDING TO THE FAR RIGHT IS THE PARISH'S TEN-ROOM SCHOOL COMPLETED IN 1886. ON THE FAR LEFT IS THE SCHOOL BUILT IN 1892 AND DEDICATED IN 1893. THE SCHOOL'S LARGE HALL SERVED AS THE CHURCH OF ST. AL'S FOR SEVENTY YEARS.

the Northwestern railroad tracks south-eastward from Fullerton to Wood; Wood and Wolcott (Lincoln) south to Division; west on Division to Leavitt, and Leavitt south to Lake.

Rev. Thiele called on two German orders of nuns, the Sisters of Christian Charity and the Poor Handmaids of Jesus Christ, to assist in developing the parish. In August 1884, the Sisters of Christian Charity in Paderborn, Germany agreed to establish a grammar school in St. Aloysius parish and to send a group of able Sisters to begin the work. By December the first of the Sisters had arrived.

Sisters Eduarda, Honoria, Patentee, and Laetitia went to work and quickly opened a parochial school in the neighborhood with twenty-five students. Classes were conducted in both English and German. A combination church-school was erected of brick on the west side of

Claremont (Davis St.) just north of LeMoyne at a cost of $20,000. The German Catholic families in the neighborhood were impressed with the "zeal, competency, and tact" of the Sisters of Christian Charity, and enthusiastically supported their work. By June 1885, 141 students were enrolled, and the school building was getting crowded. As a result, a new two-story brick school containing ten rooms was planned and opened in 1886. Father Thiele lived in a small house on Claremont until 1888 when a spacious new rectory was completed on LeMoyne.

In 1909 St. Aloysius parish celebrated its silver jubilee. In 25 years the parish had grown from forty-six to more than 600 families. In the next few years so many Polish families moved into the neighborhood that St. Helen's parish was established at Augusta Blvd. near Western a few blocks south of the St. Aloysius parish complex.

1886 — ST. ELIZABETH'S HOSPITAL CORNERSTONE LAID

In an attempt to make St. Aloysius parish more attractive and the northwest side a desirable place for Catholics to live, Father Thiele began plans to establish a Catholic hospital in the area. Learning that the Poor Handmaids of Jesus Christ were seeking permission to build a hospital in Chicago, he invited them to join him in his efforts. The Poor Handmaids had been founded in Germany in 1851 by Mary Katherine Kasper. Kasper, born in Dernbach,

Plate 3.6

ST. ELIZABETH'S HOSPITAL, DEVELOPED BY ST. ALOYISIUS PARISH AND THE POOR HANDMAIDS OF JESUS CHRIST, WAS BUILT IN 1887 ON A SQUARE BLOCK OF LAND BOUNDED BY CLAREMONT, LEMOYNE, OAKLEY AND HIRSCH. THIS PHOTO SHOWS THE HOSPITAL WITH THE ADDITION OF A NEW WING COMPLETED IN 1892.

Germany in 1820, formed the Poor Handmaids by "building a small house where she and four other young women lived together, prayed together and accepted those who needed help— a sick girl, homeless widow, orphaned children." The came to Chicago to work in an orphanage while they cared for people in their homes. During the smallpox epidemic of 1880, they were particularly active. In 1886 Archbishop Feehan asked the Poor Handmaids to establish and conduct a Catholic hospital in the city.

Later that year the Sisters, led by Sister May Palycarpa, purchased a square block in the Wicker Park District bounded by Claremont, LeMoyne, Oakley and Hirsch for $20,000. The cornerstone of St. Elizabeth's Hospital was laid on October 17, 1886. The following day St. Aloysius Church held a "Fair" for the benefit of the new hospital at which more than $1,600 was collected. St. Elizabeth's Hospital opened its doors in the fall of 1887 in a beautiful, four-story brick building that, in the end, cost nearly $65,000 to construct.

The hospital originally had 100 beds. During its first year it treated 370 patients, with an average stay of forty days each. St. Elizabeth's became progressively more overcrowded, however, and in 1892 a new wing was added. By 1897 the hospital was serving five times the original number of patients. In 1898 St. Elizabeth's established a branch in suburban Austin to care for patients suffering from tuberculosis. The Austin branch was renamed St. Anne's Hospital in 1903. The Sisters at St. Elizabeth's served a Catholic population primarily, although they prohibited any discrimination on the basis of nationality, creed, sex or ability to pay. A part of their original mission was to educate the public on the advantages of hospital care as opposed to traditional home care that was common at the time.

1889 — JOSEPHINUM ACADEMY BREAKS GROUND

Shortly after their arrival in Chicago in 1884, Sister Eduarda and the other Sisters of Christian Charity at St. Aloysius School became interested in opening a high school for Catholic girls in the neighborhood. Father Theile was very supportive of the idea because neighborhood girls had to travel out of the area to go to high school at that time. On a bitter cold day in December 1884, Sister Eduarda and Sister Regina set out to pay a visit to Archbishop Patrick A. Feehan, to present him with their plan and seek his approval.

The Archbishop's residence was located on North opposite Lincoln Park, a long distance from the Sisters' convent in Wicker Park. At the time, the North Ave. horse-car line terminated at Milwaukee, and the two Sisters trudged through heavy snow to make this connection. After a long and cold ride they arrived at the Archbishop's residence only to be told that he was not at home. His sister, however, greeted them cordially, expressing sympathy for their arduous trip and great interest in their plans for the school. In spite of the fact that Sister Regina suffered a frozen finger from the biting cold on the way home, she and Sister Eduarda resolved to make another visit to the Archbishop the following week. This time they were not disappointed, as the Archbishop received them graciously and gave them his blessing.

Father Theile immediately began searching for property in the neighborhood on which to build the school. By the mid 1880s this part of the city had become highly desirable for development, and property values were rising dramatically. In January 1887 Sister Eduarda wrote, "A lot that cost $500 last spring has now been increased to $800 and should be worth $900 to $1,000 by summer. Corner lots are $1,000."

In addition to the Archdiocese's approval, Sisters Eduarda and Regina needed the support of the provincial superior of the Sisters of Christian Charity Congregation, Mother Philomena (headquartered in Wilkes Barre, Pennsylvania) before they could proceed. Mother Philomena, herself an immigrant from Germany, came to Chicago in 1886 to discuss the proposed girls' academy with Father Theile and the Sisters. They were all very persuasive.

Convinced of the soundness of the venture, Mother Philomena and Sister Eduarda walked over to inspect a plot of land that Father Thiele had asked the realtors to put in reserve. Digging a hole with the tip of her umbrella, Mother Philomena placed a little statue of St. Joseph in it and asked that the undertaking be entrusted to his paternal care. Father Thiele was overjoyed when he heard what had happened and exclaimed, "Now St. Joseph has become proprietor. He will provide further, for now he cannot let the building site go to anyone else." Approval from Germany came later that month and ten lots were purchased. A jubilant Father Thiele credited St. Joseph with the success and declared that the school would be called St. Joseph's Academy. The name was later changed to Josephinum Academy. Eventually the total amount of land purchased for Josephinum equaled five acres, more than the amount of land occupied by Wicker Park itself.

Josephinum Academy's groundbreaking was held on the Feast of St. Joseph Day, March 19, 1889. Work progressed rapidly through the spring and summer months and by late fall the building was standing.

In the spring of 1890 work began on the interior and in August the building was ready for occupancy.

During the summer of 1890, the Sisters moved into Josephinum. Sister Eduarda was appointed the superior with a staff of nineteen other sisters who helped run the school and teach the classes. In the fall, the Academy was officially dedicated with the usual pomp and ceremony.

The stated goal of Josephinum was "To give a solid, comprehensive and practical Christian education," and thereby "prepare young girls by cultural and practical training to take their place in the world as good Christian women in the home and society." With its emphasis on moral training and etiquette, the new school was considered a finishing school as well an academic academy. The discipline of the school was said to be "wisely maternal, combined with mild-

Plate 3.7
JOSEPHINUM ACADEMY, A BOARDING HIGH SCHOOL FOR CATHOLIC GIRLS RUN BY THE SISTERS OF CHRISTIAN CHARITY, WAS BEGUN ON THE FEAST OF ST. JOSEPH'S DAY IN 1889. COMPLETED IN 1890, THE SCHOOL STOOD ON FIVE ACRES OF BEAUTIFULLY LANDSCAPED GROUNDS AND GARDENS. THIS EARLY PHOTO OF JOSEPHINUM IS TAKEN FROM ACROSS OAKLEY LOOKING SOUTHEAST.

ness and energy..." Josephinum Academy offered both a high school and elementary school curriculum and its courses were taught in both English and German.

Josephinum's domestic science curriculum established the academy as a pioneer in this area. Classes in homemaking, food preparation, ironing, needlework, sewing, as well as German composition, Bible study and piano were offered. During the first year Josephinum had an equal number of boarding and day-school students, with the boarding students coming from as far as St. Louis, Detroit, Minnesota and Iowa, although most of them originated from Chicago. The steep tuition of $200 per year meant that Josephinum girls were from upper-middle or upper class families. Most were from German heritage.

In 1897 a kindergarten for day students from the neighborhood was added. By 1900 Josephinum had introduced a two-year commercial course to train women for white-collar office work and was beginning to phase out the domestic training. Many of the academic students at Josephinum set their sights on being teachers during this time.

In 1907 an addition was attached to Josephinum Academy that extended the building seventy feet on the north side and provided new dormitories and classrooms, a laboratory and museum, a large dining room, a spacious gymnasium and a new chapel with a seating capacity of 300. The chapel, built in Romanesque style, contained stained glass windows made by the firm of Mayer and Company in Munich, Germany. The dedication of the chapel was held on November 21, when the windows

arrived from Europe and newly installed electric lights were turned on for the first time. Mother Eduarda wrote: "What an impressive sight when the sanctuary was suddenly illuminated by electric lights..."

By 1913 Josephinum no longer considered itself a finishing school; its bulletin described the school's aim to be student preparation "for the liberal arts and scientific course in college," giving "special attention to the preparation of students for the Chicago Normal College. The two-year commercial course that had begun at Josephinum in 1900 continued to be very popular during this period.

In the 1920s a nation-wide movement to bring Catholic secondary schools within the reach of the common citizen ushered in a new era for Catholic education in Chicago and transformed Josephinum Academy. Archbishop Mundelein planned a system of district schools in his archdiocese that would make Catholic institutions available to girls of average means. In 1923 Josephinum was designated by Mundelein as a district school. *The New World*, (the organ of the Chicago Catholic Church) June 15, 1923 stated:

"The Josephinum Academy, Oakley Avenue and North Avenue, in September will be known as the Josephinum High School, throwing open its doors for high school pupils exclusively....the school will be for girls, under the direction of the Sisters of Christian Charity."

Accordingly, tuition was reduced and the boarders at Josephinum were eventually eliminated. By 1928 Josephinum was acknowledged as the district high school for Catholic girls living on the northwest side of Chicago.

1892 — NORTHWEST DIVISION HIGH SCHOOL / TULEY HIGH BUILT

In the late 1880s there were only three public high schools in Chicago: the West Division High School at Monroe and Morgan, the South Division High School at 26th and Wabash, and the North Division High School at Wells and Wendell. All offered a four-year course of study. In 1892 the Wicker Park District received its first public high school when the Northwest Division High School was built at the corner of Claremont Ave. and Potomac Ave. (Bryson St.). Northwest Division High School had begun in 1889 when the North Division and West Division High Schools were crowded to over-

flowing, and pupils were accommodated in a part of the Columbus School on Augusta St. between Hoyne and Leavitt.

The new two-story high school building on Claremont was thoroughly up-to-date with sixteen classrooms, four recitation rooms, a large lecture room, a third floor assembly hall, a chemistry room and the first indoor gymnasium and life drawing room in a public school. The building was formally opened with graduation exercises for students transferred from Columbus in June 1892. During the World's Columbian Exposition held in Chicago in 1893, the

Northwest Division High School was heralded as Chicago's model high school and it became a center of attention for education-oriented visitors to the city.

Elsewhere in the neighborhood the Drummond School, a primary school, was built at Cortland (Courtland) and Honore (Girard) in 1893. The school was named after Thomas Drummond, a Judge in the U.S. District Court of Illinois.

An addition to Northwest Division was erected in 1898. Then in 1901, Norwegian-born Knute Rockne, with an interest in attending college, entered the school at the age of thirteen. While many students were involved in sports others had an after-school job, Knute did both. His grades suffered and his father was so angered that he told Knute that higher education was now "out of the question." Leaving school at sixteen, it would take Knute another six years before he would enter Notre Dame where he would gain fame as a football player and even more

fame as Notre Dame's football coach, from 1918 until his death in 1931.

In 1906 the name of the school was changed to Tuley High School, after Murray F. Tuley, a Chicago attorney, politician and judge. In 1913 the city purchased land lying adjacent to the school for another addition that was begun in 1917 and completed in 1919. With this new building, Tuley again became one of the most modern high schools in Chicago with up-to-date classrooms, laboratories, a gymnasium, swimming pool, shop rooms and a large assembly hall that seated 1,500 people. Two well-known students at the time were Saul Bellow (class of 1915) and Sidney J. Harris (class of 1917). Both wrote for the school's literary magazine. Bellow went on to become an internationally renowned novelist and winner of the Nobel Prize for literature, while Harris became a nationally syndicated columnist and commentator.

Plate 3.8

NORTHWEST DIVISION HIGH SCHOOL, LATER NAMED TULEY HIGH, ON THE CORNER OF DAVIS (CLAREMONT) AND BRYSON (POTOMAC) STREETS WAS BUILT IN 1892. THIS VIEW LOOKING SOUTH ON DAVIS AFTER THE TURN-OF-THE-CENTURY SHOWS TYPICAL NEIGHBORHOOD HOUSING AND THE TOWER OF ST. ELIZABETH'S HOSPITAL IN THE DISTANCE.

1894 — St. Mary of Nazareth Hospital Established

Plate 3.9

A POSTCARD VIEW OF ST. STANISLAUS KOSTKA CATHOLIC CHURCH, THE MOTHER CHURCH OF CHICAGO'S POLISH ROMAN CATHOLIC CONGREGATIONS. THE PARISH WAS ESTABLISHED IN 1869 AND THE CHURCH BUILDING PICTURED HERE, MODELED AFTER A BASILICA IN KRAKOW, POLAND, WAS ERECTED IN 1881.

Large numbers of Poles began moving up Milwaukee Avenue and settling in the Wicker Park District in the 1890s. Poles had originally settled on Chicago northwest side in the vicinity of Potomac and Nobel where they established St. Stanislaus Kostka Church in 1867. This parish grew at a remarkable rate during the late 1800s and eventually became the mother church of all Polish Roman Catholic congregations in Chicago. The Fathers of the Congregation of Resurrection took over the parish in 1869 and, led by the dynamic Father Vincent Barzynski, were effective in spreading the Polish community throughout the northwest side of the city.

By the turn of the century, St. Stanislaus was one of the largest Catholic parishes in the world, with a membership of 5,000 families. The area around Milwaukee Ave., Ashland, and Division St. contained the largest Polish community in the United States, and the intersection was known as the "Polish Downtown." In addition, the community acquired a national reputation as the center of American Polonia because nearly every major Polish organization in the United States had its headquarters here. *Chicago City of Neighborhoods (1986)* offers this description:

> "The Polish Roman Catholic Union and its rival the larger Polish National Alliance, both had their national offices here. The Polish Women's Alliance occupied a building on Ashland just north of Milwaukee. The Polish Welfare League occupied a building in the 1300 block of Ashland. These provided a strong institutional base for Polonia in the West Town community area. Polish-owned businesses occupied storefronts along Milwaukee and Ashland Avenues as well as east and west on Division Street...Most area banks, businesses and manufacturing were Polish owned."

By 1885 Chicago had sixteen hospitals for a half-million people. Religious organizations administered 11 of them, but only four of them were Catholic. And, the Polish community did not administer any of them. This was seen to be a great hardship for Poles; and St. Stanislaus parish sent out a call to establish a hospital in which Polish people might receive medical care in familiar surroundings, both culturally and religiously. The Sisters of the Congregation of the Holy Family of Nazareth responded.

The first St. Mary's Hospital was established in 1894 in an abandoned three-story brick building at Division and Paulina. Mother Mary Lauretta Lubowidzka, the provincial superior for the United States, headed the venture. The original hospital contained twenty-four beds. In the basement were the dispensary, the laundry and the kitchen. On the first floor were the chapel and offices, while private rooms, wards, and an operating room were located on the upper floors. Mother Mary Lauretta and a group of indomitable sisters expanded their hospital during the coming decade, despite a severe financial depression. To keep the facility operating

Plate 3.10

A NEW ST. MARY'S HOSPITAL, PICTURED HERE, WAS BUILT ON A CITY BLOCK BOUNDED BY HADDON, THOMAS, OAKLEY AND LEAVITT IN 1902. THIS BUILDING REPLACED AN EARLIER ST. MARY'S HOSPITAL FACILITY THAT HAD BEEN ESTABLISHED BY THE SISTERS OF THE CONGREGATION OF THE HOLY FAMILY OF NAZARETH IN AN ABANDONED BUILDING IN 1894.

the Sisters turned to the community for help, sometimes driving through the neighborhood in a horse-drawn buggy asking for donations. In 1899 a two-story frame house, adjacent to the original building, was acquired for a women's hospital. In 1900 the Sisters began Saint Mary's School of Nursing, a nurses training school that three years later graduated its first class of seven students.

Demands for health care in the community were ever increasing, however. As a result, a new and much larger hospital structure was planned. An entire city block, bounded by Haddon, LeMoyne, Oakley, and Leavitt, was purchased in 1901, and construction of the new hospital began. On March 12, 1902, the second St. Mary of Nazareth Hospital was dedicated; and the next day patients from the old building were transferred to the new facility. The new St. Mary's was a thor-

oughly modern facility. Constructed of fireproof materials, it stood six stories high and incorporated many advanced features including laboratories, an outpatient emergency room, x-ray room, obstetrical and surgical suites, and a morgue. By 1910 the staff included an anesthetist, ophthalmologist, neurologist, orthopedist, dermatologist, pathologist, and pediatrician.

In 1919 St. Mary's celebrated its twenty-fifth anniversary and the *Chicago Daily News* praised it as evidence of the "turning point of the social life of the American Poles."

"Launched with a small, inexperienced, but determined band of Sisters, a few dedicated physicians, modest physical facilities, and irregular and discouraging financial prospects, St. Mary's did not merely survive, it grew and prospered. Emerging from obscurity, it became a respected center for the practice and teaching of medicine in Chicago."

1897 — Deaconess Home and Hospital Opened

In 1885, twenty-two women from the community founded the Norwegian Lutheran Tabitha Society (Den norsk lutherske Tabitha Forening). The Tabitha Society in Chicago was organized to provide health care to seamen and immigrants and to form a Lutheran deaconess home and hospital. In 1897 the Lutheran Deaconess Home and Hospital opened in two small rented buildings on the corner of Artesian Ave. and LeMoyne with 25 beds. Its mission was to serve the people of the neighborhood, particularly women and children. In 1905 the motherhouse and the hospital of the diaconate moved to the corner of Haddon and Leavitt, just south of the Wicker Park District.

Sister Ingeborg Sponland arrived from Minneapolis in 1906 to become head of the Norwegian Lutheran Home and Hospital, as it was then called. In her autobiography Sponland recalls her impression upon arrival of "the lone little building...in the midst of the swampland." Sponland remained administrator of the hospital for 30 years, during which time she fought to expand its facilities and programs. In 1911 a kindergarten was opened and soon after a day nursery, classes for mothers, and a Sunday school for children. In 1924 a wing was added with areas for surgery, pathology and obstetrics; and in 1926 a school of nursing was established.

1899 — St. Mary of the Angels Church Founded

Due to the enormous growth of the Polish population in this part of the city, several new parishes were established in the late 1800s. A new church founded in 1899 by Father Vincent Barzynski of St. Stanislaus Kostka, was St. Mary of the Angels Church, at Cortland and Hermitage Ave. This part of the Wicker Park District was previously served by the Church of the Annunciation, originally an Irish parish. The large numbers of Poles flooding the neighborhood, however, merited a new Polish-language institution. Accordingly, two city blocks, totaling ninety-six lots, were purchased at a cost of $60,000. One block was sub-divided and sold for residences while forty-eight lots bounded by Cortland, Bloomingdale, Wood and Hermitage became the site of St. Mary of the Angels parish.

The cornerstone of the first building, a three-story brick structure designed in the Renaissance style by Henry J. Schlacks, was laid on July 2, 1899. This building would later house St. Mary of the Angels School, although it was originally built to accommodate the church, convent quarters, living quarters for the priests, four large meeting halls, twelve classrooms, an auditorium, and a gymnasium. Nearly 20,000 Chicagoans attended dedication ceremonies on December 10, 1899, which were led by Archbishop Patrick A. Feehan and witnessed by Mayor Carter

Plate 3.11
St. Mary of the Angels Church built in 1899 became the school.

Harrison II. In 1900 St. Mary of the Angels School was opened by the sisters of the Congregation of the Resurrection with an enrollment of 425 students.

By 1912, St. Mary of the Angels parish had grown so rapidly that it had become one of the largest parishes in the Archdiocese, with a membership of approximately 1,200 families. Nearby Annunciation parish, once a dominant institution in the area, continued to decline as Irish families moved away from the neighborhood, to be replaced by huge numbers of Polish Catholics. In 1911 work on a new St. Mary's Church was begun under the direction of Father Francis Gordon, C.R., although the cornerstone of the building was not laid until 1914. The building of the new church took more than eight years, due to numerous strikes, World War I, and a shortage of building materials. The church, also designed by Schlacks, was dedicated on May 30, 1920, by

Archbishop George W. Mundelein.

With a remarkable resemblance to St. Peter's Basilica in Rome, St. Mary of the Angels Church has been acclaimed as one of the finest specimens of Roman Renaissance architecture in the United States. The new church, built at a cost of $400,000, is 230 feet long and 125 feet wide at the transepts. With twin bell towers and a magnificent dome, its sanctuary can seat more than 2,000 people. During the 1920s, St. Mary of the Angels parish supported a school under the direction of the Sisters of the Resurrection (in which 1,099 students were enrolled), two building and loan associations, twenty-eight confraternities, sodalities, fraternal societies and clubs, and a Home for Working Girls. Father Gordon continued to serve the people of St. Mary of the Angels parish until his death in 1931. Later Gordon Tech Vocational Training School was named in his honor.

Plate 3.12
ALSO DESIGNED BY HENRY J. SCHLACKS, THE SECOND ST. MARY OF THE ANGELS CHURCH WAS BEGUN IN 1911. THE DEDICATION DID NOT OCCUR UNTIL 1920, THOUGH THE CORNERSTONE WAS LAID IN 1914.

1899 — ASSOCIATION HOUSE ESTABLISHED

Plate 3.13
JANE ADDAMS, HEAD
RESIDENT OF HULL-
HOUSE, ADDRESSES A
CROWD OF NEIGHBOR-
HOOD RESIDENTS AT
CEREMONIES CELEBRAT-
ING THE LAYING OF THE
CORNERSTONE FOR
ASSOCIATION HOUSE'S
NEW BUILDING IN 1905.

The Association House, a settlement house, was established as the Young Women's Christian Association Settlement in June 1899. It was incorporated as Association House of Chicago on March 29, 1901. Initially, it was "to carry on a gospel settlement work adapted to women and children" and as a training school for Y.W.C.A. secretaries (later called social workers). Settlement house work had begun in Chicago with the establishment of Hull-House in 1889 by Jane Addams and Ellen Gates Starr on the city's Near West Side. The settlement house movement originated in England in the mid 1880s with Toynbee Hall, which was founded in London's East End by Canon and Henrietta Barnett and a group of Oxford University students. The Barnetts took up residence among the industrial poor to develop educational opportunities and work with neighborhood people to improve working and living conditions in the area. During the 1890s the settlement movement spread quickly in industrial cities throughout the United States. It was welcomed as a means of dealing with the social problems that arose as a result of rapid urbanization and industrialization.

The North Side Y.W.C.A., under the auspices of the American Committee of Y.W.C. Associations,

was originally established in Chicago to carry on work among young women. Like all social settlements Association House was neighborhood-based and was run by a live-in staff called "residents." *The History of Association House*, by Janice Johnson, states:
"In 1899, it was estimated that 1,500 young women lived in the neighborhood of Milwaukee, Damen (then known as Robey Street), and North Avenues, and were employed in the many factories, tailor shops, stores, and laundries in the area. Most of these gave employment to from 15 to 500 young women."

From 1899 to 1906 Association House rented quarters in a brick, three-story building at 2013 W. North (formerly 474 W.), the first floor of which had formerly been a saloon. (See *Plate 4.12*) Here, under the directorship of head resident Carrie B. Wilson, they established several social clubs, classes in sewing, cooking, millinery and a kitchen garden club for children. Gradually the program was expanded to include men and boys and a manual training program was begun along with reading circles, storytelling, musical activities and Bible classes.

By 1902 activities had expanded so much that more space was needed and the Board of Association House purchased the "Gray House," a wood-frame residence on a large lot with 200 feet of frontage located across the street on North and about a block and a half west. An additional seventy-five feet of frontage was also purchased. The Gray House (See *Plates 2.38 and 4.11.*) had been built during the civil war era and owned for many years by William T. Johnson, a state senator and treasurer of Cook County. It provided space for clubrooms, resident rooms for the staff, and eventually a day nursery. To accommodate the growing program, a new building was planned to be built just west of the Gray House.

The cornerstone for the new Association House building was laid on September 9, 1905, at groundbreaking ceremonies that featured prominent

Plate 3.14
CONSTRUCTION OF THE NEW ASSOCIATION HOUSE BUILD-
ING IN 1905. IN THE BACKGROUND IS A NORTH AVE.
STREETCAR AND A BUILDING ON THE SOUTHWEST CORNER
OF NORTH AVE. AND LEAVITT.

Chicago settlement house personalities. Jane Addams, founder and head resident of Hull-House, gave the keynote address and Graham Taylor, head resident of Chicago Commons, was also on the program. The new building cost $40,000 to construct. When complete it was a striking red brick structure, 70 feet wide and 110 feet deep, with two floors in the largest section and three floors in another section. The new structure had almost forty rooms that provided a gymnasium, shower baths, manual training rooms, domestic science room, many clubrooms, and eleven bedrooms for residents and guests. (See *Plate 4.11*) When the new building was opened, the settlement

gave up the rented space at 2013 W. North.

In 1900, Association House established a playground for children. By 1905 this facility had a permanent shelter, four shower baths, a sandbox, ten swings, two teeter-totters, two large rope swings, four lawn swings and two giant slides. Daily attendance

Plate 3.15
NEIGHBORHOOD CHILDREN GATHER IN ASSOCIATION
HOUSE PLAYGROUND ON NORTH AVE, GENERALLY CONSID-
ERED TO BE THE BEST PLAYGROUND IN CHICAGO.

was reported to be from 500 to 1,000 and the number of baths given in two months was 4,000! The playground was eventually conducted as a public facility and the Chicago Park District furnished some of its equipment. Located just east of the settlement buildings and open during the summertime from 9:00 a.m. to 10:00 p.m., the playground became an important social center in the neighborhood and a draw for other Association House activities. In time it was known as the best playground in Chicago.

In 1911 the *Handbook of Settlements* stated that Association House maintained a kindergarten, a milk station (that offered sanitary, pasteurized milk to its neighbors) a library and reading room, domestic sciences classes, educational work in mechanical drawing, electricity, cobbling, pyrography, manual training, photography, printing, sign painting, a chorus and orchestra, and extension religious work in nearby shops. In addition, many clubs with social, literary, educational and industrial aims met at the House, along with Bible classes, religious services, and other entertainments and lectures.

1905 — HOLY RESURRECTION SERBIAN ORTHODOX CHURCH FOUNDED

The Serbian colony in Chicago began in the middle of the nineteenth century with immigrants from Boka Kotorska, Hercegovina, and Montenegro. In 1905, Archimandrite Sevastian Dabovich was made head of the Serbian Church Mission in America and a parish priest in Chicago. Because a number of Serbian immigrants had settled in the Wicker Park District by the turn of the century, the mission purchased a modest two-story house at 1905 W. Schiller (formerly 8 Fowler); and a small chapel was created in the dwelling's reception room. On July 4, the first liturgy was served and the church was named the Holy Resurrection. A short time later, Branko Radichevich, the first and longest-lasting Serbian singing society in America, was established by this community. This society had evolved out of an original group of traditional Serbian tamburitsa musicians.

Before World War I, the Serbian community in Chicago was largely men, and Holy Resurrection Church became the center of nationalistic and church life for these people. In 1915, the Serbian Sisters Society was formed by a handful of women in Chicago who sought to serve the Red Cross and assist war orphans. This organization dissolved at the end of the war, but was revived in 1927 as the Circle of Serbian Sisters of the Holy Resurrection Church, a women's group formed to help build a new church building on the original site at Schiller and Evergreen. The new church was completed and dedicated in 1933.

Plate 3.16

HOLY RESURRECTION SERBIAN ORTHODOX CHURCH WAS ESTABLISHED IN THIS TWO-STORY RESIDENTIAL BUILDING ON SCHILLER (FOWLER) FACING THE PARK IN 1905.

1911 — NORTH AVENUE DAY NURSERY FOUNDED

In the winter of 1910 mothers with small children constantly asked Association House of Chicago's staff where they could have their babies cared for while they went to work. As a result, several young women formed a group and began raising funds to support a day nursery in the "Gray House." The nursery was to meet the needs of large numbers of women in the neighborhood who were working in nearby factories and needed a safe place to leave their young children. At first the nursery occupied three rooms, but soon eight rooms were needed. By 1913 the nursery was caring for 50 to 60 babies a day. In that year the nursery was incorporated as North Avenue Day Nursery, a separate organization no longer under the jurisdiction of Association House.

North Avenue Day Nursery regarded assimilation and acculturation to be among the major goals for attending children, along with "protection of unsupervised youngsters" and "the preservation of family life." The Nursery rented space from Association House until 1919, when it moved to 2013 W. Pierce Ave.

1914 — ST. ELIZABETH'S HOSPITAL NURSING SCHOOL CREATED

In 1914 St. Elizabeth's Hospital was undergoing dramatic expansion. It opened a Nursing School to help provide professionally-trained staff. The school was open to women of all faiths as well as to the Poor Handmaids of Jesus Christ. The first sixteen nurses graduated from the three-year course in 1917. Sister Cornelia graduated in 1919 and later became a director of the school. In 1918 she was a nineteen-year-old student at St. Elizabeth's when the great flue epidemic hit. For eight months she tended dying patients in a crowded hospital with beds overflowing into hallways. Shifts were twelve hours long and yet the sisters did not get sick. Their supervisors had instructed them to take a precaution: drink one ounce of whiskey each day before breakfast!

In 1929 ground was broken for a new St. Elizabeth's Hospital building, and in 1930 a modern twelve-story annex was constructed on Claremont between LeMoyne and Hirsch.

1914 — ELEANOR CLUB SIX OPENS ITS DOORS

Plate 3.17
THE ELEANOR CLUB SIX WAS BUILT ON PIERCE AVE. IN 1914 AS A RESIDENTIAL FACILITY FOR YOUNG WORKING WOMEN. IT EVENTUALLY BECAME AN IMPORTANT SOCIAL CENTER IN THE NEIGHBORHOOD.

Another neighborhood institution created for the benefit of young working women was the Eleanor Club Six established on the southeast corner of Pierce and Leavitt in 1914. Ina Law Robertson, who opened the first "Eleanor Hotel" in Chicago, in 1889, originated the Eleanor Club idea. These self-governing residential clubs provided each woman with her own single or shared bedroom and an array of communal spaces including parlors, reading rooms, sewing rooms, laundry facilities, and dining rooms large enough to seat all residents at once. The clubs were open to single working-women, especially the "young girl on the low wage," and aimed to provide a home-like, respectable environment for newcomers to the city.

The Eleanor Club on Pierce was the sixth to be established in Chicago. It was unusual, however, in that it was the first of the Clubs to have a new building erected specifically for this purpose according to Robertson's plans and specifications. Earlier Eleanor Clubs had been established in existing buildings that were adapted to new use. The Eleanor Record of 1915 stated that Club Six was "four stories high, equipped with a roof garden and sleeping porches; it has class rooms, a gymnasium, ample parlors and a Social Center operated by the Eleanor Association for the young women of the neighborhood." Club Six accommodated 150 young women. The Social Center, under the same roof as the Eleanor Club but with an entrance on Leavitt Street, became a true neighborhood center attracting boys and men from the area as well as women.

1915 — ALBERT R. SABIN ELEMENTARY SCHOOL IS BUILT

The beautiful thirty-two-room Albert R. Sabin Elementary School was built at Hirsch and Leavitt in 1915. It was named after an early Chicago Public School principal and administrator. In 1924 Sabin was converted to a Junior High School and its elementary school teachers were transferred to Wicker Park School. Sabin Junior High School was discontinued during the summer of 1933, and became a branch of Tuley High School and Wicker Park Elementary.

Plate 3.18
ALBERT R. SABIN ELEMENTARY SCHOOL, BUILT AT HIRSCH AND LEAVITT IN 1915

1930 — RESIDENTIAL AND INSTITUTIONAL MATURITY REACHED

By 1930 the Wicker Park District had achieved residential maturity; that is, most of the land parcels had been developed in some way. The institutions were well established and were either erecting new buildings to accommodate modern standards and growing populations, or remodeling existing structures with additions and other improvements.

— *Mary Ann Johnson*

SOMETIMES FORGOTTEN... JEWS WERE IMPORTANT PART OF WICKER PARK DEVELOPMENT

There were two different Jewish cultures that were part of the Wicker Park District. Thus, what they ate, how they dressed, the language they spoke, and their job-skills were different. Prior to the 1890s, there was a handful of German Jews who lived in the District and others who had business dealings in but did not live in the District.

In the 1890s, Eastern European (also known as Russian Jews) began moving into the neighborhood and some began opening businesses. Many of them had initially settled in the Maxwell Street area on Chicago's west side.

By World War I (1914-1919), twenty-five percent of the city's Jewish population resided in the West Town areas of Wicker Park, Humboldt Park and Logan Square. By 1930, nearly 30,000 Jews lived in these communities, comprising approximately twenty percent of the population. However, by that time many of the Jews in the Wicker Park District were moving west to Humboldt Park, or to Lawndale on the city's west side or to Albany Park on the North Side.

Dr. Julius Rappaport, who served as the Beth El congregation Rabbi from 1893 to 1896 and again from 1905 to 1917, led the congregation's efforts to purchase three lots on Crystal St. and Hoyne Ave. in 1901. The lots were for their new synagogue. Adjoining the temple was Molner Hall. Named for one of Beth El's most devoted members, it housed the Sunday school and gymnasium and functioned as a social center offering literary, musical, dramatic performances, dancing and other entertainments to young members of the congregation.

The congregation of Tiffereth Zion (Beauty of Zion) built a synagogue on north Wolcott (Lincoln St.) that was dedicated on August 25, 1904. This congregation became the most influential orthodox synagogue on the Northwest Side and its members initiated the Marks Nathan Orphan Home, the Marion

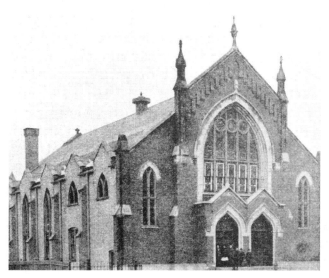

Plate 3.19
THE BETH EL CONGREGATION PURCHASED THE LAND AT CRYSTAL AND HOYNE IN 1901.

Plate 3.20
DEDICATED IN 1904, THE TIFFERETH ZION CONGREGATION BUILT THIS SYNAGOGUE ON NORTH WOLCOTT. UNTIL RECENTLY THIS BUILDING CONTAINED MARBLE TABLETS INSCRIBED WITH THE NAMES OF CONGREGATION MEMBERS.

Place Talmud Torah and the Jewish Educational Alliance, among other institutions. Members of this congregation included the Pritzker and the Crown families.

In addition to Tiffereth Zion and Beth El several other synagogues were established in the Wicker Park District. Beth Ahren, whose rabbi was Hyme Goldbogen, the father of Aron Goldbogen (Michael Todd), was located on LeMoyne west of Damen. Moses Montefiore was on Damen while Ahavas Israel was at Western and Potomac. Atereth Israel was on Bell near Division and both Beth Aaron and B'nai David were on Wood, just north of Division. Dorshe Tov occupied the same building as Beth El on Crystal. A Chasidic synagogue, Nachlas David was in a two-flat on Hoyne and Potomac from 1921 to 1926. Ohave Zedek was at 1228 North Claremont and Tomshei Shabbos was on North Leavitt for over 50 years. Bes Ha-Knesses and Ezra Israel shared a rented cottage at 1234 N. Bell (Shober).

Several Jewish organizations were established in the Wicker Park District for the education and welfare of the community. Chafetz Chayim, a Hebrew School, was located on Crystal. The Daughters of Zion Jewish Day Nursery and Infant Home was established in 1917 by a small group of women in the community. (See Page 139) The organization quickly grew into one of the largest Jewish women's organizations in the city and in 1918, the group acquired a building at 1441 Wicker Park Ave. for its day nursery and infant home. In addition, The Deborah Boys Club on Division Street provided social and educational activities for young people.

Notable Jewish personalities with roots in the Wicker Park District during this period include: movie impresario Michael Todd, author Saul Bellow and columnist Sydney J. Harris. Bellow and Harris both attended Sabin School and Tuley High School. The Arie Crown (See Page 117.) and the Nicholas J. Pritzker (See Page 129.) dynasties began in the neighborhood during the 1890s.

— Cheryl Smalling

Plate 3.21
THE DAUGHTER OF ZION JEWISH DAY NURSERY WAS ESTABLISHED IN 1917.

MARKS NATHAN ORPHAN HOME ESTABLISHED BY WILL

The Marks Nathan Jewish Orphan Home was established as the consequence of the will of Marks Nathan, a wealthy businessman, philanthropist and Orthodox Jew from Russia. Filed in Cook County in 1904, the will left $15,000 for the erection of an orthodox hospital or an orphan home. It read in part:

> "...to found and establish, either a Jewish Hospital with a Kosher kitchen, or a Jewish Orphan Asylum which shall also be conducted with a

'Kosher' or strictly orthodox Jewish kitchen in the City of Chicago, provided that the further sum of $15,000 shall be raised or subscribed from other sources..."

A committee of men from the Wicker Park District, most of them associated with Tiffereth Zion synagogue, stepped forward and offered the building of a Talmud Torah religious school for the new orphanage. They had started on Wood St.,

Plate 3.22

THE MARKS NATHAN ORPHAN HOME WAS OPENED IN THIS BUILDING AT THE CORNER OF WOOD AND BLUCHER STREETS IN 1906. THE BUILDING WAS SUBSEQUENTLY USED BY THE JEWISH EDUCATIONAL ALLIANCE, THE NORTHWEST BRANCH OF THE JEWISH PEOPLE'S INSTITUTE AND THE POLISH ARMY WAR VETERANS ASSOCIATION.

but were unable to complete due to lack of funds, for use as a home. Their offer was accepted, and with a new building in hand, they were able to raise $7,000 in one month, largely from members of the Tiffereth Zion congregation.

The Marks Nathan Jewish Orphan Home was opened in the completed and remodeled building on the corner of Wood and Potomac (Blucher) on May 13, 1906, with twenty-nine children. Dedication exercises were held in a tent in the yard with 1,200 in attendance. During the first year there were sixty-three additional admissions. The home was dedicated to Orthodox Judaism and was operated at all times in accordance with Orthodox rites. Religious training, daily prayers, attendance

at worship services and consumption of meals from a kosher kitchen were required of every child in an attempt to preserve Jewish identity.

After three years of dramatically increasing enrollment, a new building was needed and land was purchased on Albany Ave. in the Douglas Park area as the site of a new home for the institution. After Marks Nathan moved to the west side, the building on Wood St. became the headquarters of the Jewish Educational Alliance and later the Northwest Branch of the Jewish People's Institute which at that point was also located in the Douglas Park area.

— *Mary Ann Johnson*

COMMUNITY FABRIC AND GROWTH REFLECTED IN ORGANIZATIONS AND SOCIETIES

Many social societies existed at the turn of the century, and they met in Wicker Park lodge halls, back rooms of taverns, and other public spaces. Broadly, the aims or ambitions of all secret societies and fraternal organizations fall into one or more of the following categories: social, benevolent, ethnic, trade, mystical or religious, political, or criminal.

In the U.S., during the nineteenth century "pre-welfare" society, many recent immigrants felt a need to form or belong to these societies. This gave them the opportunity to associate with people of common interests who could be supportive of each other, especially in times of accident, unemployment, and illness. Many later joined with insurance companies to develop the first group insurance plans.

Social activities were also very important. Picnics were common activities on Sundays, the only day off for most. Music groups, debating teams, library services and athletic activities were also common. A popular fundraiser was the masked ball. Key to many of these organizations was preserving and using the immigrants' native language.

Swedish immigrants formed organizations of mutual assistance similar to those that had helped them survive difficult times in Sweden. In 1881 the Independent Order of Svithiod was founded as a fraternal benevolent society. In 1900, John A. Sandgren explained the needs met by Svithiod as follows:

"In talking with some of Svithiod's older members, they spoke of 'Svithiod Principles', but there is no record of what these actually were. It was the feeling of warm love towards the Swedish language, Swedish conduct, and Swedish fraternal feelings that gave the initiative to Swedish fraternal organization in America. One longed for more stable association with men of the same heritage with whom one could work and when necessary be of help to…Church associations had won quite big connections but there were many who had wider interests and wished connections outside the tight circle of the church. Many Swedes had joined American organizations but there were others who preferred to further Scandinavian fraternal organizational work."

Norwegians in Wicker Park established numerous clubs, societies and organizations in the years prior to World War I. It is said that "a veritable organizational mania" existed within the community. Societies were often based on regional loyalties as representatives from towns in Norway bound together in neighborhood groups. These organizations gave colorful masquerade balls, soirees, theater evenings and other entertainments. Another Norwegian tradition of choral singing groups for both men and women led to the formation of the Normennenes and Bjorgvin singing societies, which conducted splendid concerts in their own halls, or in larger auditoriums like the Wicker Park Hall at 2040 W. North.

Like the Scandinavians, Germans had many types of clubs, societies, and organizations. A large number of Wicker Park District Germans, in the late 1880s,

Plate 3.23
LOCATED AT 2017 W. EVERGREEN (FORMERLY 140) THIS WAS THE HOME OF THE NORTH WEST CLUB, ONE OF THE MANY ORGANIZATIONS IN THE WICKER PARK DISTRICT IN THE LATE 1800S AND EARLY 1900S.

were "club Germans," those whose primary allegiance was to secular organizations rather than religious ones. Many of these people participated in labor union activities or identified themselves as socialists or anarchists. This group gained strength from their own associations and ethnic institutions. In 1876, *Advocate,* a German newspaper, stated:

> "The Germans have their lyceums, their reading rooms, their lecture and music halls and their gymnasiums where they can meet in social concourse, discuss the political situation, enjoy an intellectual treat and improve their physical condition without money and without practice."

One of the German societies was the American Turnerbund. It promoted rationalistic thought and physical education among the other social purposes. August Spies, one of the men accused and executed following the Haymarket Riot, was a Turner and served on the education committee which taught tumbling and thinking skills to boys and girls, men and women. A picture of a Turner class in the mid 1880's shows a large group of people in close fitting clothes working on double bars and rings.

The Turners helped with the expenses and care of Spies' family after his incarceration and paid the funeral expenses after his execution. "The Aurora Trunverein," to which Spies belonged, met at their hall at Milwaukee and Huron when he was a member, and moved in 1896 to the southwest corner of Division and Ashland.

On Milwaukee, The Odd Fellows and Masonic Hall, like the Aurora Turner Hall, had an imposing appearance, expressing the high status of the members

Plate 3.24
THE NORTH-WEST HALL WAS ONE OF MANY HALLS AVAILABLE FOR THE USE OF ORGANIZATIONS. THIS WAS LOCATED ON THE CORNER OF NORTH AND WESTERN.

that built it. Thalia Hall, on Milwaukee also, was a saloon with a large back room. It was the meeting place of lodges like the Hariegari and Sons of Hermann, whose members were workers and small businessmen. A section of the Socialist Labor Party on the northwest side, and, after 1900, groups of the International Working People's Association chose Thalia Hall for their meetings.

Probably a minimum estimate of the different societies Wicker Parkers could participate in during the 1890's would be over a hundred. They varied from the Wagon Maker's Union and the Shoemakers' Union to the Swiss Men's Singing Society, one of the many musical groups that participated at the Haymarket funerals.

In 1890, at least three orders met on the third floor of Lodge Hall on Damen at North, 1568 N. Milwaukee, (formerly 1228 N.). The Richard Yates Chapter, Number 967, of the Royal Arcancon, met on the second and fourth Saturdays. It was founded in Massachusetts in 1877. Members had to believe in a Supreme Being. A restriction that was later removed was that 'Mongolians, whether of pure or of mixed blood, no matter what they believe, are ineligible". This group now is mainly a fraternal benefit life insurance company. A second group was the Wicker Park Subordinate Order of the International Order of Foresters. This group was one of the many schisms of the Royal Order of Foresters, founded in 1813, in England. At that time members were initiated by combat with cudgels, among other things.

Meeting on the first and third Tuesdays was The Jefferson Sub Grove, Number 68, of the United Ancient Order of Druids. Druids date back to 200 B.C., and there were many splits and schisms. The UAOD is headquartered in Britain. Its American branch was a fraternal benefit society. It based its teachings on principles that it attributed to Merlin the Magician:

- Labor diligently to acquire knowledge for it is power.

- When in authority, decide reasonable, for thine authority may cease.

- Bear with fortitude the ills of life, remembering that no mortal sorrow is perpetual.

- Love virtue – for it bringeth peace.

- Abhor vice – for it bringeth evil upon all.

- Cultivate the social.

— *Char Sandstrom*

Meet Some Neighbors

Throughout the decades from the 1850s to 1930, Wicker Park was home to many people in almost every walk of life and economic level. Their cultures, religions and political interests were as varied as their talents, abilities, and visions. Many enriched the lives of family members and the community. Others made contributions that had impact not just in the Wicker Park District but also throughout the city, county, state, and sometimes the world.

In the following pages you will meet some well-known and some not-well-known people who were part of the Wicker Park District.

NATHAN ALLEN AND FAMILY

Vermonter Nathan Allen, born in 1803 to immigrant parents, was an early settler in Chicago and then in Wicker Park. A letter in support of a license for a theater in Chicago in October 1838 was signed by, among others, Nathan Allen.

Based on Census Data, city directories, and abstract of title documents, it appears that Nathan, an attorney, was married to someone prior to Elizabeth H. S., to whom he was married by 1848. Nathan had a son named Omar H. in his first union.

Plate 3.25

THIS MAP, RECORDED NOVEMBER 6, 1866, SHOWS "SUBDIVISION BY ASSESSOR OF WEST DIVISION OF CITY OF CHICAGO" OF THE UNDIVIDED LANDS IN S ½ SW ¼ SECTION 31 T. 40 R. 14 E. IT WAS APPROVED BY THE BOARD OF PUBLIC WORKS ON OCTOBER 30, 1866.

IT SHOWS THE NATHAN ALLEN AND KATE JOHNSON AREAS WITH WABANSIA ON THE NORTH, NORTH AVE. ON THE SOUTH, JUST SHORT OF WESTERN ON THE WEST, AND DAMEN (ROBEY) ON THE EAST.

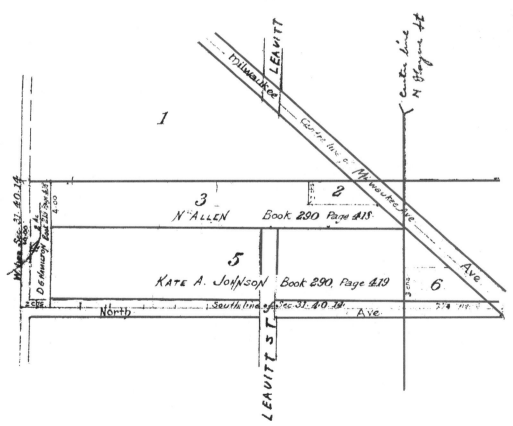

Elizabeth too was apparently previously married and had a son named Owen. Considering that she apparently had land ownership in DuPage County, it is possible that she lived outside the city limits prior to her marriage to Nathan. Elizabeth had an adopted daughter, Kate E. It is not clear whether Kate was adopted before or after Elizabeth and Nathan were married. It does appear that Kate lived with Elizabeth and Nathan by 1848.

In September 1848, William Lytle purchased the south half of the south west quarter of township 40, section 31 in range 14 E. The boundaries are Damen on the east, Western on the west, North on the south and Bloomingdale on the north. Within a few days, Lytle had an agreement with Elizabeth for her to purchase the south half of Lytle's purchase.

With his office listed on West Randolph, Nathan's residence was listed as "Milwaukee near limits" beginning in 1853. The Allen home was on the southeast corner of North and Milwaukee, "surrounded by scrubs."

One of the delegates to the Democratic Convention in Dixon, IL on September 15, 1852, Nathan Allen was elected a Police Justice, one of the first in West Town, in 1855, based on a new Police Magistrate Act in 1854. On January 20, 1858, Nathan's son Omar married Charlotte Carpenter. Then "on or about" September 10, 1859, Elizabeth died. Three years later at eighteen, Kate married William T. Johnson (See Page 120.)

Nathan was listed as a "JP" at 30 W. Randolph in 1866. At that time his residence was at 744 W. Lake. By 1869 he was once again living at Milwaukee and North, in the heart of the Wicker Park District. The 1870 Census reveals that his Maine born wife Martha M. was forty-four. On May 19, 1870, Allen and two others were appointed by the Circuit Court to assess the value of land purchased for park purposes. By 1874 his residence was listed as "931 N. Milwaukee."

Unfortunately, little else is known about Nathan's family, but it is known that he died on November 7, 1875.

NILS ARNESON

Nils Arneson learned his trade of wagon making in his native Norway. At the age of twenty-one, in 1861, he set sail for America. After working a few months in Chicago, he enlisted in Co. A., Fifteenth Regiment, Wisconsin Volunteers, serving for three years during the Civil War.

Returning to Chicago after the War, he worked in his trade for three years. In 1868 he started Arneson & Co., a furniture manufacturing company on Canal Street. It burned down in the Great Fire but was reestablished as Johnson and Arneson. Arneson and others started the Central Manufacturing Company in 1884 as an office-desk manufacturer. He served as its President and Treasurer. Arneson was also a director of the Chicago Manufacturers' Association

and of the Union Bank of Chicago. He was a member of Lyons Post No 9, G.A.R.

He and his Norwegian-born wife Hilda Tofitner had two children, a son and daughter. The daughter married Alf Norman, who served as secretary of the Central Manufacturing Company. The Arneson family lived at 1427 N. Hoyne (formerly 672 N.).

Plate 3.26
NILS ARNESON'S OFFICIAL PORTRAIT

SAUL BELLOW

Well-known author Saul Bellow was born in LaChine, Canada, in 1915 to Russian immigrant parents, and moved to Chicago at age nine. His family lived on Cortez between Leavitt and Oakley in two different buildings during the 1920s. He attended Columbus School, then Sabin School, before going to Tuley High School. Bellow left Wicker Park to attend school at the University of Chicago.

Characters in Bellows' many books are primarily Jews and Chicagoans. *Henderson the Rain King* (1959) is his only major work with main characters who are non-Jewish. According to Irving Cutler in *The Jews of Chicago*, Bellows…"has become one of the leading figures in American and world literature. Bellow received three National Book Awards, the Pulitzer Prize, and in 1976 the Nobel Peace Prize for literature."

FREDERICK W. BELZ

Frederick W. Belz built his home on Damen across from Wicker Park after the Great Fire in 1871. He moved to Oak Park in 1908 but maintained his loyalty to the Wicker Park district and his many friends in it.

His retirement from the Pennsylvania Railroad in 1911 prompted the following write up in the *Wicker Park Eagle* March 11, 1911 issue:

"Mr. Frederick W. Belz, a well known pioneer of Wicker Park, has on his own application been placed on the retired list of the Pennsylvania RR, a company whom he has faithfully served for the long period of 45 years, thirty of these as Freight Agent at Chicago.

The PA RR pension rules require compulsory retirement of an employ on reaching the age of 70, but provide that if on reaching the age of 65 and having been in the service 30 years, an employee feels that for reason of health conditions it would be advisable to leave active service, he can, upon recommendation of an examining Medical Board be retired at that age.

Mr. Belz, having just reached his 66th birthday, has taken advantage of this rule and although in good health at the time of this medical examination, the company took into consideration his previous spells of severe illness and his long and faithful service in their

behalf and granted his request, to enable him and his devoted life companion to enjoy their remaining years in peace and comfort well earned. Seeing America is one of the methods they propose to pursue to that end.

One of the pleasing incidents of his retirement was the presentation by the employees, some of whom have been with him many years, of a beautiful and costly watch and fob suitably engraved, as a lasting memento of the occasion and a mark of the respect and esteem in which he was held."

In August, two years after his retirement, Belz assured a *Wicker Park Eagle* reporter that while living in the Wicker Park District, he caught fish in the old Wicker Park Pond and ate rabbit stew from the "critters" he shot that were nibbling on his garden greens behind his home on Damen.

Belz also gave the reporter an update on how he and his wife were spending their retirement time. During winter the Belz's spent time on their Florida orange grove and divided their time up north in the summer between their Oak Park home, the "sea shore," and northern Michigan.

JOHN BUEHLER

Hard work, diverse business interests and abilities, sound business decisions in timely fashion, and possibly extreme good luck seem to typify John Buehler's business career.

Born in Dornahn, Wurtenberg, Prussia, on August 19, 1831*; Buehler's father died eleven years later. He left school at age fourteen, becoming an apprentice in the mercantile business. Except for nine months as a shoemaker's apprentice, Buehler stayed in the mercantile business until he completed his apprenticeship in 1852. As was the custom for a young man after the expiration of his apprenticeship, he started a two-year tour of other German States and Switzerland.

Buehler came to the United States in 1854 at age twenty-three, staying in New York for six months before coming to Chicago. His apprenticeships, no doubt, helped him in his first job in Chicago, which began in April 1855 and lasted for four years, as a clerk in Spring and Sons shoe store on Lake St. During that time, in 1856, he married Christina Schwartz.

*The 1870 census show Buehler's age as forty-four.

Plate 3.27
JOHN BUEHLER WAS INVOLVED WITH THE BUSINESS COMMUNITY AND ORGANIZATIONS IN THE WICKER PARK DISTRICT. HE HAD A LARGE HOME ON DAMEN, BETWEEN PIERCE AND THE ALLEY SOUTH OF NORTH.

His first entrepreneurial venture was as a grocer and provisions dealer on Milwaukee Ave. In 1864 he sold the grocery business, started a malt house at 314 and 316 Milwaukee, and went on the Board of the Huck Brewing Company, which was destroyed by the fire in 1871. In 1866 he was elected a Republican alderman, winning consecutive re-elections until 1872.

In 1867 Buehler started Union Insurance and Trust Company, serving as its secretary. Then in 1868 his wife, with whom he had six children, died.

Fortunately, for the well being of him and his family, he had the foresight to sell the insurance risk of Union in 1870, prior to the Great Fire of 1871; and his business continued under the name of Union Trust Company with Buehler as director.

As alderman, Buehler presented a resolution on September 19, 1870, to pave Milwaukee Ave. from Division to North. The Board of Public Works was, thereby, ordered to prepare an ordinance, "for curing, grading, and paving with wooden block pavement." He also presented a resolution directing the Board of Public Works to report on the delay in erecting lampposts on Milwaukee and Chicago.

Buehler owned a large parcel of land bound on the north by North, the south by Pierce, the east by Damen, and the west by the alley west of Damen. Probably built between 1871 and 1875, his very large frame home was located in the middle of the land from Pierce to the alley south of North. The remainder became commercial. The home was probably razed just before the "L" was built in 1895.

During the 1871 Great Fire, not only was Buehler saved from financial ruin due to insurance risk, but his malt house was unscathed by the fire, unlike most of the other Chicago malt houses. With the large number of breweries in the area, the post-fire malt business flourished. During his time as a maltster, Buehler developed an interest in real estate. Upon retirement from the malt house in 1873 he also resigned from Union Trust and established his own banking house at the corner of Chicago and Milwaukee, while maintaining involvement in real estate. In 1875 he was elected state senator from the 5th District. As such, he introduced the bill to tax church property.

It was his banking affiliation that almost cost him his life on January 14, 1878, according to the *New York Times* story on January 15, with the headline "An Illinois Senator Stabbed…Hon. John Buehler Attacked By An Assassin…Three Serious Wounds Inflicted—Why was the attack made?"

It was 9:50 in the morning and Buehler was about to cross the street at Chicago and Milwaukee, having just left his bank. Stepping off the curb, he was attacked by dagger-wielding Michael Marso. Buehler was only slightly wounded over his left eye by the first swipe of the knife, but received a more substantial wound on his forearm as he tried to protect himself. Struggling, clinching each other, they fell to the ground and Marso plunged his dagger into the middle of Buehler's abdomen.

Marso jumped up and ran up Milwaukee but was "soon over hauled by Policeman Schuman." Surgeons were not optimistic about Buehler's recovery.

Three years earlier, Buehler had provided Marso with a loan, for which Marso used his home and property as collateral. Treating the loan as a gift, Marso paid nothing back on the loan, nor did he pay any interest. Buehler sold the indebtedness to a third party who foreclosed on Marso's home and property. Enraged by this action, Marso vowed to kill Buehler. Marso, a real estate speculator, was about forty-six years old with a wife and family.

Fortunately Buehler recovered, continuing in banking which culminated in the institution called Garden City Banking & Trust Company.

Active in starting the Aurora Turner Hall Association, Buehler was also a Mason, and member of the Order of Odd Fellows. He helped unite several lodges and was one of the prime movers in the erection of the commodious hall on Milwaukee in 1868. In addition, he was a director of Waldheim Cemetery, serving as its secretary in, at least, 1880.

Buehler remarried in 1889 to Rose Schoppe, widow of Erdmann Schoppe. By 1894, only two of his six children were living. His son, John William, was a cashier at Garden City Banking and Trust Company and his daughter, Louisa was the wife of Otto Peuser.

Buehler was praised in *A Biographical History with Portraits of Prominent Men of the Great West* in 1894:

"During the 35 years of his residence in Chicago, John Buehler has been an important factor in its growth and prosperity and has earned the esteem of his fellow-citizens, which he enjoys. He has become widely known in business circles as a man of keen insight, rare judgment, great energy and strict integrity; while in the worlds of private life he is known for his simple tastes and habits, his benevolence, and his attachments for his friends, of whom he has a large number and who are heartily glad of this large success."

CLOUD FAMILY

Maud Cloud (fifth student to the left in the third row up from the bottom on the photo on the right) lived in the Wicker Park District for at least two or three years. Students at Wicker Park School, she and her best friend stand next to each other in the photo wearing identical collars.

Pendleton Cloud, Maud's father, was from Louisville, KY and served in the Union Army during the Civil War. He worked as building superintendent after he moved to Chicago, living in the buildings for which he was responsible. According to city directories, he and his family lived in the Wicker Park District between 1890 and 1892.

ARIE CROWN FAMILY

Arie Crown, an immigrant from Lithuania, and his wife, Ida Gordon, settled near Division and Milwaukee (1309 N. Ashland) in 1891. A successful peddler and match salesman, Arie was able to move his family to 2114 W. Potomac by 1907. Observant Jews, they attended Tiffereth Zion synagogue and increased their family to seven children. Their sons Henry, Sol and Irving attended Burr Grammar School on Wabansia.

In 1919 with $10,000, Henry and his two brothers, Sol and Irving, started Material Service Corporation. Sol was president and Henry was treasurer.

HENRY LAMARTINE HERTZ

In the 1870s and the 1880s the Wicker Park District had demonstrated a history of support for the Republican Party. Many of that party's activities focused around a triumvirate of Hertz, Pease and Lorimer. Called "Hertzville," the area on which they focused included several fast-growing northwest side wards. Henry L. Hertz was the leading "mover and shaker."

His first employment was as a clerk, while performing in amateur Danish theatrical productions. He moved on to manage a cigar store before clerking in a bank and serving as a teller for the Commercial Loan Co. From a position as a clerk in Cook County's Recorder's office, Hertz went to the Criminal Court office in 1878. By 1884, he became the Cook County Coroner.

Plate 3.28
TAKEN ON NOVEMBER 19, 1890, THIS PHOTO SHOWS WICKER PARK SCHOOL STUDENTS.

Sol died two years later and Henry, at age twenty-five became president. The sand and gravel business became the foundation for a family empire that would include interests in the Empire State Building, Hilton Corporation, General Dynamics Corporation, and the Rock Island Railroad. As Irving Cutler stated in *The Jews of Chicago*:

> The Crown family has been a major source of funds for numerous philanthropic causes including being one of the largest contributors to local Jewish causes with special support for Jewish education."

Finding himself quite adroit in the game of politics, he was elected coroner twice before becoming State Treasurer. He was later appointed Internal Revenue Collector. Over the years, he served in many Republican organizations, and on committees locally as well as in the county and state. He did all of this despite having lost his left foot on April 4, 1893, in an accident on the Milwaukee Ave. cable car line.

Hertz was a trustee of the Danish Old People's Home; member of the Social Dania; and president of the Inland Lake Yachting Assn. from 1902-04. In addition he was a member of Northwest Chicago Yacht Club; Pistakee, Fox Lake, Oshkosh Yacht Clubs as well as the Royal Danish Yacht Club of Copenhagen.

Son of a police inspector, Hertz was born in

Copenhagen, Denmark, November 19, 1847. He came to Chicago at the age of twenty-two. At the age of thirty-three he married Mary Patricia Power. They

had five children: Harriet May, Martin Power, Henry Louis, Marguerite Hannah, and Paul Power. They made their home at 1351 N. Hoyne.

JOHN CONRAD HORN FAMILY

A prominent manufacturer, John Conrad Horn was president of the Horn Brothers Manufacturing Company, a furniture factory located near Milwaukee. An alderman, Horn was born in 1852.

Horn and his wife, Paulina Steinhardt, built 2150 W. Pierce in 1890. They had three children, Conrad, William, and Frank.

Plate 3.29

HORN FAMILY WAS APPARENTLY CELEBRATING AN EVENT WHEN THIS PHOTO WAS TAKEN.

Plate 3.30

THE PHOTO BELOW IS PROBABLY PAULINA STEINHARDT HORN WITH ONE OF HER THREE CHILDREN. THE VIEW IS ON THE NORTH SIDE OF PIERCE LOOKING WEST TO THE CORNER OF PIERCE AND LEAVITT.

Plate 3.31

HOLDING THE WHIP, FRANK JOHN HORN IS THE DRIVER.

JACOB AND SARAH ISADOR

Jacob and Sarah Isador immigrated from Brissen, Germany in 1885. They first settled in Kentucky, then moved to Chicago in 1891. They had eight children.

In 1894 they built, then moved into, 2032 W. Potomac. Four years later, they moved into 2028 W. Potomac, keeping their first building as income property. Jacob had a clothing store on Milwaukee and another at 98 Market Street.

Plate 3.32
SARAH AND JACOB ISADOR POSED FOR THIS PHOTO IN 1905.

A.P. JOHNSON

Born Vinge Gjerager Johnson in 1835, he became known as A. P. His family settled in Boone County, IL on a farm in 1850. A.P. worked on the farm and attended public school until twenty, when he moved to Beloit to learn the carpenter trade. By 1861 he moved to Chicago and was employed by the federal government, assigned to the army construction corps until the end of the Civil War. Returning to Chicago, he once again worked in the carpentry trade as contractor and builder.

In 1868 Johnson and others raised money and bought out a small cane-seat factory at Green and

Plate 3.33
A. P. JOHNSON PHOTO IS FROM AN UNKNOWN DATE.

Ancona (Phillips), converting the product to wood-seat chairs. In 1877 Johnson became sole owner, incorporating as Johnson Chair Co. in 1883.

Organizer of the Mt. Olive Cemetery Association, Johnson served as director of the State Bank of Chicago beginning in 1891. In addition, he served as president of the Wicker Park Safety Deposit Vault Company and as director of the Asbestos and Iron Company of Canal Dover, Ohio. Being a "staunch Republican" he served in the City Council from 1889-91.

In his personal life, A.P. married Martha Magnussen Sattre in 1871 and they had five children. Their residence was at 1506 N. Damen (695 N. Robey). A.P. was a founding member of the Norwegian Old People's Home and was its president for two years. Having served on the building commit-tee for both Tabitha Hospital and the Deaconess Home and Hospital, he was among the first to help build those structures. As a member of the Wicker Park English Lutheran Church, he served as the board of trustees' president. The A.O.U.W. was another organization in which he had membership.

In *A History of the Norwegians of Illinois,* Johnson was described as:
> "…a quiet, consistent and faithful Christian gentleman, and in all his walks in life has been upright in his dealings, kind and considerate of the welfare of others, and is loved and respected by all who know him."

CAPTAIN WILLIAM JOHNSON

A seafaring sailor, then inland water captain, Captain William Johnson was considered the wealthiest Norwegian in Chicago, at the time of his death in 1902. Born in Arendal, Norway, in 1836, Johnson began his sailing career at age fourteen as a cabin boy. Sailing the Baltic, the North Sea and the Mediterranean for five years he nearly drowned in the St. Tubas, Portugal harbor. Saved by a Portuguese fruit and wine peddler, Johnson, came to Chicago in 1855 and soon became a pioneer Great Lakes captain and vessel owner.

Freight on the Great Lakes was a profitable business in the mid 1800s. He began his fleet by purchasing the Fish Hawk in 1857, followed by Traveler and the Richard Mott two years later. Whether he built them or bought them, the rest of his schooners were mainly given people names, including D. O. Dickenson, Paulina, Magnolia, Rosa Bell, Cecilia, Ida, Lena Johnson, Clara, Olga, Alice and William O. Goodman.

At age thirty-six, he married twenty-seven year old, Norwegian born, Eline Theodora Shoemaker. They had five children and lived at 1417 N. Hoyne from 1884 to 1903.

Plate 3.34
CAPTAIN JOHNSON POSED FOR THIS PHOTO AT AN UNKNOWN DATE.

WILLIAM T. JOHNSON

One of nine children born to Englishman Thomas and Hannah (Temple) Johnson, William T. was born on November 16, 1835. Raised on a farm in Oneida County, NY, he attended public schools before leaving his family for Chicago.

He started as a laborer in the Hayes and Morris Lumber Yard, rising to foreman. But he saw others doing better financially. So, he hired someone to teach him bookkeeping. Changing his employer to Shearer and Payne Lumber Yard, he joined them as a bookkeeper. He moved on as a bookkeeper to Mason and McArthur, proprietors of Excelsior Iron Works. Johnson's good work resulted in increased income and he established a line of credit with many friends.

At twenty-seven, in 1862, Johnson married Kate E. Allen, adopted daughter of Elizabeth and Nathan Allen. (See Page 113) In 1864, Johnson and Mr. Holder built the largest foundry in the city, which they named Phoenix. In the same year, Kate and William obtained a large parcel of land, from Nathan Allen, on the north side of North from Milwaukee to just short of Western. The land had been owned by Elizabeth Allen.

In 1866 Johnson went into a partnership with H. P. Kellogg in a wholesale/retail hardware business at Clark and Monroe. Swept away by the fire in 1871, it was rebuilt and stayed in business for another 20 years.

Involved in real estate as a planner and developer, he was quoted as saying, "I was a pioneer on this ground, and I shall not desert it until every lot feels the weight of a good building."

Politically, he took an active role in a local campaign for Abraham Lincoln. Nominated and elected for State Senator in 1878, Johnson's park bill benefited the west side parks. Nominated for County Treasurer, he was elected for a three-year term. In 1884 he became a Railroad Commission and later President Garfield

appointed him an Indian Commissioner.

The Johnsons owned an old farmhouse, known as the "Gray House," built during the Civil War. It stood on a slight hill on the north side of North Ave. Very early settlers in the territory sometimes called it "the House on the Hill" and said that it could be seen for miles around. That house was later purchased by Association House of Chicago. According to City Directories, Johnson lived at 51 Alice Place in 1902.

THEODORE DANIEL JUERGENS

Educated in Chicago public schools until 1869, Theodore Daniel Juergens was born in Chicago on November 29, 1853. His parents were Ludwig and Helen (Koehn) Juergens. According to *Edward's City Directory 1869-70*, Juergens was a student at Porter's Telegraph College.

He began his career as a telegraph operator for the Chicago and Northwestern Railroad and then became a sign painter and decorator. He followed that by

working in the mercantile business until 1892. At that point he went into manufacturing, joining the American Varnish Co. where he later became its president.

He married Mary Hemmer with whom he had four children: Helen, William, Adalia, and Edwin. They lived at 2141 W. Pierce (formerly known as 82 Ewing). Juergens was a member of the West Side Club and Royal League.

CARL LAEMMLE

Founder of Universal Studios, Carl Laemmle was a Wicker Park District resident at the end of the nineteenth century. He lived at 1423-25 N. Hoyne. Laemmle came to Chicago in 1884 as a film distributor.

He opened his first nickelodeon called the White Front Theater on February 24, 1906 at 1255 N. Milwaukee. His second theater was Family Theater at 1233 S. Halsted (pre 1909 number) on April 1, 1906.

WILLIAM G. LEGNER

William G. Legner began life on August 15, 1858, in Neustadt, W. Prussia, Germany as the son of William G. and Flora (Noetzel) Legner. Educated in Germany, he had his business school training in Troy, NY, where he worked in his father's cigar box factory from 1876 to 1879.

He moved to Chicago where his first employment was in advertising with the Chicago *Freie Presse* and *Staats Zeitung*, later becoming the business manager of the *Chicago Democrat*.

In September 1882, he married Dora Leusch and they had three children: Harriet O., Ellen H., and Roger H. Legner made another career change in 1886, when he became deputy collector of Internal Revenue. Three years later he changed careers again, this time to the brewing industry. He became the shipping clerk at the

West Side Brewing Company. There he rose to Vice President and Treasurer by 1905. Later he became President of West Side Brewing and the Conrad Seipp Brewing Company.

Like many other Wicker Park residents, he was involved with politics and government. A Democrat, he was selected as a presidential elector. In 1900, Legner became a Trustee of the Sanitary District of Chicago, and served until 1905.

A Lutheran, he was a member of Royal Areanum, Central Turn-Verein, and Teutonia Maennerchor. In addition he was a member of several clubs that included: Chicago Athletic, Germania, North West Iroquois, Columbia Yacht, Fox Lake Yacht, and Chicago Riding. He and his family lived in the 1100 block of N. Hoyne (formerly 509 N. Hoyne).

AUGUST LENKE

German immigrant August Lenke went from peddler to vice president of a local coal company and later served as the Fish Commissioner of Illinois.

Lenke came to Chicago in 1864 and worked as a peddler the next four years. First he sold feed, going into the flour business in 1870, and then coal in 1873. After 1877, he was a partner in O. S. Richardson and Co., responsible for coal mining and shipping operations. He also served as a director of the Collins Coal Co. Upon incorporation of the Richardson Co., in 1905, he was its vice-president. Governor Yates appointed Lenke, a Republican, as Fish Commissioner from 1901 to 1907.

Born in Hanover, Germany in 1844 to Henry and Christina (Schwerdfeger) Lenke, he attended public schools in Hanover until 1859. Lenke married Sophia Rauter in May 1868. They had three children: August Jr., Alvina, and Anna. Their home was at 2156 W. Pierce (formerly known as 93 Ewing.) Lenke was a Mason and a member of Cregier Lodge and the Germania Club.

SIMON PETER LONG

Pastor of the Wicker Park Lutheran Church from 1917 to 1929, Reverend Simon Peter Long appeared to have been a colorful, charismatic evangelist. Substantially increasing its congregation, he ministered to more then the Wicker Park community. Each week his sermon was broadcast on WCFL radio, and as often as possible, he spoke in other religious settings and on street corners.

The reverend related his calling to Chicago in one of his books, *My Lord and My Life*:
"God called me to Wicker Park Lutheran Church in Chicago. The call was large in its scope. I was to preach in Chicago as a center and reach the world. It looked like a hard job. It was a hard job. The people who reside around that beautiful church are nearly all Jews. What of it? Was not Jesus Christ a Jew? Were not the Prophets and Apostles Jews? I went to Chicago and met a most wonderful people. They made it possible for me to preach in the theater every Sunday and reach the masses when it costs $100 an hour. They made it possible for me to speak before the Sunday Evening Club, an honor given to a few Chicago citizens. They made it possible for me to be the Vice President of the Better Government Association. They made it possible for me to

Plate 3.35
PARTIAL TO TRAVELING BY HORSE, REVEREND SIMON PETER LONG IS ASTRIDE HIS "ASSISTANT" CHARLEY.

go to Jerusalem and see Calvary and eighteen countries 50 years after I was confirmed. They called me from a $2,000 salary to a small salary which has been raised to $5,000. They put $1,200 into my hands as a gift when I started for Jerusalem. They gave me many train letters last week when I left home to come to Glacier Park to write these words and the Sunday School letter had a check for $50 saying they love me. The Vice President of the C. B. and Q., Mr. W. W. Baldwin gave me a pass to go to Portland, Oregon, next week to teach the Bible one week there. Who is doing all this? Open your eyes and look. It is my Lord Jesus Christ. Who sent me to Jerusalem? My Lord!… "

Born in McZena, OH, on October 7, 1860, Long was the seventh child of French parents. As a boy he learned the shoe trade. At the age of twenty, like his siblings, he was to receive $1,000 "for a start in life." He was given a choice to have the entire sum at once for a business or to gradually take amounts for further education. He chose education and calculated that it would take eight years to finish preparatory, college, and seminary courses.

It would appear that his period of formal education was also a time for him to hone his skills of people reading, thinking and persuading. For the first three years, he earned $50 per year and board. Then he started selling books. Long relates some of his experiences:

"If you want to know people, touch their pocket-books. It was on a Monday morning I started. The first man I met could not read, but I took his order. By Saturday night I had sold enough books to clear $60. In one month I cleared $240. September came and I left my good home with a blessing to prepare for the ministry. For a little while I felt that I had wasted many years of my life when I saw little boys who never did anything but go to school in my classes. I soon discovered, however, that going to school is one thing and thinking is another. Education is far greater than all schools and universities. What most of our universities need today is a real education. Let me be as brief as I can. I shortened my eight years into seven and spent one year in Philadelphia. Gradually I drew my $1,000 from home and earned the rest, doing most of my own washing, acting as janitor of the church and cutting the students' hair on Saturday at 10 cents a head. Many of the beneficiaries smoked and grumbled about the poor meals and rode on the street cars while I walked to the city most of the time, never smoked, paid for all my meals… "

HENRY W., CAROLINE, AND H. ERNST NIEDERT

The Neiderts are representative of many people who have "appeared" during the course of research for this book. Like so many others, a morsel of information whets the appetite, then one searches and searches, but little else can be found. In this case, a photo of a house on the northeast corner of Pierce and Hoyne was the starting point. (See *Plate 4.19.*) Questions abound. What was their age and occupation? Were they involved in the community? What were their family relationships?

For you mystery fans, here are a few clues about the Niederts. Perhaps you can learn more about them or make up a fictional story about their family. Though not listed in any of the biographical listings available for the 1800s through 1926, there were city directory entries that present some information.

In 1866 Henry W. Niedert was listed in a business called Katz & Neidert with a residence on "Front bet Carpenter & Grove." In 1886, Henry W. Niedert's Sons was a business at 61 Market that was in flour. Henry W. was listed as living at Pierce and Hoyne. W. H. Niedert was listed as commercial merchant at 61 Market and as a boarder at 718 Hoyne. Henry E. and son were listed at 718 Hoyne. Frederick G. was listed at 814 Leavitt and Caroline was also listed at 718 Hoyne.

In the 1899 *Lakeside City Directory,* Charles Neidert, a driver, had 1184 N. Milwaukee as his residence, as did William, a salesman. At the same time, Miss Minnie Niedert, a stenographer, lived at 726 N. Hoyne. By 1902, only Frederick G. Niedert was listed as a machinist with his home at 1125 Milwaukee.

What do you think the relationships were among these Neiderts, and what happened to them?

The Noel Family

Noel family members (See *Plate 3.1*) were not only multi-generational residents and participants in organizations in the Wicker Park District, but they were also involved with manufacturing, banking, and real estate development.

Beginning in 1900, they were "…identified with the construction of various buildings, which in the order of their erection" were: 2102 W. North; 2118 W. Pierce; 2134 W. Pierce; Harriet Apartments (later Fountain Court Apartments), 2108-2118 W. North; Noel State Bank (northeast corner of North and Milwaukee) ; North West Tower Building (northwest corner of North and Milwaukee); and the Dara Building at 1638-40 N. Damen.

Theophilus Noel

The patriarch of the family Theophilus was born in 1840. A native of Texas, he was in the Confederate army as a youth. Returning home, he became involved in Texas politics, railroads, and journalism. Prior to the Civil War he became aware of a natural product mined in the southwest, and attempted to market the product in the late 1870s, before the project was aborted. In 1878 Theophilus moved to Chicago and became involved in many different enterprises, finding his greatest success in the proprietary medicine business. In 1883 he renewed his interest in the natural product; but it was not until 1896 that his Vitae Ore formulation produced a more consistent product, and financial success began to be a reality. (See Page 39.)

There is no indication that his struggles influenced his opinion of himself or his eagerness to judge others. On the introductory page of his memoirs, Theophilus writes in a very large bold script with an even larger signature: "If you don't like my bacon, don't come to my smokehouse again." The following pages, figuratively speaking, drip with pomposity and egotism. Several years later in a booklet about the Noel family, he writes in the Foreward:

> "When one becomes three-quarters of a centenarian as I, the pride he has in looking backwards as well as forward is pardonable, and will not be considered egotistical, excepting by those who have no excuse for having lived or for not dying quickly."

In Chicago: Its History and Its Builders, Theophilus is characterized as follows:

> "He is what is familiarly known as an original character, practicing few of the conventionalities of life. His large frame, commanding presence, indomitable will and tireless energy

Plate 3.36
Smoking a cigar, Theophilus Noel sits in a rocker on the porch of his Michigan country home.

make him a conspicuous figure and these attributes together with his varied experience, extensive travels, keen perceptive power and natural gift of oratory, have brought him into more or less prominence in local affairs."

There is a glimmer of a softer side in his first, and possibly only, attempt at poetry. Inspired by love for Harriet Sarah Harris, who would later became his wife, he wrote in 1856:

> "I love thee because thou hast ever
> A smile and a kind word for me,
> When those who should cherish me, never
> Can aught but my foibles see.

I'll quench not the flame that arises
From perishing hopes of my youth,
If reason the weakness despises,
At least 'twill be counseled by truth.

Thy love o'er my sad spirit beameth
Like the moon on the dark brow of night,
Till again in its glory it seemeth
That even its shadows are bright.

How sacred the hope I have cherished
That still in some region divine,
When all which is earthly has perished
My spirit shall mingle with THINE."

In 1903 Theophilus and his wife Harriet built and moved into 2118 W. Pierce, though he had his business on North prior to 1903.

Plate 3.37
HARRIET NOEL

Plate 3.38
THEOPHILUS NOEL'S UNIQUE PERSONALITY IS ILLUSTRATED IN THIS PICTURE FROM HIS FAMILY PAMPHLET.

Joseph R. Noel

Theophilus's only child, Joseph Roberts Noel, was born in Waco, TX on March 3, 1872. Joseph was educated in the Chicago school system, graduating from Irving Grammar School in 1887 and West Division High School in 1891, before attending Rush Medical College in Chicago for two years. After one year at Jefferson Medical College of Philadelphia, he graduated in 1894. The following year he interned at Cooper Hospital in Camden, NJ and married Alice Mabel Warner of St. Paul, MN. He returned to

Plate 3.39
LOOKING QUITE DAPPER, JOSEPH NOEL STRIKES
A POSE IN THE LATE 1890S.

Chicago, practicing medicine until 1897.

Learning the value of a dollar was an important business lesson for Joseph and his career. He credited learning this lesson to his experience as a newspaper boy while attending public schools. Joseph began his business career as manager for Theophilus's proprietary medicine business. When Theo. Noel Company incorporated in 1900, J. R. became vice president and secretary. He also served as general organizer of the National Association of Retail Druggists from 1901 until 1905, when he went into banking.

Like his father, J. R. was involved in many business and personal activities. Being apparently more humble than his father, he preferred being addressed as "Mr." after he went into business, as he felt he was no longer entitled to use "Dr."

At a time when failures of local private banks were numerous and attitudes hostile toward small private banks, J. R. visualized the prosperous future of the Wicker Park District. With the lack of support to open a state bank, he had the confidence and faith that a small bank could be successful. So, with the capital of $25,000, he founded the North West Savings Bank, in October 1905. In February, it moved into its own building, the Milnoro Building on the northwest corner of Milwaukee and North. The failure of the Milwaukee Avenue State Bank (Paul Stensland's bank), in 1906, had a major effect on Noel's private bank Just as they were coming through this rough period, the panic of 1907 hit; but they made it through that too, with the capital increased to $50,000. Noel maintained his sole proprietorship

Plate 3.40
JOSEPH IN A PLAID CAP RELAXES AT 2134 W. PIERCE WITH
HIS DAUGHTER, HARRIET ON THE LEFT AND VIRGINIA ON
THE RIGHT. PHOTO TAKEN BETWEEN 1903 AND 1905.

until 1909 when the bank was organized as a state institution, the North West State Bank, with a capital of $200,000. (See Page 36.)

In his personal life, J. R. and his wife Alice had three children: Harriet, born in 1896; Virginia, in 1899; and Theophilus II, in 1907. They purchased 2134 W. Pierce in 1903, living in a frame and brick home built in the 1800s until sometime after August 1904. Razing the old home, they built a two-flat graystone and brick building and coach house on that property in 1905. Though they moved to a home in Oak Park, in 1912, J. R. continued his business life in the Wicker Park District.

The bank name changed to the Noel State Bank in February 1917, at which time it was announced that it would build its own building across Milwaukee on the northwest corner of Damen and North. That building was opened in 1921.

J. R.'s belief in the district's value and future apparently led him to the belief that it was up to him to promote and develop the intersection of Milwaukee, Damen and North. An article in the February 1929 issue of *Greater Chicago Magazine* gives more detail:

"There are many dilapidated structures in this immediate community which are not doing either the owners or the community any good. This deterioration will continue each year, and cause both the income and the value of such buildings to depreciate more and more. Wherever these properties can be purchased at a price not to exceed the reasonable value of the ground on which they are situated, Mr. Noel and his associates are willing and prepared to purchase them and to improve them with structures which will be a credit to the community. Further more, after these properties are improved and rented, Mr. Noel and his associates are willing to resell them at cost.

The community is rapidly learning, particularly through the medium of the Wicker Park Chamber of Commerce, that in order to attract more merchants, and more residents, the district must be made more attractive.

After careful consideration of all the factors involved, Mr. Noel and his associates visualized what it would mean to the Wicker Park district to have a tall office building, such as North West Tower.

...Mr. Noel has devoted an unusual amount of time, effort, and strength to various public, civic, philanthropic, religious and patriotic activities. These are world-wide, nation-wide, state-wide and city-wide in extent.

Plate 3.41
ALICE NOEL IS ON THE FRONT STEPS OF 2134 W. PIERCE, PROBABLY IN 1908, WITH HER THREE CHILDREN. THEOPHILUS II IS IN FRONT WITH VIRGINIA BEHIND HIM AND HARRIET ON THE RIGHT.

Mr. Noel is a great exponent of the countless opportunities which continually confront us. His theory is that these opportunities constantly surround us, like the air we breathe, few of us being able to see them any more than we can see the air. Opportunity is not dependent on either time or circumstances. All that is necessary is to have the vision, courage and co-operation to see and to seize the golden opportunities that exist everywhere about us today."

Noel was involved with various organization as well as being a member of the Board for the Association House of Chicago.

— *Elaine A Coorens*

LUCY AND ALBERT PARSONS

Lucy Parsons was born Lucy Gathing in Johnson County Texas about 1853. Her exact ancestry is unknown, although she is claimed by Mexican-Americans, African-Americans, and Native-Americans. Lucy and her husband Albert moved to Chicago in 1873 when Lucy was 20 years old. Albert worked as a printer and joined the typographical union in 1874.

In Chicago in the 1870s, the Parsons found themselves in the midst of a nationwide economic depression and labor agitation. During the 1877 national railroad strike Albert Parsons emerged as a leading figure and participant in the newly formed Socialist Labor Party of North America. Lucy supported herself and her husband by opening a dress shop. During the 1880s the Parsons moved from democratic socialism to anarchism and direct action, calling for strikes, boycotts and when necessary, revolutionary action to achieve their goals.

Albert became editor of the *Alarm*, the new journal of the International Working People's Association, and Lucy began to write for it. In 1885, on Thanksgiving Day, Lucy led a protest march down wealthy Prairie Ave., ringing doorbells and calling people to action in support of the poor. On May 1, 1886, a general strike was called and Lucy and Albert led 80,000 workers up Michigan Ave., singing and marching.

The Haymarket bomb incident on May 4, 1886, led to the arrest and indictment of Albert, along with nine others, most of whom were members of the International Workingmen's Association. Their trial (which was considered highly unjust by many) resulted in the conviction of seven and the execution of Albert and three others on November 11, 1887. After the hanging, the bodies of the executed men were returned to their families where they were held until their funeral on November 13th.

Although the Parsons had previously lived at a number of locations in Chicago, in 1887 Lucy resided in a third floor apartment at 1129 N. Milwaukee in the Wicker Park District. As is noted elsewhere, the Haymarket funeral procession wound its way through Wicker Park and along Milwaukee, stopping to pick up Albert's body and those of the others, then down through the loop and out to Waldheim Cemetery on the west side.

Plate 3.42
LUCY E. PARSONS, WIFE OF ALBERT PARSONS, LUCY DEDICATED HER LIFE TO EXPOSING THE INJUSTICE OF THE HAYMARKET INCIDENT.

After the funeral, Lucy Parsons dedicated her life to exposing the injustice of the Haymarket incident and to advocating revolutionary socialism. She saw a revolutionary press as essential to keeping these ideas alive and through her writings she struggled for worker's liberation, and against racism, lynching and women's oppression. During the 1915 economic crisis she planned a mass demonstration and led a march of the unemployed through the streets of the Hull House neighborhood on the near west side. In the 1920s Parsons joined and became a leader in the communist party. Lucy Parsons died in 1942 as a result of a fire in her home. Although she had maintained a collection of nearly 3,000 books, extensive papers, and letters, all were missing from her home on the day after her death. There were accusations that they had been taken by the police "red squad" or the FBI. She was cremated and her ashes were buried in the German Waldheim Cemetery in Forest Park, IL.

— *Mary Ann Johnson*

C. HERMAN PLAUTZ

Like many men in the district in the late 1800s and early 1900s, C. Herman Plautz was involved with diverse businesses, often at the same time.

Born in 1844, Plautz founded the Chicago Drug & Chemical Co. in 1861. He was secretary of the German-American Publishing Co., and president of the Northwestern Brewing Co. on Clybourn Ave. In 1866 he was listed in a city directory as a clerk at C. Wuensche and living at 165 N. Milwaukee (old number). The next year he was listed as a druggist at 513 N. Milwaukee

He built a home at 1558 Hoyne in 1878. Of considerable prominence in local politics, he was the City Clerk in 1886 and City Treasurer in 1887–8. In the 1890s, he served as Ambassador to Russia. He died in his home at the age of fifty-seven in 1901.

NICHOLAS J. AND ABRAM NICOLAS PRITZKER

Arriving in Chicago at the age of ten, Nicholas J. Pritzker had been born in Kiev, Russia, July 19, 1871. From a poor family, he had to obtain his education in night school while working. He became a bookkeeper, working at Nelson Morris & C. Eager. Spending several years studying pharmacy, he changed his focus and entered the Illinois College of Law, from which he was graduated with the L.L.B. Degree.

Nicholas married Anna Cohen on March 4, 1891 and they had three sons: Harry, Abraham N., and Jacob N. The family lived at 2045 W. Evergreen.

Nicholas was actively involved with the founding of the Marks Nathan Orphan Home as well as other organizations and institutions.

Nicholas and Anna's son Abram Nicholas, known as A.N., was born in 1896; and in his later years, he became involved with the Wicker Park community before his death in 1986. (The Wicker Park Grade School was renamed A. N. Pritzker School.)

A. N. served as a navy chief petty officer in World War I, before attending Harvard where he received a law degree. Together, A. N. and his brothers built a very large, diversified group of companies including the Hyatt Hotels, the Marmon Group, Hammond Organ, and McCall's magazine.

NILES THEODORE QUALES

Norwegian born and educated as a veterinary surgeon, Niles Theodore Quales emigrated to America, arriving in Chicago on July 6, 1859 at the age of 28. He enlisted in Company "B" first Illinois Artillery, stationed in Cairo, IL. He remained in the army until 1864. Upon his return to Chicago, he entered Rush Medical College, graduating in 1867.

After a competitive examination by the medical board of Cook County Hospital, he interned there for two years. In the midst of a smallpox epidemic, Dr. Quales was appointed city physician and put in charge of the smallpox hospital located on the lakeshore at the foot of North Ave. The Great Fire of 1871 cut short his 1870 appointment as surgeon to the U.S. Marine Hospital located at Michigan Ave. and Rush Street Bridge.

After the Fire, the Chicago Relief and Aid

Plate 3.43

NILES QUALES BEGAN HIS MEDICAL CAREER AS A VETERINARIAN IN NORWAY. PHOTO PROBABLY DATES TO THE LATE 1860S.

Society appointed him a visiting physician. In 1891, he was appointed physician to the Norwegian Deaconess Hospital on Humboldt Blvd. He chaired the organizing committee for the Tabitha Society, and afterward was a member of the board of directors, serving as secretary on the executive and building committees. He became a member of the new hospital's medical board and served as its first president.

Severing his connection with Tabitha Hospital in 1895, Quales organized the Norwegian Old People's Home Society of Chicago. He followed the same pattern of organization and involvement as he did with the Tabitha organization.

Quales, one of the organizers of the Norwegian Lutheran Deaconess Society in 1896, was elected as a member of the board of directors. He was on the attending staff when the hospital was located at Artesian and LeMoyne. When a new building was erected at Haddon and Leavitt, he served on the building committee as well as other committees.

In 1903, Quales was elected physician to the Tabitha Hospital and in 1906 he was appointed physician in chief at Deaconess. A member of the Illinois State, Chicago Medical, and Scandinavian Medical Societies, he served as president of the Scandinavian Medical Society. He was honored with the Order of St. Olafin, which he received from Norway's King Haakon VII in 1910.

He moved to 1951 Schiller in 1873, three

Plate 3.44
DR. QUALES DONATED MUCH TIME AND EFFORT TOWARD THE MEDICAL WELL-BEING OF EARLY CHICAGOANS.

years after marrying Carrie L. Lawson, with whom he had three children. He was one of the founding members of the Wicker Park Lutheran Church in 1879. In politics, he considered himself, "as a matter of principle, to be a steadfast Republican."

KARL FERDINAND MARIUS SANDBERG

Dr. Sandberg received a PhD and MD in Norway, serving an internship at a general hospital and an insane asylum. He came to Chicago in 1882 at the age of twenty-seven.

His general practice included responsibilities as the attending gynecologist and obstetrician at Cook County Hospital and the National Temperance Hospital. He was also surgeon-in-chief at Norwegian Tabitha Hospital.

In 1895, he married Inga G. Stensland, a stepdaughter of Paul O. Stensland. Politically, Sandberg, like his father-in-law, was a Democrat. Shortly after 1900, he left the Democratic party to support and speak enthusiastically on behalf of the Socialist Party.

Sentenced to one year in prison, Sandberg only served two days for his indictment for anarchist activities. Some time after 1905, the Sandbergs moved to 1345 N. Hoyne.

Plate 3.45
THIS KARL SANDBERG PORTRAIT WAS TAKEN SOMETIME BEFORE 1905.

KICKHAM SCANLAN

Of Kickham Scanlan it "may be stated unhesitatingly and beyond fear of question, that no young lawyer today in Chicago gives nobler promise of future grand achievement," raved a write-up in the *Biographical History of the American Irish in Chicago*. Fulfilling that prognostication, Scanlan went on to be prominently connected with many noted criminal cases in Cook County. In addition, one of the promising young members of the Chicago Bar associated with Scanlan's practice was Edgar Lee Masters, who was also well known for his literary abilities.

Scanlan's father, Michel founded the Irish Newspaper *Irish Republic* in 1866, moving to New York and then Washington, D.C. Kickham attended public school and high school in Washington and attended Notre Dame studying English and classics for a year. His next three years were spent working for a mine and coal merchant, running their Detroit office for the last year. Returning to Chicago he studied law at the Chicago College of Law.

Born in Chicago on October 23, 1864, Kickham was admitted to the bar in 1888. He established his own office in 1893, and handled a number of well-known criminal cases. In 1909, he was elected Judge of the Circuit Court of Cook County, a position he filled until 1921, when he became Judge of the Appellate Court of Illinois for the First District.

Sadie Conway, daughter of Chicago fire inspector Michael W. Conway, married Scanlan on January 2, 1890. They had one child, a daughter. In about 1891, 2146 W. Pierce was built for the Scanlans.

In the 1894 *A Biographical History with Portraits of Prominent Men of the Great West*, the author states:

"....Scanlan is a gentleman of culture, and has a marked taste for literature, music and a partiality for outdoor sports. He has fine social qualities, and enjoys the companionship of his friends whenever release from the cares of business will permit, and while the circle of these friends is large, attracted by his sterling worth, it is ever increasing. As aptly expressed by one who knows him thoroughly, Mr. Scanlan is a man to be depended on at all times. And, this is the highest praise."

Kickham apparently felt strongly about proper credit going to the people of his heritage, the Irish. In the February 10, 1910 issue of the *Wicker Park Eagle*, the following article appeared:

**"IRISH IGNORED IN HISTORY PLEA
Judge Kickham Scanlan Says Latter Day Writers
Slight the Race**

Unfairness and slanderous statements regarding the parts taken by Irishmen in the Revolutionary War, the War of 1812, and the Civil War, are conspicuous in some late histories of the United States, according to Judge Kickham Scanlan of the Circuit Court, who spoke at the weekly luncheon of the Irish Fellowship Club at Hotel LaSalle on February 5.

Plate 3.46
KICKHAM SCANLAN APPEARED TO BE AS PASSIONATE ABOUT HIS LEGAL CAREER AS ABOUT HIS IRISH HERITAGE.

'In Washington Irving's Life of Washington, the writer mentions the names of many Irish colonels at Valley Forge as of colonels of all other nationalities who were there,' said Judge Scanlan. 'Here are the names of some of those Irish officers at Valley Forge, mentioned by Washington Irving, but forgotten by the later historians: Gen Sullivan, Gen. Conway, Col. Moyhan, Col. Conner, Col. Shea, Col. McGaw, Col. Fitzgerald, Col. Crogan, Col. Miles and Col. Kelly. These sound Irish enough.'

'Historians like to keep before the reader's eye the parts taken by the Polish, Pulaski and Kasiuszko, the French LaFayette, and the German Steuben, but they say nothing of the many Irish officers who served this country so well.'"

— *Elaine A Coorens*

SISTER EDUARDA SCHMITZ, S.C.C.

Sister Eduarda Schmitz, of the Sisters of Christian Charity, was an influential figure in the Wicker Park neighborhood as a teacher, administrator and institution builder. She was born Maria Schmitz, January 20, 1855, in Salzkotten, near Paderborn in Westphalia, Germany. In 1871 she entered the Sisters of Christian Charity in Paderborn, and in 1873 she professed her first vows.

The Sisters of Christian Charity had been founded in Germany in 1849, by Pauline von Mallinckrodt. Mother Pauline was originally dedicated to the care and education of the poor, particularly the blind; but she soon expanded her work into education of the sighted as well. When Bismark instituted his "Kulturkampf" (a series of anti-Catholic laws in 1870), many Sisters were expelled from schools in Germany and, at that time, some of them emigrated to the United States.

Sister Eduarda came to America in 1874. She taught elementary school in Scranton, PA, from 1874 to 1884. In 1884 she moved to Chicago to help Rev. Aloysius Theile establish St. Aloysius School in the Wicker Park area, becoming its first principal. Sister Eduarda was also instrumental in establishing Josephinum Academy, a boarding and day school for girls in the neighborhood. First she helped to secure the land. Then she headed up the group of Sisters who raised money for the building. Once the school was built, she served as its first principal and head administrator from 1890 to 1895 and again from 1896 to 1903. She was the Provincial of the North American Province from 1905 to 1921 and again from 1924 to 1927. When the North American Province was split in two in 1927, she became Provincial of the Western Province until 1930.

— *Mary Ann Johnson*

THE SCHULZ FAMILY

Mathias, the Schulz family patriarch, made his home in the Wicker Park District in 1871. Two more generations remained in the district through 1930. The memoirs of Mathias' grandson Otto, Jr. and other biographical writings have provided an opportunity to see a family from inside-out as well as outside-in. In addition, there is a glimpse of some of their family and neighbors with hints of relationships. — E. A. C.

Many terrible events occurred early in Mathias Schulz's life. Any one of them could have caused him to choose an unsuccessful, unfulfilled life. But he didn't; Mathias chose success.

At the time of his birth on July 14, 1842, in Warburg, Westphalia, Prussia, Mathias Schulz was fatherless. Unable to care for him, his mother placed Mathias with relatives. At the age of eleven, as the son of a fallen soldier, he became "entitled to the privileges of the military orphan asylum at Potsdam." Uprooted from family life, he lived at the asylum until beginning an apprenticeship as a cabinetmaker, at age fourteen. At the completion of his apprenticeship, he headed home to visit his mother, only to learn that she had died two weeks earlier.

Plate 3.47
MATHIAS SCHULZ, PATRIARCH, POSES WITH HIS FIRST WIFE, MARIA AUGUSTE.

Plunged into loneliness, he longed for comradeship and for someone to take care of him and be interested in his well-being. He chose to surround himself with a family-type environment — the military. A day before his physical examination, however, he broke his shoulder blade and, therefore, could not pass the physical, dashing his plans for having the military as his "family."

Plate 3.48
EMMA SCHULZ, MATHIAS'S SECOND WIFE, IS PICTURED WITH OTTO JR., IN JULY 1906.

Good fortune entered his life when he arrived in London, where he intended to earn money for passage to America. According to his grandson, Otto, Jr., two very important things resulted from that move for Mathias. He learned the English language and he learned another trade. The completion of Mathias' second year of work in a London piano factory coincided with the American Civil War's completion in 1865, making travel in America safer. So Mathias departed London for New York, and then on to Chicago.

The American piano industry, in 1868, was in its infancy; so Mathias used his skills as a cabinetmaker

*Dolge, Alfred, **Pianos and their Makers**, 1911

to earn a living after he arrived in Chicago. He even tried his hand as a grocer, but decided that there were too many nickel-and-dime sales in that type of business. Within a year, he and two colleagues opened their own business, primarily manufacturing cabinets for sewing machine companies. By 1871, the company expanded its operation to include manufacturing for furniture factories.

At about the same time, he married Maria Auguste L. Horlbeck and they lived on Front St., two blocks from his factory at Morgan and the Chicago River. The 1871 Fire consumed both buildings. The factory was rebuilt on Erie and Carpenter. The home was built on the edge of the city on Damen, just north of Wicker Park Ave. (See *Plate 4.27*.)

Mathias and Maria Auguste had four children: Otto (August 1870); Franz (February 1872) died in infancy; Ida Anna (December 1872); and Maria (September 1874).

A few months after Maria Auguste's death, on September 3, 1875, Mathias married Emma Beck, with whom he had four children: Oskar Karl Friedrich (September 1876) died April 1877; Emma Christina P.H. (September 1877); Clara Amalia Dorothea (July 1879); and Amanda Otilie Bernhardine (January 1882).

In 1876, Mathias bought out his business partners. According to one account:

"With remarkable energy he overcame all the difficulties which beset a young manufacturer who lacks experience as well as capital, and his superior craftsmanship, extraordinary capacity for work, together with his inborn honesty and integrity, soon brought prosperity and his business grew steadily."*

Son Otto, after attending public grade school, spent 1880 at the Morgan Park Military Academy, followed by a year at Bryant Stratton Business College, and then time in his father's factory.

Concerned for his family's well being, particularly after the depression of 1883, Mathias wanted to make sure that there would be income even if something went wrong with this business. So, he constructed a multi-unit building on the east side of N. Damen (1537-9) as an investment, in 1885. (See *Plate 4.27*.) That same year, Otto, age fifteen, took a "minor clerical position" with the American Varnish Company for about eight months, while taking night classes.

Otto went back to work in his father's factory, learning every detail of the business. The company was incorporated as M. Schulz Company in 1889, specializing in pianos and organs. Otto followed in his father's footsteps outside the company as well as in. He too built a multi-unit building on Damen. His was on the west side of Damen from Pierce north to the "L," which was opened in 1895.

In the business, he followed his father as president of M. Schulz Company when Mathias died unexpectedly in 1899. The company was reorganized and the other officers were Emil W. Wolff, Vice President; Frederick P. Bassett, Second Vice President, and Frederick A. Luhnow, Secretary and Treasurer. All three were brothers-in-law to Otto. Wolff was the Factory Manager. The youngest of the three, Bassett, was a Yale graduate, though it is unclear as to what his position was. Otto Jr. revealed that Bassett's college education impressed Otto Sr., "who was largely self-taught and had the inferiority feeling of one who lacked formal education." Luhnow was Treasurer and ran the retail store in their office complex. According to Otto Jr.:

"He (Luhow) was the only one of the uncles who invested some of his own money — $5,000— at the time the company was reorganized… For this investment he was receiving dividends of 300% annually plus his salary, and like the other uncles was getting to the point where he didn't work too hard. He was on embarrassingly bad terms with Papa and they scarcely spoke. It was partly due to the opposite sides they took on the War, with Papa a staunch supporter of Wilson 'making the world safe for democracy,' while Fred Luhnow clung to a deep affection for the Kaiser and all things German."

In the midst of this business turmoil, Otto married Emma Jung. They lived in an apartment on Schiller (Fowler) where the first three of their five children were born: Marie; Otto, Jr.; Carl, George, and William. They moved to Caton St. in 1906. According to Otto, Jr.'s memories of age three:

"I remember lying against the bank of grass that came down from our front yard to the sidewalk… watching the movers unloading… The 'L' was right behind our house, running northwest, paralleling Milwaukee out to Logan Square. It was so close to our house that Carl and I (who later had the room closest to it on the second floor) could hear the loud roar of the trains, and, in the winter, when

Plate 3.49
OTTO SCHULZ, SR. AND EMMA JUNG
IN WHAT WAS PROBABLY THEIR WEDDING PHOTO.

the brushes would arc on the icy third rail, there would be flashes of blue light that would light up our little bedroom.

Except for one three-flat, Caton was a street of homes, and the heads of the households were also the owners of their own small businesses. Mr Hansen, next door, was President of the Security Bank, which he had helped organize with the backing of Mr. Forgan of the First National. On the other side, the Ronnes had a food business. Across the street, Mr. Reudi processed licorice for chewing tobacco. His son took some of us kids to the factory one day and I've never forgotten the wonderful sweet smell. Mr. Thoresen, next to him, had a plant on Robey Street (Damen) that made ornamental iron used to decorate buildings. His twin sons 'Johnny and Jimmy' were great friends of mine in the early days. They were Norwegian and the mother took the twins back to see her folks one summer before World War I. Mr. David, who owned the David Storage Warehouse, was next to the Thoresens and beyond was another family named Hanson. This Mr. Hanson was a partner of Mr. Wieboldt's in the dry goods business, and a brother-in-law of the Bensons, who owned Benson & Rixon, a men's clothing store that became famous because they originated the 'two-pants suit.' There was the Hollander family on the corner, who also owned a storage warehouse, and on our side the Taubers, who built a livery stable on the vacant land north of us.

One hot August night the fat, teen-aged Tauber boy ran down the street in a 'union suit,' shocking the ladies, and shouting fire. In a few minutes we realized the stable was ablaze and we heard the horse-drawn fire engines under full draft, with smoke pouring from their stacks, come galloping down our street. They tried to get the horses out of the barn but dozens were burned to death, and the smell of burned horse flesh permeated the air for weeks."

Telling about how he and his sister, Maria, went to school, Otto, Jr. also remembers the teachers who affected their lives:

"Twice a day, Marie and I made the round-trip to Bancroft School. It was a half mile west and we walked down Wabansia, four long blocks, with-

Plate 3.50
OTTO, JR. AND HIS SISTER MARIE ARE DEPICTED AS THEY FLY OUT OF THE HORSE-DRAWN CARRIAGE DRIVEN BY THEIR FATHER, OTTO, SR.

out cross streets, and vacant (of buildings) on both sides. It was ideal for roller-skating, and I often took my skates. In the winter the adjoining land would freeze and as it was lower than the sidewalk we could ice skate or slide most of the way to school. There was only Western Avenue to cross which was real busy with street cars and lots of wagons, but when we got to school, if there was time, we would have roller-skating races around the block. Bancroft was in an old building but it was a good school with a very capable faculty. The principal was Miss Patterson, a Vassar graduate, who was probably instrumental in heading Marie toward Vassar. I can remember other names, Miss Fuchs the German teacher, and Miss Wilson, who taught me seventh or eighth grade. On real cold winter days Mama would give us money to buy our lunch so we could avoid the long trek back and forth to Caton. There was a little Norwegian restaurant on North Avenue, around the corner from school, where we could get lobskaus, or meat balls with gravy, and potatoes, plus milk and pudding, and bread and butter for 35 cents, or perhaps it was only a quarter."

Though adept in business, Otto, Sr. appeared to have problems with driving both horses and automobiles:

"In later years we had a car and chauffeur and he would occasionally take us to school. The chauffeur was the result of my father's decision not to drive. He had bought a small runabout while we were still on Fowler Street (Schiller) but he only owned it for a few days. He tried to drive it out to Waldheim Cemetery where his mother and father were buried and somewhere out in the country near the cemetery he ran into a ditch. He got a farmer and his team to pull him out and ended up selling the car to the farmer and resolving never to drive again. He kept his promise.

After that, for a few months, we owned a racy little gig and a quite spirited horse, which we kept in Spranger's livery stable on Alice Place. Papa was quite good at handling the reins, but I recall two trying moments. One was when we went under the 'L' on Humboldt Boulevard, just as a train passed overhead. The skittish horse took off with a jump that almost threw Marie and me out of the seat and it was several blocks before Papa could stop him. The other time, we were going north on Milwaukee when the narrow wheel of the buggy dropped into the cable slot, breaking the wheel and throwing us precipitously into the mud and cobblestones of the street. I believe that was the end of Papa's horsemanship."

Sunday was devoted to family and church activities at the Wicker Park Lutheran Church. Pastor Austin Crile's son Herman was a University of Chicago freshman who played on the football team and taught Sunday School. Much to the delight of Otto Jr., Herman, "a husky kid," strayed from the normal Bible lessons by diagramming football plays on the back of the lesson sheets. As Otto said:

"…we knew all about Alonza Stagg even if we weren't too familiar with Peter and John.

The real treat came after Sunday School, when we went a block and a half farther down Hoyne Avenue to Aunt Sade's. Sadie Luhnow was my Mother's sister. She lived with her husband Fred in a second-floor flat. The Luhnows had no children of their own, but Aunt Sade had us, and she was certainly a second Mother. She would be as anxious to see us as we were to get there, and before we got up the stairs, we could smell the taffy boiling away. She would take it out on a marble slab and start pulling and twisting it and cutting it into bite-size pieces. Or in the fall, we would dip Jonathan apples into it, and we would have delicious apple taffies.

Plate 3.51
OTTO, JR. AND GRANDMA SCHULZ ARE DEPICTED AT RIVERVIEW.

In the very early days my Grandfather and Grandma Jung lived with the Luhnows, and Ohpa, as we called him, would read the jokes to me, or give me a quarter and tell me to go over to Engle's candy store, and bring him back two Tom Palmer cigars. I was very proud when I made this purchase, as I hoped they would think I was a four-year-old cigar smoker.

Uncle Fred Luhnow was usually in bed during our Sunday morning visits. When he would get up to go to the bathroom, we would sneak in and feel under his pillow, because we knew he kept a revolver there. He worked for my father in the piano company, and was in charge of the retail store on Milwaukee Avenue. It stayed open on Saturday nights, as did most retail stores, and that was his excuse for staying in bed until noon."

As a child, Otto, Jr., like most children, spent most of his time with the women in the family. Sisters, mothers, and daughters were always "visiting" or doing activities together which included the children. The pre-school children, in particular, had closer ties with the women of the family. In speaking of his experiences with his aunts and grandmother, Otto Jr. said:

"They (his aunts) were all very good to me and so was their Mother (grandmother Schulz), who took me everywhere, including Riverview (Amusement) Park, where her favorite exhibit was the Incubator.

For a quarter you could walk past illuminated showcases with a prematurely born baby in each, and a card that gave their name and weight at birth, and age, and other statistics. The whole thing was terribly boring to me, as I would have preferred a second ride on the miniature railroad, or an exciting descent on the Chutes, where a flat-bottomed boat was taken up to the top of a tower so tall you could see the Masonic Temple, the Loop's largest building, and then the barge was tilted and started down a slide at breakneck speed into a pond of water, where it bounced three times, almost throwing out all of its inmates, though it never did. But my grandmother loved to see the tiny, wrinkled figures behind the thick glass cases and I would stand in the dark passageway waiting for her to have had her fill.

It was more fun when she took me downtown to the toy departments at Christmas time. I remember one occasion when I stayed at Robey Street for several weeks while Marie was down with scarlet fever, and Grandma took me downtown to the stores, and we came home on the Milwaukee avenue streetcar. As she got off at North avenue, she fell while holding me, and of course, so did I, into the mud that covered the street, oozing up around the paving blocks, and people helped us. We were quite a mess when we walked down Robey Street to the big frame house at the Park.

Aunt Clara was a big woman, slightly taller than her husband, and inclined to be heavy. She had boundless energy and was 'into everything' as the saying went. … (her) husband seemed to be quite rich by our standards, and she soon was driving her own car, which was akin to having your own private airplane now. She had a Rouch Lange electric with lots of glass all around, and a lever to steer instead of a wheel. It… was ideal for a woman to use to drive to the grocer, although nobody ever went to the grocer – the cook would call up and do the ordering and the groceries would be delivered within a few hours by horse and wagon."

Aunt Clara's husband was Henry Goehst. According to Otto, Jr., he was "a short stout man, about ten years older than my father, very jovial, usually smoking a cigar." He worked as private secretary to Samuel Insull, head of Commonwealth Edison. When they started Federal Electric Company, Goehst was its president.

By 1917, with their main office at 711 N. Milwaukee, M. Schulz Company had a wholesale branch in Atlanta, GA, and a series of factories in Chicago. They employed more than 700 people. Their subsidiaries included: Werner Piano Company, Brinkerhoff Piano Company, and Magnolia Talking Machine Company. More than 120,000 pianos and player pianos had been manufactured and sold, including Walworth and Irving pianos.

Otto, Jr. describes the office in his memoirs:
"The bookkeepers sat on stools with their legs dangling and their heels catching in the circular rung. Sometimes they did their figures standing and then would climb onto the stools to rest. It was like a Dickens counting house. There was only one private office at the far end of the floor where Papa worked at a table with his back to the big roll top oak desk, the plate-glass windows let in the hot afternoon sun, only partly shielded by wide black shades. Papa didn't draw them very often, as he preferred to look out at Schindler's movie house, and at the Milwaukee avenue streetcars rumbling by."

Otto Jr. went to work at the factory in 1923, after graduating from college and taking a trip given him by Aunt Sade. Since he had worked in the factory for six or eight years during summers, he was on a

Plate 3.52
The Schulz Co. bookkeeping department may have looked this way.

first name basis with the foremen, and working in the factory was familiar and comfortable. However, a few months later he was catapulted into the position of factory manager when "fun loving" Uncle Emil Wolff took off on a world trip and never returned.

By 1924 the radio began to be popular and Schulz sales fell off by 20% in 1927 and 50% in 1928. By 1929 they had just about stopped making player pianos. As Otto, Jr. recalled,

"Papa, who had had heart trouble ever since he was sick with rheumatic fever as a boy, had an attack in 1928 and for the last two years of his life… he was in bed, so it was up to me to try to stem the tide that was running against us. We tried hard by making smaller 'spinet' pianos, and a smaller grand piano reproducer which I called the Marionette. This latter was only three feet six inches long, with six octaves, and a complete electric reproducing action.

… Papa died in the fall of 1929 and immediately the uncles all returned (offering advice), Emil

Wolff, who had been gone since 1924, Fred Luhnow, who had been gone for several years, Fred Bassett, who was a permanent fixture, and even Joe Johnson, who had a successful chair factory with his brothers (Johnson Chair Company), and who was a director of the M. Schulz Co. through his marriage to Aunt Amanda... Uncle Emil was elected President and after looking over inventory, said we were too low on oak pianos, and ordered us to make 200.

I tried to convince him we hadn't sold that many since he left in 1924, and right then couldn't even sell mahogany or walnut pianos, but he went ahead. After a year, he got disgusted, and quit, and I had to take the 400 oak sides and convert them to bookcases and sell them... Fred Luhnow tried his hand at being President for a year or two, and by that time we had stopped manufacturing, so they said I could be President and wind it up. Fortunately we had a log of 'paper,' dealer's notes secured by retail piano time-payment contracts. Between repossessions and the discounts we gave for cash, these were shrinking very fast but we had about two million to start with and we were able to pay substantial liquidating dividends to our stock holders."

As Otto, Jr. was making collection calls, a customer, Jack Powers, talked to him about putting money into his company, the American Automatic Typewriter Company. Though not interested in putting money into Powers' company, Otto was interested in his product, the Auto Typist. Otto, Jr. and his

brothers decided to purchase the Auto Typist for $12,000, of which $10,000 was borrowed from their mother in 1932. That family business would continue for several more decades beyond the scope of this book's time frame.

— *Elaine A Coorens*

Plate 3.53
OTTO, JR. SCHULZ IS SHOWN AT ABOUT THE AGE OF TWENTY-NINE.

SAMUEL SIGAL FAMILY

"Jews fled Russia and Eastern Poland, which was under Russian rule, to avoid the twenty-five year draft. They couldn't marry, keep Kosher, or really have a life. The Russians loved to draft the young Jewish boys," said Joy Sigal Frank, during an interview in the summer of 2002, as she explained why her father, Samuel, emigrated to America in the 1890s.

Samuel was from Vyszkow, Poland, a small town near Warsaw that was under Russian rule. His wife Marie was from Gorlitz, Poland, a town near Krakow that was under Austro Hungarian rule. Their first business endeavor was a pottery store on Maxwell St. They did well and Samuel gave that store to his father when he moved "uptown" to 1266 N. Milwaukee Ave. by 1905.

Their Milwaukee Ave. store was a three-story

ladies' ready-to-wear called The Empire. It was an elevator building with coats on the first floor, millinery on two, and dresses and children's wear on three. Joy was born there in 1908, six years after her sister Flo, and three years after her sister Ruth was born. Brother Marshall came into the world six years later.

When they could afford to buy a home, they moved to Evergreen Ave. in about 1910. In 1915 or 1916, they purchased and moved to 2118 W. Pierce. The Sigals occupied the first floor and the basement. The Greenstones, who had a furniture store on Milwaukee, were their second-floor tenants. The two families had good enough relations that doors between the two units were rarely closed. Explaining how inclusive her family was with people, Joy said:

"We always had people in our house. We

Plate 3.54
IN THE LOWER DINING
ROOM OF THE SEGAL FAM-
ILY'S HOME AT 2118 W.
PIERCE. PICTURED SIT-
TING LEFT TO RIGHT:
LOUIS REIGER; PHILIP
KLAFTER, HANNA
KLAFTER, DAVID
GOLDMAN, MARY
GOLDMAN, ISRAEL SIGAL
(SAM'S FATHER),
UNKNOWN MAN, RABBI
ROSENBLATT, SAM SIGAL,
AND SIX UNKNOWN MEN.
STANDING LEFT TO RIGHT:
RUBY SIGAL EVANS,
FLORENCE SIGAL FISHER,
GERT SHURE (MARIE
SIGAL'S SISTER; MARIE
SIGAL, TWO UNKNOWN
PEOPLE, AND GERT
GLASS.

had a dining room on the first floor, but it wasn't used as a dining room, even though it had dining room furniture. There was a large table in the basement where about twenty people could sit. That is where we generally ate.

I remember my mother ordering a case of salmon and a case of something else! People were always staying with us. We had a family with an open-door policy."

One of their many frequent visitors was a very renowned Cantor, Yosevah Rosenblatt. He came to Chicago periodically to help raise funds for the Daughters of Zion Day Nursery and Infant Home. Joy's great aunt, Mrs. Charna Reiger, was the Founder and President of the organization. An immigrant from Austria, Mrs. Reiger saw a Jewish mother and her two children leave a non-Jewish nursery one day, and make the sign of the cross. Mrs. Reiger stopped the woman and asked why she brought her children there. "I have to work and there is no other place to leave my children," explained the mother. That meeting motivated Mrs. Reiger to establish the Day Nursery and Infant Home. "Mrs. Reiger was a powerful woman and she didn't even speak English correctly," Joy commented. The organization's first location

was at 1444 Wicker Park Ave. A few years later it moved to a larger more modern building at California and Hirsch.

"When Cantor came, everybody wanted to visit, hoping he would sing. But, he wouldn't, until 1:00 in the morning, when they were all gone. I remember that very well," reminisced Joy.

Joy went on to explain that additional organizations, other than synagogues, were also founded during the post World War I period. These included the North-West Fellowship Club. It was established as a social and cultural club, with its own clubhouse in a large former residence.

Talking about some of the early neighbors, Joy also comments on her family members:

"There were many prominent people in the neighborhood then. The Langendorffs had two sons and a daughter, Lena. They had a bakery. Across the street at 2121 W. Pierce, were the Teitelbaums. Evelyn was a flower girl at my sister's wedding. Evelyn became the wife of Jerome Stone, Stone Container, a very prominent family. Beatrice Spachner was a musician who after World War II spearheaded the Auditorium Theater's renovation. The Sabinoffskis were in the fabric busi-

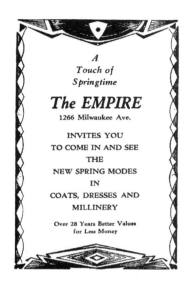

Sportsy Spring Coats

These swagger, little coats with their big shaggy collars or scarfs will be seen at the smartest events this spring. They are of high grade imported and domestic tweeds, and are tailored with expert attention to all details.

$15.00 to $89.50

Plate 3.55a, b, and c
Sam Sigal's store, The Empire, produced promotional booklets.
These three pages are from a 1929 Spring Opening booklet.

ness, possibly on Milwaukee Avenue. They had a son and daughter. Their daughter Maria was married to a Balaban of Balaban and Katz (theatres).

My sister Ruth married David Kapp. He was Vice President of Decca and his brother Jack was President. David eventually started his own company, Kapp Records.

My father loved real estate… he had had pieces all over. Marshall, my brother, followed suit. He got MacDonalds to rent 1266 N. Milwaukee where they built the MacDonalds. That is where I was born.

I liked going to my family's store, though my older sisters did not. Once I was being paid for some work I had done. They gave me my pay in an envelope, but by the time I got upstairs in the elevator it was gone. Somebody swiped it! I cried and cried."

A student at Wicker Park Grade School, Joy remembered the Uihlein mansion on Pierce:

"The teachers, on their lunch hour, would go into the Uihlein grounds. It was beautiful. It was a big show place.

In my time there were many different things. There were wealthy affluent business people and there were very non-wealthy people. When I graduated from Wicker Park School, I did a dance with a girl, from the neighborhood, who couldn't afford very much.

I remember this distinctly because The Empire (Joy's father's store) made an outfit for me. But, the other girl didn't have a new dress. I was thirteen years old, and I felt so badly."

Joy has vivid recollections of the many events

Plate 3.56
Joy Sigal's graduation photo from Wicker Park School.

surrounding her 1921 graduation from Wicker Park Grade School and the following summer:

"Mama took my sisters and brother to New York because my oldest sister was a bridesmaid at a relative's wedding. But, my father stayed here so that he could attend my graduation.

As soon as I graduated, he took me to Atlantic City where we spent the summer. Later in the summer, I got sick and had to have my appendix removed. My father was so concerned, that he took Dr. Zak, who lived on Hoyne, out of his office and took him to a train, so he could take him to me in Atlantic City. There were no airplanes then.

That was August and they wouldn't let me go to school in September. I was supposed to go to Milwaukee Downer where my sister Ruth was, in Milwaukee, Wisconsin. Instead, I went to Tuley High School for a year and a half and then to Miss Spade's School for Girls on Buena. I was in a very big class when I graduated…there were four of us!

Miss Spade wanted me to go East to school to upgrade her standing, she needed it. But, I went to Northwestern University in 1926. I lived at home. I never graduated."

In 1924 the Sigals moved to 446 W. Aldine, an area where other friends had moved. According to Joy, they moved away from Pierce because the neighborhood was changing. It was going down. "And, our family friends were moving north."

Facts Not Fiction…
SMULSKI, PADEREWSKI, AND 2138 W. PIERCE

John F. Smulski (businessman, banker, and politician) and Ignace Jan Paderewski (famed composer and pianist) had one common interest – Poland's independence. Both were avid fund raisers and proponents for efforts to create an independent Poland.

Paderewski came to Chicago three days prior to the 1915 dedication of the Kosciuszko statue in Humboldt Park. (Kosciuszko was a hero of the American Revolution, and in the first uprising in Poland against partitions.) Though he normally traveled and lived in his private railroad car, Paderewski chose not to do so on this journey, since it was to be a fund-raising trip. His early arrival was due to a meeting of the exiled heads of the Polish government at John Smulski's Pierce Ave. home. At that meeting, the National Polish Committee was formed with Smulski as its head from 1916 to 1919. It was head-quartered in the 2138 W. Pierce mansion.

The efforts of the National Committee were most helpful in Paderewski's efforts to be elected the Premier of Poland in 1919, the first democratically elected head of Poland. He held that position for a year.

Since that time, urban legends have claimed that Paderewski owned the 2138 mansion, that it was the Polish Consulate; and that Paderewski performed a memorial concert for Smulski on the exterior porch. While it is possible that before the dedication of the Kosciusko statue Paderewski spent the night in the

Plate 3.57
JOHN SMULSKI IS SHOWN TO THE LEFT OF IGNACE PADEREWSKI.

Pierce mansion, he never owned nor lived in it. It is also possible that he played the piano while he was there. However, there is no information that states he ever gave a concert at the mansion. Paderewski was in the city at the time of a memorial service for Smulski in 1928. It is, therefore, possible he gave a concert in Smulski's honor, but there are no reports about such an event.

It is also not true that the mansion was the Polish Consulate. Poland would have had to own the property for that to be true; and it never did.

John Smulski (originally Jachimski) was born in Posen, Poland on February 4, 1867, the son of Wladyslaw (William) and Euphemia (Balcer) Smulski. William emigrated to Chicago in 1869 and established the first Polish newspaper in the United States, "Dziennik Narodowy." John was educated in Polish schools prior to accompanying his mother to join his father in 1881. Completing his high school in Chicago, he spent two years in St. Jerome's College in Berlin, Canada.

John then entered Northwestern University Law School. After graduation at age 23, he was admitted to the bar in 1890 and immediately began his law practice in the partnership of David, Smulski & McGaffey, for which he worked until 1905. Later David became Judge Joseph B. David and Ernest McGaffey became known as a poet and writer.

Smulski began holding political offices in 1898 when he, a Republican, was elected for the first of three times as Alderman in a staunchly Democratic ward. In the midst of his first term, he married a public school teacher who was also an accomplished singer, Harriet Mikitynski, in 1899. Their first home was at 2145 W. Caton. In 1902 they moved to 2138 W. Pierce. In the late 1970s, Virginia Noel Long, daughter of Smulski's Pierce Ave. neighbor Joseph R. Noel, reminisced, "Mrs. Smulski was an opera singer and they had wonderful parties. My sister and I used to watch and listen out our windows. It was wonderful!"

Smulski served as City Attorney 1903-5, during which time he broke up a combination of unscrupulous lawyers who had been defrauding the City of millions of dollars through crooked damage suits and settlements. He served two different times on the West Park Commission Board, from 1908 to 1912 and from 1917 to 1920. He served as its president in 1908 and 1917.

From 1905 to 1907, he served as the State Treasurer of Illinois, establishing sweeping reforms in handling State monies. A major change was to make sure that the interest received on State funds deposited in various banks, was paid into the State Treasury instead of politicians' pockets. He did have one unsuccessful political effort, which was for the Republican Chicago Mayoral nomination in the February 1911 primary election.

Plate 3.58
THIS IS A PORTRAIT OF SMULSKI THAT IS SEEN IN MANY PUBLICATIONS.

While State Treasurer, Smulski founded the Northwestern Trust and Savings Bank in 1906. According to a March 19, 1928 article in *The Chicago Herald*:

"Until he founded the Northwestern Trust & Savings Bank he was a struggling lawyer who was not bent on amassing a fortune. The organization of that bank with the assistance of Vice President Charles G. Dawes, B. A. Eckhart, Roy O. West and Charles S. Deneen was the keystone of his financial career, which has made him among the richest men of Polish descent in this country.

He was a patriotic American, but he always retained a deep love and devotion for the native land of his fathers—Poland. When the world war broke out he worked incessantly to help the cause of relief of the needy ones in Poland and also of the cause of securing a free and independent Poland. In this he was associated with Jan Ignace Paderewski, M. Dmowski and other Polish leaders.

During the world war, this influence was of great value in his organization of the National Polish Committee. For this service to the allies, the French government bestowed upon him the distinction of the Legion of Honor.

The Polish government recognized his attainments by making him commander of the Polonia Restituta.

Smulski's services to his native land following the world war were admirable. He was instrumental in sending great quantities of food there to remedy conditions resulting from the fact Poland long had been compelled to meet food levies from Germany.

In 1919 he visited Poland, studying conditions at first hand, and upon his return to the United States negotiated loans totaling a billion dollars.

Three years later he was summoned to Poland again to assist in stabilizing exchange."

At the request of his father, he remained the publisher of his father's newspaper for many years. In addition he served as president of Pulaski Lumber and sat on the boards of Depositors State & Savings Bank and Fullerton-Southport Savings bank.

He served as treasurer for Chicago Association of Commerce in 1911 while in 1914 he chaired the Convention Bureau.

Smulski took his own life on March 18, 1928, in his Hotel Seneca apartment, due to incurable cancer that caused extreme pain despite three surgeries and medication. The *1940 Who's Who of Polish Americans* states that Smulski was the only person for whom the city ever held a memorial service. Attesting to his prominence are the lists of active and honorary pall-bearers. Active were: George R. Benson, William H. Schmidt, Cedric Fauntleroy, Julius Smientanka, August J. Kowalski, and Joseph Korzeniewski. Honorary were: Vice President Charles G. Dawes, John F. Devine, Judge Henry Horner, Anton J. Cermak, Judge John R. Caverly, Robert E. Crowe, Congressman Stanley Kunz, Mayor William Hale Thompson, Judge Joseph B. David, William E. Dever, Postmaster Arthur C. Lueder, District Attorney George E. Q. Johnson, Edward R. Litsinger, Julius Rosenwald, Senator Charles S. Deneen, Charles V. Barrett, George M. Reynolds, Oscar Foreman, Judge E. K. Jarecki, Judge S. R. Klarkowski, Judge Peter H. Schwaba, Edward J. Brundage, and Judge Kickam Scanlan.

Prior to his death, he and his wife had adopted twins, John F. Smulski, Jr. and Harriet.

PAUL O. STENSLAND

A prominent, well respected Wicker Park resident, Paul O. Stensland, who came from humble beginnings, enjoyed thirty-five years of fame and fortune until greed and lust caused a bank failure that resulted in Stensland fleeing the country in 1906.

Born in Sandied, near Stavanger, Norway on May 9, 1847, Stensland grew up on a farm with eight siblings. Obtaining what education he could, he left at eighteen for Hindustan and India. With an interest in the cotton and wool industry, he became a supplies buyer, traveling extensively for five years.

Returning to Norway, Stensland found his parents in failing health. Following their deaths, three months later, he set sail for America, arriving in Chicago in the spring of 1871. In August of that year he married Karen Querk of Sonhordland, Norway,

Plate 3.59
PORTRAIT OF PAUL O. STENSLAND

Plate 3.60
AUGUST 6, 1906, SCENE OUTSIDE PAUL STENSLAND'S
MILWAUKEE STATE BANK

with whom he had two children. They lived at 2017 Evergreen.

After focusing his energies on the dry goods business, importing and exporting, he established a private bank and entered the insurance and real estate businesses. From 1889-94, he also owned the Norwegian language newspaper, *Norden.*

He was appointed to the Chicago Board of Education by Mayor Carter Henry Harrison I and served for nine years. Stensland served on the board of directors of the 1893 Columbian Exposition and was involved with the expo's Horticultural Building, along with Edward Uihlein.

Stensland was described as "a man of substantial means, large experience and sound business judgment" in *Chicago, The Marvelous City of the West"* in 1891. "The judgment and forethought of Mr. Stensland

has been such that in no case any one trusting him with investment found reason to regret it," according to the *Illinois of To-Day and Its Progressive Cities.*

Then on August 6, 1906 the doors of the Milwaukee Avenue State Bank closed due to mismanagement and dishonesty. Stensland was accused of embezzling large amounts of money. According to rumor, the almost sixty-year-old widower had spent fortunes on women, especially Leone Langdon-Key, a

Plate 3.61
THIS PHOTO WAS TAKEN IN THE MIDST
OF THE RUN ON PAUL STENSLAND'S BANK.

former music critic for the *Chicago American.* Stensland fled the country, but a $5,000 reward prompted someone to provide information that led to his arrest in Tangier, Morocco.

— *Elaine A Coorens*

FATHER REVEREND ALOYSIUS J. THIELE

Reverend Aloysius J. Thiele was known as the German boss of the archdiocese because of his great influence on the parishes of Chicago. He was born in Westphalia, Germany, and came to the United States in 1863. After completing his studies in Milwaukee he was ordained by Bishop Foley in Chicago in the Church of the Holy Name on December 17, 1870. He served a short term as pastor in Sterling and then at St. Peter's Church in Niles Center in 1872. From there he went to Waukegan and DesPlaines to serve

German parishes, then on to Elgin to act as chaplain of the poorhouse and insane asylum there. He was transferred to the pastorate of St. Henry's parish in Rosehill in 1879 and in 1884 he was appointed by Archbishop Feehan to establish the Wicker Park parish that was to bear the name of his patron saint, St. Aloysius.

Father Thiele became a dynamic leader of St. Aloysius parish and a central figure in the development of the surrounding neighborhood. He built

St. Aloysius Church and School and supported development of two neighboring German churches, St. Francis Xavier and St. Philomena, until they had pastors of their own. He initiated and oversaw the erection of Josephinum Academy and St. Elizabeth Hospital and sponsored other pioneering parishes in the city. He was profoundly interested in the welfare of the poor, especially orphans, and for many years was the spiritual director of the Guardian Angel Orphanage in Rosehill, an innovative social welfare institution. In 1877 he founded *Katholische Jugenfreund*, a monthly magazine published for the benefit of the orphans, which he edited for the next

ten years. Rev. Thiele demonstrated extraordinary business ability and great organizing skills. Archbishop Quigley appointed him Vicar General of the archdiocese in 1909, and six years later Pope Benedict XV conferred on him the dignity of Domestic Prelate with the title of Right Reverend Monsignor. For many years he was also the spiritual director for all the St. Vincent de Paul societies in the Chicago area. Monsignor Thiele remained a friend and adviser of the Sisters of Christian Charity at St. Aloysius until his retirement in 1932. He died in Niles Center on August 2, 1935.

— *Mary Ann Johnson*

WILLIAM THORESEN

Plate 3.62
WILLIAM THORESEN WAS IN THE ARCHITECTURAL
SHEET-METAL BUSINESS.

Architectural sheet metal ornaments are what made William Thoreson a successful businessman. Having emigrated to this country at age twelve with his parents O. C. Thoresen and Sidonia Andersen, he cut his education in Chicago short.

At about fourteen, he went to work, becoming a cornice work apprentice less then a year later. He mastered his trade by eighteen and was offered the foremanship in one of Chicago's largest cornice shops. After seven years he opened his first factory on Western Ave. and secured a contract with the Board of Education.

Over the next five years, William Thoresen

developed an interest in metal ornamentation. He started studying and then designing and making ornaments. By 1897 he expanded his sheet-metal cornice business, devoting his company's manufacturing to architectural ornamentation. The demand for products was so great that he built his own building at 1914-1916 W. North (formerly 419-421 W.), near the intersection of Milwaukee and Damen.

Married to Norwegian-born Sarah Ornes on May 22, 1891, they had four children and made their home at 2147 W. Caton in 1906.

Plate 3.63
SARAH THORESEN, WIFE OF WILLIAM, AND THE FOUR
THORESEN CHILDREN LIVED AT 2147 W. CATON.

Ole A. Thorp

At the age of thirty-four, Ole Thorp explained that he had to overcome prejudice suffered because of birth into the lowly cotter class in Eidsberg, Norway, in order to become successful.

Shipping cargoes of merchandise directly between Europe and Chicago was Ole A. Thorp's earliest professional dream. Thirteen years after arriving in Chicago in 1880, he succeeded in bringing the *Wergeland*, filled with fish, from Norway to Chicago. The ship returned with a cargo load of provisions. Thorp founded O. A. Thorp & Co. and served as its head for twenty years.

As a result of demonstrating the feasibility of making Chicago a port for Atlantic vessels, Thorp was made a member of the deep waterways commission. He was appointed as a commissioner to the World's Columbian Exposition in 1893 and decorated with the Order of St. Olaf in 1899 by King Oscar of Sweden and Norway. He was the first Norwegian American honored with this knighthood.

In 1891, Thorp purchased the part of Mason's sub division that goes from Milwaukee to Leavitt on the south side of Caton, becoming its developer.

Like many other people of the time, Thorp was involved in civic matters and private endeavors. As a member of the board of education for three years, he served as chairman of the buildings and grounds committee. Interested in charitable projects, he contributed in "quiet ways." His residence, at 2156 W. Caton (formerly known as 59 Columbia Place), was known to every Chicago Norwegian. Thorp paid par-

Plate 3.64
Ole Thorp was first Norwegian American decorated with the Order of St. Olaf. He developed part of Caton St.

ticular attention to the welfare of his countrymen.

Ida Amelia Johnson married Ole Thorp on May 23, 1885, at the age of twenty. Ida was born in Chicago to Andrew and Mathilda (Peterson) Johnson and educated in the Chicago public schools. She and Ole had four daughters, two of whom preceded Ole in death. Following an operation for an abscess, Ole died unexpectedly January 25, 1905, in St. Mary's Hospital at the age of forty-nine.

Edward G. Uihlein

One of nine children born to Benedict and Katherine (Krug) Uihlein, Edward Gustav Uihlein was born on October 19, 1845 in Wertheim-on-the-Main Baden, Germany, the third of seven sons. He learned a strong work ethic early in life from his parents who were innkeepers along the Tauber River. He also learned at an early age that springtime and the overflowing of the river could mean much sacrifice, including moving all possessions and food to the top two levels of their building.

By age ten he was butchering; carrying drinking water from the nearest well; working in the inn setting the tables in the guest dining room, carrying the noon meal to and serving the guests in the dining room, clearing tables; and washing dishes. In addition, he was attending school in the morning and afternoon and arts and crafts classes in the evenings from 7:30 to 9:30.

At age fifteen, Uihlein went into an apprenticeship at the general store of Joseph Knapp, Jr. in

Miltenberg, fifteen miles from his home. Two years after his apprenticeship began he was given three days vacation to go home. Two months before the end of his apprenticeship, he decided to go to America. His work at Knapp's was so good that Knapp gave him his apprenticeship certificate early.

In the company of family friends, the Uhrig Family from St. Louis, MO, Uihlein left for America in 1864. After a stop in Chicago, they spent a week in Milwaukee, WI before going down to St. Louis where Uhrig's Brewery was located. It was one of the leading businesses in the U. S. and August Uihlein, Edward's brother, was its manager.

With the recommendation of his brother, Edward was hired in a grocery business where he was able to work and master English. His previous work experience, intelligence and work ethic caused his salary to increase from ten dollars per month to thirty dollars per month, enabling him to move from one task to another. Eight months later, he was offered a bookkeeper's position at Kruz & Hofmeister Brewery for seventy-five dollars a month.

With the financial help of his brothers August and Henry, Edward rented a three-story building in St. Louis in 1866. By sub-leasing part of the building, Edward covered his rent. He formed a partnership with Charles Grath for the manufacture and wholesale of metal wagon parts and oil. Their best customer was Chase, Hanford & Company in Chicago. To save freight costs, Uihlein went to Chicago while Grath stayed in St. Louis. Uihlein open a small factory on West Chicago. Business went well and he opened a small retail store within the factory.

In 1872, Joseph Schlitz offered Uihlein the Chicago Agent position for Schlitz's brewery business, with compensation being a commission per barrel. Though the commission would not equal the profit he was getting from his own business, he felt that the potential with Schlitz was greater so he took the job. Two years later Schlitz founded the Jos. Schlitz & Company brewery with $400,000.

Edward Uihlein had a rich, fulfilled life beyond the business world too. He explains:
> "In the Summer of 1874, I met a Miss Manns, she won my heart. As I had, already attained age 29, I decided to pursue the matter and approach the good nature of Augusta's mother."

They married in January 1875, had four daughters and one son. They enjoyed their home on Pierce as well as a home with twenty-two acres and a 500-foot frontage on Lake Geneva, WI.

His violin lessons at age eight are possibly what instilled a sense of musical interest in Edward. He and his brother Karl played duets and went on to be part of larger groups playing operatic and other classical pieces. Edward went on to sing in the Catholic Church Choir as a child, renewing that expe-

Plate 3.65
A CHILD OF INN KEEPERS IN GERMANY, EDWARD UIHLEIN LEARNED ABOUT HARD WORK AS A CHILD.

rience when he came to Chicago. His invitation to join the St. Peter's (German Roman Catholic) Church choir was followed by being among the first in the German Men's Choral Society. His membership in that group (which included being its perpetual president) continued for more than fifty years.

Edward's interest in gardening was evident by his spectacular conservatory and gardens on Pierce as well as his involvement with the West Park Commission and the Chicago Horticultural Society. In addition, he was a member of: Chicago and Milwaukee Brewers' Association, United States Brewers' Association, and President of German Hospital, later known as Grant. His participation in clubs included: Germania, Orpheus, Teutonia, Maennerchor, and German Press. (See Page 46 and Page 190.)

— *Elaine A Coorens*

Carrie Wilson

Carrie B. Wilson was Head Resident (director) of the Association House of Chicago settlement house from its founding in Wicker Park in 1899 until 1910. She also owned Ridge Farm near Danville, IL, which became the settlement house camp, and was its director from 1910 to 1912. In 1912 she returned to Association House and was its Head Resident until 1916.

Before working for Association House, Wilson worked in the office of the Y.W.C.A. where she was discovered and recruited by Ellen Holt, a founder and leading member of the House's Board of Directors. Wilson was described as "blond, blue-eyed, deeply religious, yet with a sense of humor, and a deep compassion for all." After 1916 she continued to be involved with the settlement house, retiring in 1925. Although she was not a trained social worker, she made Association House her life's work and was dedicated to its development throughout the years.

— *Mary Ann Johnson*

Plate 3.66

Carrie Wilson was the first Executive Director at Association House of Chicago in 1899.

An Afternoon with Emilia

Emilia Skrzypkowski Sherman is a delightful, sparkly Chicagoan who first moved into Wicker Park in 1920 at age six.

Q: **What are some of your earliest memories?**

A: "I remember when I was one and a half. I woke up in a darkened hospital room surrounded by empty beds. Only a nurse came in from time to time…probably to see if I was still alive!"

Q: **That sounds scary, what happened?**

A: "It was *very* scary. Not even my mother could come in. I guess I had something like diphtheria."

Q: **What do you remember of this area from that time?**

Plate 3.67

Teen aged Emilia, laying on the sand, is on the left of her cousin, Amelia. Emilia's mother Apolonia Skrzypkowski is between the girls and Amelia's mother Helen stands behind them.

A: "Well the address was 62 Columbia (2159 W. Caton) and I was six years old when we moved in. People lived in the neighborhood for years. It was safe. Now, people often move in and out within two years."

Q: Where did you go to school?

A: "I went to Sabin for grade school and graduated from Tuley High School. Teachers were much older. Of course, anyone 25 and older is *old* to a child. (She chuckles.)

One day in grade school, someone took a girl's quarter. The teacher said, 'I am not going to ask who did this because I don't want you to be ashamed. Each of you, walk through the cloakroom. The quarter may be left there and NEVER do that again.' We walked through the cloakroom, one at a time. The quarter was there!

Oh, in high school, a boy punched a teacher!"

Q: What did the teacher do?

A: "He fell over! We were all shocked! He was ok. That is the only time we ever heard any such thing happening. Teachers were strict but we listened and did what they said."

Q: Aside from school, what else did you do?

A: "I went to Association House. They had so many wonderful classes and things to do. They had ballet lessons. I, of course, *had* to take that! (A gleam of remembrance dances in her eyes as she smiles.) We had Robins (maybe Bluebirds), Girl Scouts…the boys had baseball and basketball. We played games like drop the handkerchief. It was wonderful!

The Noel State Bank was originally where the Tower Building is now. They built the building where Fairfield Savings (changed to MidWest Bank in 2003) is now. They had a contest for kids with the first prize being a pair of ice skates. I really wanted those skates. A boy won first prize and I won second. I got a box of candy! Boy was I mad! I wanted those skates! (She emphasized her ire with a thump of her fist on the table.)

Plate 3.68
STANDING ON THE LEAVITT SIDE OF HER CATON ST. HOME, EMILIA, POSES AGAINST A FENCE.

Honey, the daughter of Mr. (Ole) Thorp, who originally developed half of Caton St., lived across the street with her husband, two daughters, two Irish Wolfhounds, and five Pekinese. Oh those Irish Wolfhounds were very elegant. Honey's husband Colonel Trygve Siqueland was a very dashing and handsome young man. Their daughters were Alyce and Margo. Margo was the youngest and my age. We were friends.

Honey and her husband were society people and often had parties. Their guests came in chauffer-driven limousines that lined the streets. Guests would come out singing on the porch from time to time. It was very nice. One time I was invited for dinner during a party, but the children were *not* part of the party.

Several very nice Jewish families lived on Alice (now Concord). I had several friends there."

Q: What did you do after you graduated from High School?

A: "I gave a big sigh of relief! (She chortles deeply.) I couldn't get a job. It was the depression. I knew a woman who was a professional physiologist. She worked in a bakery!

My father, who was a tailor with Kuppenheimer, had his job reduced to part time. Do you know that the union did nothing for their members during the depression but they made them pay dues every month! My mother took in roomers, everyone did. They were desperate But…we got along.

Later I worked in a dentist office but got bored and left. I eventually became a bookkeeper. Each morning I took the North Ave. streetcar east to Halsted. There were breweries along there. Many taverns were located east of Halsted where comedians performed. I retired in 1980."

Q: **How did you travel to other places in the city?**
A: "We traveled to my Aunt Harriet's who lived west of Humbolt Park on the El that paralleled North Ave. When we went downtown, we took the Milwaukee Ave. streetcar. At one point it went through a tunnel under water."

Q: **Where did you shop for food?**
A: "Some things were delivered. The iceman delivered the ice. The milkman delivered milk, butter, sour cream, and eggs. You'd walk out the door and it would be there for you! During the summer, Saturday was a special day because the produce man would come with all kinds of fresh fruits and vegetables. We could get 13 bananas for 12 cents. During the winter we didn't get fresh produce very often. Oranges and sometimes a shriveled apple would be a treat.

There was a drugstore on the SouthEast corner of Leavitt and North with an ice cream counter. Across Leavitt was a National grocery store. You went to the counter, told the clerk what you wanted and they would get it for you. Now it takes me half a day to find what I am looking for in the super markets.

Also along North was another grocery store, drugstore, produce store, bakery, and Dr. Kramps office."

Q: **Have you gone to St. Paul's Church since you were young?**
A: "Oh *no*! Only the Norwegians went there. Each Sunday there would be a parade of well-dressed ladies going to church.

By the 1980s the Norwegians moved to the suburbs and neighborhood people, including me, started going there. That was also a period in my life when I traveled. I went around the world once in 1965 and spent Christmas 1984 in Siberia. It was warmer there than in Chicago!"

Q: **Earlier you said that you felt safe when you first moved here. Did that change over the years?**
A: "Yes. I married and moved away in 1953 and 54, but then I moved back home. In the 60s I got my own apartment. I moved back in 1971 after my father died and my mother became ill. During the 70s and 80s, someone grabbed and ran with my purse three times. Then one Sunday I was on my way to church, a 14 year old put a gun to my head. I wouldn't give him my purse, I thought he probably had a play gun. I started screaming and a car came along North Ave., he ran.

The police came, I gave them the description. Later they came back. I cry when I think of it. They brought a skinny little kid of about 12 who was sucking on a lollipop, looking around as though this happened to him all the time. I just couldn't believe they could think this little kid was the person I described.

Things are better now and improving."

Elaine Coorens interviewed Emilia on May 12, 2001
— Elaine A. Coorens

Communications Are Agents Of Change

Plate 3.69
CHICAGO'S FIRST POST OFFICE IS DEPICTED IN THIS PAINTING

Man has always had a need for communicating with others. Whether from cave to cave, door to door, neighborhood to neighborhood, city to city, or continent to continent, options for delivery systems of the written, coded, or spoken messages have not always been great in number. The voracious appetite for communications caused industries to be created and then flourish.

Native Americans delivery systems included feet, horseback, drums and smoke signals in the Chicago area. White men, with their desire to get more information distributed to further points more quickly, expanded their delivery systems to include stagecoaches, steamboats, railroads, wires, telephones, automobiles, and airplanes.

POSTAL SERVICES

With no wire, voice, or visual communications possible for early settlers, the written word was the primary method of communications. Letters and packages were sent and received by individuals and companies using individual travelers or private delivery services such as the Pony Express, stagecoach, and others, as well as military messengers.

Though a United State Post Master General position was established in 1775, steamboats didn't begin carrying mail for short distances until 1831. The railroad was awarded its first contract in 1836, and was constituted as a post road in 1838. Chicago was made a distribution point in 1837.

Locally, people gave verbal messages or written messages from one person to another, or they hired someone to make the delivery. To use the Federal Postal System, one had to go to a facility to mail and pick up mail until the 1860s, when street boxes began appearing.

One of the reasons to create towns was to establish a post office. As an example, Humboldt Park Post Office was established in 1878. Chicago annexed the Humboldt Park Post Office eleven years later in 1889, and the first carrier station was established in July of that year at 1576 N. Milwaukee.

Between 1894 and 1900, the Chicago post office stations were named by letters, "A","G", "U", etc. Operations in the Wicker Park and Humboldt Park areas were then divided into two stations, the Wicker Park station at 1263 N. Milwaukee and the Logan Square station at 1911 N. Milwaukee.

By an Act of Congress on June 25, 1910, the post office also became a place for residents to save money as of January 1, 1911. Since many immigrants were accustomed to postal services including savings functions in their home countries, the legislators determined that this new service would encourage people to take money out of hiding and get it into circulation. With hours that were convenient to the working people, six days a week from 8 a.m. to 6 p.m., people put aside some of their fears and apprehensions about trusting institutions to hold their money, after the bank panic of 1907.

Plate 3.70
THE POSTAL CANCELLATION STAMP SHOWS THIS MAIL WENT THROUGH POSTAL STATION A.

TELEGRAPH SERVICES

Telegraph communiqués to and from Chicago began zinging across the wires on January 15, 1848, when a message traveled from Milwaukee to Chicago. By 1877, the telegraph dominated communications in Chicago. Several companies provided the service that employed an army of delivery boys. Decked out in special uniforms, the boys scurried about town on foot and bicycle. Telegraph poles were prevalent, and wires were strung in profusion. Telegraph communication had two major problems: speed of delivery and accuracy. Customer satisfaction was low in the 1880s.

TELEPHONE SERVICES

Alexander Graham Bell made the first telephone call on March 10, 1876. "Mr. Watson, come here, I want you!" In May 1877, Gardiner Greene Hubbard brought six telephone instruments to Chicago. He and Thomas Watson distributed flyers offering telephone leases…"for social purposes… will be $20 a year, for business purposes $40 a year, payable semiannually in advance."

"Well, what is new in the world?" Edward Uihlein was asked during a Sunday visit at the family home of Augusta Mann, his intended wife. All present were fascinated and eager to hear Uihlein's description of the new invention, the telephone. One of Augusta's uncles, however, pulled Augusta's mother aside. In his memoirs, Uihlien's quotes uncle Mathias Hahn's advice, "If I were in your place, Sophie, I would consider, twice, very carefully, before I would decide to let such a Chicago Humbug marry my daughter!"

Many shared Mathias's disbelief in the sensibility or usefulness of the new instrument. However, in June 1878, two exchanges opened in Chicago on LaSalle St. The first was American District Telegraph (ADT); and one week later came the Bell Exchange, with 267 subscribers. In 1881 the two companies came together as one. The next year there were 2,610 telephones within the city limits; and the count was 6,518 by 1890. The subscriber count jumped to 26,661 by 1900, leading to 575,840 by 1920. It was not unusual to have one phone located in a business such as a drugstore, and many people using it. This sharing made it possible for many families to have limited access to the use of this new miracle of modern day.

RADIO

Twenty-five years elapsed before Marconi's invention started the broadcast industry. Guglielmo Marconi of Bologna, Italy, invented his spark transmitter with antenna in December 1894. It was not until RCA incorporated in 1919, that the meteoric ball of the broadcast media would begin to roll.

AT&T toll broadcasting began in 1922, and the first commercial advertisement aired on August 28. NBC was formed in 1926 by RCA, GE, and Westinghouse. William Paley, who was in Chicago's cigar manufacturing industry (LaPalina Cigar Co.), helped create the United Independent Broadcasters in 1927, which became the Columbia Broadcasting System (CBS) in 1928.

In his memoirs, former Wicker Parker resident Otto Schulz, Jr., explains how radio popularity was tied to radio instrument production:

"The radio was beginning to be popular by 1924. That summer the Democratic Convention, that ran to more than 100 ballots in Atlantic City, was broadcast nationally. Al Smith failed to get the nomination, but radio was established as a necessity for every home.

The sets were big, clumsy boxes with separate speakers and batteries. The better music dealers wouldn't buy them as they didn't think they would last," he continues, "so they were sold by electric shops. By 1926 there were 'battery eliminators,' which meant you could plug the radio into any electric socket and the following year the 'dynamic speaker,' with a much wider range of tone, was introduced. In 1927, Majestic offered a handsome cabinet that incorporated chassis, speaker, and battery eliminator into a single unit for $150 and the radio business was off and running. Atwater Kent, Sparton, Stromberg, RCA, Philco, Crosby, and many others followed suit and all found a lush profitable market."

This invention changed many things. People learned of news more quickly and had a center of entertainment that partially started the erosion of families communicating with each other through conversation, playing cards, or games.

NEWSPAPERS

Chicago is rich in history of citywide newspapers, beginning with publication of the city's first newspaper, *Chicago Democrat,* on November 26, 1833. A four-page weekly, it had six columns by John Calhoun. He sold it to Mayor John Wentworth in 1836. *The Chicago American* was the second newspaper. Its first weekly publication was on June 8, 1835, by O. T. Davis. In October 1842, a daily, *The Chicago Express,* was published by William W. Brackett, followed by *The Chicago Daily Journal* in April 1844, published by Richard L. Wilson and J. W. Norris, who also were responsible for the editorial management. *The Chicago Republican* had its first issue on December 14, 1842. A weekly, it was produced by A. R. Niblo. *The Chicago Tribune* came on the scene for the first time on July 10, 1847. *The Chicago Tribune* would affect much more than the dissemination of news. It became embroiled in local and national politics as well as product success for people such as Wicker Park's Theophilus Noel (See Pages 40).

Though there were neighborhood newspapers as early as the late 1800s, only one has surfaced that served Wicker Park. Entitled *Wicker Park Eagle,* it was published by Albrecht Bros. Printers & Publishers, located at 1632 N. Winchester. This monthly publication professed to be "Published in the interest of Wicker Park and the North West Side" and was "The North-West Sides Most Exquisite Monthly Newspaper. Spicy and Clean." Providing information about area activities, events, crimes, weddings, births, deaths, helpful hints, and recipes (as well as advertising), it began publishing in 1900 and was still publishing in 1916, though it is unclear as to when and why it ceased being published.

— *Elaine A. Coorens*

POST CARDS ARE WINDOWS FOR VIEWING LIFE

Three by five inch postcards from the late 1800s and the early 1900s are open windows on everyday life of the period. Their pictures recorded scenes, buildings, people and events. Their messages conveyed need for help, romantic teasing, love, appointment setting, family news, general news, and greetings in celebration of personal events, as well as public and religious holidays.

When the penny postal card was authorized in 1872, only the recipient's name and address and the printed postage were allowed on one side. The other side was printed with a greeting or advertising. No space was designated for a message.

Plate 3.71
THIS WAS ON THE ADDRESS SIDE OF THE FIRST POST CARDS ISSUED BY THE GOVERNMENT IN 1872, WITH STAMPED ON POSTAGE .

Though an Act of Congress on May 19, 1898 permitted privately printed cards with no imprinted postage, they were to show the phrase "Private Mailing Card." As before, only the addressee and postage were to appear on one side. This change had no effect on the space allotted to a written a message. With virtually no telephones available, post cards were a way to send a message, though small, to someone more quickly than visiting or asking someone else to deliver your note or message. It was also less expensive than hiring a courier.

Plate 3.72
AN ACT OF CONGRESS IN 1898 ALLOWED CARDS TO BE PRINTED PRIVATELY WITHOUT POSTAGE PRINTED ON THEM.

In 1907, the post card came of age when the Legislature permitted the postage side of the card to contain message, address and postage. For one penny, postcard users relied on their messages being delivered the same or the next day! Multiple postal deliveries per day generally meant same-day service was assured.

These charming, fun, and informative cards have allowed cities and neighborhoods as well as family histories to be discovered, preserved, and cherished. In her collection, this author not only discovered a sweet romance between her Norwegian maternal grandparents, who like

so many other immigrants lived along North Ave., but that the family name was changed, as happened to so many immigrants, from possibly "Bengtson" to "Benson."

Lack of delivery timeliness and reliability has relegated post card use in current times to travelers and advertisers. They send greetings or taunts such as "Wish you were here." and "When in ___ be sure to see this spot."

— *Elaine A. Coorens*

Plate 3.73
IN 1907 THE CONGRESS PASSED LEGISLATION THAT ALLOWED A MESSAGE TO BE WRITTEN ON THE ADDRESS SIDE OF THE CARD.

Plate 3.74 a and b
ROMANCE WAS DEFINITELY IN THE AIR WHEN JOHN E. BENSON SENT THESE CARDS TO ANNA JOHNSON PRIOR TO THEIR MARRIAGE ON AUGUST 24, 1907. (JOHN E. BENSON BORN AS JOHANNES BENG(Y)STEN IN OSLO, NORWAY IN 1877 AND ANNA M. JOHNSON, BORN IN ODALEN, NORWAY IN 1884). CAPTIONS ARE: "WHY DOES HE KEEP ME WAITING?" AND "AT LAST WE HAVE THE HOUSE TO OURSELVES."

Wicker Park Eagle REPORTS ON NEWS OF THE TIME

In 1900 a publication called the *Wicker Park Eagle* produced its first issue. Albrecht Bros. Printers at 1632 N. Winchester were the publishers. Though the date of its last issue is unknown, following are excerpts from several issues dated April 1909 to January 1916.

You will recognize some people mentioned elsewhere in this book and you will learn about others not previously mentioned. Some news is good, some is not, other is amazing, and yet other is fun or funny. Additional excerpts may be found in the Walking Tour section at the back of this book.

Published in the interest of Wicker Park and the North-West Side. :: :: :: ::

Wicker Park Eagle

The North-West Sides Most Exquisite Monthly Newspaper. Spicy and Clean.

Single Copy 5c   Chicago, August, 1913   Vol. 13 No. 6

Plate 3.75
ABOVE IS A PHOTO OF THE AUGUST 1913 FRONT PAGE FROM THE *Wicker Park Eagle*.

PIONEER RESIDENT DIES
—Herman Kirchhoff

Herman Kirchhoff, a pioneer resident of Chicago and one of the oldest settlers on the North West side, died at his home, 1344 N Hoyne Ave., on Sunday, February 27, at the age of 63 years.

Mr. Kirchhoff at one time had the largest sash, door and blind factory in the West. During the panic of 1893, immediately after the World's Fair, he was forced to close his doors. After strenuous efforts to retain what he had lost, he at last gave up in despair. The direct cause was his placing too much confidence in two men whom he thought trustworthy.

He was born in Germany in 1847. Upon his arrival in this country he immediately went to Honey Creek, WI. Being a carpenter and contractor he finally came to Chicago to follow his trade. He was a man of wide experience, having traveled extensively, not only in this country but abroad.

He leaves a widow, Mrs. Elizabeth Kirchhoff, and three daughters, Mrs. H.C. Burdt, Mrs. R. D. Strong and Mrs. E. E. Utz. The Burial was a simple one. Burial was at Waldheim. *–February 1910*

FIRE DEPT. REPORT

Fire in a three story building at 1734 West Division Street, last week, drove four families to the street and caused a loss of $1000 damage.

When Engine Company No. 30 in charge of Battalion Chief Heaney arrived at the scene they detected the odor of oil and later found matches saturated in alcohol lying about the floor, which was occupied as a cigar and confectionery store by Nathan Israel. The building is owned by M. Marcus. *–February 1910*

WICKER PARK WOMEN'S CLUB

It was eighteen years ago that twelve women from the Northwest Side decided to form a club which would share in the efforts to elevate humanity. They wanted also to benefit themselves socially and intellectually and they decided to make their organization one that would be lasting. So the Wicker Park Woman's Club was formed with a limited membership of 200. It is now full with a waiting list and the work that has been done has far exceeded the expectations of the original twelve members.

The founders of the club. Mrs. Kickham Scanlan, Mrs. William Severin, Mrs. Henry Hertz, and Mrs. Henry Schroeder, started a culture club, but the name was changed to read "Woman's Club" in 1909. Its work now includes art, literature, domestic science, philanthropy and civics.

Mrs. John F. Devine, is the club president being the eleventh one to hold the office. *–January 1916*

REAL ESTATE MARKET ACTIVE

An interesting transaction made during the week was the conveyance by H. Escher to Miss Clara C. Nieman of the property at the northeast corner of Milwaukee Ave. and Division St., 24 x 62 x 102 x 119.7 feet, with brick business improvements, for $60,000. Miss Nieman gave back a trust deed to the Chicago Title and Trust company, for $45,000 ten years at five percent.

L. Hoeft is erecting at a cost of $75,000 a two-story store and loft at 1441 Milwaukee Ave. Fritz Lange is the architect.

Michael G. Mayer, carrier at Wicker Park Postal station, has purchased from A. Stoltze the three story flat building at 2507 W. North Ave., near Campbell Ave. at a cost of $9,590 with an encumbrance of $4,900.

Other transfers recorded were, Premises at 1418 N. Paulina St., west front, 221x100 feet, Fred Mayer to John Mayer for $4,250. Armitage Ave., 236 feet east of Oakley, north front, 24x100 with an encumbrance of $1,700. M. Huth to John Cichowski, for $4,000. *–February 1910*

CLUBS and NOTES

On February 1st, known as Philanthrophy Day, Mrs. Kickham Scanlan, presided at a meeting of the Wicker Park Woman's club.

Mrs. Ringland, Superintendent of the Visiting Nurses Assn., spoke of the good work in this district and of the cooperation of the Women's Clubs in this noble work.

The visiting nurses are indeed a blessing. Anybody desiring their services may apply to the organization for help in the care of the sick. If you are able to pay a small amount it is always acceptable from .25 a visit to $1.00 per day—when you have the services of the hourly nurse. This is without a doubt a great help to those with but a moderate income, as the trained nurses generally ask an outrageous fee.

A St. Patrick's party will be held at Clubhouse, 1634 N. Winchester Ave., on March 17.

Miss McClemmens, teacher at the Burr School, was welcomed by her scholars, upon her return to her duties, after a successful operation upon her eye.

Theodore A. Ottow, 1640 N. Winchester Ave., of the United States Marines, has arrived in Cuba with his company. They are stationed at Guantanamo Bay.

Miss Margaret Johnson, 2020 Wabansia , daughter of Mrs. Johnson, was operated upon for tonsillitis. She was confined at the Norwegian Lutheran Tabitha Hospital. She is doing nicely.

The cigar store and billiard room owned by S. B. Blumenfield, 1311 N. Western Ave, was damaged by fire at 2.a.m. on February 10. Loss was small.

Miss Catherine Ingeborg Erickson, 1937 N. Hoyne Ave., chaperoned a theatre party at the Crown Theatre Monday evening, February 21. –*February 1910*

GIRL'S PLEA TO LEAVE SCHOOL
FOUND ON WALK—*Pathetic Note Says Writer Will Die of Grief if She is Not Allowed to Return Home*

A little girl's pathetic appeal for permission to return to her home and loved ones from whom she has for the first time been parted and evidently placed in an educational institution by her parents, is made in the following note penciled upon a slip of paper dated March 3 and found on the pavement at Crystal and Robey Streets early Saturday morning by W. Frankel of 1943 Crystal St.

"Dear Mamma: 'Oh, I am so tired of this place. I cannot learn so many things at once and I cannot bear going to bed without kissing you. You know, mamma, I have never been away from you before and I feel as if I should die of grief. If you do not let me come home again. Do, mamma, do, and I will love you forever. Your miserable Child, Mamie." –*March 1911*

CHAMBER OF COMMERCE ORGANIZED

Permanent organization of businessmen and property owners of the North-West side into an association which will provide the benefits of a "Chamber of Commerce" for this section of Chicago was effected at a meeting at Gersten's hall, Ashland Ave and Division St, Friday. evening, Feb 24

The association will cooperate with the improvement and commercial organization and foster the work being carried on by these branches. Public questions, which the new body plans to take up include: street cleaning, garbage removal, street illumination, adoption of street signs and through routing of street cars.

Officers elected at this meeting were: Pres. R.I. Terwilliger, VP-Otto Schulz, Edward Alswede, Moritz Bendheim, Sec-Geo. L. McCararon, Treas- Jens C. Hansen. The directors are Richard Parroll, John S. Edwards, Iver L. Quales, Thomas F. Deuther, Joseph R. Noel, A.C. Sievers, F.A. Mauer, Chas. Lange, Paul Drysmalski and Chas. C. Breyer. –*March 1911*

BRIEF MENTION

The Baraca Boys' club beat Mrs. Gales'class in a debate, "Resolved that young women are more frivolous than young men," at the church parlors, on Friday, Feb 17.

Mr. Carl Whitengen and Miss Hazel Nestle were united in marriage on Feb 18. Mr. Whitengen formerly resided at 1221 N .Robey. Pastor Gale of the Wicker Park M.E. Church, performed the ceremony. –*March 1911*

BUSINESSMAN KILLED

Funeral services for Emil Iverson, the Milwaukee Ave. businessman killed in an auto crash with his companions, Richard Carroll and John Gauer, were held at the chapel of Frank Mueller, Ashland and Milwaukee avenues and at the Wicker Park Lutheran Church, Hoyne and Lemoyne st on Sat. June 14. Vast throngs filled the streets as the funeral cortege wended its way to the church. A detail of police kept the crowds in order. At the church the Rev. Anda and Rev. Dent lauded the dead merchant in impressive sermons. –*June 1913*

FIND NOBLEMAN WAS VICTIM OF
ARSENIC—*Accused his wife*

Jan N. De Latour, slain Galician nobleman and Russian exile, died of arsenic poising. Analysis of the viscera of De Latour by the Coroner's physician revealed large quantities of the drug. Coroner Peter Hoffman immediately took steps to reopen the inquest later in the week.

The chemist's findings, which were reported to Coroner Hoffman were communicated to Lieut. Duffy of the Rawson street Police station.

De Latour died at his home, 1520 North Wood street, Aug. 8. Before he died in great agony he accused his wife, Wanda De Latour, of having poisoned him. Two days before death he had written a letter to the Polish National Alliance, of which he was a member, in which he asked a thorough investigation if he should die suddenly.

On complaint of Attorney Max Kaczmarek of the Alliance, Mrs. De Latour was arrested on a charge of murder. She was released on $5,000 bail.—*August 1913*

HOLD UP MILLER'S RESTAURANT
— *Men Easily Escape*

On Friday, August 15, two youthful highwaymen held up Miller's Restaurant at 1546 N. Robey street and escaped.

At 2:55 a.m. the pair entered and after giving their order pressed revolvers before the eyes of the astonished cashier and waiter.

After looting the cash register of $35, the men escaped. The Robey street Elevated station is only a few feet from the restaurant and a train going down town had passed just a short time previously. Police of the West North avenue station searched the neighborhood but no trace of the men was found. .—*August 1913*

STENSON BREWING FINED

Stenson Brewing Company, North Winchester Ave. and Bloomingdale road were fined as violators of the smoke ordinances of Municipal Judge Scovel. –*February 1910*

Bath Houses and Hygiene
Are Old Wicker Park Traditions

Plate 3.76
**GIRLS LINE UP IN THE
PLAYGROUND AREA OF
ASSOCIATION HOUSE
ON NORTH AVE. FOR
THEIR BATHS.**

From 1600 through 1899 public and even private bathing in Chicago was not a frequent experience of most residents. By the beginning of the 1900s, people began to appreciate that good hygiene was related to good health, and bathing gained popularity.

Bathrooms and hot running water were still novelties in many buildings in the late 1800s and early 1900s. Sewers and water services gradually came into the neighborhood starting in 1873. It was therefore understandable that hundreds of thousands of Chicagoans would stand in long lines to take hot showers at the city's expense. The Chicago Board of Health opened the first free public bathhouse in the world in 1894.

The concept of public baths was not totally embraced by everyone because many people thought illicit activities were going on in these facilities. Even as late as 1906, an entry in the Biennial Report of the Chicago Health Department explained:

"…(bath houses) have not been established as places of diversion and pleasure, but to promote habits of personal cleanliness and of enabling those who are not provided with bathing facilities at their homes or places of lodging, to observe the fundamental rules of health and sanitation."

With great praise for Chicago, New York's Dr. Simon Baruch, originator and proponent of the "free cleansing bath," wrote in 1905:

"Chicago was the first city in the world to take up my idea that Public Baths should be free. You have demonstrated to the world that the view, I announced in 1890, which regarded the public bath as a hygienic necessity, to be approved by cities, like public parks, and which was at that time regarded as utopian, was sound and practical. I could not convince any one of the 3 mayors to whom I appealed for this boon to the working people of New York even after your city had offered a practical demonstration that the people would use these baths."

Each bather was given a free bar of soap and a towel. Allowed twenty minutes to undress, shower, and dress. Seven to eight minutes of that time was for the water to run "full force." By 1919, nineteen bathhouses were built in Chicago. However, the reduction in city revenue, due to prohibition, caused the city to charge bathers five cents for the soap and towel.

Plate 3.77
BOYS WAIT FOR THEIR TURN AT THE BOYS' BATHING FACILITIES AT ASSOCIATION HOUSE.

Public bathhouses were in areas with concentrations of rooming houses and apartments with no bathing facilities. Medill Bath at 2138 W. Grand was the public bath closest to Wicker Park. Total cost for four city staff people in 1904 was $2,380.00 in salaries. That year they served 588,596, and 621,893 in 1905. Medill's usage in 1919 was approximately 43,000; in 1920 it was 25,000, and in 1921 it went back up to 32,300. In that time frame, Medill's male caretaker was paid $1,440 annually, and the female attendant $1,080. By 1930 there were nineteen city-owned facilities.

Two days a week were scheduled for the exclusive benefit of women and girls, while the rest of the week, except for Sundays, were reserved for men and boys. School children and working men were the predominate users.

Social service agencies such as Association House of Chicago provided free bathing facilities as well as many other child- and adult-oriented programs.

Private bathhouses began to open at the beginning of the 1900s. They offered other types of bathing experiences including dry heat rooms (saunas), heat with steam created by throwing water on red hot stones; and a small room filled with steam so hot, it required stooping low with a towel over your mouth to insure that you keep breathing. Some had a swimming pool, whirlpool, sleeping rooms, and massage rooms. In the steam room, most had oak leaf brushes, which were soaked in buckets and soaped. One bather would assist another by scrubbing them with the wet soapy leaves. Almost all facilities had a restaurant area.

Be they public or private baths, they all had women's areas and men's areas, each of which had their own exterior entrance.

The Division Street Bath at 1916 W. Division became a vital and thriving part of the neighborhood in 1906. It took another twenty years before the North Avenue Baths (later called the Luxor) was built at 2039-41 W. North.

Bathhouses have always been a "melting pot" for the neighborhood. Many Wicker Park residents of various ethnicities, ages and backgrounds have enjoyed the experiences of the bathhouses since their inception. As one story goes, according to a bathhouse owner, a Judge was at the bathhouse. He recognized a man whom he had given a harsh sentence, several years prior. The Judge suggested to the bathhouse owner that he might not want people *like him* at the bathhouse. The owner asked if the man had in anyway hurt the Judge. The judge said, "No." "Then," the owner replied, "if he did not do anything wrong, he is welcome." A few weeks later, the owner was taking a bath himself and noticed that the Judge was giving an oak leaf scrub to the man he had given a harsh sentence. This is just one of several examples of barriers that separate us in daily life, but vanish upon entering the bathhouse. It is a safe place where people are treated with respect and become like family.

Rumor has it that many a mob (gangster) meeting has taken place inside Wicker Park bathhouse walls. Since it is a bathhouse and most people are wearing little to nothing, it would be quite difficult to hide a wire or a weapon. If only walls could talk.

Researched by Elaine A. Coorens and Carol Scheidelman

— *Elaine A. Coorens*

Entertainment explodes with…
Nickelodeons and Theatres

Plate 3.78a and b

THE STAR THEATRE, WHICH OPENED IN 1887 AT 1455 N. MILWAUKEE, WAS IN BUSINESS UNTIL AFTER
THE TURN OF THE CENTURY AS CAN BE SEEN HERE AND ON THE NEXT PAGE.

Nickelodeons and cinemas exploded as an entertainment opportunity for all economic levels of the community's residents, as the 1800s turned into the first two decades of the 1900s. There was a production studio and up to thirty-one theatres in the community.

A wide variety of theatre types were in the area. They ranged from full theatre stock theatres which were equipped for presenting plays (such as the Crown on Division) to typical nickelodeons, and cinema only buildings such as the Wicker Park/Bell. No large movie palaces were possible, because of the cost of assembling parcels of land. The closest "palace" is the Congress a few blocks north on Milwaukee, with its 3,000 seats. Of the same size, the Harding, just above Logan Square, was its sister theatre.

In 1887, there was one theatre in Wicker Park at 1455 Milwaukee. It opened as the Star Theatre, and was the Royal Theatre from 1907-1976.

Between 1905 and 1921, storefront nickelodeons appeared overnight and disappeared almost as quickly.

THEATRES OF WICKER PARK

(Years below indicate span of building existence, not years of operations.)

NAME	ADDRESS	YEARS
PREMIER	1237 ASHLAND	1915-?
BANNER	1611 DAMEN	1910-1950
CHOPIN	1541 DIVISION	1918-1923
HARDING		1926-1930
CHOPIN		1932-1948
PIX		1948-1950
CHOPIN		UNKNOWN
MOZART	1606 DIVISION	1912-1913
CROWN	1607 DIVISION	1909-1959
ASHLAND	1609 DIVISION	1910-?
PASTIME	1949 DIVISION	1914-1987
BILTMORE/SAN JUAN	2046 DIVISION	1921-1991
NEW STRAND	2111 DIVISION	1915-?
MONARCH	2123 DIVISION	1912-1915
LYRIC/PEERLESS	1217 MILWAUKEE	1911-1933
IOLA	1238 MILWAUKEE	1907-1921
AMERICAN/BISMARK	1252 MILWAUKEE	1907-1927
WHITE FRONT	1255 MILWAUKEE	UNKNOWN
FAIRYLAND	1254 MILWAUKEE	1909-1912
ASHLAND	1257 MILWAUKEE	1906-1910
TRY IT/WONDERLAND	1335 MILWAUKEE	1908-1913
ROYAL	1369 MILWAUKEE	1910-1915
GEM	1390 MILWAUKEE	1910-1912
UNKNOWN NAME	1391 MILWAUKEE	1909-?
UNKNOWN NAME	1398 MILWAUKEE	1907-1908
UNKNOWN NAME	1435 MILWAUKEE	UNKNOWN
STAR	1455 MILWAUKEE	1887-?
ROYAL		1907-1976
HOME/BELL	1539 MILWAUKEE	1912-1921
WICKER/W.PARK		1929-1955
PALACE	1915 MILWAUKEE	1908-1912
REX	1926 MILWAUKEE	1910-1912
GRAND	1937 MILWAUKEE	1910-1912
NORTH AVE.	1819 NORTH	1908-1909
UNKNOWN NAME	2031 NORTH	1907-1909
PAULINA	1335 PAULINA	1913-1985

Source: Joseph R. DuciBella, Chicago Director   Theatre Historical Society of America, 152 N. York Road, Elmhurst, IL. 60126

Plate 3.78b

Theatre licensing was non-existent; anyone could offer the cinema experience. Furthermore, it was inexpensive entertainment for the theatregoers.

Mostly mom and pop operations, funded by family savings, a projector was bought or rented. Sometimes old chairs were used for seating and a white painted square or sheet became the screen. Aunt Effie played on a beat-up piano to accompany the silent flicks, in theatres such as the Iola and Peerless.

By the 1900 teen years, cinemas were constructed, many by previous nickelodeon owners, usually larger, with better air circulation, décor, and music, such as the Bell/Wicker Park and Strand. The large Royal was actually a roller skating rink around 1880, remodeled into a theatre with full stage in 1907. Certainly the neighborhood's largest theatre was the Biltmore/San Juan/Alameda on Division Street.

Famous theater architect John Eberson designed the Crown Theatre, his first Chicago-area theatre. Carl Laemmle opened one of the nickelodeons at 1253 N. Milwaukee. He later founded what is now Universal Studios.

— Joseph DuciBella

ANOTHER THEATER FOR NORTHWEST SIDE...
OLD ROBEY RINK THE LOCATION FOR NEW ENTERPRISE

Old Robey Rink, 1611-15 N. Robey St. (Damen) is new theatre which will open its doors to the public. Entirely renovated for $10,000, will contain a large stage with steel curtain and balcony with a seating capacity of about 800. F. C. Smalley, of the Smalley Manufacturing Company 1835 W. Lake St., who has the lease for the theatre, says "nothing but

high class numbers will be staged." Wm. J. Van Keuren with offices at 78 La Salle St. is the architect.

—From the Wicker Park Eagle, Feb 10, 1910...

Plate 3.79
NEAR THE END OF THE 1920S, BERNICE SNOW AND WALTER BARCZYKOWSKI (ON THE LEFT) POSE IN FRONT OF THE THEATRE WITH THEN BANNER OWNER, H. S. MACDONALD (ON THE RIGHT.).

Plate 3.80a and b
THE OUTDOOR ENTRANCE OF SITTNERS BANNER THEATRE WAS ORIGINALLY ORNATE IN 1910 AS SEEN HERE. BY THE LATE 1920S (BELOW), THE BANNER'S FRONT LOOKED QUITE DIFFERENT.

Plate 3.81
THIS MID-1920S CLOSE-UP OF THE BANNER'S LOBBY SHOWS BERNICE SNOW IN THE BOX OFFICE AND WALTER BARCZYKOWSKI IN HIS USHER'S UNIFORM

Taverns, Saloons and Restaurants

Specific information about food and drinking establishments in early Wicker Park has been elusive. Quaife in *Chicago's Highways Old and New* paints interesting images about pest conditions in public and private dining areas. He cites a quote from *Illinois in the Fifties* that describes the village tavern:

"There were, he relates 'Flies everywhere! Flies in everything! Flies on everything! But little wonder, for at no great distance from the kitchen door was a big manure pile—an ideal incubator for hatching these household pests.'

To combat them, in private homes as meal-time approached, someone procured from a convenient bush or tree a branch well supplied with leaves, and by plying this vigorously during the meal the flies were to some extent kept from the table. People in better circumstances signified their station by substituting for a branch from a tree a brush made of ostrich feathers.

In the tavern, still another device was employed. 'About three feet above the dining-room table and extending its whole length was a strong cord to which was attached strips of paper that nearly reached down to the dishes. At meal time it became the duty of someone to manipulate this cord in such a way that the papers hanging below it were set in motion and the flies kept for the time being from alighting on the food.'"

Food fare in the mid 1800s in taverns included such breakfast offerings as corn-meal griddlecakes or biscuits, buttermilk, coffee, fried pork and venison. Dinners might include large pots with savory fragrances. Though guests would contemplate the possibility of it including turkey, venison, or prairie chicken, it was often rabbit.

Taverns and saloons were part of the culture of many immigrant groups. Many establishments, particularly if they were owned by Germans, had special family entrances. Eating and drinking as a family was part of their culture.

City directories from 1876 listed roughly ten saloons in the district with several restaurants along Milwaukee Ave., but all were south of Chicago Ave. The 1886 saloon count in the Wicker Park District was about seventy, while the restaurant count was two. The directory saloon count soared to 149 by 1917 before plummeting to zero, due to Prohibition, by 1923. Restaurants increased from twenty-six in 1917 to thirty-four in 1923.

Though a 1943 *Chicago Tribune* article identified "Penzhorn & Sauerbrei, and Hagedon's White Horse tavern," as restaurants of note in early Wicker Park, there appears to be no additional information about specific restaurants (including these two).

TWO FAMILIES PURCHASED TAVERNS AFTER PROHIBITION BEGAN

Prohibition began in January 1920. Some taverns transitioned into ice cream parlors, others into restaurants, and others were closing their doors. Yet two families purchased taverns in the Wicker Park District in 1920. They were Charley and Mary Schroeder and Frank and Sophia Bolit.

According to the May 1, 1920, Bill Of Sale between the seller, John J. Dietz and the purchaser Charles Schroeder, $800 was to be paid by the purchaser for:

"The following goods and chattels, to-wit:
One back bar; one front bar; one ice-box; one cash register; one cigar case and all the chairs, tables,

kitchen utensils, glassware and other chattels contained in and about the premises known as 1256-58 N. Paulina Street, Chicago, Illinois.

The Bolits purchased two Wicker Park bars. The first was 1850 N. Damen (Robey) and the second was 1809 N. Hoyne.

Both Schroeders worked two jobs. While Charley worked as a cook and bartender for Henry Katnig at the Wicker Park Hall, 2040 W. North, Mary tended to the restaurant/saloon and taking care of their one daughter Elsie. Although they had help from a a friend who tended bar, a waiter, and a woman who

Plate 3.82
PURCHASED IN MAY 1920, THIS RESTAURANT/TAVERN AT 1256-58 N. PAULINA BELONGED TO MARY SCHROEDER METZGER (RIGHT) AND HER SECOND HUSBAND NICHOLAS METZGER (BEHIND THE BAR) AT THE TIME THIS PHOTO WAS TAKEN BETWEEN 1921 AND 1927. THE OTHER PERSON IS UNIDENTIFIED.

Plate 3.83
FRANK AND SOPHIA BOLIT, ALONG WITH THEIR FIRST CHILD PETER, ARE BEHIND THE BOLITS' FIRST BAR AT 1850 N. DAMEN

cooked, it was a very busy and hectic time.

Diagnosed with prostrate cancer in February 1920, Charley's health continued to decline. Prior to his death on June 7, 1921, Charley wrote a letter to his wife and daughter wishing them well after his demise; and another to Mary with the following instructions:

"...when I have passed on, the pathological death certificate has to be brought to Wicker Park Hall, only ask at the office for Mr. Vigerske or Mr. Raeding, because of the continual dedication to his work as an undertaker, so that the funeral costs do not come too high. Notify the insurance companies so that you receive your money. You know the funeral home, turn to either Ernst Schwizerhof or Jerry Raeding.

Within three months, Mary, who then had to do all the work at the business, married Nicholas Metzger, in order to maintain the business and her family. Unfortunately, a tubular pregnancy caused Mary to have peritonitis. She lost her life on May 5, 1927; and the business was sold shortly thereafter.

The Bolits, on the other hand, appear to have not just survived prohibition but they thrived with their establishments. Built in 1886, 1850 N. Damen appears to have been a bar even prior to October 16, 1909, when Joseph Jankowski purchased it. Bruno Wojnowski bought the bar from Theodore and Karolina Spanger on January 1921, just ten months before Wojnowski sold it to the Bolits on November 15.

Polish-born Frank Bolit came to this country in June 1912, and Sophia Postrozna arrived in October of the same year. They met, and later married, on January 30, 1915. Both worked. Frank had several different jobs that included being a porter, roofer, and construction worker. According to the Bolits' grand-daughter Lynn Horn, Frank "bartered and traded for things." It is believed that Sophia worked as a maid at the Lincoln Hotel.

The Bolits' first of three children, Peter, was born on July 23, 1920; and their second, Stanley, was born on January 2, 1923. Business at the Damen bar apparently went well enough that they were able to obtain 1809 N. Hoyne, possibly in 1923.

At some point, Frank was arrested for bootlegging. "My uncle used to tell me about how he stirred the brew in the bathtub," Lynn Horn related. "They moved to California Ave. by 1930, when their third child, Rose (Lynn Horn's mother), was born on January 28, 1930.

Though they owned a saloon/soda pop/ice cream parlor and two buildings on California, it is possible that the move was a result of the St. Valentine's Day Massacre. The *Chicago Daily Tribune*'s February 16,

1929, account of The Massacre reported that State's Attorney John A. Swanson ordered the police commissioner and his deputies (in addition to fifty police captains) to demand that all saloons, speakeasies, and beer flats be notified of being closed.

— *Elaine A. Coorens*

Plate 3.84
FRANK AND SOPHIA BOLIT ON THEIR WEDDING DAY,
JANUARY 30, 1915.

Plate 3.85
THOUGH CITY DIRECTORIES DID NOT LIST TAVERNS AFTER
THE BEGINNING OF PROHIBITION, THERE WERE OTHER
WAYS TO MARKET. THIS IS AN EXAMPLE OF A METHOD THE
BOLITS USED, A BUSINESS CARD.

Phone Armitage 7778   Ladies Invited

MRS. S. C. BOLIT TAVERN
1809 NORTH HOYNE AVE.

Whiskeys and Wines   Best Beer in Town
Music Every Saturday   Free Sandwiches

The Haymarket Events 1886–1887

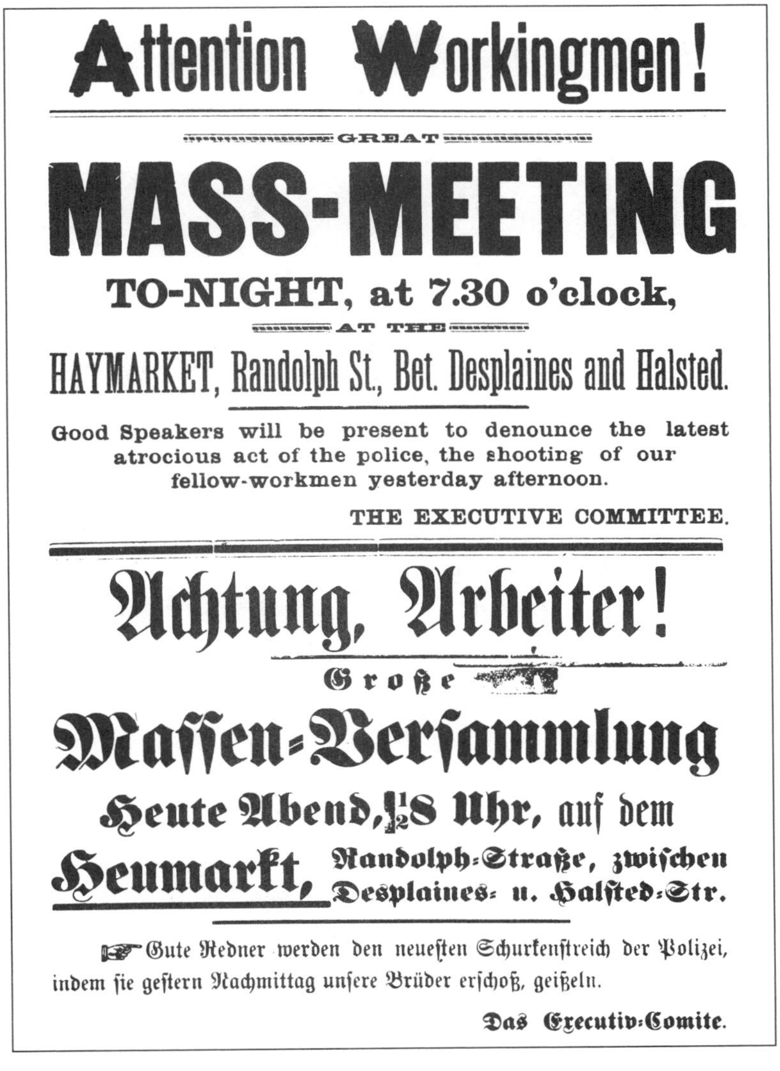

Attention Workingmen!

GREAT
MASS-MEETING
TO-NIGHT, at 7.30 o'clock,
AT THE
HAYMARKET, Randolph St., Bet. Desplaines and Halsted.

Good Speakers will be present to denounce the latest atrocious act of the police, the shooting of our fellow-workmen yesterday afternoon.

THE EXECUTIVE COMMITTEE.

Achtung, Arbeiter!
Große
Massen-Versammlung
Heute Abend, ½8 Uhr, auf dem
Heumarkt, Randolph-Straße, zwischen Desplaines- u. Halsted-Str.

☞ Gute Redner werden den neuesten Schurkenstreich der Polizei, indem sie gestern Nachmittag unsere Brüder erschoß, geißeln.

Das Executiv-Comite.

Plate 3.86

THIS BI-LINGUAL NOTICE HERALDED A MASS LABOR MEETING IN HAYMARKET ON RANDOLPH ON MAY 4, 1886.

Many working-class people from the Wicker Park area were involved in the Haymarket Riot, which was a key event in the history of the anarchist labor movement.

There was widespread labor strife across the country during the 1870s and 1880s. In Chicago, many immigrants had come to help rebuild the city after the Fire of 1871. Many were enduring conditions worse

Plate 3.87
DURING THE MASS MEETING, A DYNAMITE BOMB EXPLODED.

than those they had fled, including hunger, poverty, and illness. Workdays were ten to twelve hours. Workers were often not paid, victimized by unscrupulous employers; and workers wanted free education for their children.

May Day, 1886, was declared as a day of demonstration for the "Eight Hour Day Movement." In Chicago, 80,000 workers marched peacefully with their families. Two days later, two of the striking workmen were killed while protesting at the McCormick Harvester Works on Blue Island Ave. To denounce their deaths and police brutality, the "Haymarket Protest Meeting" was organized for the next day.

August Spies printed and distributed the handbills. Approximately 1200 to 1300 people gathered at Haymarket Square. At 8:30 August Spies addressed the crowd, followed by Albert Parsons and Samuel Fielden. At about 10:00 it began to rain and the speeches ended. At the same time, 180 policemen arrived to disperse the already dispersing crowd. Then, there was a loud explosion.

A bomb landed in front of the police ranks. One officer was killed immediately, seven died later, and sixty to seventy were injured. The police opened fire, killing three and wounding many. Hundreds of suspected anarchists were rounded up and thirty-one were indicted. Eight were charged with inciting to murder. They were Samuel Fielden, Michael Schwab, Oscar Neebe, George Engel, Adolph Fisher, Albert Parsons, August Spies, and Louis Lingg. Fielden, Schwab, and Neebe were given prison terms. Engel, Fisher, Parsons, Spies, and Lingg were sentenced to be hanged. At the time, Spies, Fisher, and Parsons lived

Plate 3.88
THE FUNERAL PRO-
CESSION FOR THOSE
CONVICTED OF THE
DEATHS RESULTING
FROM THE
HAYMARKET RIOT
PASSED THROUGH
THE WICKER PARK
DISTRICT AND UP
MILWAUKEE AVE.

in Wicker Park, and Engels had a toy store on Milwaukee Ave. The police dug up Wicker Park looking in vain for more bombs.

The trial of the eight was highly publicized. Openly admitting their bias, the jury found the eight guilty because of their ideas, not their actions. After the verdict, Lucy Parsons, Albert's wife, traveled to sixteen states giving speeches and raising thousands of dollars for an appeal, to no avail. Later in her life she continued speaking on behalf of the labor movement in this country and in Europe.

November 11, 1887, was the day Parsons, Spies, Engel and Fisher were hanged and Lingg committed suicide. In 1903, Joseph R. Buchanan, a pallbearer for Albert Parsons, wrote the following account of the funeral:

"The bodies of the executed men, and that of Louis Lingg, the suicide, were laid in the temporary vault, at Waldheim Cemetery, on Sunday, November 13. The funeral cortege was said to be the largest ever seen in Chicago. The five hearses were followed by thousands of mourners, and the newspapers estimated the vast crowds that lined the streets through which the procession passed at nearly two hundred thousand.

As one of Albert Parson's pallbearers I marched through three miles of crowded streets that day, and upon every one of the thousands of faces I saw about me there was a look of sorrow. I noticed that some of the policemen bared and bowed their heads as the hearses passed them. The police department had issued an order prohibiting the carrying of banners or flags of any kind. With a single exception the order was obeyed.

Just as the procession began to move down Milwaukee Avenue, a veteran of the Civil War stepped quickly in front of the first rank and unfurled a small American flag. The old veteran was not molested by the police; he carried the flag to the end of the march. At the cemetery, short addresses were made by Capt. Black, Thomas J. Morgan and others, and chants were rendered by several of Chicago's singing societies.

On Sunday, December 18, the caskets containing the mortal remains of "the boys" were placed side by side in an underground vault which had been built in Waldheim to receive them. A vast concourse of people assembled to participate in and witness these final ceremonies. After reaching the cemetery I was requested by the committee to preside. I accepted the honor, making a short speech in the opening exercises. Addresses were made by Captain William P. Black, Paul Grottkau, and Albert Currlin. Capt. Black's address was the most eloquent and most impressive funeral oration I have ever read or heard."

— *Char Sandstrom*

Wicker Park's St. Valentine's Day Massacre Connection*

The legendary St. Valentine's Day Massacre in the S. M. C. Cartage Company garage at 2122 N. Clark has been reported as having connections to Wicker Park. Reported repeatedly as brutal and brazen, members of George "Bugs" Moran's gang were gunned down at 10:30 a.m. on February 14, 1929.

What appeared to be a police car and an unmarked police car (1920s touring car) drove up to the Clark St. garage. Four or five men got out. Two wore police uniforms, and the remainder carried what appeared to be riot guns. Rapid successions of gunshots rang out shortly after the men entered the garage. In response to calls, the police arrived sometime later and found the carnage. Five members of Bugs Moran's gang and two others lay in pools of blood on the garage floor. One of Moran's men lived long enough to say that the gunmen were policemen.

What apparently precipitated the massacre, according to former fireman and fire department historian Ken Little, was another murder in Wicker Park. Pasquale (Patsy) Lolardo, a friend of the infamous Al Capone, lived on North Ave. east of Damen on the south side of the street and frequented a bar on the southeast corner of North and Paulina. Lolardo was shot to death by one of Bugs's men. In retaliation, Capone planned to "take out" Moran.

Capone's men created a "police car" and parked it and another "unmarked car" in a brick garage in the 1700 block of Wood. Lookouts were posted in second floor bay windows across from the Clark St. garage. When Bugs, who traditionally dressed all in brown, arrived, the lookouts were to signal a motorcyclist who would relay the news to the men waiting in the Wicker Park garage.

A man dressed in brown entered the cartage company. The lookouts, not realizing that the man was not Moran, started the chain reaction that would end in the assassinations. Receiving the signal from the lookouts, the messenger headed his motorcycle to the alley behind Wood St., tapped on the garage door and drove off. The garage door opened, and the squad car and the sedan headed toward the 2100 block of Clark.

Following the shooting, fake "cops" arrested "the shooters" and they headed back to Wicker Park. In an attempt to destroy the evidence, Capone's men smashed the fake cop car and set it on fire. A fire alarm was called in, and Wicker Park's Engine #35 appeared on the scene. In the process of "downing" the fire, the alert fireman noticed there was something not quite right with the squad car. The firemen called in the police and the car became evidence in the St. Valentine's Day Massacre.

Though this crime was never solved, it triggered the cleanup of Chicago's criminal activities that had intensified during the Prohibition era. Citizens and government officials alike were so outraged by this gangland act that police turned to the new science of ballistics in an attempt to solve the crime. Chicago became the first city in the country to set up a scientific criminal-detection laboratory.

— *Elaine A. Coorens*

*Many written news stories only report one vehicle and do not include any connection to Engine #35.

Buildings

Plate 4.1
UIHLEIN ESTATE ON 2000 BLOCK OF W. PIERCE WAS DEMOLISHED IN 1924

Commercial Intersection Changes Over Time

Overview

The Wicker Park District gained historic designation both locally and nationally, not just because its buildings were well made, but also in recognition of the people who built the community, and who created its historical significance by living here. Details of specific structures and many of their residents appear in the *Walking Tour* section at the back of this book. Many former residents visit us in the pages of the *"Development"* and *"Life In Wicker Park"* sections. However, there are other views of the neighborhood's structure.

They are the many aspects of the building exteriors and where and when they were built as well as a glimpse of the building interiors. The following stories introduce you to Commercial, Institution, and Residential views.

Plate 4.2
VIEW OF NORTHEAST AND NORTHWEST CORNERS OF NORTH AND DAMEN FROM THE SOUTH OF THE SOUTHWEST CORNER OF NORTH AND DAMEN. TO THE LEFT, OUT OF CAMERA VIEW, IS THE MILNORO BUILDING. (THIS PHOTO WAS TAKEN BETWEEN 1899-1906)

Over time, structures in the Wicker Park District have appeared and disappeared, each change transforming the cityscape. Focusing on the main intersection of North, Milwaukee, and Damen, written accounts paint a rural scene, well into the 1880s.

Judge Allen's mansion, surrounded by shrubs and trees on an acre of land, sits on the southeast corner of North and Milwaukee. An old oaken bucket is perched atop the well on the northwest corner of North and Damen. Farmers pause to water their horses and exchange the latest news as they have their lunch. The northwest corner of North and Milwaukee is the location of a house, which moves to Winchester and Wabansia in 1885. It is a few years later that the southwest corner of Milwaukee and North will be occupied by what is now 1568 N. Milwaukee, a multi-story, mixed-use building. It is probably in this period that the Milnoro Building replaced the

home that moved from the northwest corner of North and Milwaukee.

In the same time frame, Mathias Schulz lived down Damen just north of Wicker Park Ave. and built 1537-1539 N. Damen. Memoirs of Otto Schulz, Jr. give some insight into the decision to build at that time, adjacent to his own residence:

"To show how conservative Grandpa was, in 1885 he built a six-flat building on the north end of his property, right close to the house. There were no windows on the north side of the house so it (the new building) didn't darken the living quarters (of his residence). I imagine the panic of 1883 gave him pause and made him want some insurance in the event the cabinet business faltered."

Plate 4.3
THE MILNORO BUILDING PRECEDED THE NORTH WEST TOWER ON THE NORTHWEST CORNER OF NORTH AND MILWAUKEE BETWEEN 1885 AND 1928.

Plate 4.4
THIS VIEW LOOKS SOUTH ON MILWAUKEE WITH SOUTHWEST CORNER OF DAMEN AND MILWAUKEE STRAIGHT AHEAD AND THE SOUTHWEST CORNER OF NORTH AND MILWAUKEE ON THE RIGHT.

FLATIRON BUILDING BUILT FOR $250,000 IN 1912

A three-story, white-glazed, terra-cotta-faced building is constructed on the southeast corner of North and Milwaukee, in 1912. The architectural firm of Holabird and Roche designed the flatiron building for office and retail space. Its cost was $250,000. An article in the *Wicker Park Eagle* gives the details:

"The building is being erected by Peter C. Brooks of Massachusetts under a twenty-five-year lease, closed last October, to Carl Hansen, formerly of Wieboldt's, and George R. Benson of the Benson & Rixon Company. The structure will have a frontage of 234 feet on Milwaukee avenue and 248 feet on West North avenue... The corner 100 feet of the building will contain five single stores fronting on both streets, while the second and third floors will contain about

Plate 4.5
FLATIRON BUILDING ARCHITECTURAL RENDERING

forty offices. The eastern section of the proposed building, which will front 134 feet on each street with a depth of 190 feet, will be built for use as a department store. This section will contain 17,500 square feet of floor space on each of the three floors. Benson and Hansen report having already sublet about one-half of the available store and office space."

WICKER PARK'S FIRST SKYSCRAPER... NORTH WEST TOWER OPENS APRIL, 1929

"The new North West Tower lifts its cupola-crowned head in graceful beauty," proclaimed an article in **Greater Chicago Magazine** in its 1929 Vol. IV No. 2 issue. Located on the northwest corner of North Ave. and Milwaukee, the building was designed by Perkins, Clatten and Hammond to be as high as zoning permitted. It opened in April 1929. According to the 1929 article thirty thousand people and twenty thousand vehicles passed the site each day. Describing the building, they said:

"The builders of the North West Tower, in this new structure, have created an outstanding example of superior office building construction. With its walls of Indiana limestone, rising from a granite base to a sheer height fourteen stories above the sidewalk, it is the tallest office building on the northwest side. Surmounting its stone cupola, a great bronze lantern illuminated at night by floodlight will be visible for miles

Plate 4.6
SHOWING CONSTRUCTION UNDERWAY ON THE NORTH WEST TOWER BUILDING, THIS VIEW LOOKS WEST ALONG NORTH AVE. (BETWEEN 1928-1929)

in all directions. Besides calling attention to the merits of the North West Tower as a fine business home, this beacon will serve to advertise the entire district in which it stands.

The interior of the North West Tower was carefully planned to achieve both beauty and utility. Tenants and their patrons enter vestibules and a large elevator lobby, tastefully finished in beautiful Grecian marble, mosaic and fluted plasters from handsome entrances on both North and Milwaukee avenues.

Elevator doors, mailboxes, lobby entrances and window frames of bronze afford a pleasing contrast to the fine paneled ceiling. All through the building a uniform beauty combined with utility and economy of space prevails.

The North West Tower offers a dignified home to physicians, dentists, lawyers and others, who will become its tenants and one ideally suited to their requirements. Everything is characterized by a noiseless efficiency through the building. Two high speed new type elevators, equipped with the latest automatic leveling devices, afford excellent service to the building and remove all need for 'step up' or 'step down, please.' The danger of stumbling is non-existent. In place of the old fashioned, unsightly outside fire escapes, the North West Tower is provided with an enclosed fire shield stairway, which insures increased safety for the building's occupants.

There are many special features... Electricity is sub-metered at wholesale rates to all tenants from a master meter. Heating is by vacuum steam radiation from oil-burning boilers, with a resulting absence of all dust and noise usual in coal deliveries. Utilities, such as compressed air, gas, electricity and water for use in medical, dental, surgical and laboratory work, are piped and wired to each suite of offices where and when required.

Several floors are equipped with large reception rooms to be used in common by eight offices. Other floors have private reception rooms with each suite of offices. By virtue of the location and unique shape of the building, each office has outside light."

Stockholders of the Noel State Bank owned the building and chose Charles F. Noyes National

Plate 4.7

This 1929 drawing depicts the six-corner area of North, Milwaukee, and Damen with the newly erected Tower Building. Noel State Bank was heavily invested in the six-cornered intersection and elsewhere in the neighborhood.

Realty Corporation of Illinois to rent and maintain it.

The building replaced the Milnoro Building, which was formerly the home of the Noel State Bank. Noel State Bank built and moved to a new building, across Milwaukee at the intersection with Damen and North, in 1906.

DARA BUILDING PROVIDES STORE AND APARTMENT SPACE

Another 1929 addition to the Wicker Park District is the Dara Building. It has fifty feet of frontage on Damen (Robey) and eighty on Concord (Raymond Court). Perkins, Chatten and Hammond, also designers of the North West Tower building, designed this three-story modern brick structure for stores and apartments with red face brick on the two street fronts. An article in *Greater Chicago Magazine*, No. 2, 1929, described the building:

The first floor contains three stores, which will be divided to suit the tenants. Copper and plate glass fronts offer the opportunity for attractive window displays. Back of these stores are two apartments, one consisting of one room and bath, and the other, two rooms with bath. These are especially adaptable to the use of store tenants. They have an independent entrance on Raymond court separate from the entrance to the apartments above.

There are three apartments on the second floor, and three on the third floor. One apartment on each floor contains a living room, two bedrooms, dining room, kitchen and bath; another apartment on each of the two floors is designed for a living room, two bedrooms, kitchen and bath. The remaining apartment on each floor is laid out for a living room, bedroom, kitchen and bath. In this way provision is made for the accommodation of large or small families, with plenty of space for their comfort.

All modern conveniences have been put into the Dara Building to insure the satisfaction of the tenants. Tiled bath room floors, kitchen and medicine cabinets, art metal doors, from the apartments to the stairway, Abso-pure electric refrigerators, gas ranges, door mirrors, roll-away beds and other up-to-date labor saving devices all add to the charm of these apartments. The entire building is heated by steam.

The site of the Dara Building was formerly occupied by a dilapidated structure, over forty years old. The new building, owned and built by Mrs. Joseph R. Noel, represents another substantial contribution of the Noel family to the development of the Wicker Park District."

— *Elaine A. Coorens*

Plate 4.8

DARA BUILDING RENDERING, 1929, SHOWS THREE-STORY BRICK BUILDING NORTH OF NORTH AT CORNER OF DAMEN AND CONCORD, DESIGNED BY PERKIN, CHATTEN AND HAMMOND, ARCHITECTS.

Institutions Have Many Faces

Plate 4.9
St. Elizabeth Hospital opened these doors in 1886 at Claremont and LeMoyne.

Like all structure types built in the Wicker Park District, the institutions had many faces from small and simple to massive and ornate. Institution's interiors also reflected the fashions of the day. Here is a sampling of the exteriors and interiors of this major component of the neighborhood.

— *Elaine A. Coorens*

Plate 4.10
St. Aloysius Church had its first service on June 20, 1884, in this structure on the northwest corner of North and Western.

Plate 4.11
ASSOCIATION HOUSE MOVED
INTO THE GRAY FRAME HOUSE AT
2150 W. NORTH IN 1902 AND
THEN BUILT A LARGER FACILITY
TO THE WEST IN 1905. NOTICE
THE HORSE WATER TROUGH IN
THE RIGHT FOREGROUND.

Plate 4.12
ASSOCIATION HOUSE OF
CHICAGO BEGAN DELIVERING
SOCIAL SERVICES IN AND FROM
THIS BUILDING
AT 2013 W. NORTH IN 1899.
THEY WERE AT THIS LOCATION
UNTIL 1906.

Plate 4.13
THIS GOTHIC STRUCTURE ON THE NORTH WEST CORNER
OF HOYNE AND LEMOYNE WAS WICKER PARK LUTHERAN
CHURCH'S FIRST CHURCH, DEDICATED IN JANUARY 1880
AND REPLACED IN 1906.

Plate 4.14
JOSEPHINUM ACADEMY OPENED
IN 1889 AS A DAY AND RESIDEN-
TIAL SCHOOL FOR GIRLS.

Plate 4.15
A SCIENCE CLASS ROOM IS FEATURED
IN THIS JOSEPHINUM PHOTO.

Plate 4.16
ST. ELIZABETH'S HOSPITAL LABORATORY

Plate 4.17
THE RESIDENTIAL AREA
OF THE JOSEPINUM
ACADEMY
HAD THIS PARLOR.

Plate 4.18
ST. ELIZABETH'S HOSPITAL
SOLARIUM

Residential Development Ties to Ethnic Background

Wicker Park's development pattern is not unusual for late nineteenth century urban neighborhoods, however it is one of Chicago's most exaggerated examples of 'city within the city.' The uniqueness of this pattern is even more evident when we compare it with more recent examples of residential construction.

There are, of course, commonalities between late nineteenth century and late twentieth century residential development; proximity to transportation, to shopping, and to institutions such as schools, churches, and hospitals. For Wicker Park's settlers these amenities were readily available: transit via streetcars on Damen, North, and Milwaukee, and later by elevated train; shopping within walking distance on Milwaukee and North; and the development of institutions and the park at the center of the community.

However, our present development pattern is largely determined by demographics. Each new real estate development, or entire suburban community, can be clearly demographics. Each new real estate development, or entire suburban community, can be clearly defined by the educational, career, and economic profiles of its residents. The demographics of places such as Chicago's Gold Coast, or the suburbs of Lake Forest or Wilmette, for example, depict a highly educated, professional, and affluent population. In comparison, areas such as Englewood, Lawndale, or Ford City, with their relatively low levels of education and high rates of unemployment and poverty, can be characterized quite differently. The contrast is indeed striking, and is largely

Plate 4.19
LOCATED ON THE NORTHEAST CORNER OF PIERCE AND HOYNE, THIS MANSION WAS PROBABLY TORN DOWN IN THE EARLY TO MID 1920S. IT WAS HOME TO THE NIEDERT FAMILY.

founded on differences of class and race.

Our nineteenth century forbearers would not have recognized this development pattern, not only because they did not have such tools as the automobile, but because their socialization pattern, and ultimately the expectations they derived from their world view, were so different from those of the present time. Most Americans of the late nineteenth century were immigrants or the children of immigrants. This is particularly true of the fast-growing industrial centers such as Chicago.

The common pattern of immigration was for one individual, or small group, to leave their birthplace for the New World, to find work and settle with people who shared at least some of their heritage. They would then send word back home: there are jobs, there is housing, there is a future; come on. This is the reason that some European and Asian towns or regions sent so many people to America, and others did not; if there were no intrepid first emigrants to test the waters, the conceptual as well as the physical distance was too far to travel.

The immigrants and their children tended to settle in proximity to those who understood the problems of their Old Country and the exertions of creating a life in the new one. Their need for familiarity is the reason that immigrant peoples settled with others who spoke their ancestral language, shared common religious beliefs, and saw themselves as a definable group in spite of their differences in educational level, career status, or relative poverty or affluence. The glue that held these communities together, and the socialization pattern that defines Wicker Park, is the connection to what was left behind in the Old Country.

As a result, Wicker Park included the entire social gamut in educational level, career achievement,

and economic status. And it is not surprising that we find in the neighborhood one of Chicago's broadest ranges of surviving nineteenth century residential building types. From the simple worker's cottages on Crystal and Potomac, to the middle class flats on Leavitt and Claremont, to the early mansions of Beer Baron Row on Hoyne, and the later great houses on Pierce and Caton Avenues, Wicker Park provides a cross section of the entire social register. These buildings represent a development pattern based on the settler's heritage. They came form Prussia, Pomerania, and Silesia, areas that are today parts of eastern Germany and western Poland, but that were then all in the German Empire. They spoke German and Polish, shared a common world view. Like the Germans, the Scandinavians, made up of Norwegians, Swedes, and Danes, also congregated together in support of each other as fellow travelers from the same points of origin.

The housing shows the ethnic background of its original builders and owners in its materials and details. A house in brick, for example, was more desirable here because it was seen as more substantial 'back home.' The desire for decorative detail, evident on such modest buildings as those found at 2025 W. Evergreen, at 1511 N. Bell, or at 1559 N. Hoyne, only further indicated the success its owner had achieved. The scale of these houses also marked their owners as suc-

Plate 4.20

S. E. GROSS & CO. BILINGUAL ADVERTISEMENT FOR HOMES AT DIVISION AND WESTERN SHOWS THE INTERIOR LAYOUT.

Plate 4.21
THESE MULTI UNIT BUILDINGS IN
THE 1920S LINED ONE OF THE
STREETS IN THE MILWAUKEE,
ASHLAND, AND DIVISION AREA,
NORTH OF MILWAUKEE.

Plate 4.22
IN JANUARY 1916, THIS WAS THE
VIEW OF 1628 N. WESTERN.

Plate 4.23
THIS 1912-13 PHOTO (BELOW) OF A WORKER'S COTTAGE
AT THE BLOOMINGDALE RAILROAD TRACK AND HONORE
(GIRARD.) NOTICE HOW FAR BELOW CURRENT
STREET GRADE IT WAS BUILT.

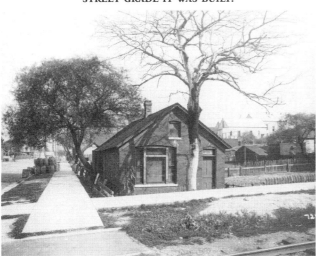

Plate 4.24
JULIAN, A SHORT STREET BETWEEN ASHLAND AND WOOD,
WAS THE LOCATION FOR THIS HOME AROUND 1880-1885.

Plate 4.25
IN THE AREA OF MILWAUKEE, ASHLAND AND DIVISION,
THERE ARE STREETS THAT ARE SHORT AND ANGLED NORTH
AND EAST OF MILWAUKEE. AS SEEN TO THE RIGHT.
AMONG THEM IS BAUWAN. (PHOTO TAKEN AROUND 1920)

cessful; the Hansen House at 1417 N. Hoyne (1879), the Runge House at 2138 W. Pierce (1884), and the Thorp House at 2156 W. Caton (1891) manifest the dream of the New World realized.

A common background did not, however, guarantee community unanimity. Some of the leaders of the labor movement who organized the Haymarket Incident rallies lived in the modest houses of Wicker Park; some of the business owners against whom they were protesting lived in the area's mansions. The shift from an ethnic allegiance to an economic one is a division that would anticipate new social and residential developments in the twentieth century.

— *Timothy N. Wittman*

Plate 4.26
GEORGE RAHLF, A WEST PARK
COMMISSIONER, LIVED HERE
AT 2040 W. PEIRCE AVE.
(33 EWING PLACE) ACROSS THE
STREET FROM ANOTHER
COMMISSSIONER,
EDWARD UIHLEIN.

Plate 4.27

BUILT IN 1885 AS INVESTMENT PROPERTY BY MATHIAS SCHULZ, THE MULTI-STORY BRICK BUILDING ON THE LEFT IS 1537-1539 N. DAMEN. NOTE THAT THE WINDOWS ARE ALL RESIDENTIAL IN APPEARANCE AND THAT THE BUILDING WAS BUILT PRIOR TO THE RAISING OF THE STREET.

TO THE RIGHT (SOUTH) IS MATHIAS SCHULZ'S BRICK HOME WITH A GREAT DEAL OF WOODEN DETAIL BUILT JUST AFTER THE FIRE IN 1871. (SEE STORY ON PAGE 189.) PHOTO WAS PROBABLY TAKEN JUST BEFORE OR AFTER 1900.

Plate 4.28

IN AUGUST, 1904 MRS. J. R. NOEL STANDS BY THE FRONT FENCE OF 2134 W. PIERCE WITH DAUGHTERS HARRIET AND
VIRGINIA. THE TWO-STORY BRICK HOME AT THE BACK OF THE PROPERTY HAD A WOODEN FRONT.
TO THE LEFT (WEST) THERE IS A BRICK STABLE AND TO THE RIGHT (EAST) IS A WOODEN STRUCTURE.
THE 1886 ROBINSON MAP SHOWS THE HOME AND A STABLE ON THE EAST WITH NO STRUCTURE ON THE WEST.
AT THIS TIME, 2134 WAS A WORKER'S COTTAGE BETWEEN TWO MANSIONS.

Plate 4.29

BY JULY, 1905 THE LARGE GRAY
STONE FRONTED BRICK TWO-FLAT
WITH BRICK COACH HOUSE AT
THE REAR OF THE PROPERTY
REPLACED THE OLD HOMESTEAD.
IDENTITY OF THE BOY IS
UNKNOWN BUT THE GIRL IN THE
MIDDLE IS HARRIET NOEL AND
ON THE RIGHT VIRGINIA NOEL.

Plate 4.30
KNOWN AS A LUMBERMAN'S DREAM OR "STEAMBOAT MANSION",
THIS RESIDENCE AT 2138 W. PIERCE WAS BUILT BY LUMBERMAN HANS RUNGE.
IT HAS BEEN INCORRECTLY CALLED THE "POLISH CONSULATE" AND
THE "PADERWESKI HOUSE." (SEE PAGE 141.)

Plate 4.31
THE ROONE FAMILY LIVED IN
THIS CATON ST. MANSION.

EARLY HOMES WERE SIMPLE AND SPARSELY DECORATED

Only a few houses dotted the Illinois plains of the 1700s. They were one or two room log cabins, where the fireplaces acted as oven, kitchen stove and the primary source of heat.

Jean Baptiste Point de Sable probably had a dwelling similar to the French settlers' low-slung house with a balcony around it constructed with vertically placed logs forming a wall. There was probably a bedroom with a bed-frame strung with rope (hence the expression sleep tight). A chest to hold clothing and linens might have been the only other piece of bedroom furniture. The other room would serve as living, dining room, kitchen and parlor. Its furnishings would include a solid table, a few wood chairs and kitchen utensils.

As the city began to grow vigorously after 1830, the Greek Revival style was ubiquitous, from small prairie houses to large mansions and municipal buildings. A few balloon frame wooden houses of this period can still be seen on the periphery of the Wicker Park area.

Initially the interior walls of these houses were probably painted a white or light pastel color. A small table in the front parlor, a few chairs, perhaps a sideboard with a few valued plates or bric-a-brac, the furnishings were probably modest.. The dining room, if it was separate from the kitchen, would have a table, chairs, and if they were "wealthy" some candelabra or a chandelier. Going upstairs, there would be a small hallway with small bedrooms on either side. In general, there was just enough room for a bed and a small chest for clothing. The windows probably didn't have curtains but relied on external shutters for privacy and protection from the elements. In the more modest buildings, heat would be provided by a wood stove while the larger, well-to-do homes, would have fireplaces replete with mantles.

— *Nick Sommers*

Plate 4.32
ITS FIRST OWNER POINT DE SABLE BUILT THE KINZIE HOUSE. FRONTED BY LOMBARDY POPLARS IT WAS LOCATED ON THE CHICAGO RIVER'S NORTH BANK (NORTH END OF THE CURRENT MICHIGAN AVE. BRIDGE.)

Interiors Reflect
Their Time

Plate 4.33
THIS IS A VIEW OF NILES T. AND CARRIE QUALES' PARLOR .

Wicker Park home interiors reflected the age in which they were built. It was the mid to late Victorian era; the industrial revolution was in full swing. Parquet floors were made available to the upper middle class, thanks to the modern industrial techniques. At that time they were called wood *carpets* and allowed even modest homes to pretend that they were in the same class as the Vanderbilts. New machinery made wall coverings affordable, some even imitated damask coverings. Paint technology had improved and organic chemistry had introduced new colors. Furniture was no longer the province of craftsmen cabinetmakers, but was mass-produced. Replicas were almost as good as the originals which they copied.

Plate 4.34
MR. AND MRS. ROONE IN THEIR DINING ROOM ON CATON.

Much of the ornamentation, which was visible on the exterior, was also reproduced in the interior. Ornate gingerbread porches with their elaborate machine turned pillars and spindles were echoed inside with spandrels and archways of delicate wood lace. The metal cornices and tower facings were mirrored on the inside with embossed metal ceilings. An additional benefit from this use of metal was its fireproof quality. After 1871, Chicagoans were a bit touchy about fire.

The most important room in the house was the front parlor. This and the dining room were the only rooms that visitors saw. Before the telephone, telephone book, and television, there was a blue book, which listed the hours when people could come to call. The front parlor was where guests were received. It was also where, when people died, their coffin was placed, hence today's name of *Funeral Parlor*.

The front parlor announced the wealth and prestige of the family to the visitor and was generally the fanciest room in the house. Here, family portraits were hung framed with lavish detail. Furniture groupings allowed for different occasions. A table and chairs were necessary for the after dinner card and parlor games. Stuffed chairs and sofas along with numerous corner chairs and footstools were crowded into the room for conversation groups. There were rarely matched sets of furniture in the latter part of the Victorian era and exotic furniture reflected the tastes and travels of the occupants.

A curio cabinet was generally seen in wealthier homes. Here one could display exotic porcelain and figurines, mementos from trips to foreign lands and other curiosities meant to impress the visitor.

Numerous textiles filled the Victorian parlor. An oriental rug might be placed as a tablecloth. The window treatment could consist of several textile layers with a lace curtain and heavy damask drape and valences over every window. Heavy curtains would also be used in doorways to help reduce drafts. A tapestry on the wall and in a fire screen would also speak reams of the owner's travels and tastes. Fringed shawls were draped over chairs and some of the stuffed furniture was protected with antimacassars.

The new wood carpets allowed a parquet border, extending a few feet from the wall, around the room. As Charles Eastlake observed in his *Hints on Household Taste,* the border allowed for a quality carpet to be purchased which was smaller and adaptable to other rooms. If good wood was either too expensive or difficult to come by (as was the case after the Chicago fire) pine could be easily shaped and then false grained to look like more expensive wood. Sometimes wood would be painted to look like marble and, conversely, marble would be painted to look like exotic wood.

Next to the parlor, the dining room was another center for social gatherings, a place where guests could be impressed with their host's sophistication. It might contain a large table capable of being extended to accommodate groups as large as 12 (the number 13 was to be avoided). A handsome, frequently ornately carved sideboard would be present as well as a glass cabinet in which the best china and crystal could be seen and displayed. The dining room fireplace and mantel might be simpler than that in the front parlor and probably was home for a vase or two and some candlesticks.

Most likely the dining room table was bedecked with layers of textiles. The table had at least two layers of table cloths, one on top of the other. When the dinner was finished, the first tablecloth was removed and dessert service was set. When that course was finished, the second tablecloth was removed and fruit and coffee were placed on the bare table. A dining room rug was probably under the table to catch the errant scraps of food and drink and protect the floor. Lighting in the dining room was provided by both candles and an elaborate gasolier, or later a combination gas and electric fixture.

The second parlor, or sitting room, would later evolve into what we call today *the family room*. It was rarely seen by outside visitors and was reserved for relaxation, craftwork, and generally also housed the piano or parlor organ. Since the front parlor was the more formal room and generally kept in readiness for company, the sitting room was much more relaxed and informal. Window treatments were plain curtains, the walls might be painted or wallpapered in light colors to give it an airy feeling. Sometimes a small conservatory was attached where exotic plants could be grown. The floor was generally carpeted, particularly since this room would not generally have the more expensive parquet or wood flooring. Lighting would be provided by small lamps around the room. In earlier Victorian times these lamps would be kerosene and later they were electric. Windows would be treated with simpler shades or maybe chintz curtains.

Many Victorian kitchens were in the basement, to keep food odors away from the front parlor and dining room. With the advent of gas lines and plumbing in the late 1870s and 1880s, the kitchen was often moved upstairs to the first floor at the rear of the house. Wooden wainscoting was often used in Victorian kitchens and the advent of linoleum began to brighten kitchen floors. In later Victorian times the kitchen reflected an almost laboratory like feel as a result of increased concerns over the spread of disease through contaminated food. Wooden wainscoting was replaced with white tiles and white enameled porcelain sinks with exposed plumbing. By the late Victorian period, oak ice boxes were in place and closed cupboards could be safely used since so many goods were now available in sanitary tins.

Emphasis on sanitation also influenced bathroom design and furnishing. At first Victorian bathrooms had tin tubs enclosed in oak cabinets, rugs on the floor and pictures on the wall. There were fancy marble surfaces and elegant brass fixtures. By the 1890s, concern over germs and disease transformed the bathroom into another sanitary room. Porcelain tubs

and sinks with exposed pipes were the rule as they were easy to keep clean. Tile flooring replaced wooden floors for similar reasons.

Victorian bed rooms were generally a simpler, though they still had more furniture than many of today's bedrooms. The floor would be wood with a few scatter rugs. A dressing-table, a few chairs or even a small sofa or day bed might be found in the master bedroom.

In the later Victorian period there was great concern over a constant source of fresh air. For this reason, you will see air registers with ornate metal grills. These registers could be opened or closed. They were meant to help the bad air escape from the room. In keeping with their fear of germs and disease, Victorians used canopied, brass, or steel beds, since they were easier to clean. Ever modest, the Victorians also frequently used oriental room dividers behind which they dressed and undressed.

By the late 1870s central steam heating had made its debut and radiators and the pipes that led to them were prominently displayed. Some of the radiators were quite ornate. In general however, bedrooms had smaller radiators since a bedroom shouldn't be overheated.

Because most houses had narrow staircases, many had a *coffin niche* at the top of the stairs. Since people in those days frequently died in their own bed, rather than in a hospital, the remains were carried downstairs to the front parlor in a coffin. To navigate the narrow staircase the *coffin niche* came into play allowing the long coffin to be turned and brought down the staircase.

While the wealthier inhabitants of the area had indoor plumbing and all the amenities that accompany this luxury, the majority of the people in the area still used outhouses and some still obtained water from wells. Indoor plumbing didn't come to some houses in the Wicker Park area until after World War II.

The influx of central Europeans to the area was the catalyst for the development of neighborhood bath houses. The North Avenue Baths and the Division Street Baths served the German, Jewish, Polish and Russian immigrants who had settled in the area.

— *Nick Sommers*

MEMORIES OF MATHIAS SCHULZ'S HOME BRING INSIGHT

Though wide steps led to the second floor main entrance of Mathias Schulz's four-story home, to the south of the 1537-39 Damen building and just north of Wicker Park Ave., the most used entrance was at ground level at the side of the steps. Built prior to street raising, access to either entrance from the sidewalk required walking down a few steps before reaching the building.

Describing entering through the ground level door, Mathias's grandson, Otto Jr. wrote in his memoirs:

"Here was a small hall and at its side, facing Robey Street (Damen), a small living room, and behind that a dining room and then a large kitchen with a big wood-burning stove, sinks, tables, and cabinets. There was also a winding basement stairway in one corner that went down to an earthen cellar, which was particularly fascinating to me, as salami and summer sausages hung from the ceiling, along with smoked hams and briskets of beef. Of course, there were barrels of pickles, and shelves with preserves and vegetables in mason jars.

I thought the second floor was particularly grand. It consisted of two large parlors that stretched the length of the house with a small front room and a little library on either end of the side hall. The parlors were lavishly furnished with satin-covered sofas, and lace antimacassars, and there was statuary that my grandmother and aunts had brought back from their visits to Europe. A large grand piano was in the rear parlor.

There were full-length mirrors, and pendulum clocks, and innumerable vases and pictures. The room wasn't used except for parties and weddings, as most of the living was on the ground floor.

The third floor had the bedrooms. My grandmother's was in the rear, and I was told the furniture had been made in my grandfather's factory. It was heavily carved black walnut, with a huge bed, where I slept with my

Plate 4.35

THIS IS A LINE DRAWING OF THE MATHIAS SCHULZ HOME, LOCATED ON THE CORNER OF DAMEN AND WICKER PARK AVENUES.

grandmother when I stayed there during the period when my sister was down with scarlet fever, and also when Mama was having a baby. (Otto's family lived across the Park from his grandparents.) … the fourth floor was mostly a large ballroom, with one or two maid's bedrooms and there was another winding stairway up to a cupola, and a widow's walk in the center of the roof. In 1910 we climbed up there and looked at the night sky until we found Haley's comet moving slowly across the horizon. I remember they said it would come back in 80 years…"

Comparing his grandparents' home to others, Otto said their home was "not nearly as pretentious a place as some of the homes the Scandinavian and German businessmen were building in the area." Many of the houses were limestone or brick, with stained glass windows and elaborate wood carving on the porches and lintels. Only a block away, Ed Uihlein's mansion included a glass conservatory, with wrought iron fence, statuary, and beautiful stained glass windows.

— *Elaine A. Coorens*

TASTE AND AFFLUENCE CAUSED INTERIOR CHANGES

Interiors are easily and, therefore, frequently changed with the whims of taste and affluence. There were no professional *decorators* or *interior designers* until well into the 1900s. Those who sought advice, back then and now, might be inspired by something they saw in someone else's home or a publication.

Selections of interior furnishings are influenced by experience (what grandma may have or have not had), ethnicity (some cultures influence color and stylistic choices), and availability (catalogues of furnishings, such as Sears, etc. allowed mass production of furnishings that was available to everyone).

The lack of durability of interior surfaces and furnishings (and their modest cost of change, as compared to architectural items) make them easily changeable, even to whim. One can change the entire effect of a room by rearranging furniture, paint or wallpaper changes, and adjusting a few pictures and accessories.

— *Joseph R. DuciBella, A.S.I.D*

View Inside and Outside Victorian Estate

Plate 4.36

THE UIHLEIN MANSION SAT ON THE WEST EDGE OF THE PROPERTY ON AN ALLEY AT 2041 W. PIERCE

Edward Uihlein's mansion at 34 Ewing Place (2041 W. Pierce) was a showcase opened on a regular basis to Wicker Park students and faculty and most likely to others. Uihlein purchased the land in 1877 and built his home for approximately $10,000. As head of the Schlitz Brewing Company in Chicago, the expanse of his estate seemed to match his position in the industry.

His interest in horticulture was evident in his domed conservatory, built some time after the residence. He explains in his memoirs:

"I decided to erect a conservatory for the cultivation of rare plants, such as palms, anthuria, maranthas – in fact, as many tropical plants as the green houses could accommodate – to which I added a little collection of orchids. I had the good fortune of obtaining an experienced gardener, under whose care everything succeeded

Plate 4.37
THE DOMED CONSERVATORY WAS HOME FOR OVER 5,000 RARE ORCHIDS.

splendidly, however, after six years of service, he left me, and a gardener named Skjoldager took the vacancy. Under his good care, the orchid collection was much enlarged, and, today, some 5,000 of the rarest orchids from all parts of the world, are to be found in various parts of my conservatories. It will be 25 years, this summer, since Skjoldager took his position and he is, apparently, in good health."

Uihlein was President of the Chicago Horticultural Society and also served, for three years, on the West Park Commission at the request of Governor Altgeld. Born in Wertheim-on-the-Main,

Baden, Germany in 1845, he and his wife, Augusta Manns, had five children. Two of their four daughters, Ella and Melita, married Seipp brothers. (The Seipp family was also in the brewing industry.) Their other children were Clara, Olga and Edgar.

The Chicago branch of the family pronounces their last name as "Uline" while the Milwaukee branches pronounce it as "Eline." According to Edgar Uihlein, Jr., that is because Edward said, "At least they will *start* to spell it (Uihlein) correctly!" It is said that when Edward's wife was ill and close to death at their

Plate 4.38
CLOSE UP VIEW OF THE FRONT OF THE UIHLEIN HOME.

Plate 4.39
ALL FOUR UIHLEIN DAUGHTERS RELAX ON THE FRONT PORCH. LEFT TO RIGHT: ELLA (SEIPP) (1886-1960), CLARA (TROSTEL) (1876-1976), MELITA (SEIPP) (1893-1919), AND OLGA (BENEKE) (1879-1971).

Plate 4.40
NOTICE CLARA AND MELITA'S SURROUNDINGS. THOUGH THIS IS A REAR EXTERIOR PORCH, ONE GETS THE FEELING THAT IT IS AN INTERIOR ROOM. THE CONSERVATORY IS TO THE LEFT IN THE BACKGROUND.

Plate 4.41
**LOOKING FROM THE SITTING ROOM INTO
THE DINING ROOM.**

Pierce Ave. home, Edward had straw spread along the street and alley, so the noise of wagons and horses would be muffled.

Probably the death of Edward in 1921 and the economic decline for the "beer barons" due to prohibition caused Edgar Uihlein to sell this property in 1924. The purchasers demolished the complex. They also had the alley west of Uihlein's house closed. The alley land became the center of a large multi-unit building that covered the space of the Uihlein house and an equal space to the west. By constructing the new building from close to lot line to lot line, the cityscape and population density on the residential streets changed substantially.

— *Elaine A. Coorens*

Plate 4.42
**A STEINWAY PATENT GRAND PIANO IS IN A ROSEWOOD
CASE IN THE SITTING ROOM.**

Plate 4.43, 4.44, 4.45
A PANORAMA OF THE PARLOR IS POSSIBLE BY VIEWING THESE THREE PHOTOS.

Reference

About the Creators

Elaine A. Coorens

Elaine Coorens immigrated from Lincoln Park to Wicker Park in 1976, though her Norwegian ancestors chose a different route to Wicker Park. She quickly became involved with local businesses and organizations, first as a member of the Milwaukee/North/Damen Business Assn., and then with the Greater Milwaukee Ave. Chamber. She chaired the coalition-building effort that resulted in the Greater Milwaukee Ave. Economic Development Corporation (GMAEDC). Its goal was to bring the National Trust for Historic Preservation's Urban Demonstration Program to Chicago. With a budget of over $100,000.00, the project focused on the Milwaukee Ave. business strip. Elaine served as the corporate president of GMAEDC until 1987, when the program ended.

Old Wicker Park Committee (OWPC) received much of Elaine's volunteer service beginning in 1977. She chaired the Greening Festival in 1979, when house tours and the first house tour booklet were first launched. She wrote and produced the 1988 *OWPC Circa, The Magazine*, and has served on and chaired many committees since then. Elaine also served on the Association House Board from 1978 to 1987, filling several positions, including President in 1984.

Elaine credits two years at Mac Murray College as the starting point for her journalistic pursuits. A graduate of the University of Illinois - Champaign in Marketing/Advertising, Elaine has been a writer, editor, and publisher with major corporations and small companies for many years. Currently she is President of Coorens Communications, inc., a computer consulting company that analyzes client needs, recommends, installs and maintains hardware, and provides software solutions and training for business clients. In professional organizations she is active with the International Association of Microsoft Certified Partners (IAMCP) and National Assn. of Women Business Owners (NAWBO). Elaine is Past President of the Chicago IAMCP Chapter, and is serving a second year as Treasurer on the IAMCP International Board.

Mary Ann Johnson

Mary Ann Johnson is a native Chicagoan, born and raised in the south side neighborhood of Hyde Park. A graduate of Iowa's Grinnell College, she subsequently did graduate work in Urban Studies at Roosevelt University and American History at the University of Illinois at Chicago. Mary Ann's love of Chicago history, neighborhoods and architecture led her to purchase a home on Caton Street in Wicker Park in 1979 where she lived until the late 1980s. While a resident of the neighborhood she developed a deep interest in the history of the area, and subsequently she initiated the Wicker Park Neighborhood History Project, an archive of photographs, documents, artifacts, oral history interviews and other historical materials.

Mary Ann has directed numerous public history projects in the Chicago area and for many years was director of the Jane Addams Hull-House Museum at the University of Illinois at Chicago. She is author of *Walking With Women Through Chicago History* (Salcedo Press) and editor of *The Many Faces of Hull-House, The Photographs of Wallace Kirkland (University of Illinois Press.)* She is also associate editor of *Women Building Chicago 1770-1990, A Biographical Dictionary (Indiana University Press.)*

Currently Mary Ann is President of the Chicago Area Women's History Council, a local organization that supports women's history. She is also an accomplished photographer and a consultant to museums and archives.

Joseph R. DuciBella

Licensed as a professional interior designer in Illinois, Joseph DuciBella works in both the residential and commercial markets. He is a member of the American Society of Interior Designers (ASID). In his twenty years as a sole proprietor, Joe's projects have ranged from private homes to theatres, including the Chicago Theatre, and a railroad parlor car.

Educated in both architecture and the arts, Joe has specialized in historic structures, in projects for more than twenty theatres in several states. Instrumental in the Wicker Park District being placed on the National Register for Historic Places, he became a Wicker Park resident in the mid 1970s.

He is co-founder of the Theatre Historical Society of America, which he served as President from 1989-93, and is currently the Chicago Area Director. In addition he has volunteered for Chicago Landmark Commission projects and served on the Old Wicker Park Committee Board.

Char Sandstrom

Char Sandstrom moved to Wicker Park during 1983 to rehab one of the community's 100+ year old buildings. She has been actively involved with the OWPC and the CAPS program. She is a founding member of the Nelson Algren Committee.

Art, history, and the development of a healthy community are her avocations. Char has a master's degree from New York University in social work and community development.

John Scheidelman

John Scheidelman is a technology professional who moved to Wicker Park in 1997. A member of OWPC, he enjoys reading about the history of the neighborhood and the City of Chicago.

Cheryl Smalling

Cheryl Smalling became a Wicker Park resident in 1990. Since then, she has served on the Old Wicker Park Committee Board for eleven years. Her many responsibilities have included being Secretary, V. P of Historic Preservation, and a member of the Planning and Development Committee.

For several years, Cheryl also organized the Wicker Park House Tour, which was given in conjunction with the annual Greening Festival, which was discontinued several years ago.

Nicholas H. Sommers

Nicholas H. Sommers retired from Akzo Nobel in 1998 after 32 years of employment that began in 1967 as Technical Writer. Subsequently he was Advertising Manager, then Product Manager, Communications Manager, and finally Director of Communications.

Majoring in languages with a minor in the sciences at Beloit College, Nick was awarded a Graduate Fellowship in Linguistics at Brown University in 1962. He has also studied at the University of Freiburg in Germany and at the University of Chicago.

In 1969, shortly after moving to Wicker Park he published a booklet called *The Historic Homes of Old Wicker Park*. Other publications include chemical technical brochures and articles.

Since his early retirement, Nick has become a board member of The Holland America Music Society and Treasurer of The Wicker Park Advisory Council. He continues to restore his 1870's Victorian house, plays the cello in a local chamber music group, substitute teaches at Lincoln Park High School and consults for a number of companies and organizations.

Ed and Mary Taminga

Residents of Wicker Park for several years, Ed is an architect, and Mary works in sales and marketing. They were attracted to Wicker Park by the remarkable historic quality and residential heritage of the neighborhood. Appreciative of the small-town character of Wicker Park, Ed and Mary work to preserve architectural integrity within the community.

Timothy N. Wittman

A preservation consultant and educator in Chicago, Timothy Wittman teaches at the School of the Art Institute and Columbia College.

He was a member of the staff of the Commission on Chicago Landmarks for twelve years, during which time he was responsible for the local designation of the Wicker Park Historic District as a Chicago Landmark.

Larry E. Clary

Larry Clary, who has served as editor of this book, moved to Chicago's Hyde Park community in 1967 to attend college, where he received a bachelor's degree in English from the University of Chicago. He lived in Hyde Park for twenty-five years before moving to Wicker Park, where his roots run eleven-years deep.

Work experience during college included several opportunities to work as a freelance editor, primarily for University of Chicago Press, and on small portions of the major 1970s revision to Encyclopedia Britannica. His first work after college was in fundraising for nonprofits, which he pursued for more than fifteen years, at University of Chicago, Field Museum, Chicago Commons Association, Erikson Institute, and Ingalls Hospital. When it was time for a change, Larry joined ranks with Coorens Communications in 1990, to consult and provide service in computer networking and database support.

Plates

Illustrations

Bibliography

A Biographical History with Portraits of Prominent Men of the Great West. Chicago: Manhattan Publishing Co., 1894.

Adams, Rosemary, Ed. *Wild Kind of Boldness, The Chicago History Reader.* Grand Rapids and Chicago: William B. Eerdmans Publishing Company and Chicago Historical Society, 1998.

Adelman, William J.. *Haymarket Revisited.* Chicago: Illinois Labor History Society, 1976.

Album of Genealogy & Biography Cook County, IL with Portraits. Chicago: Calumet Book Engraving Co., 1897.

Album of Genealogy & Biography Cook County, IL with Portraits. Chicago: LaSalle Book Co., 1900.

Andreas, A. T. *History of Chicago from the Earliest Period to the Present Time, Vol I & Vol II.* Chicago: The A.T. Andreas Company, 1884.

Andreas, A. T. *History of Chicago From the Earliest Period to the Present Time, Vol III.* New York: Arno Press, 1975 (1886)

Andreas, A. T. *History of Cook County Illinois, From the Earliest Period to the Present Time.* Chicago: A.T. Andreas, Publisher, 1884.

Avrich, P. *The Haymarket Tragedy.* Princeton: Princeton University Press, 1984.

Bluestone, D. *Constructing Chicago.* New Haven, CT: Yale University Press, 1991.

Bowes, L. M. *A History of the Norwegian Old People's Home.* Norwood Park, IL, 1940.

Bregstone, P. P. *Chicago and Its Jews.* Chicago: Privately Published, 1933.

Buchanan, Joseph R. *The Story of a Labor Agitator.* New York: The Outlook Co., 1903.

Buettner, Paul. *Wicker Park Evangelical Lutheran Church 115th Anniversary Commemorative Book, 1879-1994.* Chicago.

Casson, Herbert N. *The History of the Telephone.* Chicago: A. C. McClurg & Co., 1910.

Chamberlin, E.. *Chicago and its Suburbs.* Chicago: T. A. Hungerford and Co., 1874.

Chicago Census Report. Chicago: The Chicago City Directory, 1871.

Chicago Transit Authority Historical Information, 1859-1965. Chicago: Chicago Transit Authority, 1966.

Colbert, Elias and Everett Chamberlin. *Chicago and the Great Conflagration.* Cincinnati and New York: C. F. Vent, 1871.

Cronon, William. *Nature's Metropolis.* New York: W. W. Norton & Company, 1991.

Curry, J. Seymour. Chicago: *Its History and Its Builders Vol III, IV.* Chicago: S. J. Clarke Publishing Co., 1912.

Cutler, I. *The Jews of Chicago, From Shtetl to Suburb.* Urbana, IL: University of Illinois Press, 1996.

Danckers, Ulrich and Jane Meredith. *A Compendium of the Early History of Chicago to Year 1835 When Indians Left.* River Forest, IL: Early Chicago, Inc., 2000.

Dedmon, Emmett. *Fabulous Chicago.* Chicago: Atheneum, 1983.

Drury, John. *Old Chicago Houses.* Chicago and London: The University of Chicago Press, 1941.

Falk, Jr., Byron and Valerie R. Falk. *Personal Name Index To The New York Times Index 1851-1974.* Succasunna, NJ: Roxbury Data Interface, 1976.

Fishbein, J. I., Ed. *History of Chicago Jewry 1911-1986.* Chicago: Sentinel Publishing Co., 1986.

Flinn, John J. *History of the Chicago Police.* Montclair, NJ: Patterson Smith, 1973.

Flinn, John J. *Chicago, the Marvelous City of the West, A History, an Encyclopedia and a Guide.* Chicago: Flinn & Sheppard, 1891

Foner, P. S. Ed. *Haymarket Martyrs.* New York: Monad Press, 1969.

French, Charles. *Biographical History of the American Irish in Chicago.* Chicago and New York: American Biographical Publishing Co., 1897.

Furetz, Howard B. *Chicago A Chronological & Documentary History 1784-1970.* Dobbs Ferry, New York: Oceana Publications, Inc, 1969.

Gale, Oscar. *Remembrances of Early Chicago.* Chicago: Fleming H. Revell Company, 1920.

Gilbert, Paul and Charles Lee Bryson. *Chicago and It's Makers.* Chicago: Felix Mendelsohn Publishing, 1929.

Hartmut, K and J. B. Jentz. *German Workers in Industrial Chicago, 1850-1910*: A Comparative Perspective. DeKalb, IL: Northern Illinois University Press, 1983.

Hayner, Don and Tom McNamee. *Streetwise Chicago: A History of Chicago Street Names.* Chicago: Loyola University Press, 1988.

History of Illinois & Chicago Railroads.

Hofmeister, R. A. *The Germans of Chicago.* Champaign, IL: Stipes Publishing Co., 1976.

Holland, T. A. *Hollalnd's Directory of Milwaukee Avenue for 1875-76.* Chicago: Western Publishing Company, 1875.

Holli, Melvin G and Peter d'A Jones. *Ethnic Chicago.* Grand Rapids, MI: William B. Eerdmans Publishing Co., 1977.

Holli, Melvin G and Peter d'A Jones. *The Ethnic Frontier, Group Survival In Chicago and the Midwest.* Grand Rapids, MI: William B. Eerdmans Publishing Co., 1977.

Howatt, J. *Notes on the First One Hundred Years of Chicago School History.* Chicago: John Howatt, 1940.

Hoyt, H. *One Hundred Years of Land Values in Chicago, the Relationship of the Growth of Chicago to the Rise in its Land Values 1830-1933.* Chicago: University of Chicago Press, 1933.

Hutchinson, Thomas, Compiler. *Annual Directory of the City of Chicago: 1876-77, 1878-79.* Chicago: Donnelley, Loyd and Company

Industrial Chicago. Chicago: The Goodspeed Publishing Company, 1891.

Kantowicz, E. R. *Polish-American Politics in Chicago 1888-1940.* Chicago: University of Chicago Press, 1975.

Karlen, Harvey M. *Chicago's Crabgrass Communities The History of The Independent Suburbs and Their Post Offices That Became part of Chicago.* Chicago: The Collectors Club of Chicago, 1992.

Keil, H. A. J. and John B, Eds. *German Workers in Chicago, A Documentar History of Working-Class Culture from 1850 to World War I.* Urbana, IL: University of Illinois Press, 1988.

Leonard, John W. *The Book of Chicagoans, A Biographical Dictionary of Leading Living Men of the City of Chicago.* Chicago: A. N. Marquis & Company, 1905.

Little, Kenneth and Kirk Rosenhan. *Chicago Fire Department Engines; Sixty Years of Motorized Pumpers, 1912-1972.* Chicago, 1972.

Long, D. D., Simon Peter. *My Lord and My Life.* Burlington, IA: Lutheran Literary Board, 1924.

Lovoll, Odd S. *A Century of Urban Life — The Norwegians in Chicago Before 1930.* Champaign, IL: The Norwegian-American Historical Association, 1988.

Marquis, Albert Nelson. *The Book of Chicagoans, A Biographical Dictionary of Leading Living Men and Women of the City of Chicago.* Chicago: A. N. Marquis & Company, 1917.

Mayer, Harold M and Richard C. Wade. *Chicago: Growth of A Metropolis.* Chicago and London: The University of Chicago Press, 1969.

Meites, H. L, Ed. *History of the Jews of Chicago.* Chicago: Chicago Jewish Historical Society and Wellington Publishing, Inc., 1990.

Moffat, Bruce. *"L" The Development of Chicago's Rapid Transit System 1888-1832*. Chicago: Central Electric Railfans Association, 1995.

Montay, S. M. I. *History of Catholic Secondary Education in the Archdiocese of Chicago*. Washington, D. C.: The Catholic University of America Press, 1953.

Moses, John and Joseph Kirkland. *History of Chicago, Illinois*. Chicago & New York: Munsell & Co., 1895.

Notable Men of Chicago and Their City. Chicago: Chicago Daily Journal, 1910.

Pacyga, Dominic. *Polish Immigrants and Industrial Chicago, Workers on the South Side*. Columbus, OH: Ohio State University Press, 1991.

Pacyga, Dominic and Ellen Sherrett. *Chicago City of Neighborhoods, History and Tours*. Chicago: Loyola University Press, 1986.

Peyton, John Lewis. *Over the Alleghenies and Across the Praireis (1848) 2nd ed.*

Peyton, John Lewis. *Over the Alleghanies and Across the Prairies*. Chicago and New York: Rand McNally & Company, 1896.

Pierce, Bessie Louise. *A History of Chicago 1848-1871*. Chicago: University of Chicago Press, 1940.

Pierce, Bessie Louise. *A History of Chicago Volume I The Beginning of a City 1673-1848*. New York and London: Alfred A. Knopf, 1937.

Poles of Chicago 1837-1937, A History of One Century of Polish Contribution to the City Of Chicago, Illinois. Chicago: Polish Pageant, Inc., 1937.

Pritchard, Edward Randolph. *Illinois of To-Day and Its Progressive Cities*. Chicago, 1897.

Quaife, Milo M. *Checagou 1673-1835*. Chicago: The University of Chicago Press, 1933.

Quaife, Milo M. *Chicago Highways Old and New From Indian Trail to Motor Road*. Chicago: D. F. Keller & Co., 1923.

Quaife, Milo Milton. *The Development of Chicago 1674-1914*. Chicago: Caxton Club, 1916.

Renumbering Plan of City of Chicago. Chicago: The Chicago Directory Co., 1909.

Republicans of Illinois. Chicago and New York: The Lewis Publishing Company, 1905.

Sanford, Charles. *A History of Healing, A Future of Care Saint Mary of Nazareth Hospital Center: Celebrating a Century of Catholic Hospitality*. Flagstaff, AZ: Heritage Publishers, Inc., 1994.

Schultz, Rima L. and Adele Hast, Eds. *Women Building Chicago 1790-1990 A Biographical Dictionary*. Bloomington, IN: Indiana University Press, 2001.

Schick, L. *Chicago and Its Environs a Handbook for the Traveler*. Chicago, 1891.

Sheahan, James W and George P. Upton. *The Great Conflagration — Chicago: It's Past, Present and Future*. Chicago: Union Publishing Co., 1871.

Shufeldt, Jr., Geo. A. *The History of the Chicago Artesian Well*. Chicago: Religio-Philosophical Publishing Association, 1867.

Simon, Andreas. *Chicago The Garden City*. Chicago: The Franz Gindele Printing Co., 1894.

Skerrett, Ellen and Edward Kantowitz and Steven Avella *Catholicism, Chicago Style*. Chicago: Loyola University Press, 1993.

Souter, Gerry and Janet. *Northbrook, Illinois, The Fabric of Our History*. Northbrook, IL: Northbrook Historical Society and Northbrook Centennial 2001 Committee, 2001.

St. Mary of The Angels 100 Years of Blessings 1899-1999.

Strand, A. E. *History of Norwegians in Illinois*. Chicago: John Anderson Publishing Company, 1905.

Straus, Terry. *Indians of the Chicago Area*. Chicago: NAES College Press, 1990.

Tanner, Helen. *Atlas of Great Lakes Indian History*. Norman, OK: For Newberry Library by University of Oklahoma Press, 1987.

The World's Fair Being A Pictorial History of The Columbian Exposition. Des Moines, IA: M. L. Dudley & Co., 1893.

Thenstrom,, S., Ed.. *Harvard Encycolopedia of American Ethnic Groups*. Cambridge, MS: Belknap Press, 1980.

United States Biographical Dictionary and Portrait Gallery, Etc., Illinois. Chicago and New York: American Biographical Publishing Co., 1876.

Waterman, A. N. *Historical Review of Chicago and Cook County and Selescted Biography*. Chicago: Lewis Publishers Company, 1908.

Winchell, Samuel R. *Chicago Past and Present*. Chicago: A. Flanagan Company, 1910.

Woodruff, Marjorie. *Lucy E. Parsons*. Chicago, 1997?.

Woods, Robert A. and A. J. Kennedy, Eds. *Handbook of Settlements*. New York: Arno Press, 1970.

Young, David M. *Chicago Transit, An Illustrated History*. DeKalb IL: Northern Illinois University Press, 1998.

Directories

Bailey's City Directory: 1864-65, 1865-66;

Business Advertising of Chicago 1844. Chicago: J. W. Norris, 1844.

Chicago Census: 1850, 1870, 1880

D. B. Cooke & Company's Directory 1858

Edward's City of Chicago Directory 1866, 1869-70

Fergus's Directory of the City of Chicago 1839, 1843. 1844, 1855-56

Halpin City of Chicago Directory 1864-65

Lakeside City of Chicago Directory: 1867, 1870, 1871, 1872, 1874-75, 1882, 1889, 1890, 1899, 1901, 1917, 1923.

Land Tract Books For: Twp 40 Sec 31 Range 14E, Twp 39 Sec 6 Range 14E, and 18 Additions.

Norris's Chicago Directory 1846-47, 1848-49.

Articles, Newspapers, Dissertations, Booklets, Reports, and Other Documents

Abstract of Title and other documents for property in Twp 40, Sec 31, Range 14E.

Alden, William C., geologist, 1896. Economic Geology Sheet. Il (Cook) Chicago Quadran: US Geological Survey, 1902.

"An Illinois Senator Stabbed". New York: New York Times, January 15, 1878.

Bell, C. E. "Wicker Park Commercial Area Revitalization Plan". Chicago, 1984.

Baumann, Edward. "The Haymarket Bomber". Chicago: Chicago Tribune Magazine, April 27, 1986.

Beardsley, H. E. "Milwaukee Avenue Holds Great Assets, District is Axis of large Manufacturing" and "Business Section". Chicago: Chicago Tribune, 1928.

Bruss, S. L. "History of Josephinum High School". M.A. Diss., DePaul

University, 1945.

Bureau of Parks Recreation and Aviation 1930 Directory, City of Chicago, 1930.

Chicago Daily News, 1908.

Chicago City Council Proceedings, September 1858–1900.

Chicago City Manual, 1909.

Chicago Daily Tribune: February 15-16, 1929; April 5, 1973, August 2, 1987.

Chicago Herald and Examiner: March 19, 1928.

Chicago History: Spring 1982, Vol 11, Number 1; Spring-Summer 1990, Vol 19, Number 1 & 2. Chicago, 1990.

Chicago Public Works Annual Report 1870-71. Chicago, 1871.

Chicago's West Parks Commissioners Annual Reports: 1870, 1871.

City of Chicago Number Conversion Tables. Compiled under W. P. A. Project Number 673.

"City's Old Tollgates Pioneer Residents of Chicago Recall Time When Tribute Was Collected". Coorens, Elaine. "Wicker Park Begins", *Circa Magazine*. Chicago: Old Wicker Park Committee, Fall 1988.

Dolge, Alfred. "Pianos and their Makers".

Duis, Perry. "The Saloon in a Changing Chicago," *Chicago History*. Chicago, Winter 1975-76.

Eckhoff, G. "Transformation of Milwaukee Avenue from Indian Trail to Modern Boulevard", *Edison-Norwood Weekly*, 1927.

"Historical Register of the Twenty-Two Superseded Park Districts". Chicago: Works Progress Administration and Chicago Park District, 1941.

"Historic City: The Settlement of Chicago". Chicago: City of Chicago Dept. Of Development & Planning, 1976.

"Ice Age Geology". Lockport, IL: Illinois & Michigan Canal NHC, 2001.

Ludwig Drum Co. Catalog Fifty-seven. Chicago, 1956.

MacBain, Ed, Merle. *The Greater Chicago Magazine*. Issues from 1920 through 1930.

Marohn, M.D, Richard C. "The Arming of the Chicago Police in the Nineteenth Century", *Chicago History*. Chicago: Chicago Historical Society, Spring 1982, Vol 11, Number 1.

Muller, Charles M and Roderick A. Manstein. Chicago 1891 - Annexation. Chicago: Globe Lithographing and Printing Co., 1891.

Noel, Joseph R. "A Policeman's Place in the Community", *Main 13*, Sept/Oct, 1921.

Noel, Joseph R. "Data Pertaining To Vitae Ore and V. O. Preparations," Chicago, April 15, 1932.

Noel, Theophilus. *Autobiography & Reminiscences of Theophilus Noel*. Chicago: The Noel Company Print, 1904.

"Notice to Pre-emption Claimants", *Chicago Democrat*, Chicago, March 25, 1835.

Notz, Jr., John Kranz. "To Cathect or not to Cathect". Chicago: Presented to The Chicago Literary Club, 1996.

Piehl, Frank J. "Our Forgotten Streetcar Tunnels," *Chicago History*. Chicago: Chicago Historical Society, Fall 1975.

Posadas, B. M. "Community Structures of Chicago's Northwest Side: The Transition From Rural to Urban, 1830-1889". Ph.D. Diss., Northwestern University, 1976.

"Potawatomi History", Potawatomi Histories Site

Report to the City Council on Garbage Collection and Disposal by the Department of Public Works Chicago, 1905.

Report of the General Supt. of Police of the City of Chicago, Fiscal Year Ending 1882. Chicago, 1883.

Sandstrom, Char. "The History of the Park", Circa Magazine. Chicago: Old Wicker Park Committee, May, 1987.

Schoenherr, Steven E. "History of Radio," August 2001.

Schulz, Jr., Otto. "Otto F. Schulz Memoirs", Volume One.

Sommers, Nicholas H. "The Historic Homes of Old Wicker Park". Chicago: Old Wicker Park Committee, 1979.

Stehman, J. H. "The Story of Milwaukee Avenue". Chicago: 11, 1936.

Stillwell, R. F. "A Parish History and Study of the Fourth Congregational Church of Chicago". Chicago, 1927.

The Greater Chicago Magazine: Feb. 1929 Vol. IV Number 2;

"The Squires of Wicker Park". Chicago: The Chicago Tribune Newspaper, July 19, 1943.

Uihlein, Edward Gustav. "Memories of My Youth."

"Up From The Mud". Chicago: Board of Education of Chicago, 1941.

Werth, J. T. "Wicker Park Oral History": A Research Draft, Written for the Neighborhood Planning Unit of the Dept. of Development and Planning, The City of Chicago. Chicago, 1976.

Whelan, M.D., Chas J. "Biennial Report of Department of Health", City of Chicago. Chicago, 1906.

Wicker, C. M. Letter to his family describing the Chicago Fire.

Wicker Park District, Preliminary staff summary of information. Chicago: Commission on Chicago Landmarks, March 1989.

Zimmerman, B. "Milwaukee Avenue", *The Chicago Guide*, 1973.

Maps

Muller, Charles and R. A. Manstein. "Map Showing Territorial Growth of the City of Chicago", accompanies Annual Report of the Map Department. Chicago: Globe Lithographing and Printing Co., 1891.

Chicago 1830 Map.

City of Chicago Map, 1867.

Map of City of Chicago, Warner & Beers, 1876.

Rascher's Fire Insurance Map 1892.

Robinson, E. Robinson Fire Insurance Maps, 1886.

Sanborn Fire Insurance Maps 1894-1928.

Wicker Park Planting Plan, 1905.

Electronic Sites

Chicago Historical Society. www.ChicagoHS.org

Chicago Public Library Digital Collections. www.ChicagoPublicLibrary.org

Illinois Secretary of State Website. www.sos.state.IL.us

"Knute Rockne's Adolesence". http://home.no.net

"Legacy of Success". www.CrownTheaters.com

Library of Congress. www.loc.gov

National Trust. www.NationalTrust.org

Newberry Library. www.newberry.org

Oakland Health Club. www.OakLeafBroom.com

Telephone History. http://TelephoneTribute.com

Index

Walking Tour

Plate WT 1

Built in 1888 for Herman Weinhardt this home is located at 2137 W. Pierce.

Street Numbering & Name History

STREET NUMBERS AND NAMES HAVE HISTORIES OF THEIR OWN. CHICAGO STREET NUMBERS AND NAMES HAVE CHANGED OVER TIME. THE INITIAL NUMBERING WAS INCONSISTENT. THE CITY WAS DIVIDED INTO THREE DIVISIONS AND EACH HAD ITS OWN SYSTEM. THE BASES FOR THESE SYSTEMS WERE THE CHICAGO RIVER, ITS TWO BRANCHES, THE LAKESHORE AND LAKE STREET.

In 1909 the Brennan numbering system was introduced. This system used State and Madison as the base line for the numbering. Madison is where North and South numbering begins and State is where East and West numbers change.

Though street numbering is now consistent, the street names continue to change. Following are current streets, listed alphabetically, in the Wicker Park District, if there is at least one structure with historical information listed. A short history of each of these street names is given below.

Descriptions of the buildings on each street begin on the pages listed to the right of the name. Street name information is shown below each name.

BELL AVENUE   Page WT5
Named after either Alexander Graham Bell (1847-1922) or Lt. George Bell. In 1861, Lt. Bell led the 37th Regiment of the Illinois Volunteers, which was mustered into service in Chicago to fight in the Civil War. (Former names: Shober and Irving).

CATON STREET   Page WT7
Originally named Columbia Place, in anticipation of the Columbian Exposition planned for 1892, Caton St. was laid out and platted in 1889-90. It and the next parallel street, Concord St., were the last streets created in the area. Only one block long, Caton had a gate on each end. The foundations remain.

　　　It was later named for Chief Justice of the Illinois Supreme Court, Judge John Dean Caton (1812-1895). A New York native, he settled in Chicago in 1833 and was admitted to the bar two years later. He opened what may have been Chicago's first law practice. His daughter was Delia Caton (Marshall) Field.

Plate WT 2
POSTCARD ANNOUNCES STREET NUMBER CHANGES SHOWING THE OLD (502) AND THE NEW (1627) NUMBERS FOR A. BECK'S ADDRESS ON GRAND AVE. THIS POSTCARD SHOWS ONE WAY PEOPLE USED TO NOTIFY FAMILY AND FRIENDS THE RESULT OF THE NEW BRENNAN STREET NUMBERING SYSTEM. POSTMARKED 1:30 A.M. AUG. 28, 1909, MR. BECK WAS SURE JOHN BENSON WOULD KNOW HIS NEWS LATER THAT SAME DAY.

CLAREMONT AVENUE   Page WT11

Named after Robert Fulton's steam boat, this was formerly Davis St.

CONCORD PLACE   Page WT13

Originally laid in 1889-90, this street was called Alice Place. It was later changed to Concord Street, in honor of the New Hampshire town.

CRYSTAL STREET   Page WT15

May have been named for the mineral.

DAMEN AVENUE   Page WT17

Named in 1927 after Father Arnold Damen (1850-1890), a Jesuit priest who was a founder of Holy Family Catholic Church, St. Ignatius High School and Loyola University (1870). Named Robey in 1895, it was originally Grove Street.

ELK GROVE AVENUE   Page WT19

Named after a grove of the same name that existed here before the land was developed. It was a popular picnic site, and yes, Elk roamed here.

EVERGREEN AVENUE   Page WT21

Named for the tree.

HONORE STREET   Page WT27

Henry Hamilton Honore (1824-1916) was a Chicago real estate developer. His work in helping to establish Chicago's parks and boulevard system established his place in Chicago's history. Daniel Burnham said, "...wherever his hand appeared, there has been big, broad development. ...he has ever looked into the future." Of French ancestry, Mr. Honore was in the wholesale hardware business in Louisville, Ky., before coming to Chicago in 1855. This is why some historians credit him with naming Ashland Ave., which ran through his subdivision, after Henry Clay's home in Kentucky. Mr. Honore's daughter, Bertha, married Potter Palmer and became Chicago's leading socialite in the late 1800s. Formerly Girard from Milwaukee north and Fontenoy between Milwaukee and Wicker Park Ave. Fontenoy was formerly Park Ct.

HOYNE AVENUE   Page WT29

Thomas Hoyne (1817-1883) served as Chicago's disputed mayor for three months in 1876. As mayor, he abolished the city's practice of borrowing money on certificates, a move credited with placing the city's credit rating on solid ground.

In 1853, as newly appointed United States attorney for the district of Illinois, he prosecuted a mail robber. Mr. Abe Lincoln defended the accused, but Mr. Hoyne won the case. The victory secured Mr. Hoyne's legal reputation. Despite their initial encounter, Mr. Lincoln and Mr. Hoyne were friends. When President Lincoln was slain, Mr. Hoyne was part of the escort that brought the body to Chicago to lie in state. Hoyne drew up Chicago's first Thanksgiving Day proclamation in 1840. Hoyne Ave. was formerly Horan Avenue.

LEAVITT STREET   Page WT37

David Leavitt was a banker who came to Chicago from New York. He was appointed a trustee of the Illinois and Michigan Canal in 1844.

LEMOYNE STREET   Page WT41

John Le Moyne was a lawyer and congressman from Chicago in the late 1800s. He was born in Pennsylvania in 1828 and moved to Chicago about 1852. He served in Congress in the 1870s and was a founder of Chicago's Philharmonic Society and other organizations devoted to music. Street formerly known as Thompson.

MILWAUKEE AVENUE   Page WT43

One of the original Indian paths and later a plank, toll road, it was named for an Algonquin Indian village that is now the site of Milwaukee, WI. "Fine land" is the English translation.

NORTH AVENUE   Page WT47

This was the northern boundary of the city when Chicago was incorporated in 1837.

OAKLEY BOULEVARD   Page WT51

Charles Oakley (1792-1849), an Illinois politician, was one of the first state-appointed trustees of the Illinois and Michigan Canal in 1844. Possibly one of the earliest Chicago politicians accused of patronage, Oakley worked to obtain financing overseas and back East for the massive Canal project.

PIERCE AVENUE   Page WT53

Originally named Ewing Place for William Lee Davidson Ewing (1795-1846). Mr. Ewing was a lawyer, colonel of the Spy Battalion during the Black Hawk War, an Indian agent, president of the Illinois Senate in the 1830s, and governor for fifteen days in 1834.

Ashael Pierce came to Chicago in 1833 and worked as a blacksmith. He and his brother M.J. Pierce started the Pierce Brothers' land development firm, and in 1869 developed about eighty acres of land.

POTOMAC AVENUE   Page WT57

Formerly Bryson, west of Wolcott and Blucher east of Wolcott. This avenue was named for the Union's Army of the Potomac, which took its' name from the Potomac River. Potomac is a variation of Patowomek, an Indian village and tribe in Virginia. The word means, "a place where something is brought".

SCHILLER STREET   Page WT61

Johann Christoph Friedrich von Schiller (1759-1805) was one of Germany's greatest literary figures. He is considered to be the founder of modern German literature. Formerly "Fowler", this street was probably named by German sub-dividers to honor their heritage.

WICKER PARK AVENUE   Page WT65

Originally named Park St. it was changed to Wicker Park Avenue in honor of the park.

WOLCOTT AVENUE   Page WT67

Dr. Alexander Wolcott (1790-1830) came to Chicago from Windsor, Conn. as an Indian agent in 1820. He married Ellen Marion Kinzie. Their wedding is said to be one of the first in Chicago. This avenue was formerly Lincoln Street.

WOOD STREET   Page WT67

Alonzo Wood was a real estate sub-divider in the 1880s.

In the mid 1970s, the first step in applying for listing in The National Register of Historic Places was to identify significant buildings. Over 450 sites were selected in the Wicker Park District. Most of them remain, though some have been destroyed. Those buildings plus a few others are described on the following pages. Ratings, shown below as per the 1970s listing, are to the left of a number in parentheses at the end of each address description. The number is used for locating addresses on maps. Example: AH(337)

> **A** = **Architectural Significance**
> **H** = **Historical Significance**
> **M** = **Major contribution to the fabric of district**

For your convenience, building descriptions on the following pages are organized by street. Streets are listed alphabetically. Addresses are in numeric order. Use the map at the back of the book to customize your tour.

Buildings by Street

BELL AVENUE (NORTH)
1304, 1318, 1320, 1322
These four structures were built as residences in the Italianate style that features a flat cornice with brackets and dentils; indented facade or rectangular bay windows with a unified appearance with stone hoods and stringcourses. M(1)

1308
Italianate styled two-flat with stone hoods and continuous stringcourse. M(2)

1316, 1317
These four two-flats are of the same Italianate styling as the first four addresses listed above. M(3)

1311, 1353
Italianate is the style for these residences with a peaked gabled roof. M(4)

1321, 1333, 1341, 1349, 1352
Built around 1883, these are a highly simplified one to one- and-a-half story cottages with a gabled roof, as advertised by S.E. Gross in 1883. M(5)

1337
This residence is in Queen Anne styling. M(6)

1340, 1342, 1344, 1349 REAR
Little is known about these residences. M(7)

1350, 1351, 1354
A flat front is one of the characteristics of this Italianate style. Flat cornice with brackets and dentils and individually treated windows are also typical of this style. M(8)

1356
This building was built as a store with apartments.

The exact construction date is not known but it is in the same style as 1304, 1318, and 1322. M(9)

1400, 1408, 1410, 1434, 1438, 1440, 1452, 1456
All eight of these homes are of the same Italianate style as described for 1304, 1318, 1320, and 1322 above. M(10)

1456 N. BELL

1406, 1412, 1416, 1422, 1454
All of these residences were built around 1883 in an Italianate style similar to 1321. M(11)

1420
This is an Italianate style residence similar to 1350, 1351 and 1354. M(12)

1418, 1430
The difference between these two structures and 1420 is the window treatment. Notice these windows are unified. M(13)

1432
Windows on this Italianate style are treated individually.

Characterized by an indented facade or rectagular bay, the cornice is flat with brackets and dentils. M(14)

1441

A three-flat, this structure is in the Queen Anne style. M(15)

1442

Queen Anne style single-family residence. M(16)

CORNER OF BELL AND HIRSCH

The date of construction of Albert P. Sabin Public School is unknown. However, there is no doubt about its classical revival style.

In the 1500 block of Bell, the western most edge of both the National Historic District and the Chicago Landmark District, you'll see an eclectic mix of housing stock, a bridge between both halves of Wicker Park. A large Victorian convent used to stand on the west side where the schoolyard is now. A(17)

1507

This Queen Anne two-flat, with many classical and Romanesque details, was built in 1890. Up until 1990 it was a rooming house. It has been extensively renovated, returning it to a two-flat. At one time the building was used as an auto shed!

Brick and sandstone surfaces have been chemically cleaned to reveal scallop detailing, bead and reel moldings and foliate detailing at the end of the columns. M(18)

1511

This is an example of the smaller high quality residential buildings built in the 1890s. It was built for Mrs. Emma E. Peters, whose son or husband, Charles, was a deputy marshal. The architecture is a mixture of Romanesque and Queen Anne Styles. The cornice design of two facing swans was obscured by years of "paint-over" and neglect until repaired. There originally was an entrance below the main one, apparently for the servants' quarters, but it was closed up at some point. M(19)

1523, 1537

Built circa 1883, this Italianate cottage is like the six described above in the 1400 block. They all have gabled roofs. M(20)

1525

This single-family residence is the same Italianate style as 1354, 1351, and 1354. M(21)

1531

The coach house on this property was one of the first buildings on this block, built in 1888. C.E. Lohman is listed as the architect. It may have been moved to the rear of the lot to make room for the later addition of the two-flat in 1905. The metal cornice has fine detail and is in excellent condition. Much of the original woodwork and ceiling moldings and medallions remain in the two-flat. M(22)

1535 N. BELL

1535

This basic red brick building was built as a worker's three-flat for $5,000 in 1891. The cornice was long ago removed, and would have been destroyed anyway on August 8,1988, when lightning struck the upper right corner causing a four-foot gash. The basement floor was dirt in 1988. M(23)

1541, 1545

Both of these homes were built in the Queen Anne style. M(24)

1649

This two-flat, built in 1903 at the rear of the lot, has a drive-through access to the yard from the alley, indicating it may have been a coach house. The original trims, including raised panel wainscoting in the kitchen, remained intact. Renovation into a single-family home has retained its farmhouse charm. M(25)

CATON STREET (WEST)

Scandinavians built most of the structures on Caton. They were also probably responsible for building St. Paul's Norwegian Evangelical Lutheran Church on North Avenue. Interiors of these homes contain every embellishment from polychromatic parquet to ornate plaster ceilings and stained glass windows, either intact or painstakingly restored.

2131 W. CATON

2131

Built in the 1890s, this Queen Anne Victorian two-flat was converted into eight units and painted bright pink by the early 1970s. Fortunately, it has been revamped into a tasteful pair of duplex apartments with modern appointments and a "wooden deck." M(26)

2135

Notice the beautiful porch with spindle-like wood supports and the unusual metal balcony. This Queen Anne styled residence is a near twin to 2151. They were both built in 1892 by the same builder. M(27)

2137

Notice the similarity to 2141. Ole Thorp built them as a pair of two-flats in 1893-94. Note the beautiful wood doors, roof turret and decorative eaves. M(28)

2138

Built in the Romanesque Revival style in 1891, it was the home of Dr. George Thilo. This exterior is virtually unchanged except for new landscaping and the iron fence across the side yard. The house has always been a single-family dwelling and was never divided up as a rooming house.

All the leaded glass windows are original to the house. The carved oak leaf motif on the stonework and front door is repeated in the carved oak woodwork of the interior. Exterior details include the bulbous three-dimensional cross, which serves as the finial for the domed turret. Notice all of the outside sills are different (the second story has what appears to be a window box, the first floor has two different patterns). M(29)

2141

One of Ole Thorp's buildings, it has a flat facade with brick pilasters. Notice the sunburst patterns on the cornices and over all the openings. Its "mate" is 2137. (30)

2142

Built in 1891 for Nels Nelson, a local businessman, this Romanesque Revival styled 14-room mansion contains some of the finest interior and exterior details on the street. The facade is of rusticated pink sandstone at ground level, changing to textured brick on the upper levels. Of particular interest is the freestanding Romanesque column supporting the ominous turret with its spike finial. Polished granite columns support the front porch.

Most spectacular, however, is the restoration work inside: original woods have been carefully cleaned and finished; the built-in sideboard and original gas chandelier are complimented by the more modern addition of mirrors between the original beams of the dining room ceiling; and a striking pair of griffins face each other on the mantel of the decorative parlor fireplace. New French doors lead out to a garden of various woods and ground cover. A concrete deck is a contemporary addition; it overlooks the lily pond and steps, which cantilever from the main structure in the rear. M(31)

2142 W. CATON

2145

Though this looks like many Chicago two-flats, it is a spacious four-bedroom home built in the 1890s. It is the original Wicker Park home of John F. Smulski (originally Jachimski). His father was the publisher of the first Polish newspaper in Chicago. He moved to 2138 W. Pierce in 1902. (32)

2146

Built in 1891-93 for Luis Lambeau, this Romanesque single family red-brick residence features two impressive semi-circular arches supported by miniature stone columns with basket-type carved capitals. Notice the picturesque balcony and the pair of small turrets. Lambeau became vice president of the Lambeau Leather Company on Elston Ave. in 1899. A(33)

2147

This is the newest home on Caton. It was built by William A. Thorsen in 1906. He was the owner of an architectural metals mill. Owned by the Thorsens

until 1949, it was converted into a two-flat, then a three-flat, and then eleven one-room apartments. Renovated in the early 1970s, it is now a five-bedroom single-family residence. The rectangular facade of this building exemplifies the Beaux Arts style. Constructed of flat cut greystone, the structure is fitted out with metal ornamental trim. There are balustrades at both the roof and second floor porch, with the porch supported by Roman-composite columns of Ionic and Corinthian styling. The ornamentation on the porch frieze contains garlands of grapes and flowers tied with bows, and little lions' heads at either end. The interior also contains a great deal of ornamental metal work, including an ornate dining room ceiling. M(34)

2147 W. CATON

2151

Built in 1892 as a "honeymoon house," this building is of Queen Anne styling. It originally had a master bedroom connected directly to a nursery, with no other bedrooms. In keeping with the style, it lacks symmetry in the layout of rooms, the position of doors and windows and the placement of decoration. Sometime after WWII, probably in the mid-1960s, it was divided into three apartments, then converted back to single-family use in the late 1970s. It is a near twin to 2135. A(35)

2152

Essentially Gothic Revival in style, it was built in 1891. The first owner was Max Tauber, the largest livery contractor for the city and a friend of the mayor.

His first wife thought he had died in a fire at work and she died of a heart attack. He remarried in the 1920s and lost everything in the 1929 crash. He did not declare bankruptcy, but started over in a partnership with banker Joseph Noel. He paid back all his debts before murdering his wife and committing suicide in the 1930s, after which the residence became a rooming house.

There are innumerable art glass windows in this house, including triple sash stained glass windows. Note the coiled dragon above the door and the terrella to the left and right. M(36)

2151 W. CATON

2155

This three-story single-family residence was built for C. Hanson in 1899-1900. The style is Classic Romanesque and Queen Anne. It has a rusticated stone facade and a classical porch with fluted pillars. M(37)

2156

The largest structure on Caton, the house and coach house cover three city lots. It was built for and by Ole A. Thorp (1856-1905), the Norwegian developer of the Caton Street Subdivision. It cost $7,500 while other buildings on the street, of the same era, cost between $3,600 and $8,000.

A large domed turret rises from the flared and rusticated foundation. The finial was replaced in 1986.

Small granite columns support the front entry arch. There is a stone sunburst design above the second story faux porch. By 1971, this mansion had become a rooming house; now it is a two unit building. A Norwegian coat-of-arms exists above the large fireplace in the rear parlor.

The lower level originally contained a terrazzo-floored ballroom with wine cellar, kitchen facilities and furnace room. The small coach house has space for two horse-drawn buggies with a hayloft. The brick arch from the original door is visible above the current metal one.

Thorp, a Norwegian native who was in the import-export business, built 2137, 2142, 2152, and 2156. The Queen of Norway reportedly stayed frequently with the Thorp family when visiting Chicago. A(38)

2159

This large home was built in 1891 by William Hopkins. The original address was 62 Columbia—you can see the number 62 in the stained glass above the front door. The style is Queen Anne, with two small Queen Anne porches on the front and side. Both have turned columns, ornamental brackets and turned spindles. Up above the first floor windows you'll see a pressed brick stringcourse; near the cornice is another decorative stringcourse. M(39)

WICKER PARK EAGLE
EXCERPTS

FOR SALE

$800 will buy a lot on Claremont near Potomac Ave. Call at once. T.W. Schulze & Co., 419 W. Division St.
—April or May 1909

LOCAL INTEREST

Mr. And Mrs. Joseph Hollander 2159 Columbia St., announce the engagement of their daughter Sadie to Samuel G. Orenstein. They were at home to their many friends Sunday, February 20.
—March 1911

Mr. And Mrs. Otto Schulz and family, 2142 Columbia court, returned from a five weeks' trip to the east. The greater part of the time was spent at Martha's Vineyard, an island in the Atlantic ocean. 85 miles from Newport, R. I. Mr. Schulz is vice-president of the Northwest Side Commercial Association.
—August 1913

HORSES LOST IN BARN FIRE

The origin of fire at Max Tauber's barns at Wabansia avenue and Leavitt street has not been established, but it seems that crossed electric wires, probably started the disastrous fire on August 10th in which nearly sixty horse were burned to death.
—August 1913

James O'Connor has sold to Theodore Juergens what is known as the old Keeley flats for $23,050, subject to an encumbrance of $9,300. The improvements comprise six two flat and four three flat buildings. In part payment Mr. Juergens conveyed the twelve room residence at 2141 Ewing place, for $18,000 with encumbrance of $4,000. Hessey and Kirkley represented both parties to the transaction.
—February 1910

CLAREMONT AVENUE (NORTH)

1325

This Gothic Revival building was built in 1891. Formally opened with the graduation ceremony on June 22, 1892, Northwest Division High School was one of the best and most modern in the city. It was the site of tours during the Columbian Exposition in 1893.

The name changed to Murray F. Tuley High School in 1917 when the building was expanded. It became Tuley High in 1939 with the dedication of a new structure, replacing the original fire ravaged building. Note the elliptical-arched entrance.

This building was the home of Tuley Middle School beginning in 1975 and then became the Jose de Diego Community Academy in September, 1982. Famous names who were educated on this site include: Knute Rockne, Abe Stollar, Sidney Justin Harris, Saul Bellow and Sam Wanamaker. M(40)

1328

Essentially a Gothic Revival, this is a three-flat building with other eclectic detailing including a Romanesque arched entrance. A(41)

1332

These three-flats are both in an eclectic French Chateau and Beaux Arts style. M(42)

1338

Built in 1895, this two-flat is in a similar eclectic style as 1332 and 1342. M(43)

1431

St. Elizabeth's Hospital, main building, was built in 1929. Art Deco inspired portions of the main entrance are intact. The five-story addition to the north is not part of the original structure. German born Father Aloysius Thiele, who founded St. Aloysius Church, was instrumental in bringing the Poor Handmaids of Jesus Christ to the community. This order of nuns was dedicated to care for the sick. They laid the corner stone for the original hospital on October 17, 1886 at 1405 N. Oakley. That building, Margaritas Hall, was torn down in the late 1990s. M(44)

WICKER PARK EAGLE
EXCERPTS

DROWNS AS HE BATHES IN TANK AT Y. M. C. A.

William Meier, a civil engineer, son of Rev. Jacob Meier, superintendent of the German Baptist Missions of the Northwest, was drowned on Feb 14 in the swimming pool of the central department of the YMCA, 153 LaSalle Street.

Meier was a graduate of the engineering school of the University of Illinois and was 32 Years old. He lived with his parents at 2152 Alice Place and is survived by them and four brothers and one sister.
—*February 1910*

REAL ESTATE

Carl Schiffmann of Schiffmann Bros. Lumber Company has purchased from K.A. Johnson and M.E. Baker, 175 x101 feet on Milwaukee Ave., between Alice Place and North Ave. It was purchased with the intention of getting more space as their present quarters are too small for the rapid growth of business. —*February 1910*

NOTES

The Nos Intimes Whist Club met at the home of Mrs. Henry L. Hertz, 1351 N. Hoyne Ave., on February 7th. On February 23, Mrs. Charles B. Knudson entertained the same Club at her home 2146 Alice Place.

Judge Oscar M. Torrison, 2129 Alice Place, was on the sick list for a few days.

Mr. And Mrs. Phillip Jackson of 2152 Alice announced the engagement of the daughter, Ruth Dorothy to George Washington Bromberg, son of Mr/Mrs. M. Bromberg, 2333 Racine.
—*February 1910*

CONCORD PLACE (WEST)

2053-61

A flat building designed in Romanesque Revival style, this was built as a stable. Delbert S. Mills was the architect. M(45)

2102-4-6-8

This is the last building to be built on this block, dating from shortly after World War I (1926). Originally it contained thirteen small one-bedroom apartments, designed with all the architects' ingenuity to serve families of four or even more. Units were complete with double Murphy beds in the living room closets and truly modern amounts of closet space for such small apartments. (46)

2124 W. CONCORD

2112, 2116, 2120, 2124, 2134, 2152

These buildings were all eight-room three-flats originally, later most were divided. Other buildings nearby on Leavitt, Bell and Oakley, are remarkably similar and probably were constructed by a speculative builder. The squared bay of 2112 compares with that of 2120, and the rounded Romanesque styled bay of 2116 with that of 2124. The second story porch balustrade continues in relief on the facade of 2112, while 2120 is distinguished with a decorative frieze on the neatly styled cornice. The simple design of the ironwork that serves as the railing for the second floor porch is repeated in the ironwork of the front stairs. 2124 exhibits columns in an abstracted or decadent Corinthian styling. After the late Victorian period and before more innovative modern styling, decorations often adhered less strictly to traditional motifs; altering Classic columns for new structural needs as well as the ornamental appearance was considered au courant. M(47)

2113, 2117, 212L, 2125

These four buildings were built as a single project in 1893 and were originally identical except for differences of facade and interior decoration. The old Humboldt Park branch elevated line ran through what are now the back yards of these buildings, so they were built with a continuous, windowless brick wall along the south to shield them from the noise. Hence the back porches face Concord and not the alley, and you can most easily see the original plan, indeed the original porch, between 2121 and 2125. All except 2117 have been extensively, if not entirely, renovated. The facades are interesting, if not particularly special: notice the Beaux Arts style oval window in the pediment structure at 2113; the longer flat narrow bricks employed in the structure at 2117 (they were particularly popular around the turn of the century); the rusticated quoins in 2121 and the foliated bas relief under the second story bay window. M(48)

2125 W. CONCORD

2129

This was the first building on Concord (then known as Alice Place) and predates other structures by about 15 years. It was probably a farmhouse, and the similar two-flat across the street at 2140 reportedly was built by the same family. The front of the building was extended several feet and equipped with a new facade, which still is older than its neighbors. Notice the semi-circular and full-circle openings also seen on 1951 W. Schiller and 2137 W. Pierce. M(49)

2132

An unusual building with distinctive Prairie School details, this two or three-flat was built in the 1900s. (50)

2134

Built as a two or three-flat, this Gothic-revival inspired structure was constructed in 1895. M(51)

2137-39

This apartment building was built after the elevated came through behind it, and therefore has few southern windows. It was a burned out hulk in 1975.

Notice the rather interesting detail in the pediment cornice, which is of unusual character. The high

pilaster columns spring from acanthus leaf scrolled (and non-structural) corbels. M(52)

2156

John Anderson, a prominent realtor in the area, built this Victorian Romanesque-style home in 1893. Note the tower with conical roof, steeply pitched gabled dormer and transom windows. Thirteen different cabinet woods have been found in the house. Parquet floors, a white marble fireplace and a wine cellar highlight the interior. M(53)

CRYSTAL STREET (WEST)

2014
The National Register of Historic Places classifies this structure as typical of Italianate style that is characterized by a flat cornice with brackets and often dentils; a flat front; and individual window treatment. M(54)

2015
This is classified as Italianate with the flat cornice but with an indented facade or rectangular bay and individually treated windows. M(55)

2023, 2024, 2025
These three workman's cottage residences are further examples of Italianate but with a peaked gabled roof with brackets and/or dentils. Construction dates span at least eight years. First was probably 2025 followed by 2023 in 1886 and finally 2024, which was built in 1904. M(56)

2028
The current street grade was completed in the 1870s. This was built prior to that in the style described for 2023. M(57)

2027, 2030, 2035, 2043
All of these two-flats have the same styling as 2015 except that the windows are unified with continuous hoods and/or stringcourses. Their construction occurred in the 1880s. M(58)

2033
Built in 1892, this style transitions Italianate to Queen Anne. M(59)

2027 W. CRYSTAL

2034
This is another example of a workman cottage as described for 2023 above. M(60)

2038
A residence designed in the Queen Anne style, it joined the neighborhood in 1890. M(61)

2114
Another workman cottage, this was built in 1889. Unfortunately the structure was lost to fire in 2001. M(62)

2124
Listed in the permit records as 2120-22, this structure was built in 1902 by Bob Leafgrau. Construction costs totaled $15,000 for the Beth El Temple. It is a two-story brick church with two adjacent entrances.

Since about 1970 it has been the home of the Original New Morning Star Missionary Baptist Church. M(63)

2125

A two-story residence dating to 1904, it was built by G. N. Nelson for H.G. Guttermeister. For $3,000, it was less costly then the religious structures. This was structure was destroyed in 2002. M(64)

2126-2128

Named Molner Hall, it included a two-story flat and a one-story hall when it was built in 1905. Joseph Todd constructed this at a cost of $14,000 for the Beth El Congregation. M(65)

2127

Built in 1904, the architects were Worthmann and Steinbach. Designed in Gothic revival styling, this church was originally the Evangelical Lutheran Church of our Savior for the Deaf. More currently it was the home of the Peoples' Missionary Baptist Church. M(66)

DAMEN AVENUE (NORTH)

1215, 1216, 1222

All three of these structures were built as two or three-flats in the 1880s. They are essentially Queen Anne in design with some Italianate influenced detailing. M(67)

1217

The flat cornice with brackets, the flat front and individually treated windows are typical of one type of Italianate design. It was built as a two or flat in 1892. M(68)

1233

An 1880s building, notice that this Italianate style has a mansard roof. M(69)

1235

Like many structures on this commercial street, this was built as a store with an apartment above in the 1880s. The cornice detailing is original, however the storefront has been modified. M(70)

1237-39

A manufacturing site, this four-story building was constructed in 1888 as a pair of two-flats with Italianate detailing. Its address was 572-4 Robey. A(71)

1243

Like 1215 in design, this residence was built in the 1890s. M(72)

1245

Built in 1886, this was built as a two or three-flat in the style of transitional Italianate and Queen Anne. M(73)

1246

This Italianate multi-unit 1886 building includes the following characteristics: flat cornice with brackets and dentils, indented facade or rectangular bay, and windows unified with continuous hoods and/or stringcourses. M(74)

1247

Built in 1886, this is an example of a workman's cottage. M(75)

1249

Constructed in the 1880s, this was built as a two or three-flat. M(76)

1255

A single-family residence, this cottage Italianate design is characterized by gabled, peaked roof with brackets and dentils. M(77)

1311

Like many homes in Wicker Park, the original dwelling was built around 1890 and now serves as a coach house for this recently remodeled multi-apartment building. The simple cottage, adorned only with a metal cornice of brackets and dentil work.

The front dwelling was constructed as a "middle class" workers' three-flat between 1895 and 1900. Reflecting a more affluent status by the owners, more ornamentation is found on the metal cornice and medallion limestone lintels over the entry way and windows. M(78)

1311 N. DAMEN

1338

Built as essentially as a Gothic Revival styled church, it is the current home of the Chicago Missionary Society. M(79)

1351

The flat cornice with brackets, the flat front and windows unified with continuous hoods and/or stringcourses are typical of this type of Italianate design. It was built as a three-flat. M(80)

1530

Though the original date of this Classical Revival style building is unknown, it served as a professional building prior to occupancy by Illinois Bell Telephone Co. It is now the home of North Ave. Day Care Center which occupied the residence at 2024 W. Pierce (around the corner). M(81)

1537-9

Built as an investment by Mathias Schulz in 1885, Schulz was owner of a cabinet shop that later made organs and player pianos. He lived in a home next door that stood where the former auto shop now cafe is at Damen and Wicker Park Avenues. This Italianate style building is typified by a flat cornice with brackets and dentils; indented facade or rectangular bay; and windows unified with continuous hoods and/or stringcourses. M(82)

1542

Schulz's son, Otto, built this complex of storefronts and living units. This was built on the site of a wood-

en mansion just after the "L" came through.

A neighborhood institution, Sophie's Busy Bee Restaurant occupied 1546. It was the main neighborhood eatery for over 30 years. Featuring Polish foods, its Polish immigrant owner, Sophie Madej, and her family served breakfast, lunch and dinner to an ever-changing unbelievable mix of humanity including neighborhood residents, police, film crews, artists, sanitation crews, former residents, and visitors. Opened in 1965, they served their last pierogi on June 28, 1998. M(83)

1551

The date is unknown for this business block with apartments on the upper levels. It is considered to be typical of the Italianate style with a flat cornice of brackets and dentils, a flat front, and unified windows with continuous stone hoods and stringcourses. M(84)

1560-62

Built in 1894 by the Metropolitan E. Railroad the number of this commercial block was 733-43 Robey. Like 1551, it is an Italianate style building with rusticated stone hoods and continuous stringcourses. M(85)

1568

On March 10, 1885, Joseph Sokup took out a building permit for a three-story building for a store and dwelling that was to be 24 ft. on the front, 60 ft. deep, and 36 ft. high. The original address was 1228 Milwaukee Ave.

In 1890, typical of the community's mix, the first floor housed the professional offices of Drs. Jeffis B. Grant and Norman Kerr, physicians and surgeons and Dr. Rudolf Hasselrus, dentist; the Nielson, Gehrke, & Rusler, Clothiers; and a saloon owned by Daniel McCarthy. McCarthy lived on the second floor, as did two clerks, Joseph Luby and Edward Olson, and a policeman, John R. Looby. The third floor was a large Lodge Hall. (86)

1621

Originally this brick and brownstone structure housed the Chicago Fire Department Station. M(87)

ELK GROVE AVENUE (NORTH)

1410

Italianate style similar to 1422, there is not much more known about this residence. M(88)

1412

This flat building was originally built to an earlier, lower street grade. It is considered to be in an Italianate style with the following characteristics: flat cornice with brackets and often dentils; a flat front; and windows unified with continuous hoods and/or stringcourses (horizontal lines). M(89)

1422

Built in the Italianate style, the peaked gable roof originally would have had brackets and dentils. This residence was built to the same lower street grade as 1412. M(90)

1424

Different than most of the buildings on this street, this has a mix of styles; Queen Anne, Gothic and Romanesque. M(91)

1428

This residence is an Italianate style similar to 1422. M(92)

1432, 1523

Both of these three-flats were built in a Queen Anne style. M(93)

1441

Built prior to the current street level, this is Italianate style home has a mansard roof. M(94)

1500

Like 1514 and 1524, its origin is unknown, except that it was built as an apartment building. M(95)

1508, 1508 REAR

This three-flat and the rear building are in the transitional Italianate-Queen Anne style. M(96)

1514

Like several structures in the 1500 block, this residence was built prior to the construction of our current street level. The cornice and some of the original brickwork has been modified. M(97)

1518

This is a three-flat Queen Anne style building with stone hoods and a continuous stringcourse. M(98)

1519, 1520, 1529

These three residences are an Italianate style similar to 1428. M(99)

1522

In the traditional Italianate design, this has a flat cornice with brackets and individual window treatment. M(100)

1524

Not much is known of this building except that it was built as a two-flat. of Italianate style with stone hoods and continuous stringcourse. M(101)

1528

Of Italianate style characterized by a peaked gabled roof with brackets and dentils, this was built to house blue-collar families, it was a two-flat with relatively large kitchens, no dining rooms and two tiny bedrooms per apartment. Now it is an open, duplexed space with decks, skylights and spa room. M(102)

1528 W. ELK GROVE

EVERGREEN AVENUE (WEST)

1819

Built by 1889 for Matthias J. Seifert, this residence and flat were created in Italianate characterized by a flat cornice with brackets and (often) dentil; indented façade or rectangular bay; and windows treated individually. M(102)

1829

This residence is an Italianate style similar to 1819 but has a polygonal bay. It was built in 1877. M(103)

1833

Charles Heinze was the original owner of this 1880s residence built in a Queen Anne style. M(104)

1837

Built as a two-flat in 1887 for Morris and Theodore R. Schlesinger, this Italianate design has a mansard roof. M(105)

1903

This 1881 two-flat Italianate style is characterized by a flat cornice with brackets and (often) dentils; indented façade or rectangular bay; windows unified with continuous hoods and/or stringcourse. M(106)

1919

Built between 1875 and 1880, this residence was designed as a two-flat. It is classified as Italianate characterized by a flat cornice with brackets and (often) dentil; a flat front; and windows unified with continuous hoods and/or stringcourse. Look at the large elaborate cornice design with a gabled false upper-story window as a center motif. A(107)

1921

This two-flat was designed in 1882 and built as single-family home. It is an Italianate style with flat cornice with brackets and (often) dentils; a flat front; and individual window treatment. M(108)

1927 W. EVERGREEN

1927

Like 1921 in design and vintage, except the windows treatment is continuous hoods and/or stringcourses, this is a residence. M(109)

1930

An original worker's cottage with an early addition, its classical styling includes knee braces and dentils. This home was built in 1881. (110)

1931

Built around 1883 for Jacob Deutsch, this Italianate style has a mansard roof. M(111)

1934

This 1880s residence with its peaked roof is a type of Italianate design that has brackets and/or dentils. M(112)

1935

Like 1930, this residence was also built in the 1880s. M(113)

1937

Note the careful restoration of the façade on this 1883 Italianate with a peaked, gabled roof. M(114)

1945 W. EVERGREEN

1945

This three-flat was built by 1892. It is essentially a Romanesque revival. M(115)

1945 REAR

Classic Italianate revival style from the 1880s, this home has its original large doors. Surrounding trim matches the door panels. Note the initial "H" on the tympanum of the cornice pediment. M(116)

1948

The cornice and the front porch fretwork are restored on this 1890s "painted lady" style. This is a fairly typical Victorian three-flat with six-room apartments. Originally there was a stairway on the front of the building leading to a second floor entrance. Conversion to an interior stairway was made in the '40s. The ground floor porch is a reproduction, as is

the cornice. Note the similar design motif on the cornice and porch fretwork. If you look toward the back of the building on the east side, you'll see the same motif used on the top panel of the fence. (117)

1951

Cornices of the bull's eye pattern are featured on this 1880s structure. Notice another pattern on 1953. (118)

1952

This Italianate style built in 1888 for August Frank has a mansard roof. M(119)

1953

This residence style is Italianate characterized by a flat cornice with brackets and (often) dentils; indented façade or rectangular bay; windows unified with continuous hoods and/or stringcourses. Note the cornice with the "raised diamond" or "nail head and rosettes". It was built in 1883. M(120)

1955

The exact date of this building is not known. It is presumed to be between 1880 and 1885. Its style is Italianate characterized by a flat cornice with brackets and (often) dentils; indented façade or rectangular bay; windows unified with continuous goods and/or stringcourses. A(121)

1956

Built in 1889, this Queen Anne styled structure was constructed as a two or three-flat. M(122)

1958

This 1889 Victorian Romanesque has some interesting detail. Notice the griffin in the keystone, the urn with the sunflower and the angels in the baroque-like bas-relief. The geometric patterns include the Greek symbol of unity.

Built as a three-flat, the third floor was home for Nelson Algren, author of "Man With The Golden Arm," during most of his years in Chicago. In his honor, there is bronze plaque on the building, presented by the Nelson Algren Committee. There is also an information marker on the parkway. M(123)

1958 W. EVERGREEN

1959

A mix of Queen Anne, Gothic, and Romanesque design, this was originally a 1904 two-flat. It became a rooming for 17 people by the 1950s. It was de-converted to a single-family residence in 1988.

This greystone holds the Department of the Interior's highest rating in the Wicker Park National Historic District. The building was completely gutted, with all architectural millwork reinstalled and refinished. The original first floor plan was preserved, along with the quarter-sawn oak and parquet flooring, with the addition of a powder room and bar area under the stairs. The original staircase has been restored, along with three beautiful beveled and stained glass windows. M(124)

1966

This was built in 1880s as a two- or three-flat. M(125)

1970

Built by 1885 for Charles Lusk, it is considered to be of the Italianate characterized by a flat cornice with brackets and (often) dentils; indented façade or rectangular bay; windows unified with continuous hoods and/or string-courses. Notice the elaborate "painted lady" cornice.

Built as a two-flat, the coach house was added in 1912 designed by architect, Perley Hale. M(126)

1973

Built around 1874 the first owner was John Stut, a

carpenter and contractor. It is classified as Italianate characterized by a flat cornice with brackets and (often) dentil; indented façade or rectangular bay; and windows treated individually. A(127)

1959 W. EVERGREEN

2009

This Italianate-style workers' cottage was constructed in 1877 for Henry Thompson, a machinist. Thompson came from England and lived with his wife and children until his death in 1890. Circuit court documents reflect that in 1890 the Thompsons owned a horse, a cow, a calf and a sheep. His wife resided here until 1902.

Architectural details that remain include brackets and dentils under the steeply pitched roof. The front windows have interior pine shutters, which fold into the casements. The Indiana limestone lintels above the arched windows depict an unusual cross design. M(128)

2013

This three-flat, built in 1887, is essentially Queen Anne in style. M(129)

2017

This three-story red brick building was built as a single-family residence circa 1883 for Paul 0. Stensland, a local prominent Norwegian businessman.

In the 1950s the building became a rooming house and then converted to a three-flat. In the conversion, it was discovered each floor has a unique decorative treatment. Preserved under a layer of canvas on the ceiling of the front parlor of the first floor were four medallions, each painted with a portrait of a famous artist or writer, entwined with a center medallion with the original owner's initials. This room also has the original carved oak fireplace mantel. The second floor has heavy decorative plaster detailing, and the third floor (probably once a ballroom) has a curved plaster cove ceiling. Fragments of stencil work and traces of gilded trim were also discovered under layers of wallpaper and canvas.

Take a moment to view three different types of working class housing at 2019, 2023, and 2025. AH(130)

2019
Built as a residence with flats in approximately 1885, this is an example of an essentially Queen Anne style. It was the home of Jacob Dal. M(131)

2023
This 1880s Italianate peaked, gabled roof structure has brackets and dentils. M(132)

2025
Built sometime between 1876 and 1887, like 2019 it is in the Queen Anne style but with a mansard roof. M(133)

2035
This residence was built in 1890. M(134)

2039
Designed in Italianate, it is typical of the type that is characterized by flat cornice with brackets and (often) dentils; polygonal bay; and windows treated individually. It was built in 1876. M(135)

2045
Built in the 1870s, this Italianate cottage served as the home of one prominent Chicago family, the Nicholas Jacob Pritzker family in the 1880s. M(136)

2051
A Romanesque revival style two-flat, it was built around 1894 for Emil A. Holmes. M(137)

2053
Essentially a Queen Anne style building, circa 1890, this structure was totally intact until the mid-1970s when fire and vandalism robbed it of everything except its ornate rounded masonry shell. After years of neglect, it was remodeled. M(138)

2057
This three flat was built around 1890 in the style of Queen Anne structures. M(139)

2107
Styling on this structure is Italianate characterized by a flat cornice with brackets and (often) dentils; indented façade or rectangular bay; windows unified with continuous hoods and/or stringcourses. M(140)

2109
Circa 1888, this building is the same Queen Anne styling as 2057, 2133, 2137, and 2143. M(141)

2115
Built in 1889 in the essential Gothic revival style, this building's interior of "The Widow Johnson House" has been used as a set for motion pictures and television, including ABC-TVs "The American Dream" series about a suburban family moving back to the city. The home has one of the grandest turrets in Wicker Park, as well as one of the most dramatic stairwell bays. The east wall is face brick rather than common brick masonry. Also noteworthy is the modified bay with its shell support, the decorative inserts under the first floor bay and the entire decorative chimney structure. M(142)

2120
This house was probably built before the Great Fire, making it another one of Wicker Park's oldest structures. (143)

2128
The greystone in front was built in the 1890s, using stone mined in Indiana. Each floor consisted of two apartments, a three-bedroom in front and a two-bedroom in the rear. Both were rented as one unit: the renter and his family lived in the front and the house-

hold staff lived in the rear. In 1984 it was gutted and de-converted into a three-flat, with 2,000 square feet of space in each unit.

The two-story frame coach house was built prior to the greystone, probably before The Great Fire of 1871 after which frame structures were prohibited. It may have been built in the front of the lot and later moved. When purchased in 1987, the building had two apartments. It has since been gutted and rehabbed as a single family home. (144)

2128 W. EVERGREEN (BACK)

2128 W. EVERGREEN

2133
This building, constructed in 1882, and 2137 were both built as residence in essentially Queen Anne style. M(145)

2137
This essentially Queen Anne styled structure was built in the 1880s. M(146)

2143
Built in 1896, this three-flat is the same style as 2133 and 2137. M(147)

WICKER PARK EAGLE
EXCERPTS

CLUB NOTES

The Wicker Park Woman's Club held their regular meeting at the North-West Clubhouse, 2017 Evergreen Ave., Tuesday, Feb 21. The topic was "The Short Story," by Prof. J.G. Carter Troop. *—March 1911*

The NW Club will disband after July 1. *—June, 1913*

FOR SALE from T. W. Schulze & Co.

Beautiful 9 room 11/2 story residence on Hoyne near Div. Must be sold. $3300 Store and four 4-room flats on Division near Robey, in good condition. Rental $1,100 annually. Price $10,500. *—April 1909*

OFFICERS' GOOD WORK

— Capture Women Thieves

While walking down Lincoln street with three pairs of trousers on her way to Olsen's tailoring shop, Ms. Josephine Alfono, 1832 N. Winchester avenue, was stopped by Elizabeth Laskowski, 1643 N Lincoln street, and the trousers taken from her. Miss Alfono informed Officers Hubman, Grams and Gasing and they gave chase. At Robey street and North avenue she was taken by Officer Huhman, who took her to the station.

At the West Chicago Avenue Police Court she was fined ten dollars and costs and sent to the house of correction for thirty days. *—January 1916*

HONORE STREET (NORTH)

All the structures listed below were built to Chicago's earlier street grade. It is, therefore, presumed that they were erected before the raising of the grade, which was completed in the mid 1870s.

1532

This large multifamily residence was built in the 1870s in the Italianate style featuring a peaked gabled roof with brackets and/or dentils. A(148)

1549, 1550

Another gabled roof is featured, but this time it is a highly simplified workman cottage. It is of the kind advertised by S. E. Gross in 1883. Both homes where built prior to the streets being raised M(149)

1551

This building was designed in the same Italianate style as 1532 with a bracketed cornice and stone hoods. M(150)

1552

Though a two-flat, this too is of the same design style as 1532 and 1551. M(151)

1558

A two-flat, the unified window treatment with continuous hoods and stringcourses distinguish it from other Italianate designs having flat cornices and fronts, in addition, there is some Queen Anne detailing on this home. M(152)

1559

Details are unknown about this Italianate styled residence. M(153)

WICKER PARK EAGLE
EXCERPTS

CLUBS NOTES

Wicker Park Club Notes

A St. Patrick's party will be held at Clubhouse, 1634 N. Winchester avenue, on March 17.

A local Juvenile Protective League was organized at an eving meeting of the Wicker Park Woman's club on Fri, Feb 4. Anyone interested in this worthy work and in the interest of the community for safe guarding the children will be welcome to join this league.

A meeting of the citizens will be called shortly and a large membership solicited. The membership dues are One Dollar a year.
—February 1910

BRIEF MENTION

Fritz Braun, 1509 N. Paulina, accompanying the Swiss Singers, is spending a few months touring Europe.

Herman Smith, 1628 N. Winchester has been appointed a pipeman of the Chicago Fire Dept. and assigned to Engine co. No. 66.
—June 1913

FALL FROM LIFT FATAL

A.J. Hawley, 1658 N. Robey street, an employee of E.J. Brach and Sons, 503 LaSalle avenue, candy manufacturer, died at the Polyclinic Hospital, Mar 3 of injuries from falling into an elevator shaft.
—March 1911

HOYNE AVENUE (NORTH)

1221, 1223
Both of these buildings are essentially Queen Anne in style with Romanesque arched window treatments, and were built as two-flats. M(154)

1233
A very large three-flat with lovely granite columns and greystone details, it was designed by S. Milton Eichberg, architect, in 1908. This building combines Romanesque and French Chateau features. M(155)

1236
An example of gabled roof simple Italianate styled workman's cottage, this home was built in 1886. M(156)

1237, 1246
These residences are in the Italianate style characterized by a flat cornice with brackets and (often) dentils; indented facade or rectangular bay; and windows unified with continuous hoods and/or stringcourses. Like 1236, 1237 was built in 1886, while 1246 was constructed in 1890. M(157)

1239
Built in 1888, this residence is an Italianate style home. M(158)

1248
A Chateauesque style three-flat with fine details, it was built in 1891. Its beautiful stonework, windows and front door, all with curved details, help us envision what others might have been before renovation. M(159)

1249
This was built in 1887 as a two-flat in the style of 1237 and 1246. M(160)

1251
This two-family landmark was built in 1885. Thanks to the preservation efforts of past owners, many of the original elements of this Victorian home can be seen. Most striking is the ornate metal facade topped by a cast iron roof cresting. The mansard roof entry is the original design bottomed out by a cut limestone stairway weighing over five tons. Eight chimneys once adorned the roofline of this home; two hand-carved marble fireplaces remain. The interior retains much of its historical character, including two sets of ten-foot high pocket doors in the front parlors, ornate plaster cornice work and eleven-foot high vaulted ceilings on the second floor. (161)

1252
This was built in 1899 as a two-flat in the style of 1239. M(162)

1253
Built as a Romanesque style residence in 1891, the wonderful small top floor turret is a very difficult albeit pleasing (and actually useless) detail. Purely to delight the eye, it is too small to hold furniture or allow for a better view. M(163)

1300
This was built as a two-flat in the style as 1239 and 1252. M(164)

1301
Converted from a thirty-room boarding house into a luxury five-apartment building, this is a turn-of-the-century structure. Take note of the limestone arch over the entryway, the bold dentil molding below the painted cornice, balconies on the south side and the rooftop decks. (165)

1301 N. HOYNE

1305

Styled in a mix of Gothic and Romanesque, it was built in 1894 as a two-flat. M(166)

1308 N. HOYNE

1308

Designed by architect Alexander L. Levy, this greystone was built in 1907. It has characteristics of Queen Anne, Gothic, Neo-Classical and Romanesque styles. All of the original wooden trim and floors have been preserved. Take note of the limestone medallions and cornice. Most Chicagoans think of this type as a typical "Chicago Greystone." Most were built between 1890 and 1910. M(167)

1309 & 1311

Two brothers built these buildings in 1887. You'll notice the matching stained glass windows on the front of both buildings. M(168)

1310

Built in 1886 as the Berentson residence and flats, this is in the Queen Anne style like 1239, 1252, and 1300. Note the Romanesque conical tower on the small porch roof. M(169)

1317

Of Italianate style, this residence is characterized by its peaked gable roof with brackets. M(170)

1336

This very large structure, built in 1888-89 for druggist Henry Schroeder, predates most mansions on Hoyne. Note the simple face brick facade and elaborate Victorian porch designed by Treat & Foltz. The very few details may reflect a Spartan household, but one of means.

After serving as a "hippie" commune, it was a burned out hulk in the early 1980s.

1343

The Greek temple entry with fluted columns distinguishes this Georgian style home designed in circa 1898 by Henry Worthmann. Notice the double-windowed dormer and the fleur-de-lis pattern on the architrave. Look across the street to 1344, an 1870s 'Octagon Front' Italianate so typical of this era. (172)

1344

Note the Octagon Front of this Italianate 1887-constructed residence. Designed by Christian Hansen, its style typically has a flat cornice with brackets and dentils; polygonal bay; and individually treated windows. M(173)

1345

This Second Empire style house, with a combination of Romanesque columns and classical egg-and-dart patterned designs, was built in 1895. A prominent Chicago surgeon, gynecologist and professor, K.F.M. Sandberg, who was a native of Norway, lived here.

The foundation of alternating smooth and rusticated stone is Tuscan in nature, which style is distinguished by its combination of colors and textures. Denticulate lintels and oak-leaf patterns repeat. AH(174)

1351

This is massively elegant greystone with unusual customized details and the rounded tower-like corner. It was built in 1897 for Harry Hertz, a Denmark native who was formerly Cook County Coroner and Treasurer for the State of Illinois. AH(175)

1352

Though this 1899 three-flat is ornate and a typical greystone style, it looks 'spindly' in comparison to its neighboring buildings. (176)

1356

This was one of the first houses and one of the very few frame structures built in this area. The Italianate styled house was almost certainly built in 1871 (unless it was constructed without a building permit) since Hoyne Avenue did not extend north of Division Street before 1871. Although presently covered with asphalt siding, many of the wood decorative details remain. It also may have been moved to this site, as this was a common practice before viaducts and power poles made house moving impractical. AH(177)

1362

Built in the 1880s as a residence in the Italianate style with a flat cornice with brackets and dentils; a flat front; and individual window treatment. M(178)

1363

Built in 1889 it is referred to as the John Wigren House and is essentially a Queen Anne style. M(179)

1400

This pre-fire frame structure may have been a one-story building moved to this site and raised. Note the unique second floor window trim west of the south bay and the interesting trim on the two-story small front porch. The window bays of this brick and frame structure are obvious later additions, probably an attempt "to keep up with the Raaps" across the street at 1407. (180)

1406

This three-story red brick, built in 1887 as William H. Thompson's first home, now has a duplexed-unit with apartments on the garden and third-floor levels. Most woodwork was gone or not in restorable condition, so the Victorian feel was replicated with woodwork, cut in the same style, and oak in-laid floors. A gorgeous oak staircase and the fireplaces are original. M(181)

1406 N. HOYNE

1407

This Second Empire style house commands the attention of residents and first-time visitors alike. Noticeably the largest private structure in the Wicker Park Historic District, this house, with its impressive tower, is surrounded by an expansive lawn and cast iron fence. The unusual detailing of the iron porch is also worthy of mention. John H. Raap, a prosperous wine merchant, whose store was located on Milwaukee Avenue, built the house in 1879. The matching coach house (now a separate property) and the original fence make this building quite distinguished. A(182)

1417

The Italianate style house was built in 1879 and the Second Empire coach house constructed in 1893 for Edward Warnecke, owner of a sewing machine manufacturing business. The second resident from 1884 to 1903 was William Johnson, a lake captain and vessel owner in the Great Lakes trade. A beautifully detailed wood-columned side porch, rolling lawn and a summer gazebo were typical of Victorian architectural and landscaping sentiment. Unfortunately, the disrepair of this home makes it difficult to imagine that elegance.

The English basement design placed the kitchen on the ground floor to keep the odors and heat away from the living area. A(183)

1417 N. HOYNE

1421

This large mansion was built in 1891, just after its southern neighbors. It has face brick for the front, with the common brick on the sides. The detailing of the front ballroom window is Sullivanesque. New art glass windows are probably more ornate than the originals would have been. M(184)

1421 N. HOYNE

1422

Built 1892 as William H. Thompson's second residence with flats for rent. It is in the mixed styles of Queen Anne, Gothic and Romanesque. It was once the home of a tailor whose father was a Rabbi. A Seder House stood in the back yard at that time. M(185)

1423-25

This once was a single-family residence (see the coach house behind) converted to apartments early on. One early resident was immigrant Carl Laemmele. A fire in the mid-1970s destroyed its northern neighbor and structurally weakened the North Bay staircase, melting the art glass windows. It is now an upscale multi-unit building. (186)

1427

This Romanesque Revival structure was built in the late 1880s by Nils Arneson (1840-1911). A Norwegian businessman, he came to this county in 1861.

The third floor was once used as a ballroom. Notice the short smooth columns supporting the second floor windows and tower with conical roof. Fine decorative patterns on the facade include modified Minoan scrollwork on the cornice, a basket-weave pattern over the windows and doors, and swirling drape on the stairwell bay. AH(187)

1502

This is the second structure for the Wicker Park Lutheran Church. It was built in this Romanesque style in 1906, modeled after the 12th century Holy Trinity Chapel in Caen, France. The mica-flecked stone came from a house of "ill fame" on Michigan Avenue. Queried about the appropriateness of using the stone, the pastor replied: "It has served the devil long enough, now let it serve the Lord."

In the 1870s, there was an unfinished gothic frame church at this site. The Scandinavian and German founders of WPLC purchased the property for $3,000 from mortgage holder, Mr. Henry Holden. The first Lutheran church structure was completed and the church was dedicated on January 18, 1880. A(188)

1510

Particularly noteworthy of this 1875 Italianate-Queen

Anne town home is the splendid restoration of the façade and grounds. Time and effort have obviously been spent wisely in paying attention to details such as chemically cleaning rather than blasting the face brick masonry, reconstructing the entry stairs and walks faithfully, and re-painting the cornice and trim appropriately. The cornice pediment now readily reveals a sunburst pattern on the tympanum and stallion and bull's eye motifs at either end. The limestone keystones supporting the windows and door openings are particularly handsome. What appears to be a pineapple motif supports the iron rails on the front steps. M(189)

1510 N. HOYNE

1512

This was built in 1884 as a residence in the Italianate style characterized by a flat cornice with brackets and (often) dentils; indented façade or rectangular bay; and windows unified with continuous hoods and/or stringcourses. Architect was C. Boyington. M(190)

1513

Note the intricate artistry of the stained glass window transom on this 1888 home designed by Frederick Faber. This is in the Queen Anne with mansard roof style. M(191)

1520

Designed by G. Bloedner in 1886 for Henry Grusendorf, a Russian lumberman, this Second French Empire style mansion with its tall, steeply pitched mansard roof and double-gabled Queen Anne porch is much larger than it appears from the street. Spanning nearly two city lots, this house's structural support is massive 3x12 floor joists, eight inches apart and over thirty-two feet in length. Thirteen-and-a-half-foot ceilings are decorated with marvelously ornate plaster medallions and moldings. The capitals of the door trim in this house are among the most unusual found anywhere. Interior and exterior detail abound: notice the supports for the iron banisters at the front stair are cast in the form of human hands. The ornate paintwork is typically Victorian. A(192)

1521

Built as a single-family residence there are two stories about its origin. One is that it was built between 1875 and 1880 by Isaac Waixel, who sold $20 million worth of meat to the Federal Government during the Civil War and came to Chicago when the meat packing industry became centered here. It was then sold to Adolph Bergmeier, treasurer of Johnson Chair Company in 1890. The second story is that Bergmeier built it in 1890. The National Register nomination states that Waixel lived his entire life on Washington Blvd. and that the style of the house is not that of the 1870s.

This Queen Anne style mansion became a rooming house, during the 1920s. When de-converted in 1972, reportedly twenty-three sinks and nineteen bathtubs were removed. The third floor ballroom is now a photo studio. Note the elegantly embellished porch and turret on this house displaying a wide variety of symbols in the metal trim: egg and dart, rosettes, flowers and scrolls.

Observe classic dentils, nail-head pattern plates and cabled or scrolled Ionic columns in relief on the large dormer. The square billet or checkerboard pattern appears in the stonework. Take special note of the turned wood of the front porch, as well as the unusual ornate brick patterns on the south side of the building. A(193)

1524

This building was built in 1886-1887 for Kolben Johnson, a native of Norway, who was the proprietor of Eureka Foundry, which made castings of every description. He specialized in printing press work and had a prosperous business. This is French Second Empire style. Its large steep mansard roof, dormer windows and ornamental trim give the mansion an elegant, romantic character. The porch has exquisite and delicate gingerbread work with acorn finials. Other original features include shutters that fold into pockets and solid oak carved double entrance doors. The cast iron fence continues the romantic feel of the home. You can see the carriage stone on the parkway. (195)

1526

This two-flat was built in the 1870s in the Italianate characterized by flat cornice with brackets and (often) dentils; polygonal bay; and windows treated individually. M(196)

1530 N. Hoyne

1530

This residence was built in the grand style of many homes on "Beer Baron Row." An early owner was William Legner, a German native. The original structure, with both Romanesque and Queen Anne elements, was three stories with a ballroom and servants' quarters on the third floor. Both the interior pine woodwork and the exterior large wrap-around porch were painted, typical of the Victorian era. The coach house was a working stable. A fire in the 1930s destroyed the third floor, beginning the decline of the structure, which became a boarding house for thirty-five boarders after WWII.

While the exterior could be restored to its

Victorian splendor in 1986, only the original interior staircase was salvageable. A new cornice was added in 1990 and is made of wood and composite products. An enclosed back porch was removed, leaving the four support columns. A gabled roof was added, in keeping with the lines of the coach-house, making a dramatic outdoor space. AH(197)

1553

Built in 1891 as Frank P. Schreiber's first home in the district, it is in the Queen Anne style. M(198)

1554

A large-scaled simple Italianate house, it is believed to have been built before 1885. George Casper Mages, Milwaukee, WI native, was its owner in 1885. He had various jobs in Chicago until becoming a partner in the firm of Saul and Bolton. After 1884, when fire destroyed the firm's premises, he bought his partners' interests, and incorporated the George C. Mages Company in 1897. The company made moldings, frames and mirrors. A(199)

1555

Built in the Romanesque style around 1902, this was Frank P. Schreiber's second house in the district. A(200)

1558

This modest mansion, one of the oldest homes in the area, was built in 1878 in a modified Queen Anne style. The walls are eighteen inches thick. Ornamental pressed metalwork adorns the tower, the cornices and the conservatory on the south side. Inside, the parlor contains a marble of fireplace, a carved mantelpiece, original faux bois shutters and blinds, and an unusual coved plaster molding on the ceiling. The front hall ceiling is embossed tin. A low wrought iron fence exaggerates the size of the house as does the separate tower room, which is higher than the attic.

It was built for C. Herman Plautz (1844-1901). He founded the Chicago Drug & Chemical Co. in 1861. He died in his home in 1901.

From 1927 to 1972 this was an American Legion Hall. A remnant of a prohibition era bar remains in the basement. In May 1934, the cannon was placed there. It is a 1912 U. S. Navy cannon mounted on a Studebaker 47" caisson wheel carriage with wooden spokes. The cannon was "stationed on" Navy Pier during WW II. AH(201)

1559

Built in 1876, it is considered to be a "text book" Italianate style. Notice the original street number, 742, in the stained glass of the transom. Several of the details were probably copied from other buildings or catalogs of the period. Albin Greiner, a local brew master, was its first owner. He began his career as maltster and went on to become quite prominent in the brewing business. The interior of this house has survived virtually in tact. AH(202)

1563

Designed by Frederick Faber, this is a typical three-flat in a type of Italianate style characterized by a flat cornice with brackets and dentils; polygonal bay; and windows treated individually. It was built in 1894. M(203)

1564

This 1870s Italianate style residence features a flat cornice with brackets, polygonal bay, and individually designed windows. M(204)

1566

Built as a residence in the 1880s in a type of Italianate style characterized, it has a peaked gable roof with brackets and/or often dentils. M(205)

1619

This unique building served Wicker Park in the 1890s as a livery service with horses and carriages awaiting the call of wealthy residents. Note the tall windows on the south side. Quarters for drivers were upstairs. By WWI, the building was converted to factory use and abandoned by 1975. (206)

WICKER PARK EAGLE
EXCERPTS

REAL ESTATE

A transaction of interest to Northwest siders was that made by George C. Mages of 1550 N. Hoyne Ave. to Fred K. Bartlett. It consisted of 4 houses at 4917 to 4927 Champlain Ave. at $5,000 a piece, or $20,000 all told.
– *February 1910*

BRIEF MENTION

Miss Hellen Thon, 1529 N. Hoyne ave, wishes through the Wicker Park Eagle, to inform her schoolmates that she, her mamma and papa and brother are enjoying a very pleasant winter among the roses in the beautiful sunny Riviera of France and Italy. They are at present stopping at Monte Carlo but expect to leave soon for the Azores.

A very successful musicale and social was given by the Ladies' Aid Society of the Wicker Park Ev. Luth. Church on Feb 20. Much credit must be given the ladies for the artistic program and the dainty manner in which the cake and coffee was served.
–*March 1911*

Mr. Peter Larson and Family are dividing their time between their summer cottage at Paw Paw Lake and the windy city on Lake Michigan. The Larsons reside at 1340 N. Hoyne.
–*August 1913*

Geo. Morris of 1361 N. Hoyne has entered the auto business. His cars will be at service during any part of the day or night for all occasions. It at any time you are in need of automoile service, kindly give him a trial.
–*August 1913*

Mr. W. H. Lansten, 1546 Hoyne left Chicago on July17 and came by steam boat to Mackinac Island, Mi then by steamer to Detroit and again by steamer to Buffalo. From there he went to Niagara Fall, Montreal, Canada, and Atlantic City. He reported the weather very pleasant although cold enough for an overcoat at times.
–*August 1913*

Mr. And Mrs. H. Misch, 1410 N. Hoyne Ave. spent ten days at West Baden, Indiana.
– *February 1910*

LEAVITT STREET (NORTH)

1121

The Holy Trinity Orthodox Cathedral and Rectory was designed by Louis Sullivan. Built in 1901, it was partially financed by a $5,000 grant from Czar Nicholas II, and consecrated by a Bishop who became the Patriarch of the Russian Church.

The exterior is simple with occasional exotic touches in curved shapes or angular window hoods. The bulbous domes found in Russian Church architecture must have inspired the onion-like shape above the lantern. M(207)

1241, 1243, 1309

All in the Italianate style with a flat cornice with brackets, indented or rectangular bay and windows that are unified. They were all constructed in the 1880s. M(208)

1312

Built in 1900, this structure gained notoriety in 1991 when the TV program, "This Old House", sent fix-it expert and star Bob Villa to feature both the front greystone and the coach house in his syndicated show. They took this turn-of-the-century two-flat and converted it into a two-level owners' unit by duplexing into the basement, leaving a rental unit on the second floor. (209)

1367

This structure was built as a combination store and apartment. M(210)

1411, 1456

These Italianate buildings are typical of the type that features a flat cornice with brackets; a flat front and windows treated individualistically. M(211)

1415

Featuring a peaked gabled roof with brackets, it differentiates itself from other Italianates at 1411 and 1423. It was built in 1887 for C. Riemer. M(212)

1423

A two-flat, this shows yet another Italianate style. This style is characterized by a flat cornice with brackets and dentils; an indented facade or rectangular bay; and windows that are treated uniquely. M(213)

1459

Built in the 1880s, this three-flat is a Queen Anne styled structure. M(214)

1461

Italianate with a flat cornice and brackets, an indented façade or rectangular bay, and unified windows are the characteristics of this 1888 two-flat. M(215)

1465

Like 1459, this building was constructed in the 1890s. M(216)

1501

Built in 1892, this is a two-flat. M(217)

1504

A two-flat residence, this was designed in a Queen Anne style. M (218)

1505

An example of the transition from Italianate to Queen Anne, this two-flat was built in 1893. M(219)

1507

Also Italianate in style, this two-flat features a peaked, gabled roof with brackets and dentils. It was built in 1880. M(220)

1512

Like 1514 and 1518, this 1887 two-flat is of the same Italianate design. Its architect was Henry Sierks. M(221)

1514

Another product of architects Lutken and Thisslew, this 1888 residence is like its neighbors at 1512 and 1518. (222)

1518

Architect G. Isaacson designed this residence in 1887. Style wise, it is characterized as Italianate with a flat cornice with brackets and dentil; polygonal bay and unified window treatment. M(223)

1528

Essentially Queen Anne in style, this 1880s structure has a Romanesque façade. It is exhibited in the typical contrast of brick and sandstone and the decorative inserts of terra cotta. There are suggestions of a medieval castle here in the unusual cornice with "sentry posts" decorated in a swirling motif supported by leaf-decorated corbels. Lintels and braces stretch the distance between the posts. M(224)

1530, 1534

These two-flats were built in1887 and 1888 respectively. Their Italianate style features an indented façade or rectangular bay, flat cornice with brackets and dentil and unified window treatment. M(225)

1538

The design of this building, as in 1528, incorporates a Romanesque style rounded front bay. Here the lower floor windows are in square inserts into the bay while the upper story fenestration respects the curves of the bay with appropriately arched openings. Except for the door transom, the building displays a complete set of fine stained glass windows. It was built as a two-flat in 1890. (226)

1540

Like 1542, this two-flat is essentially Queen Anne in design. It was built in the1880s. M(227)

1542

This two-flat is dated to the 1880s by the use of archi-tectural elements of terra cotta, sandstone and brick. The decorative arch rests on the corbelled plain brick supports and encloses a multitude of terra cotta decorative inserts. The Dutch Colonial cornice is not original to the building but is part of the exterior renovation. M(228)

1547

A Romanesque styled church, this structure was built in the 1890s. This structure has been converted into residential units. M(229)

1620

Another example of Italianate styling, this 1887 two-flat has the flat cornice with brackets and dentil, a flat front and windows that have a unified appearance. M(230)

1624

A peaked, gabled roof with brackets and/or dentils typifies this Italianate styled multi-unit building dating to the 1880s. It was built as either a two or three-flat. M(231)

1630

This frame residence may have been built prior to the Chicago Fire of 1871, but the Commission on Chicago Landmarks estimates it as built sometime between 1880 and 1886. Since frame residences were illegal after 1871, it could have been built without a permit or it could have been moved to this site.

The style reflects the "catalog components" of the popular "Carpenter's Architectural Elements," which contained many wood and window details used by builders in the 1860s and 1870s. M(232)

1644

Designed as a mix of Queen Anne, Gothic, and Romanesque, this single-family residence, which has been converted into a 3-flat was built in 1896.

The third-floor window in the south curved corner is artificial. A turret roof, which existed above this corner, was removed sometime after 1920. This building is similar to the five-flat buildings on Concord St. around the corner. M(233)

1644 N. LEAVITT

1646

Built in 1897 by Contractor Fred A. Miller, this two-flat building is best described as Beaux Arts. Later occupied by a doctor, the second floor was used as the family quarters while the first floor was used as the doctor's office. The façade is of rusticated grey limestone with a stepped cornice of painted zinc-coated copper that is a complete restoration of the original cornice. The unique oval leaded glass window in a decorative stone frame above the main entrance sets this house apart from its neighbors. Each floor has a different floor plan as evidenced by the odd array of windows on the north wall. M(234)

1658

This three-flat is of the same mix of style as 1644. M(235)

1658

The rear building is a residence that was built in the 1870s. M(236)

1660

Built in 1891 as a mix of Queen Anne, Gothic and Romanesque styling, this two-story residence was severely altered in the 1960s.

The stained glass in the transoms, spells A. Ohlhorst, probably the original owner. The original street number, 897, was also in the glass, but it was covered. Take time to admire the enormous two-lot wide garden. M(237)

WICKER PARK EAGLE
EXCERPTS

BRIEF MENTION

Robert Murback, 1644 N. Leavitt street, was confined to his home for a few days with an ulcerated tooth.
—*February 1910*

Mr. Colon Johnson, 1538 N. Leavitt is rapidly recovering from his recent painful injury.
—*June 1913*

The wedding of Miss Elsie Adeline Huber, daughter of Mrs. Ida Dreiske Huber, 2136 LeMoyne St. to Mr. Wallace a. Nieske took place on We, June 11. The ceremony in the fourth German M E Church, Augusta and Robey St. was the first marriage to be celebrated in the church.
—*June 1913*

Mr. And Mrs. I. Feuer, 2030 LeMoyne, were at home Wednesday afternoon and evening June 18 in honor of the son and daughter Milton and Loretta.
—*June 1913*

Mr. & Mrs. Edward Mohr, 2024 LeMoyne are receiving congratulations upon the arrival of a little stranger at their home. It's a boy, born Aug 13.
—*August 1913*

AUTO CRASH KILLS BUSINESS MAN

— Emil Iverson

Funeral services for Emil Iverson, the Milwaukee ave business man killed in an auto crash with his companions, Richard Carroll and John Gauer, were held at the chapel of Frank Mueller, Ashland and Milwaukee avenues and at the Wicker Park Lutheran Church, Hoyne and Lemoyne st on Sat. June 14. Vast throngs filled the streets as the funeral cortege wended its way to the church. A detail of police kept the crowds in order. At the church the Rev. Anda and Rev. Dent lauded the dead merchant in impressive sermons.
—*March 1911*

LeMoyne Street (West)

Many of the original buildings on the 2000 block were razed in the 1960s and 1970s.

2034 W. LeMoyne

2034

The facade is of plain cut grey limestone, with only an ornamental ribbon scroll molding accenting the top of the porch cornice. One can speculate what the missing top cornice design might have been. Most assuredly an elaborate embellishment of the ribbon scroll of the porch cornice was dominant in the design motif. This residence was the boyhood home of movie producer Michael Todd and stands as a reminder of other buildings once on the block that were destroyed in the 1960s and 1970s.

The 2100 block of LeMoyne is an eclectic mix of many building types and a few fun details. Brick two-flats (like 2133) workers' cottages (like 2129) and greystones (like 2136) make this block representative of almost forty years of development, and shows considerable modern adjustments. (238)

2112

Essentially Queen Anne in styling, this residence was built in the 1890s. M(239)

2119

A great example of a "spite wall", the massive stone wall was to shield it from its neighbor following a Victorian feud. It was built in 1897 in Queen Anne style. M(240)

2122

This workman's cottage was built in the 1880s. M(241)

2123

This Queen Anne two-flat was built circa 1886. M(242)

2126

This 1875 Italianate two-flat, is of a style characterized by a flat cornice with brackets; indented façade or rectangular bay and unified hooded windows and/or stringcourses. Like many structures in Wicker Park, it continues to be and appear as it did when it was built. It accommodates the life style needs of two families and blend in with its neighbors. M(243)

2127

This two-flat is nearly identical to 2123. M(244)

2128 W. LeMoyne

2128

Wicker Park's answer to San Francisco is this 1875 brick and wood "painted lady." It is thought this structure pre-dates many of its neighbors and served as a four-room worker's cottage with a summer kitchen lean-to addition in the rear. The bay windows on the brick first floor reflect simple brick arched lintels with a crown shield adorning each window. The ornate wood second floor bay and peak roof cornices were the architect's whimsical statement, which set the pace for many buildings to follow in this area. M(245)

2129, 2131

These two buildings were probably built before 1875. They are typical of the Italianate style described for 2126. The difference is for 2129, which has a different window treatment. A(246)

2133

An Italianate style residence probably built in the 1880s, little more known about this structure. M (247)

2137

A three-flat, this too was built in the 1880s. It is Italianate with unified window treatment. M(248)

2138

This three-flat was built circa 1881. M(249)

2139

Like 2137, this two-flat has individually treated windows. M(250)

2140

The pitched roof on this 100-year-old brick residence is remarkable in that it is unlike most of the residences in this area. The wood cornices have been painted in the Victorian style similar to its neighbors on the street. Originally built as a single-family dwelling, it was converted into a multi-dwelling structure in the mid-1950s after which it fell into disrepair. It was rescued in the spring of 1988 and restored. M(251)

2141 W. LeMoyne

2141

Built in the 1880s as a two-flat, this red brick building is a classic example of an architectural style often found in Wicker Park. Aside from the number of units, it was built like 2137. M(252)

2140 W. LeMoyne

MILWAUKEE AVENUE (NORTH)

1129

At the time of the Haymarket Protest, this was the site of the home of Albert and Lucy Parsons. Albert was born June 20, 1848 in Montgomery, Alabama. When he was thirteen he joined the Confederate Army. In 1873 he came to Chicago as a typesetter for the Inter Ocean & Times. He was an active socialist, as was his wife. Lucy was born in 1853. (254)

1400

A four-story structure with commercial on the ground floor and residence above, the original cornice has been lost. M(255)

1401-09

Like many structures along commercial streets, these structures were built for mixed use of commercial on at least the ground level and residential on upper floors. They are typical of the Italianate styled structure with a bracketed cornice. M(256)

1408

Commercial and residential combination, this building was built in 1883. Its style is Italianate characterized by a flat cornice with brackets and dentils, a flat front, and individually treated windows. M(257)

1418-20

Little is known about these three-story Italianate commercial structures. M(258)

1422

Built in 1885, the J. Helmke Building is identical to 1426 except for the two end bays versus the single end bays at 1426. M(259)

1426

This mixed-use structure was built in 1881. M(260)

1427

The C. Strauss Building was erected in 1887 as an Italianate styled building. M(261)

1429

The J. Jensen Building was built a year after its neighbor at 1427 in a similar Italianate style. M(262)

1431

This mix of Queen Anne and Neo-Classical revival structure was built in 1888. M(263)

1439

The C. J. Zuehlke Building was designed in the Queen Anne style. M(264)

1440

This Italianate styled structure was built in the 1880s as a mix of a store and apartments on the upper floors. M(265)

1444

Essentially Queen Anne in style this structure was erected in 1892. M(266)

1455

Designed in Classical Revival or Heavy Classical, this housed The Star Theater in 1887, then The Royal Theater in 1907. M(267)

1459

This is a four-story structure with terra cotta storefront surround and Italianate styled terra cotta cornice. M(268)

1460

Another combination of a store and apartments, the original masonry structure was covered with aluminum siding in the early 1970s. M(269)

1462

The architectural firm of Worthmann & Nee designed this 1890 building. They used Queen Anne styling. M(270)

1471

This is considered a commercial block. Unlike most other buildings along the street the cornice and storefront frieze are terra cotta.. M(271)

1476

This is yet another example of mixed use commercial structure with Italianate detailing. M(272)

1501, 1505

Built prior to 1871, these structures are designed like 1408. Detailing is, however, Queen Anne. The majority of the facades have been covered with vinyl siding. Note the eave brackets that are still visible M(273)

1511

This is a simply two-story structure with Italianate detailing. M(274)

1514

Built in 1902, this is another example of Queen Anne styling. M(275)

1520

Designed in 1921 by Jens J. Meldahl in a Classical Revival style, this was the former Peoples Gas, Light and Coke Co. office. A(276)

1524, 1534

Similar to 1514, these buildings are in the Italianate style. It is known that 1524 was built in 1891, but the construction date of 1534 is unknown. M(277)

1538

Built in the 1870s, this is typical of other mixed-use structures on the block with Italianate cornice details, stone hoods and stringcourses. M(278)

1540

This four-story commercial building was built over 100 years ago. It is one of the more unique buildings on Milwaukee Avenue because of its grape ornamentation on the front windows. The building has been restored to its original wooden store front, with beautiful Italian columns. What was formerly a neighborhood bakery in 1877 has served as a restaurant in more recent times. The upstairs still has residential units. (279)

1540 N. MILWAUKEE

1542

Built in the 1880s with Italianate detailing, this is similar to1501.

1548

The G. Erickson Building is a Italianate styled building built in 1889. M(281)

1560, 1564

Both of these buildings were styled with Queen Anne features. Like many other neighbors, they were a combination of stores and residents. They were probably erected in the 1890s. M(282)

1579-83

The original building on this site was built in 1887-8. It was probably demolished to make room for the current structure that dates from 1912. Known as the "The Flatiron Building", note the terra cotta exterior. (283)

1608

The original Noel State Bank building, wrecked in May, 1928, occupied this site. The Northwest Tower Building was built in 1928-29. The architect was C. Herrick Hammond of Perkins, Chatten and Hammond. This is one of the city's finest examples of Art Deco architecture and was among the first skyscrapers in an outlying Chicago neighborhood. It still serves as a prominent landmark of the major intersection of Milwaukee, North, and Damen. A(284)

1615

Built as the second home of the Noel State Bank, this building was completed in 1928. M(285)

1616

Although the upper floors of the Hollander Fireproof Warehouse are very simple and unadorned, note the neo classical storefront and frieze detailed with terra cotta. M(286)

1629 N. MILWAUKEE

1629

This was built in 1903 as The M. Houlberg Building. Mr. Houlberg was a Danish decorative artist who came to Chicago in the 1890s to work on the World's Fair. He designed and built the metal cornice on the building. This housed both his painting and decorating business. For 35 years, in the 1950s-1980s, this was the site of N. Prehler Hardware. It was rehabbed in the 1990s. (287)

1632

A typical three-story lodge hall, it has the meeting hall on the third floor. A shoemakers' union owned this building until they sold it to the Segundo Ruiz Belvis

Cultural Center. This Center is a Puerto Rican cultural organization. Also of historic interest is that it was the site of the first Illinois soup kitchen, established during the depression. (288)

W I C K E R   P A R K   E A G L E
E X C E R P T S

FLAMES SHOOT FROM DENTISTS' OFFICE

Crossed electric wires caused a small fire in the office of Drs. Howatt and Bassett, dentists, at 1588 Milwaukee avenue. A crossing policeman at the corner saw a sheet of flame emerge from one of the windows and sent in a still alarm of fire to Engine Company 35. The fire was easily extinguished.

BRIEF MENTION

The funeral of Robert Hausen, the well known coal and wood dealer was held from his home, 420 W. North Ave, Sunday afternoon, May 2.
 —*May 1911*

A very successful concert and Dance was given by the Northwestern Business College Alumni at Wicker Park Hall on Wed, February 2nd.
—*February 1910*

After May 1st, the Library Board will dispense with the free reading on Milwaukee avenue, owing to the fact that the store is rented for other purposes and that the expense of operating same is too great. A delivery station will still be retained in the immediate neighborhood.

Mr. Paul Rommel, 1659 N. Robey street, has brought the property at 1702 N. Robey street and will, after May 1st, remove his bakery to the latter address, where he hopes to see his former patrons and friends and to serve them in the same befitting manner that he has done in the past.
—*March 1911*

The Campfire girls of Association House spent two weeks at Oak Ridge Camp, St. Charles, IL.

Mrs. M. Haulberg, residing at 1629 Milwaukee avenue, is home from a two months' trip to Europe. —*August 1913*

Ollie Sandof, accused of sawing out a panel of a door in the saloon of J. Neienstadt, 1601 N. Milwaukee avenue, and robbing the cash register of several hundred dollars, was held over to the grand jury in $5,000 bail.
—*March 1911*

NORTH AVENUE (WEST)

1821

This beautifully restored Queen Anne style four-story building was originally designed as a store and apartment. M(289)

1823

A flat cornice with brackets, flat front, and individually treated windows are characteristic features of this Italianate multi unit building. It was built in 1886. M(290)

1825

This Italianate style mixed-use property was constructed with a mansard roof. Building date is unknown but may been 1893. A(291)

1833

Like several buildings on this street, this structure was multi use. It included multi living units with an Italianate styled storefront. M(292)

1901

This building has been demolished to make way for an Animal Hospital. M(293)

1907

This is a Italianate styled residential two-flat. M(294)

1919

Designed as a Queen Anne styled structure, this was built as a residential two-flat. M(295)

1958

Built as a mix of commercial and residential use, it was constructed in 1889. It was designed in the style of Queen Anne, the original mansard roof has been lost and modified. Note the Romanesque style window hoods and stringcourse. M(296)

2001

Architect William Ohlhaber designed this commercial and residential structure in 1889. He chose to style it in Italianate like 1823 except with unified windows with continuous hoods and stringcourses. M(297)

2007

Built in 1884, the J. Schmidt Building is in the same style as 1823. M(298)

2009

This is an Italianate style building similar to 2001. Construction date is unknown. M(299)

2013

Another example of a multi-use building, this one was built in the late 1870s. This was the first home of Association House. M(300)

2013 W. NORTH

2017

There was a coach house at the rear of this property that was burned and razed in the 1990s. It was originally a stable built in the 1870s in Italianate styling. M(301)

2037

Construction date is unknown for this two-flat. It was designed in the Italianate style characterized by a flat cornice with brackets and dentil; indented facade or rectangular bay, and windows unified with continuous hoods and/or stringcourses. M(302)

2041

Built in the Beaux Arts style in 1923, this was originally a public bath. The North Avenue Bath contained both Turkish and Russian steam rooms. Many famous and infamous people passed through these portals, among them, Nelson Algren. It functioned as a bathhouse until the late 1980s. M(303)

2050 W. NORTH

2050

This three-story red sandstone and brick building with inlaid terra cotta detail dates from the 1890s. In the first floor window, note the decorative architectural motif of cast terra cotta scrolling and Acanthus leaves in high relief in the spandrel of the arch. The oversized turret finial at the top right was a very popular decorative motif of the period. No doubt its influence came from the Rookery Building on LaSalle Street downtown. Regrettably, the third floor window bay has been altered, but one can speculate what remains of the original bay roof underneath the asphalt shingles. Fortunately, the top cornice

with its Moorish circular motif enclosing the window is complete. (This can be viewed more easily from across the street.) AH(304)

2100-02

An apartment building, Bennes & Kutsch architects designed this structure in 1900. It is an example of Classical Revival. M(305)

2101-15

Also an example of Classical Revival, this was once a nicely appointed hotel, The Victor. It fell on hard times by the 1970s and was forced closed in 1990s. Unfortunately it remains an eyesore today. M(306)

2112

This apartment building is an example of the Chicago School of Arts and Crafts. It was revitalized in 1990s and turned into condominiums. M(307)

2141

At the rear of this property there is a building that was built as a three-flat. M(308)

2147

Often called the "Old Farm House" by local residents, this building was built in the mid-1870s by German settlers shortly after the Chicago Fire. Until the late 1800s, the "estate" of this house stretched from the alley on the east to Leavitt on the west. Owned by the Prehler family from 1911 to 1956, the building was used as a boarding house during the Depression. Unusual architectural features of the building include round arched windows on the main floor that begin at floor level, as well as the "Dutch tuckpointing" on the exterior, a practice in which plaster is applied over the common brick facade and the mortar is "pencil-lined" to redefine the mortar joints. The home has been remodeled extensively for the use of a social service agency. Unfortunately, the removal of a large tree on the property in the early 1990s and the structures use have caused a loss of its farm-like character. A(309)

2150

Founded in 1899, Association House of Chicago moved west from 2013 W. North in 1902. Originally occupying the "old gray house" on this site, that building (owned by William T. Johnson) was built around 1864. It was the oldest documented house in the vicinity but was razed in 1940, after they purchased 2134 W. Pierce as the residence for their staff.

Jane Addams, who laid the cornerstone for this structure on September 9, 1905, lead the settlement house movement in the US, patterned after Tounbey Hall in England. Following that social service movement, Association House's mission was to serve the needs of the immigrant population of the community. Over the years, the "House" has served all the populations moving through this community from Scandinavians, Germans, Poles, Ukrainians, and Russians through African Americans and Hispanics.

An example of the Chicago School of Arts and Crafts design, the architect was William Carbys Zimmerman. AH(310)

2156
Essentially Queen Anne in design, this created with a mixed use of commercial and residential. M(311)

2200 W. NORTH

2200
This classic braced cornice, embellished in the "painted lady" style, is striking as it runs the entire length of the facade and the side of the house. The old limestone at the base structure and in the lintel is simply and neatly ornamented with a single patera or rosette design. Built in the 1880s, the piano windows are traditionally taller than those of the upper floor. Inside

the coach house, which was altered in the 1980s into an art studio, an electric automobile was discovered in the late 1960s. M(312)

2204
The classic braced cornice runs the length of the façade and the side of the house and has been renovated. In the 1970s this was a bordello. M(313)

2215
St. Paul's Church's cornerstone was laid on August 24, 1890 and the church was dedicated in 1892. Cost of the Gothic Revival structure was $12,000, twice the original estimate. It contains the original stained glass windows and lighting fixtures. The front elevation, drawn on linen by architect G. Isaacson, is preserved in the church archives.

The interior has many interesting features. Built in the shape of an ark with sloping floors, the altar is on the west wall with a large stained glass window on the north. Built by Norwegians, the beamed and wainscoted ceiling gives a warm feeling to the space. Of musicological significance is that the Austin Company built its first pipe organ in Chicago here in 1906. A(314)

2219
Architect, Charles Sorensen, designed St. Paul's Parish House in 1908. M(315)

2216
Built around 1876, this structure was known as the C. Werden Deane House. M(316)

2225
Considered to be Trans Italianate-Queen Anne in design, this mixed-use building was built in 1892. M(317)

WICKER PARK EAGLE
EXCERPTS

BUILDING PERMITS

Armitage avenue, 236 feet east of Oakley, north front, 24x100 with an encumbrance of $1,700. M. Huth to John Cichowski, for $4,000.

A one story brick addition is being built by Carl Buschel at 2059 North Oakley for $1000.
—February 1910

BRIEF MENTION

Two men were injured on February 16, when the wagon which they were driving was struck by an east bound Chicago Ave. car near Albany Ave. They were hurled in the street, but after being revived went home. The men were August Albrecht, 2063 N. Oakley, and Patrick Hallen, 1646 N. Talman Ave.

Mr. Emil Freeman, 1534 N. Oakley Ave., has fully recovered from a severe attack of pneumonia.
—February 1910

OAKLEY BOULEVARD (NORTH)

1303
A simplified one to one-and-a-half story cottage, this home was built in 1883. M(318)

1313, 1320
Three-flats, both are designed in the style of Queen Anne. Construction for 1320 was in the 1880s. M(319)

1314
This residence is also of Queen Anne style. M(320)

1317
Characterized by a flat cornice with brackets and indented façade or rectangular bay, this residence has unified window treatment with continuous hoods and stringcourses. M(321)

1319
Built in 1891, this two-flat is of Queen Anne design. M(322)

1321, 1323, 1331, 1336, 1342
All five of these two-flats are in the same style as 1317. M(323)

1327, 1329, 1333, 1343, 1345
All five of these residences have no known construction date. M(324)

1330
Built in the 1880s, this two-flat is a transition style of Italianate and Queen Anne. M(325)

1339, 1349, 1353
A two-flat, this is essentially a Queen Anne styled structure. M(326)

1341
Like 1339 in style this is a residence. M(327)

1501
The third addition to Father Thiele's German Catholic "empire" of St. Aloysius Church and St. Elizabeth's Hospital was with the Sisters of Christian Charity community. They purchased eight Oakley lots on February 7, 1887, and increased their holdings to 4 acres later that year. Breaking ground on St. Joseph's day, March 19,1889, they opened the doors for the Josephinum Academy in September 1890.

This boarding and day school institution's popularity grew quickly, requiring an addition to be built to the original building in 1907. Imagine large Romanesque buildings with landscaped parks and gardens on the north and south ends of their property. Wrought iron fencing surrounded secluded gardens that sloped down below street grade. The current building was built in 1959. M(328)

DEATH TAKES PAUL WENIGMAN—*Ill in Recent Years*

One of the best known electrical manufacturers of this city passed away on January 9, in the person of Paul P. Wenigman, who for twenty-six years had been head of the firm bearing his name. The deceased was fifty-eight years of age. He had been in none too good health in recent years, but his condition was not considered in any way serious.

Mr. Wenigman was born in Aschen, Germany, September 1, 1857 and came to this country when a boy. In 1889 he established the electrical business, being located at 1802 N. Robey Street for the past eighteen years and was actively engaged in this line until death—which removes from the trade one of the most respected members operating in the middle west.

Quiet and unassuming, and genuine and sincere in all his transactions he was highly esteemed by all with whom he came in contact and did business with.

The funeral took place from his late resident, 2121 Pierce Avenue, Wednesday morning, January 12, and was largely attended.
—*January 1916*

BRIEF MENTION

The marriage of Miss Emma Dierssen, daughter of Mr. and Mrs. H. Dierssen, to Mr. Oscar Fleischer, was solemnized at the home of the bride's parents, 2052 W. Ewing Place, Saturday evening, February 26. Rev. Austin D. Crille officiated.

Mr. Edward Ahlswede and daughter, Miss Ruth, of 2029 Ewing Place, are sojourning through the west and southwest.

LOCALS

Misses Harriet and Virginia Noel, 73 Ewing Place visited their grandmother and aunt at Detroit, Mich.
—*April or May 1909*

Mr. Frank Horn, 2150 Ewing place, is on a business trip through the West.
—*March 1911*

Miss Ella Uihlein and Edwin Seipp were united in marriage on July 30. They are on a wedding trip through Canada.
—*August 1913*

PIERCE AVENUE (WEST)

2023

A text-book example of Italianate architecture, H. Clay was its architect. It was built 1886 for Charles H. Carter. M(329)

2024

The original building permit, dated Dec.17, 1894 was for a two-story brick building, 35' by 64' and 30' high. The rear open porch was added in 1939. Its first owner was Paul Benson, president of the Benson and Rixon Company, one of the major retail clothiers in Chicago for a number of decades. Its style is Romanesque. AH(330)

2027-2029

This building represents a rare opportunity to view the rebirth of a classical 1920s vintage apartment building into a fully functional living environment for today's city dweller. The six-flat building was constructed in 1926 based on the design from architect Benjamin A. Comm, after demolition of an 1884 mansion on this site. Fine craftsmanship was coupled with heavy structural integrity providing numerous windows and nine-foot ceilings. The vintage façade was retained when it was converted into and eight unit condo in the 1990s. M(331)

2046

This building with its red sandstone facade and heavy rustication of large cut stone blocks reminds us of what other buildings on the block may have looked. Only one other original building remains to the east. It was built in 1895 for Werner Spengler.

Above the top metal cornice is a stone gable treated in the stepped "Dutch Renaissance" style. At the beginning of this century, the rounded porch was restored. This home once faced the former Uihlein home at 2041 W. Pierce (also known as the Schlitz mansion) and garden that filled the southeast corner of Pierce and the alley east of Hoyne. Part of the multi-unit brick 1920s apartment buildings now stands over that alley. M(332)

2046 W. PIERCE

2118

Like its "sister" house 2134, it has a truncated hip roof, hip knob and finial, and the cross gable framing for a decorative stone sculpture. The architect for both was Charles Thisslew. They were designed in the classical revival style. It was built in 1903 for Dr. Theophilus Noel, the owner of a "proprietary medicine" business that marketed a questionable "cure for all ails." Noel was the father of Joseph Noel who built 2134 two years later. Reportedly Herman Weinhardt, who built 2137, lived here at some point after selling the other property. It remained in the Noel family until 1925. Later, it became a legal rooming house. Note the sidewalk. It is probably the only remaining example of the slate sidewalk. A(333)

2121

The original address was 66 Ewing Place when this

two-flat was built for Paul Wenigman by the contracting firm of Marquardt and Brunke in 1907 for $10,000, including the coach house. Architect Albert J. Fischer chose a Romanesque style, featuring a limestone facade, face brick on the sides and a steel I-beam support down the middle that was probably prompted by the San Francisco earthquake a year earlier. Note the castellated roof line and corbelling on the east side. Wenigman owned an electrical supply business on Damen Avenue but still had the buildings chandeliers piped for gas as well as electricity.

The coach house stored hay in the loft until 1979 and has the remains of a tack room. The second story loft doors are preserved here and on the coach house across the alley behind 1530 N. Hoyne.

Like so many other buildings on this block, it went through WWII rooming house days. Fortunately, none of the original features were discarded—all were stored in the coach house.

Nancy Wicker owned and lived in this property from 1992 to 1999. She is the great granddaughter of Charles Gustavus Wicker. M(334)

2121 W. PIERCE

2124

If only houses or ghosts could talk, we would learn much about Wicker Park and Chicago from this 1868 home. Purchased by John and Amelia Press in the early 1870s, the common brick structure did not include the wing to the East. They added it at an unknown date. Originally the kitchen was in the garden level with a dumb waiter taking the food up to the dining area level.

A native of Alsace, France, Press was a saloon keeper for many years prior to becoming a wine merchant. There was a two-story stable at the back. The horses and carts, that delivered the wine, occupied the first floor and goats and chickens resided on the second floor!

The Kendzior family purchased the property in the 1920s and owned it until 1992. It is possible that Kendzior was a bootlegger for Al Capone and had his distillery in the current garage, based on remnants of some plumbing. There was a fairly extensive fire that, among other damage, caused the main structure's wooden front bay and the East wing's porch to be reconstructed in brick. M(335)

2129

This single-family residence was built in 1888 with a red brick front and common brick sides and back for Julius Schuldt. The greystone wrap around porch was added in 1906. It is classified as a mix of Queen Anne, Gothic and Romanesque styles. M(336)

2134

First recorded information about the property's ownership is 1871 when Daniel Forbes purchased one lot from Clemens Hirsch and two lots from Mary L. Stewart. Built as a two-flat in 1905 by Dr. Joseph R. Noel, the building's floor plan is similar to 2118.

Although the decorative work in the stone facade is clean and simple, it is massive in proportion to many homes in the neighborhood. Notice the bay leaf garland molding on the second story window and the guilloche-like pattern that completes the framing. The front porch is handsomely supported by a juxtaposition of straight-shafted piers with the more classic fluted columns. Notice that the stained glass on the first and second floor windows is identical.

Interior lighting was originally gas and electric and there were no wood-burning fireplaces. There is a "fireplace" on each floor, which they used for gas or possibly coal fires. It is surprising that residents lived through using these "fireplaces." There are no chimneys; fires were vented between the walls! Original remaining interior features include oak floors, hall pillars and built-in dining room sideboard of classic styling. The coach house was originally home to at least one horse and carriage. Remnants of the pole used to hoist hay to the second floor are still visible on the back wall.

Association House of Chicago bought it in 1940 for $14,500. It served, as a residence (rooming house style) for their employees until they sold it in 1976. AH(337)

2134 W. PIERCE

2137

This splendid example of late Victorian ostentation is situated on an expansive lot that used to be flooded for ice skating. This architectural fantasy, which is basically Queen Anne style, was built in 1888 for Herman Weinhardt, president of the Niemann and Weinhardt Table Company and a West Parks Board Commissioner. The Kramps family occupied the house from the late 1890s until 1979. The pressed metal bargeboard is the most obvious element of a design effusive in its decorative features, which merge Victorian and Germanic aspects.

The beautiful interior trim of different woods and intricate spindlework, as well as the grand entry and staircase indicate that this house was made for luxurious living. Known for its gardens and its conservatory, the house was pictured in a German language guidebook published for the Columbian Exposition in 1893, Chicago, Die Garten Stadt. This 1893 publication served as a reference guide for exterior decorative restoration in the late 1990s. A(338)

2138

Commonly called the "Steamboat (style) Mansion", the "Polish Consulate", or the "Paderewski House", this combination of architectural types and elements (the wood and brick mixture) is unique in Wicker Park. It was built for Hans Runge in 1884-86. Perhaps the fact that he was treasurer of a wood milling company in Chicago explains the intricate wood detailing of the structure. Notice the delicate spindle columns supporting the grand veranda, the interlocking asymmetrical pattern of the balustrade, the delicately notched roof rafters for the veranda cover, and the detailed carving above the French doors.

Details of this house span almost 50 years, suggesting changes were made as time went by. It is possible that the extensive use of neatly patterned stained glass, which provides a nice frame for the front French doors, may be one of the changes or additions.

In 1902, John F. Smulski, a prominent local banker and politician, bought the house and moved here from 2145 W. Caton. He was a leader in the efforts to make Poland a free independent state. These efforts had him working with famed composer and pianist, Ignance Paderewski.

The oral legend that claims this building as a former Polish Consulate, "Paderewski's house," or as the site of a Paderewski concert are untrue.

This elegant lady experienced decades of decline but was purchased in 2001 and is once again receiving the care and attention she deserves. AH(339)

2141

Probably the most striking feature about this Romanesque-style house is the Eastern Cross atop the structure. It was added when the Ukranian Archbishop of Chicago occupied the premises from 1954-1971. Original construction was in 1895 for Theodore D. Juergens. Juergens began his career in 1868 as a telegraph operator for the Chicago and Northwestern RR then worked as a sign painter and decorator. He joined the American Varnish Company in 1895 and became its president in 1905.

Gargoyles peer down past the limestone facade at passersby, and a conservatory faces the garden on the east side of the house on the first floor. The third floor, as was typical of larger homes of the era, was a ballroom devoted to lavish entertaining. The building has since been divided into several apartments. AH(340)

2146

This is one of three side-by-side buildings that are almost identical. The other two are 2150 and 2156. All were designed by the architectural firm of Lutken and Thisslew. It was built around 1891 for Kickham Scanlan, a prominent Chicago lawyer and judge. The Scanlan family shared the house with Michael W. Conway, a City of Chicago fire inspector, and his father-in-law. AH(341)

2150

Perhaps the most striking of the three, this house is marked by a carriage stone near the driveway curb with the name J.C. Horn, who built the building in 1890. Unlike its two brownstone neighbors it is greystone.

On the exterior, the house is characterized by a full porch-cover supported with granite columns. Notice the extensive copper renovation of the roof and roof finials. The interior contains carved oak woodwork and a wine cellar with walls fourteen inches thick. A(342)

2155

This institutional structure is of an obviously much later vintage than its neighbors. It was one of several Eleanor Clubs opened in the city from 1914 to 1960. They were designed to provide respectable living accommodations for young, single, working women. This one, called Eleanor Club Six, offered rooms plus breakfast, dinner and three meals on Sunday for $6.50 per week. Also provided were "spacious parlors, homelike living rooms, roof gardens and sleeping porches; and a sewing room, library and laundry." Entertainment and parties were reportedly frequent.

Architecturally, the building is similar to many of the multiple-dwelling types of the early twentieth century. The balustrade provides a "design relief against the expansive flat roof, often thought necessary at that time. In the early 1960s the building was sold to the Winston Manor Nursing Home, which occupies the facility today.

Wieboldt was one of the financiers of this

club. The remaining Eleanor Club at the southwest corner of Dearborn and North was closed in 2001. M(343)

2156

This Victorian Romanesque home was constructed in about 1890 for August Lenke, a German immigrant who went from peddler to vice president of a local coal company and later served as Fish Commissioner of Illinois. AH(344)

POTOMAC AVENUE (WEST)

This street has a series of workers' cottage and two-flats intermixed with elaborate greystones. Many buildings were destroyed along this street by fires that plagued this area in the early 1970s.

1942-6

A double residence, they were erected in 1870. It was designed in the Italianate style that featured a flat cornice with brackets and dentils, polygonal bay, and windows treated individually. M(345)

1945

This is an example of the workman's cottage with the gabled roof. M(346)

2015

Italianate featuring a flat cornice with brackets and dentils, indented façade or rectangular bay, and windows unified with continuous hoods and/or string-courses, this two-flat was built in 1889. M(347)

2016-18

This building is of Italianate style too, however, it features a flat front and individually treated windows. It was constructed in 1895. M(348)

2017, 2019

Both of these three-flats were designed in Queen Anne style. They were constructed in the 1880s. M(349)

2022

Built in 1883, this two-flat is similar to 2015 except that the windows are treated individually. M(350)

2023-25

Like 2016, this structure was erected in the 1880s. M(351)

2024

A three-flat, this structure was built in 1892. M(352)

2026

These three-flats were built in 1896 and 1897 respectively. Their design is in the mixed styles of Queen Anne, Gothic, and Romanesque. M(353)

2027

Essentially Queen Anne in style, this three-flat was built in 1886 by John Jenson. M(354)

2028

Like 2026, this three-flat was built in 1897 in mixed styles. Look up at the leaded glass windows on the third floor. The circular top windows have the Star of David in their design—a reminder that many decades ago this community had many Jewish residents. (Two blocks west, at Potomac and Bell, there used to be two synagogues.) M(355)

2032

This three-flat greystone is noteworthy for its limestone cornice; notice the draped garland details in the limestone over the door. The home was built in 1894 for Sarah and Jacob Isador (for $3,000) who moved from Brissen, Germany, to the U.S. in 1885. Jacob Isador was a textile merchant with several stores in Chicago. M(356)

2033

This two-flat building is an excellent example of the small multi-family, basically Italianate residences, which are encountered along the more modest streets of Wicker Park. A(357)

2034

A two-flat, this was built in the 1890s. Its design is essentially Queen Anne in style. M(358)

2035

Architects Thiel & Lang designed this three-flat in 1889. Its style is essentially Queen Anne like 2034. M(359)

2038

Built in 1887 as a two-flat, this is in the same style as 2035. M(360)

2039 W. POTOMAC

2039

Built in 1889, this greystone remained a two-flat in decent condition. The original stained glass window, fireplace mantels and some woodwork remain intact. In 1990-1991, the building was converted to a single-family residence. An original tin ceiling was uncovered and stripped. New window and door trims were milled to match the original; the doors and hardware were stripped and re-used where practical. Living room and dining room plaster coves remain. During demolition, a wood rosette was found with the following inscription written by one of the original carpenters: "Thursday, June 21st A.D. 1889, Andrew West did go without beer for one day at dinner." M(361)

2040

Essentially Queen Anne in style, this two-flat was built in 1888. M(362)

2041

Charles Sorenson was the architect in 1889, when he designed this three-flat in the same style as 2040. M(363)

2042

A three-flat design in the mixed styles of Queen Anne, Gothic, and Romanesque, the stained glass windows are original. This is one of several good quality buildings that have been well maintained and barely altered through the years. (You may recall that this building was used as the exterior of the family home in "The American Dream" TV series in the 1980s.) Notice the difference in quality details and scale with nearby buildings such as 2028 and 2024. M(364)

2114 W. POTOMAC

2043

Like 2015 in style and size, this building was erected in the 1880s. M(365)

2114

The original structure on this site was built in 1893 and now serves as a seven-room coach house. The front building was built in 1903 as a three-flat. It was the home of the Crown family from 1907 to 1918, who occupied the second-floor apartment.

The construction is brick with cut grey limestone sills and trim, giving the façade a turn-of-the-century Victorian appearance typical of Chicago buildings of this era. The cornice at the flat roofline is metal. M(366)

2115

This structure is typical of the "Workman's Cottage"

2115 W. POTOMAC

and was built about 10 years later than the smaller cottages found on this street, probably between 1885 and 1890. Originally it would have been crowned with a metal cornice and typically had a dirt-floor basement. The cornice was destroyed by fire sometime in the 1950s. The building has been totally renovated. M(367)

2116
This three-flat was built in the 1890s. M(368)

2118
A residence, this structure was built in 1880s. M(369)

2119
This three-flat was built in the 1893 in a style mix of Queen Anne, Gothic, and Romanesque. M(370)

2122
Built in the 1880s, this is a single-family residence. M(371)

2129, 2131
Both of these three-flats were built in 1893 by Martin Anderson. Their mixed styling is like 2119. M(372)

2132
Built in the 1880s, this two-family residence was the home, or site of the home, of the August Spies family. August Spies, born December 10, 1855 in Germany, was one of the four principal Haymarket Anarchists hanged for their alleged participation in the

famous Haymarket Riot of May 4, 1886.

The riot was one of the famous events in U.S. labor history that pitted the West Town workingmen against the police. A mass meeting, held in Haymarket, was raided by the police. Someone threw a bomb, killing seven policemen and four other people.

Though it is uncertain whether Spies lived at this address with his family, his body was brought here for viewing after the hanging. The Haymarket funeral procession began here. It passed along Damen, Evergreen, Potomac, Crystal and up Milwaukee Avenue. Governor John Peter Altgeld later pardoned all surviving Haymarket defendants. H(373)

2133, 2135
These are the same as 2129. M(374)

2132 W. POTOMAC

2134
This residence was built in 1880s. M(375)

2140
Essentially Queen Anne in style, this three-flat was built in the 1880s. M(376)

2143, 2155
These three-flats were built in the 1880s. Their style is Italianate featuring a flat cornice with brackets and dentils, indented façade or rectangular bay and windows unified with continuous hoods and/or stringcourses. M(377)

2151
Mixed in style with features of Queen Anne, Gothic, and Romanesque, this three-flat was built in 1893. M(378)

2152
A two-flat, this building was erected in 1881. Its Italianate style features a flat cornice with brackets and dentils, indented façade or rectangular bay, and windows treated individually. M(379)

2154
This two-flat was built in the 1880s in the Italianate style that is characterized by a peaked gabled roof with brackets and dentils. M(380)

SCHILLER STREET (WEST)

1915

Built by 1885, the first person to own this parcel for any length of time was Frederich Huebner, who held it from 1873-82. He sold it to Christian Anderson. While either may have built the residence, it is believed that it was built by 1885. The first verifiable occupant was Frederick Faber, an architect. A(381)

1917 W. SCHILLER

1917

This typical two-story red brick with its original cornice has its natural sandstone window lintels and windowsill stonework still intact. The focal point of the entrance with its elaborate Victorian carved doors provides a dramatic highlight to the facade. The interior restoration and practical new kitchen designed with an adjoining family alcove is a prime example of what can be done with a former tiny pantry and small back bedroom. The French doors leading into the back deck and yard provide an open light court for the kitchen. M(382)

1919

Built in the 1880s, this building was built as a two or three-flat. It is in the style of Italianate that is identified by a flat cornice with brackets and often dentils, polygonal bay, and individually treated windows. M(383)

1925

This Italianate brick and limestone trim house was built for a single family before 1880 and was completely renovated in 1979. All original features were repaired and restored, such as the elaborate cornice on three sides of the building. The "piano" windows, second floor, suggest the eleven-foot high ceiling within. Long gone is the bay window on the side of the house.

The brick coach house was probably built as servants' quarters later in the 1880s. This poorly constructed building required major structural work when it was renovated in 1984. It is now a duplex apartment with a garage. M(384)

1935

Built in 1886 as a two- or three-flat, this structure is of the Italianate style featuring a flat cornice with brackets and often dentils; a flat front, and individually treated windows. M(385)

1937

With the original address of 38 Fowler, this building dates from 1878. The cast iron banisters on the front steps are original, while the front porch roof is a pedestrian replacement for something that must have been grand. Italianate, like its neighbor at 1935, it has a polygonal bay instead of a flat front. The huge coach house in the rear is rumored to have once been a hat factory. A(386)

1941

In Italian Romanesque style, this mansion was built in 1890-91 for Harris Cohn, a partner in the Cohn Brothers Clothing Company. Notice that the square stone columns meet the capitals of round polished granite columns. Also note the turret resting on a shell-shaped base, the checkerboard-like stonework of the second-story balcony, the denticulate lintels and the scroll and oak-leaf motif at the ends of the handrails. The structure was extensively renovated back to a single-family residence from a boarding house after a fire about 1980. It has undergone extensive interior beautification during the 1990s. A(387)

1941 W. SCHILLER

1945-7

Constructed during the 1880s, the coach house originally served as stables and living quarters for the livery help associated with the luxury homes, probably built in 1885, situated on the front of the lot. In keeping with changes brought about as a result of the horseless carriage and a housing shortage of the period, the stable area was eliminated to increase living space, in the early 1900s. Until the late 1940s, the property remained relatively unchanged at which time, additional units increased the count to twenty-two. Suburban flight and federal entitlement programs of the 1960s nearly brought the buildings to demolition by the early 1970s. Vacant and dilapidated by 1977, it was renovated providing viable housing once again. A(388)

1951

Fire was responsible for the downward spiral of this mansion's appearance, it serves to remind us of how close we have come to losing some of the most inter-

esting aspects of our architectural history. Only the sides and rear of what was originally an Italianate house built in 1873 are now visible. The Romanesque Revival façade, with Moorish (if not simply eclectic) openings on the first and second floors, was added about 1890 to the original Italianate structure. Its first owner Dr. Nels T. Quales, a native of Norway, was a prominent physician, surgeon and humanitarian. A founder of the Lutheran Deaconess Hospital, Dr. Quales received the Order of St. Olafin 1910 from Norway's King Haakon VII. AH(389)

1947 W. SCHILLER (COACH)

1947 W. SCHILLER

1955-57

Built in 1878, this Italianate double house comprises

two single-family homes with servants' quarters at the front of the third floor. The owners of 1957 Schiller chose to keep the ceiling moldings of the double parlors and dining room intact, while removing the interior walls to provide a contemporary space. The cornice has been restored in a conservative "painted lady" color style. The cut stone lintels are no doubt from a standard builders' supply catalog of the era. M(390)

1957 W. SCHILLER

1959 W. SCHILLER

1959-61

This double house, built in 1886 for Dr. Baltzar Meyer and Halver Michelson (president of the Vessel Owners' Mutual Benefit Association), is of the Second Empire style. Note that the tower, cornices and other trim have been carefully painted in a Victorian man-

ner, using a variety of colors. The large mansard roof with its straight lines and the saw-tooth decorative brick belt courses are of particular interest. A major fire in the 1990s prompted adjustment of the interior of 1961 into a modern "open" plan, although most exterior details replicate originals. A(391)

2121

Architect H. Worthmann designed this Italianate three-flat in 1889. Despite significant interior renovation the detail of the exterior has been maintained. M(392)

2128, 2130

Both of these two-flats were built in the 1880s and are classified as Italianate with a peaked roof and supporting brackets. M(393)

2129

Built in 1877, this residence is a simplified workman's cottage with a gabled roof. M(394)

2133, 2135, 2137

These are identical common brick cottages whose early residents were probably professional men and their families. Sparse in detailing, this type of house attracted would-be homeowners to move from the city to this "new suburb." Built as four-room houses in 1876, they were enlarged in 1886 as the neighborhood began to show its prosperity. Despite extensive current renovation and major floor plan modification, the basic simplicity and character of the exterior of these houses has been maintained. M(395)

2138

This residence was built in the 1880s with the same styling as 2128 and 2130. M(396)

SUICIDE ATTEMPT
—Caused by Job Loss
Rose Lusk, 19 years old, 1069 North Hermitage Ave., who attempted to kill herself by swallowing carbolic acid in the saloon of Michael Scrokas, 1154 North Ashland Ave., was freed of a charge of disorderly conduct by Municipal Judge Uhlir. "I'm sorry, now, Judge, that I tried to commit suicide," the girl said. "I was tired of life because my parents scolded me for losing my job a week ago. I looked for work, but couldn't find it."
– February 1910

BRIEF MENTION
Mrs. J. Meldahl and children, of 2018 Fowler St. are on a long visit to Los Angeles, Ca, where Mrs. Meldahl is visiting her sister, Mrs. West.
– February 1910

Dr. and Mrs. Arthur Behrendt, 2026 Fowler are spending 6 weeks on a ranch at Dallas, Oregon. Their little son, Jamie accompanied them on the trip.
– August 1913

Mrs. Agnes Johnson, 95 Fowler street, was presented with a gold medal, in acknowledgement of the good work she has done toward the Carnation Benevolent Society. In their recent dance held at Young's Hall, North avenue and Burling street. The token contains a beautifully engraved carnation. – April or May 1909

CORRECTION
We wish to make a correction in the last issue of the Eagle. The article stating that Mrs. Anderson and daughter Florence of 2031 Fowler street are on a trip to the West, should read: Mrs. C. Erickson and daugher Florence, 2031 Fowler street, are on a trip to Los Angeles, California, where Mrs. Erickson will visit her brother, Mr. Jevne.
–March 1911

WICKER PARK AVENUE (NORTH)

1317, 1326

These three-flats are both designed in an essentially Queen Anne style. While the construction date of 1326 is thought to be in the 1880s, the date for 1317 is unknown. M(397)

1322

A single-family residence, this too is a Queen Anne style structure. M(398)

1323-25

A Queen Anne styled two-flat with some Romanesque detailing. M(399)

1324

A single-family residence, this 1890s building was designed in Italianate styling. M(400)

1328, 1329, 1331

Built in the 1880s, these three structures are two-flat row houses. They are also alike in style: Italianate with flat cornice with brackets and/or dentils; flat front; and windows treated individually. M(402)

1330

Like 1326, this is a stand-alone two-flat with Italianate detailing. M(403)

1333

Designed in the Italianate style featuring a flat cornice with brackets and/or dentils; flat front; and individually treated windows, this residence was built around 1875. A(404)

1338, 1339

Though 1338 is a residence and 1339 is an apartment building, both of these structures were built in the 1890s with a mansard roof in the Queen Anne style with some French chateau detailing. M(405)

1411, 1421

Constructed within three years of each other, 1411 built in 1880 and 1421 in 1877, these Italianate designed two-flats feature a polygonal bay, a flat cornice and individually designed windows. M(406)

1415

Built in the 1890s, this three-flat is like 1317 in size and style. M(407)

1419

Like 1421 in construction date, this Italianate two-flat features an indented bay; flat cornice with brackets and dentils; and windows unified in appearance with continuous hoods and stringcourses. M(408)

1427

This house was built in 1879 and the original address was 92 Park St. The original brick house had a brick stable in the back. It still stands as a two-car garage. The house was built by a Frenchman, Paul Populorum, who came to Chicago in 1854. He married a woman from Switzerland, Marie Michon, who came to Chicago in 1871. Mr. Populorum was a farmer and a tanner and had a tannery on Fleetwood St. near Elston Ave.

After World War II the third floor was converted into two apartments. Following that there were several owners, including a Yugoslavian couple who lived there for twenty-five years. They converted the house into seven apartments, renting out units by the week. (409)

1431-33

Essentially Queen Anne in style, this three-flat building was built in the 1890s. M(410)

1509

This brick three-story residence was built in 1877 and overlooked the swan pond directly across the street in Wicker Park. The bay windows are crowned with shell medallion lintels, which are repeated over the door and above the upper floor windows. The metal cornice, that is original to the dwelling, is typical of the last quarter of the nineteenth century homes in this area and throughout Chicago. M(411)

1509 N. WICKER

1519

This unique two-color brick house is an example of masonry craftsmanship. Notice the smaller mortar joints and the corbelled dormer. Decorative wrought ironwork includes the fence, entry roof brackets, interior balustrade and the tall lighted newel posts. Although this house has a prairie style, there are Victorian details such as entry hardware and an oak fireplace. M(412)